GINO BARBIERI

DECLINE
AND ECONOMIC IDEALS
IN ITALY
IN THE EARLY MODERN AGE

Edited by
SERGIO NOTO and MARIA CRISTINA GATTI

with an Introduction by
DAVID COLANDER

LEO S. OLSCHKI EDITORE
MMXIII

All rights reserved

Casa Editrice Leo S. Olschki
Viuzzo del Pozzetto, 8
50126 Firenze
www.olschki.it

Original Edition:

Gli Ideali Economici degli Italiani all'inizio dell'età moderna, Milano, Giuffrè 1940.

Translated by:

Nicola Gelder and Marcus Perryman

Book published with the financial support of

and with the encouragement of

ISBN 978 88 222 6301 8

INTRODUCTION

If you go on the web into Google Earth and start from a distant view of earth, and begin zooming in, you see a fascinating panoply of patterns and places. As you zoom in, you lose sight of the vastness, and gain sight of the particular country, state, city, area of a city, house, pixel... that happened to be the initial focal point. In the future we might be able to add a Google Time to Google Earth, so that not only can we capture the spatial dimensional vastness, but also the temporal dimensional vastness of our reality. Our reality is an infinitesimal point in time and space. That process gives one an appreciation of our limited understanding, and at least for me, instills a humility of how little I bring to the table in my attempt to understand the social dimension of our system.

To even begin to understand our social system, one must first answer questions such as: How do we propose to gain insight into that vast domain? What lens do we want to use? And what should be our focal point? There are no right answers to these questions, but some answers may well be better than others. No matter what approach we take, it is important to recognize that the understanding we get from any particular focus, whether a far off focal point, or a close focal point, will be highly limited. Most of us choose the lens our teachers have chosen, and we build on that, and institutional structures and incentives tend to justify to us our lens as the appropriate lens, and not to emphasize its limitations and problems. So we become locked in, and, far too often, lack the humility that our infinitesimal point in time and space should have instilled in us.

Modern global economics is a case in point. It has chosen a particular lens, it sees all economics through simple highly restrictive models that almost uniformly rule out by assumption all types of issues that were on the minds of writers in the sixteenth and seventeenth century. Modern economics students are not presented with the diverse tapestry of the economy in either their geographic dimensions, or their developments over time. They seldom learn economic history or history of economic thought. But even those who learn economic history and history of thought, like me, still only get insights into small parts of the history and thought looked at through the modern lens.

For example my history of thought book[1] includes only a couple of pages on the Scholastics, and then jumps to mercantilists, which it presents in a few pages. Then it is on to Smith and Classical economics (British variety mainly) where the picture we present of economics gets a little more focused. The reality is that my history of thought book doesn't even mention sixteenth and seventeenth century economic thought, and certainly provides students with no insight into thinking of the period. Mercantilism is just a term for students to memorize – Mercantilism was a period within which economic thinkers believed that wealth meant gold, that trade surpluses were supposed to be fostered by the state, and that production took place through guilds and government monopolies. They get no sense of the diversity of thought and the different way of thinking that "mercantilists" had.

That's what made Gino Barbieri' s book, *Ideali economici degli italiani all'inizio dell'età moderna*, so exciting for me to read. It was as if I had jumped into a whole new Google Earth and Time Search, and had landed in a quite different place – sixteenth and seventeenth century Italian economic thought – than the period and a place that I study. It is a place where economists were not afraid to discuss issues of morality and interfaces of economics with social and political issues. It is a place where economists blend economics history and history of economic thought into the same tapestry. It is a wonderful place, and one that I strongly encourage the reader to visit.

While it is a wonderful place, it is also a potentially treacherous place. One of the reasons economics moved away from using a broader lens the blends issues of morality and ethics with economic analysis is that as views of morality and ethical norms change, earlier views can seem off-putting and inconsistent with appropriate ethics. For example, the discussion of Jews by Barbieri seems a bit lacking in the political correctness of today. When ethics and analysis are intertwined, debates become heated, and cannot be resolved by empirical facts. That blending led to vitriolic debates, such as debates about what capitalism is, and whether it is better than socialism.

Those debates have faded away. In my view, this is for the good, not because such debates are not important, but because there are so many different aspects to both concepts that the debate can never be resolved, and can only leave various sides feeling misunderstood. Today, we don't have capitalism or socialism; we have only pragmatism, and I see the study of the history of eco-

---

[1] H. LANDRETH – D. COLANDER, *History of Economic Thought*, Boston Mass., Houghton Mifflin, 2002.

nomic thought as the study of the pragmatic solutions societies have found to solve complex coordination problems.

One of the reasons the place hasn't been visited is that the global economics profession is highly English language/U.S./British-centric. Outside of the Italian public finance tradition, little is taught about the rich Italian economic tradition, and so little is known about it by non-Italians. My textbook[2] which is widely translated into many languages, including Italian, has essentially no mention of that (and many other national traditions.) That is a travesty which should be rectified. One of the reasons for the lack of knowledge is that English has become the common language of global economics, so unless works are translated into English, they don't get read. Until now, no English translation of Barbieri's book (which is being published simultaneously with a new edition of the Italian edition) existed. The previous 1940 edition was never translated into English, and since I (and most other non-Italian economists) do not read Italian, many of the insights of the long and proud tradition of Italian historians of thought were unknown to us. That's why the simultaneous publication of the new edition and the English translation of the book is such a wonderful occasion. The newness of it all gives it a freshness that put me back to the position of a student first being exposed to ideas that I always felt were important, but that modern conventions put out of focus, or ruled out completely.

1. The Intellectual History of Gino Barbieri

Gino Barbieri (1913-1989) is part of a line of distinguished economic thinkers from Northern Italy. He was the first student of Amintore Fanfani (1908-1999), who himself was a student of Giuseppe Toniolo. (1845-1918). Toniolo was a professor at both the University of Padua and then the University of Pisa, and he maintained an active interest in Social Catholicism throughout his life. His work blended scholarly study and social activism. In 1893 he founded the *International Review of Social Sciences and Auxiliary Disciplines* to illustrate the value of the Christian Social order, and was instrumental in the founding of the University of the Sacred Heart where Fanfani began his studies. Fanfani became Toniolo's best known scholar, and in 1936 Fanfani was given the university's Chair for Economic History, and in 1933 he

---

[2] *Ibid.*; H. Landreth – D. Colander, *Storia del pensiero economico*, Bologna, Il Mulino, 1996.

became editor of the *International Review* that Toniolo had founded. Fanfani was also active in politics, and was an Italian prime minister in the 1950s and 60s.

Barbieri was Fanfani's best known student, and his work is very much in the tradition of Toniolo and Fanfani. He is a conservative catholic who held strong beliefs about the role of individuals, and the importance of ethics to understanding economics. That comes through in Barbieri's work, and his work has a breadth that modern work in economics generally lacks. Work in this tradition spans far beyond what today is considered economics, and includes dimensions of politics, sociology the moral ethics.

Barbieri is a historian of economic thought, and thus he is very similar to me. But his history is quite different because his scope of analysis is much broader than mine and because his raw material – the texts he analyzes – is different from mine. We both reflect the traditions of our time. The broader scope of the analysis fits with the difference in raw material; with a broader scope, many more areas are opened up to his analysis, and his history of ideas blends with economic history. He considers not only economists' writings, but also poetry, writing of legal scholars, and the views of common people about the economy. By today's standards, the book would be seen as more an intellectual history book than a history of economics book.

Prof. Paolo Pecorari,[3] in his introduction to a conference volume, *Ethics and Economics in Giuseppe Toniolo*, (1997) notes that Barbieri' s last formal scientific contribution occurred in October 1988, where he introduced the papers to this conference focused on Toniolo's work. In that introduction, Barbieri noted the centrality of ethics and economics in Toniolo's work. He «advised not to see the "quaestio" as a thematic "unicum" that can be hypothesized, ...but to underline the need for a severe historicizing able to make the problem plain as to its appearance and its evolution, recognizing the different moments and phases, with the distinction between the critical and theoretical analysis».[4] That advice could as well have been for Barbieri' s own work. It blends ethics and economics, but also recognizes the different movements and the heterogeneity of thought that surround these issues.

---

[3] *Ethics and Economics in Giuseppe Toniolo*, edit. P. PECORARI, München, Springer Verlag, 1997.

[4] *Ibid.*, p. 1.

2. A Brief Summary of the Book

Barbieri's book is a history of thought book, but, as I stated above, it is quite different than a modern history of thought book. One difference is that it is designed to answer some actual questions, not just present in the thought of the period. A central question it attempts to answer is: Why did economic growth slow in Italy in the sixteenth and seventeenth center, when it had grown so fast before then? Other questions it addresses are: What were the views of wealth over this period, and how did those views affect growth? In answering these questions, Barbieri goes far beyond economics and approaches them as a social historian and scientist, not as only an economist.

The book is nicely organized and structured. Each chapter starts with a summary of the issues it will consider and ends with a summary of what his conclusions are. Chapter 1 reconstructs the solutions to the problem of wealth propounded by some of the most eminent Churchmen of the sixteenth and early seventeenth century. Chapter 2 attempts to reconstruct the economic thought of Churchmen and explain how those views affected capital and credit markets. Chapter 3 considers the economic views of historians and political commentators of the time and how they subordinated wealth and economic activity in general to the needs of the state. Chapter 4 considers the views of poets, writers, and philosophers in relation to wealth and economic activity, and notes that, although there was debate, an intellectual in the sixteenth century would likely feel pangs of remorse about focusing on making money. Chapters 5 and 6 consider the opinions of jurists in relation to wealth and wealth creation. In these chapters Barbieri discusses the legal structure and how it reflected the economic order, with a specific consideration of usury. Chapter 7 tries to capture the spirit of the times by considering the "testimony of practical men" and Barbieri finds that in the sixteenth century a new moral code developed that affected people's view of wealth. Chapter 8 concludes.

3. Views on Wealth and Wealth Creation

As you can see, Barbieri considers the period he is studying from many different perspectives, but includes threads that tie the various views together. One of the most important of those threads concerns people's view of wealth and wealth creation. For example Chapter 1 explains the movement in thinking on wealth from the Scholastic period captured in the writings of St. Thomas Aquinas to the sixteenth century and to what Barbieri calls the modern age, by which he means thinking that began in the eighteenth century which Classical economics focuses on. While the views have a close connection to the thinking of Aquinas, the movement away from Aquinas is also nicely apparent. Barbieri notes that during this period Churchmen authorized men "to seek to acquire wealth to a level above that required to preserve their status in society." (Chapter 1, p. 2) This authorization produced more social mobility than otherwise would have existed, with important implications for society. There were, however, strict limits on the methods of attaining wealth; usury was ruled out, but not surprisingly, people figured out ways around those restrictions, some of which were admired, and others of which were condemned, by writers of the time. Both how much the restrictions on usury were followed and enforced, and the views on wealth, changed over time to reflect the needs of society – so within limits we can picture morals and implicit church authorizations changing to reflect the perceived needs of society.

Later chapters continue this thread, and by the end of the book the reader has a good sense of the differing and changing views on wealth creation during this period. Thus, for example, in Chapter 4 Barbieri considers poets, writers, and philosophers to gain insight into the period. He shows how they considered wealth as a means to an end, and not the end itself. The poets saw idleness as bad, but they also saw strenuous efforts toward material gain as bad as well. There were long treatises on the benefits of city life over country life, and Barbieri explores how those views changed over time, and how those changes affected the economy. He notes that usury was condemned by writers of the time in part because the loans were often for consumption, not productive investments. Their opposition to usury had to do with its real-world effects, and they felt that too much lending would lead to unsustainability on the part of the debtor, and less work on the part of the creditor, and thus undermine the economic growth of the society.

Another thread that ties the chapters together is the way in which economic thinking interacts with problems facing society. Barbieri points out that much of the thinking of the period involved providing solutions to the practical needs of their time. That's why he blends discussions of economic history with discussions of the history of economic thought.

Another interesting aspect of economic thinkers of the time is that they did not assume given wants, but assumed that activities influenced wants. Thus, their analysis and the consideration of policy was as much about "shaping" wants as it was about "fulfilling" wants. In modern day terminology, their policy analysis involved shaping the utility function, not exploring how utility is maximized given a utility function. Their economics would not be defined as the study of how to allocate scarce resources among alternative ends as economics is today, but rather more as Alfred Marshall defined it – as the "study of men as they think and move and live in the ordinary business of life".

Thinking about policy issues in this broader framework allows a natural entry into the relationship between the Church and economic policy. Because the Church controlled access to the afterlife, which was assumed to be infinitely long, its pronouncements about what people should do to attain that afterlife acquired a central importance to the workings of the economy. Worldly wealth becomes *de minimis* when compared to an infinite afterlife, even for those individuals who held some doubt about its existence. Thus, Church doctrines about material wealth – and whether it was appropriate to accumulate wealth, or to give it away – were important to the workings of the economy.

While today, the Church is far less important in modern life, and the average individual is probably even more doubtful about the existence of an afterlife that his or her worldly actions can affect, church statements, and more so, social secular norms, remain of central importance to the workings of the economy. Modern economists don't even consider such issues. My point is that a world in which all rich individuals held to Andrew Carnegie's gospel of wealth, which holds that it is the duty of all to give away the majority of their wealth before they die, would be quite different from a world of misers, or even our world today with its complex views of the ethics of wealth.

4. THE CONTINUING RELEVANCE OF BARBIERI'S BOOK

Throughout my reading of the book, I was struck by the fact that many of the questions Barbieri was currently struggling with similar to those I am working on now. My recent research focus has been on complexity policy and social entrepreneurship and whether government can foster an ecostructure in which for-benefit enterprises can prosper.[5] My policy question concerns whether we can develop a new corporate structure – a flexible purpose corporation – that encourages individuals to be far less materialistic, but still rely on markets. The good is to be able to rely on markets and people's inherent proclivities to solve social problems from the bottom up, without having to rely on state control as our current system has done.

Our system of capitalism is often associated with materialism, but Barbieri shows that the connection is much more complicated. When tastes are endo-

---

[5] COLANDER and KUPERS, forthcoming.

genous, so is the degree of materialism, and society can solve social problems with markets just as it can solve material problems with markets. That is one of the lessons I take from Barbieri. Pragmatism is a much better description of the world Barbieri surveys than capitalism. Corporate capitalism, and the welfare state involved one possible state/corporate blending – but one that pushed out the church, and spiritualism. That is basically unstable, and in the work I am doing, I am exploring whether other options are possible.

The recognition that views of wealth are important to the working of the economic system is not totally missing from modern economics. Discussions of such issues can be found in various places in Western social and economic thought – for example in John Stuart Mill's[6] conception of the stationary state (Mill, 1844) in which individuals were no longer concerned with achieving material goods, or in Keynes's Economic Possibilities of our Grandchildren, where he writes:[7]

When the accumulation of wealth is no longer of high social importance, there will be great changes in the code of morals. We shall be able to rid ourselves of many of the pseudo-moral principles which have hag-ridden us for two hundred years, by which we have exalted some of the most distasteful of human qualities into the position of the highest virtues. We shall be able to afford to dare to assess the money-motive at its true value. The love of money as a possession – as distinguished from the love of money as a means to the enjoyments and realities of life – will be recognised for what it is, a somewhat disgusting morbidity, one of those semi-criminal, semi-pathological propensities which one hands over with a shudder to the specialists in mental disease. All kinds of social customs and economic practices, affecting the distribution of wealth and of economic rewards and penalties, which we now maintain at all costs, however distasteful and unjust they may be in themselves, because they are tremendously useful in promoting the accumulation of capital, we shall then be free, at last, to discard.

Unfortunately, these musings by Mill and Keynes are deviations of modern economic thought. Thus I see this book as both a consumption good – a book that provides knowledge and joy because it fills in patterns and adds to our knowledge, and also a production good – it sheds light on problems that society now is, or at least should be, trying to solve. In Italy, at the time of this

---

[6] J.S. MILL, *Principles of Political Economy: with some of their applications to Social Philosophy*, [S.L.], John W. Parker, 1848.

[7] J.M. KEYNES, *Economic Possibilities for our Grandchildren*, in *Essays in Persuasion. The Collected Writings of J.M.K.*, vol. IX, Cambridge-New York, Cambridge University Press for the Royal Economic Society, 2007, p. 329.

writing, unemployment stands at 25%, and the chances of an Italian youth finding a good job is low. Italy is having a growth problem similar to the one that Barbieri's analysis focuses on the sixteenth century. But, in comparison to the past, even the unemployed are rich compared to what people were 100 years ago. The ultimate goal of society is not "more goods," but sustainability. Providing as good a life for the greatest number that can be had – what the utilitarians called the greatest good for the greatest number – seems to be an appropriate goal for economic study. In a world where wants in endogenous and utilities are interdependent, so that how much one has relatively to others, matters as much, or more, than how much one has absolutely, the policy problems facing society are quite different from those modern economics deal with. Barbieri's consideration can help, if not show the way, at least to show that there are other ways than simply trying to maximize GDP.

Let me conclude by reiterating my main point. There is a consistency of problems that society faces – and those problems involve a confluence of morals with markets. It is a problem that modern economics shed no light on, but is a problem that Barbieri's work does. I encourage the reader to enjoy and learn from this book.

DAVID COLANDER
Middlebury College

ACKNOWLEDGEMENTS

It may not be evident but a large number of people – and not merely conventionally – deserve the editor's deepest thanks and sincerest appreciation for helping to make the publication of an old and perhaps forgotten book by Gino Barbieri possible. Of course, any errors are not theirs but should be attributed solely to the editor.

First, thanks go to Gianni Barbieri, who with his son Martino, has been an outstanding example of love for his parents, a devotion that encouraged us to continue in this work. We would also like to thank signora Mirella Bonomi and signora Celeste Fedele, who have always done everything in their power to honour Professor Barbieri, even after he had ceased to be part of the small group of influential people in the world.

Our gratitude goes to Giovanni Padovani, inimitable Secretary General of the Cassa di Risparmio di Vr-Vi-Bl-An at the time of Gino Barbieri, a man of rare moral and professional rectitude, without whom – put at its simplest – this book could never have been published.

Thanks to all those who believed in the initiative from the start and provided vital and unstinting support: Carlo Fratta Pasini, Chairman of Banco Popolare, Bettina Campedelli, Professor of Business Administration at Verona University, Paolo Bedoni, Chairman of the Board of Directors of Cattolica spa, and Giovanni Sala, Acting Vice Chairman of the Cariverona Foundation.

The group of colleagues and co-workers who generously contributed their time and work is particularly numerous. Elisa Dalla Rosa and Fabrizia Fabbro, who took upon themselves the work on the Italian publication, and not only that; Cristina Gatti who shared with me the editing work of the English volume; Simone Zardi for the Index of names, Giovanni Zalin and Francesco Barbarani for their friendly and helpful advice.

Many thanks to David Colander for his willingness and generosity in taking up the work of an old Italian researcher and for his Introduction to the republished edition of the book.

Thanks to Daniele Olschki and Erika Marchetti, for their patience and perseverance in continuing – these hard times – a great publishing tradition, enabling us to get the most and best from our limited skills in the realization of this project.

A big thank you to Nicola Gelder and Marcus Perryman, who not only translated the text of Gino Barbieri with skill and personality, but have done their utmost to make the work of a great Italian scholar available to the worldwide scientific community today.

S.N.

DECLINE
AND ECONOMIC IDEALS IN ITALY
IN THE EARLY MODERN AGE

CHAPTER ONE

MATTERS OF WEALTH AND SOLUTIONS PROPOSED
BY SIXTEENTH AND SEVENTEENTH CENTURY CHURCHMEN

1. The beginning of the Modern Age was characterized by a profound re-assessment of all life values. In the sixteenth century, different thinkers, including scholars and Churchmen, dealt with questions of art, science, politics and economic organization, combining, to a significant extent, the legacy of the past with original contributions of the times. Historians of the Modern Age should therefore be very careful to distinguish between heritage and new ideals in analyzing human thought and actions during this period.

With this precaution in mind, Chapter 1 examines how the most eminent Churchmen of the sixteenth and early seventeenth centuries approached the problem of wealth. To understand the origin, development and meaning of their ideas, it is important to realize that in the closing centuries of the Middle Ages, theologians and moral philosophers had already postulated principles of economic ethics. The most important of these men was Thomas Aquinas. A well-known commentator of Aquinas, Tommaso De Vio, whose life spanned the late fourteenth and early fifteenth centuries, published several pamphlets on economic arguments that bear witness to the attention given by Scholastic thought to matters of wealth.[1]

One of De Vio's most important contributions concerned the dynamics of social class. Social mobility conflicted with the duty to be content with one's lot as established by theological doctrine in the Middle Ages. As previous studies have revealed, thirteenth and fourteenth century Scholastic theologians told Christians to be content with their position in society and to give up

---

[1] T. DE VIO, *Opuscula economico-socialia*, Roma, Angelicum, 1934.

In his sober introduction, Padre P. Zammit listed the most important economic issues analyzed by De Vio, whose works are of interest not only to economic historians but also to scholars seeking to detect antecedents of economic theory in the strictest sense. De Vio alludes to Gresham's law, a further example of an idea carried down from antiquity to the Modern Age.

any aspirations to climb the social ladder. In the fifteenth century, the followers of Scholasticism proposed a similar solution. De Vio, on the other hand, solved this impasse in pre-capitalist social ethics in his comment to Aquinas's *Summa Theologiae*, asserting that an individual with uncommon qualities was entitled to pursue wealth to achieve a social standing compatible with his talents.[2] No other interpretation can be given to the following: «singulares autem personas multas ab intrinseco donatas conspicimus quadam sapientia... ita quod inter homines vel aliorum domini nati vel facti sint, quamvis domini non sint.

Et quia his naturali aequitati debetur regimen aliorum, idcirco si isti appetunt dominium, si ad hoc cumulant pecunias ut dominium temporale emant, ut cuiusque decet sapientiam, a rationis rectae tramite non recedunt».[3]

This was the first time that, in seeking to solve the problem of acquiring economic goods, a Churchman[4] actually authorized men to acquire wealth beyond the level necessary to maintain their social status, provided they really did possess the uncommon qualities he demanded.[5]

All Scholastic precepts were grounded on the principle of sufficiency, so the originality of De Vio's justification of social mobility at the start of the sixteenth century is striking. All his other economic and ethical principles remained faithful to the Thomistic tradition, particularly the canonical and evangelical rules on the acquisition and use of material goods. When De

---

[2] A. FANFANI, *Le origini dello spirito capitalistico in Italia*, Milano, Vita e Pensiero, 1933, p. 122.

[3] [It is reasonable that those with particular natural virtues aspire to positions of supremacy or wish to accumulate money]. T. DE VIO, *Commentaria in Summam theologicam angelici doctoris sancti Thomae Aquinatis*, n.t.n., 2. 2. q. 118, art. 1.

[4] I say actually authorized because Fanfani notes how San Bernardino of Siena, in his fifteenth century discussion of the concept of the superfluous, urged citizens to invest all the gold, silver and precious gems they had in their homes in the *fondaco* (merchant warehouses) and in trade. This advice apparently conflicted with the duty to be content with one's status and to donate to the poor. In fact, San Bernardino's rules on leading a frugal life and helping the poor seem to suggest that he allowed men to indulge in trade for one purpose only: to assist the needy and to offer employment to one's neighbour. This brings us back to the Thomistic view of wealth: once men had satisfied their needs according to their status, the surplus was for the poor. For further detail cf. FANFANI, *Le origini*, cit., pp. 115-118.

[5] A. TILGHER, *Le travail dans les moeurs et dans les doctrines: histoire de l'idéee de travail dans la civilisation occidentale*, Paris, Alcan, 1931, p. 33. In relation to this problem, he wrote: «Caietan, exégète de Thomas, permet de s'enrichir et de s'elever de rang social. Mais à une condition, c'est qu'on en ait l'aptitude et la vocation naturelle». Cf. also: V. BRANTS, *L'économie politique au moyen-âge: esquisse des théories économiques professées par les écrivains des XIIIᵉ et XIVᵉ siècles*, Louvain, Peeters, 1895, p. 41; W. SOMBART, *Der Bourgeois: Zur Geistgeschichte des modernen Wirtschaftsmenschen*, München [u.a.], Verl. Duncker & Humblot, 1920, p. 317. Brey ruled out any difference between the Thomistic concept and De Vio's approach to changes in social status H. BREY, *Hochscholastik und "Geist" des Kapitalismus*, Borna-Leipzig, Noske, 1927, pp. 28-29.

Vio discussed usury, for example, not only did he dismiss as illegal the profits earned from money lending, but he also condemned the desire to earn more than the sum lent, reiterating one of Bernardino of Siena's strict rules.[6]

De Vio remained true to the principle of *Mutuum date, nihil inde sperantes*[7] in considering illicit even the negligible rate of interest charged by the newly established *Monti di Pietà* to cover their administrative expenses.[8] De Vio was equally rigorous in his interpretation of the canonist rules when he declared it illegal to sell at anything but a fair price, even when both buyer and seller were willing to complete the transaction at another price.[9]

De Vio placed the contractual intentions of buyers and sellers within the context of commutative justice, in the sense that the hidden motivations of the parties could never justify *inaequalitatem rei ad rem, scilicet pretii ad rem emptam*.[10] De

---

[6] T. De Vio, *De usura quaestiones sex*, in *Opuscula economico-socialia*, cit., p. 145. «Quaeritur: utrum mutuans sub spe aliquid ultra sortem habendi, non aliter mutuaturus, absque omni tamen conventione, sit usurarius mentalis. Et videtur quod sic. Primo quia spes principalis alicuius muneris habendi ex mutuo, usuram parit; iusta illud Lucae VI: "mutuum date, nihil inde sperante", et communem sententiam doctorum. Sed in casu proposito invenitur talis spes. Ergo».

For San Bernardino's theory on gratuitous loans with greedy intents cf. FANFANI, *Origini*, cit., p. 113.

[7] MATTHEW, VI, 35.

[8] T. De Vio, *De Monte Pietatis*, in *Opuscula economico-socialia*, cit., p. 68 e *passim*; p. 75 and following. De Vio's argument that interest payments, however small, charged by the administrators of the Monte to the poor was very weak and upon closer examination, untenable. When De Vio stated that the cost of running the Monte, preserving its assets, and paying its employees were not directly beneficial to the poor, who were under no obligation to cover costs they did not incur, though he showed great skill in constructing a logical argument he went beyond common sense. However, apart from this, the issue of charging interest to the poor was a matter of great controversy at the end of the fifteenth century and the start of the sixteenth, until Pope Leone X (as we shall discover in due course) issued a papal bull to declare that the interest charged to the poor to cover the expenses of charitable institutions was legitimate. After the papal bull, scholars concerned with usury and credit pondered the question and of course declared that the minimal interest charged by the Monte was legal. Tomaso Buoninsegni (T. BUONINSEGNI, *De Montibus et illorum iustitia*, in *Tractatus ad iustas negociationes*, Florentinae, Sermartelliana, 1587) justified such payments on the grounds that the Monte had modified both their structure and their function to become, to all effects, a lending bank. Therefore it was right for them to receive interest from borrowers, since they had to divert money from more lucrative investments to do so. Also dead with the same Topic Gian Battista Lupo Geminiano, Virginio Boccaccio de' Cingulo, Lodovico Carbone da Costacciaro and Marcello Megalio, cf. U. GOBBI, *L'economia politica negli scrittori italiani del secolo XVI-XVII*, Milano, Hoepli, 1889, pp. 211, 214, 216, 233, 275.

[9] T. De Vio, *Responsio ad tria dubia ad Magistrum Conradum Koellin*, in *Opuscula economico-socialia*, cit., p. 171.

«Si res venditur pretio, quod est extra totam latitudinem iusti pretii... peccatum est». Padre Fabiano of Genoa claimed that it was illicit to buy at a price below the fair price when prices had fallen for reasons of «deceit, fraud or some other artifice». P. FABIANO, *Trattato del Cambio di Lione, o di Bisenzone, diligentemente composto, e considerato dal Reverendo padre Frate Fabiano Genovese, Eccellentissimo Teologo, e procuratore nella corte di Roma di tutto l'ordine de Frati Eremitani di Santo Agostino*, in VENUSTI, *Compendio utilissimo di quelle cose, le quali a nobili e christiani mercanti appartengono*, Milano, G. Antio degli Antonii, 1561, c. 7.

[10] De Vio, *Responsio*, cit., p. 171. Cf. V. CUSUMANO, *Saggi di economia politica e di scienza delle finanze*, Palermo, Tip. dello Statuto, 1887, p. 44.

Vio was critical of the *societas negotiatoria*, merchant partnerships based on capital and labour; he branded as usurers men who put capital into a partnership at an agreed rate of interest without bearing their share of capital risk.[11]

In the sixteenth century, merchants devised crafty schemes to evade the canonist ban on interest-bearing loans, even though medieval doctrine included the concepts of loss of expected profit, consequential damages and capital risk that effectively broadened the scope for lending. As a result, the practice of demanding increasingly high interest to compensate for loss of expected profit had become widespread, and compensation in full was claimed from debtors in arrears. De Vio spoke out against such lenders: though he acknowledged that some form of payment was due for loss of expected profit, he stressed the essential difference between actually or potentially being in possession of something, and the corresponding difference between compensation for actual or potential loss.[12] In this, too, De Vio was faithful to medieval doctrine.

As already mentioned, men used various schemes in their everyday lives to flout the ban on usury. Of these, the most important was the art of money changing: in the sixteenth century, it was not only the most sought after and profitable of professions, but also the most controversial, in terms of its legitimacy. This explains why Girolamo Sauli, Bishop of Genica, bowed to the request of citizens and appointed a commission of theologians to determine, once and for all, the legality of the Lyon clearing Fair.[13] The status of money changing was discussed in other works of the period, including the well-known *Notizia de' Cambi* by Davanzati,[14] though in this case the author

---

[11] T. De Vio, *De societate negotiatoria*, in *Opuscula oeconomico-socialia*, cit., pp. 174-175.

[12] «Sicut inter habere aliquid in actu et habere illud in potentia multum refert, sic magna debet esse differentia inter recompensationem eius quod habetur in actu, et illius quod possidetur in potentia». T. De Vio, *De lucro sive de petizione lucri cessantis*, in *Opuscula oeconomico-socialia*, cit., p. 166 and following.

See the detailed historical and theological assessement of De Vio's response by Crosara, in his essay: A. Crosara, *Sovranità dello Stato e prepotere del denaro*, «Rivista di Storia del Pensiero Economico», VI, 1937, p. 295.

[13] Cf. Fabiano, *op. cit.*, c. 1.

[14] In his historical preface on the origin of money changing, Davanzati wrote «they began to open their eyes and to see that between the one payment and the other, there being an interval of time between them, it was possible to make use of the money of another, and it seemed honest to render interest for this, or interfuit: and so they made the second payment, and some of the first, and thereby paid more than they received. Greed for this exchange has risen it to an art; and damaged money not through the need to have part of it elsewhere but to have it with interest; to take it not by transfer from another place but to make use of the money of others for a certain time, with interest; and Saint Anthony and De Vio and other theologians concur, if this be for the public good. So that if Exchange were not an art, it would be rare and it would not occur whenever goods are bought or sold, as is now the case; so less money would be exchanged and less good come of it for society and human life; which the more is agitated and made splendid, not to say blessed, the

focused on the technical workings of markets rather than questions of morality. In 1499, with remarkable foresight, De Vio discussed money changing, and formulated a set of principles later embraced by theologians when they returned to the question. Laymen also referred to De Vio whenever confronted with the moral aspects of money changing.[15] Regardless of the procedure De Vio used to analyze specific cases, his conclusions are noteworthy: as an occupation, money changing was certainly just, and it was legitimate to earn a profit for providing a service to the community. On the other hand, a private individual, rather than a campsor, who occasionally changed florins to dinars was not entitled to even the smallest reward on the grounds that it was unjust.[16] Changing currencies that had been obtained at a lower rate in one place at a second place where their value and purchasing power was higher was also legitimate.[17] Also permissable was «cum campsor moderate lucratur ex eo, quod Petrus habens certam summam pecuniae Mediolani, dat eam campsori, qui faciat aequalem summam Romae dari sibi vel alteri. Si enim ex hoc campsor mercedem exigit, iusta est exactio; campsor enim translatoris in hac parte locum tenet. Nec est aequum, ut merces suo servitio subtrahatur».[18]

On the other hand, De Vio considered usurious the transactions carried out by money changers who, rather than serving the common good, feigned contracts on the London or Bruges money exchanges to conceal usurious loans. This was the case, for example, when a money changer lent a sum to a citizen of Milan, claiming to have changed it at the going rate in another town, yet knowing full well that the sum would re-exchanged in Milan.[19] Such prac-

---

more men are active and engaged and work together for the common weal; so that even if those who exchange money have no good desire in their hearts, the universal effect is good and a large number of evils of nature are avoided for the greater good». B. DAVANZATI, *Notizia de' cambi*, in *Le opere di Bernardo Davanzati*, Firenze, Le Monnier, 1853, vol. II, pp. 428-429.

[15] Davanzati however (cf. the previous note) did not comment on De Vio's distinction between legitimate and illegitimate forms of money changing for small sums.

[16] Currency changing occurred when a *campsor* bought foreign coins with the legal currency of the town where the money changing took place. A small profit was allowed in this case, as compensation for the work of the campsor in the name of the common good. Such a profit would have been illegal if the various coins listed in the exchange contract had been wrongly itemized (T. DE VIO, *De cambiis*, in *Opuscula oeconomico-socialia*, cit., p. 94). Cf. FABIANO, *op. cit.*, c. 17. Fabiano defined the changing of coins as: *reale solo*, also known as *currency changing*, because more often than not the transaction involved petty sums of money. Cf. FABIANO, *op. cit.*, c. 2.

[17] DE VIO, *De Cambiis*, cit., p. 95. «Quando campsor lucratum ex eo, quod monetam alicubi minus valentem congregatam, transfert in locum ubi plus valet. Haec enim est negotiatio numismatum ... Et est licita, sicut ceterae negotiationes ad augendas opes licent».

[18] [A certain additional price is legitimate for those forms of exchange that require goods to be moved from one place to another]. *Ibid.*

[19] *Ibid.* Note that one of the functions of medieval and above all modern fairs was to provide

tices undermined the public utility of the money changing service, the profits of which were to be «non propter tempus sed propter loci distantiam». The Churchmen accommodated the needs of economic life by sanctioning institutions and trades that served both the private and the public good. Padre Fabiano stated on many occasions that, despite the legitimacy of the forms of exchange cited by De Vio, it was impossible to justify the «workings of the bankers, who in all their affects and turning their mind entirely to it, intend to accumulate earthly riches, laying their hearts in abeyance; and giving their money to exchange in Lyon and Bisenzone only to make more money».[20] Through an inordinate love of riches, Church rules governing the order of economic life came to be broken, the very rules that Christians were to consider a path to virtue rather than a way to satisfy their base passion for goods. «They use money – wrote Fabiano alluding to certain bankers – with too much affect for gain, which is their unending passion; and do not use money as an instrument of civil art».[21]

Returning to De Vio, it is worth mentioning his position on the Thomistic principle of donating excess wealth to the poor. Certain commentators of Aquinas (II, II, 9, 32, a. 5-6) mistakenly considered the duty to donate simply a recommendation of the Church, unless the giver had such wealth and the receiver was in such dire need that it became a true obligation. In his interpretation of Aquinas, De Vio acknowledged that both conditions were indeed necessary; however, he clarified that extreme need should not be interpreted as literally dying of poverty, and that excess wealth should not be construed on the basis of all conceivable future needs, but only those needs that were likely to arise.[22] In this way, De Vio ruled out any over-concern with future needs, and compelled the wealthy to be charitable as a matter of obedience to a principle. De Vio remained faithful to the Scholastic tradition,[23] except with regard to questions of state.

How did such an original solution square with the rest of his thought? It seems that De Vio, who lived in a century in which rising above one's station

---

usurious loans, using a series of sophisticated legal expedients. For an analysis of fairs as markets for loans, see G. MANDICH, *Delle fiere genovesi di cambi particolarmente studiate come mercati periodici del credito*, «Rivista di Storia Economica», IV, 1939.

[20] FABIANO, *op. cit.*, c. 4.

[21] *Ibid.*

[22] T. DE VIO, *De eleemosynae praecepto*, in *Opuscula oeconomica-socialia*, cit., pp. 5-7, 14-15.

[23] On the question of whether De Vio's solutions agreed or conflicted with the canonist precepts, see T. FORNARI, *Delle teorie economiche nelle provincie napolitane dal sec. XIII al MDCCXXXIV. Studi storici*, Milano, Hoepli, 1882, p. 96.

was not uncommon, justified social mobility through hard work as the sign of a true vocation. However, wealth was not to be acquired by violating the principles of justice, as men in his day had become so accustomed to doing (both in preserving or increasing their wealth). If an individual was called to a higher social standing, De Vio sanctioned new wealth in so far as it allowed him to donate more generously to the needy and to fund good works. In this respect, De Vio followed the Scholastic theologians who perceived wealth as a vehicle for charitable giving.

De Vio explicitly and unconditionally defended the principle of accumulating wealth in his treatment of money changing, when he declared that *negotiatio numismatum sicut ceterae negotiationes ad augendas opes*[24] was legitimate. This was a rather controversial claim, one De Vio motivated in the light of ancient Thomistic ideals. Nevertheless, such a principle was not enshrined in the broad legislation of the Great Council on economic ethics. And neither did it gain widespread acceptance from the pulpit that, as seen below, played such a crucial role in spreading the social effects of the Counter Reformation.

Like Fabiano and other scholars, De Vio derived his social theory directly from the Scholastic theologians, whose ideas also had a considerable influence on the virtually unknown Bishop of the diocese of Gallese, Girolamo Garimberto, author of *De regimenti de la città*.[25] Garimberto's fierce invectives against usury, concealed principally in money changing activities in the sixteenth century, are reminiscent of the severe condemnation by Scholastic theologians of this illicit means of acquiring wealth.[26] The desire for excess and luxury drove many into the hands of usurers to fund their extravagances;[27] Garimberto condemned usury with the same rigour of the Church-

---

[24] DE VIO, *De Cambiis*, cit., p. 95.

[25] G. GARIMBERTO, *De' regimenti publici de la città*, Vinegia, appresso G. Scotto, 1544.
Garimberto, who was Bishop of Gallese, died in 1565, as stated at page 686 of P.B. GAMS, *Series episcoporum Ecclesiae catholicae*, Ratisbonae, G.J. Manz, 1873. Nothing else is known about him, apart from a few observations in Curcio (C. CURCIO, *Dal rinascimento alla controriforma: contributo alla storia del pensiero politico italiano da Guicciardini a Botero*, Roma, Colombo, 1934).

[26] Garimberto did not deny the utility of a money changing service «considering the great ease that comes of having money in diverse cities and countries far away, without suspicion or danger of losing it on the way from one to another, and with it, as often occurs, life itself». However, he abhorred foreign exchange transactions that clearly deviated from this honest purpose in the desire to earn «denari in infinito» (GARIMBERTO, *op. cit.*, p. VIII). His continuing emphasis on the legitimacy of these operations shows that they had become commonplace in everyday life, in the same way as the fixed income from interest-bearing loans. Garimberto claimed that once an indisposed usurer (p. VIII) who «unable to retain his food» one day said he feared he would vomit his innards: «you have nought to compain of – a gentleman replied – because you will not vomit your own intestines; but those of the bodies you devour every moment of the day».

[27] *Ibid.*, p. VIII.

men of earlier centuries. Nor did he show any compassion for the uncontrolled urge to possess goods abhorred by Scholastic theologians on the grounds that men content with their status should give their excess riches to the poor. Garimberto alluded to this duty when he insisted that rich men should succour the poor with due compassion and generosity.[28] Up to this point, the principles of the Scholastic theologians and those of Galimberto coincide. But closer analysis reveals Plato's influence on Galimberto, as on other authors of the sixteenth century.

Garimberto scorned the humble trades: cobbler, blacksmith, woodcutter, tailor, builder and so on.[29] These men were not suited to a life of civic virtue, the supreme goal of all men. Intellect, knowledge and prudence were the cornerstones of civic virtue, a quality that enabled righteous men to defend the city and to make it a great and noble place.[30]

Merchants were not admitted to the aristocracy, though as a category they ranked well above craftsmen. By means of «navigation, or conducting merchandise with beasts or carts or carrying the goods of others» merchants accumulated the wealth that Garimberto considered an essential part of the common good.[31] Without economic goods, citizens «cannot increase or dispense the common weal of the country they are from».[32] And it was by virtue of their possessions that wealthy merchants were allowed join the ranks of the aristocracy, the governors of the city, provided they refrained from trade and lived an honest life.[33] Though Garimberto condoned trade, he was concerned that efforts to acquire goods distracted men, diverting them from noble virtue; the true source of human happiness came not from bodily goods or wealth, but rather from introspection and contemplation, far more worthy and virtuous than actions.[34] It was not Galimberto's intention to undermine the importance of wealth that it given enabled citizens to perform virtuous deeds.[35] However, in seeking the riches that were fitting and necessary for an honest and virtuous life, men should be aware that only virtue led to true happiness. Since citizens cought up freuried trading activities ranked wealth

---

[28] *Ibid.*, p. LXI.
[29] *Ibid.*, pp. XI-XIII.
[30] *Ibid.*, pp. XI-XIII.
[31] *Ibid.*, pp. VIII-IX.
[32] *Ibid.*, pp. XVII-XVIII.
[33] *Ibid.*, pp. XI-XIII, XVII-XVIII. See the analogous concept of Sarpi (chapter III).
[34] GARIMBERTO, *op. cit.*, pp. LIII-LX.
[35] *Ibid.*, pp. LIII, XVII-XVIII.

higher than virtue, the city had a duty to rein in economic instincts and thereby prevent trade from tainting the nobility of the city. Following Plato, Garimberto recommended that towns should be located not directly by the sea, but close to it, to prevent the different ideals and customs of foreign merchants from corrupting the moral integrity of the virtuous city.[36]

Having said this, it is not clear what induced Curcio, always so exacting in his scholarship, to misquote Galimberto as saying «happiness, contrary to Plato's view, is found in wealth».[37] In fact, the meaning of Galimberto's claim was entirely different. In the *Regimenti* Garimberto stated that the city should be «made comfortable with goods of fortune which are instruments of happiness». What seems to have misled Curcio was a marginal note in his copy that read «a new interpretation of Plato». This is confirmed by Garimberto's assertion that «supreme happiness lies in the contemplative part of our soul».[38] And when he wrote that riches «are instruments of a happy life» he immediately clarified that without riches, the city would be overwhelmed by poverty. Galimberto described the dire consequences for a city lacking in material wealth: its moral life could not prosper without a certain measure of economic affluence.

In a city with a mass of paupers, the rich would be obliged to provide Christian charity. In Galimberto's mind, this type of social inequality did not correspond to the ideal of the common good; unlike Plato, he argued that goods should be privately owned. The misleading marginal note that induced Curcio to attribute to Garimberto an idea in contrast with his economic thought can be summarized as follows: the virtuous city was a political and economic ideal, and riches were useful. However, since the pursuit of wealth distracted citizens from virtue, economic activities should be reduced to a minimum, leaving manual work to menial labourers and providing ample scope for the noble-minded to dedicate themselves to a life of contemplation, and in so doing, to discover true happiness. If merchants with newly acquired wealth wished to join the ranks of those who led a life of blessed virtue, they were to abandon their trades and through honest and virtuous conduct seek to rise to the ranks of the city's nobility. The virtue and grandeur of the city therefore represented an ideal for Garimberto, while farming the land after a life in the city was a sign of of poverty or even depravity.[39]

---

[36] *Ibid.*, pp. LIV-LV. Note the analogy between these principles and similar rules dictated by PLATONE in the *Republic*.

[37] CURCIO, *op. cit.*, pp. 19-20.

[38] GARIMBERTO, *op. cit.*, p. LX.

[39] *Ibid.*, p. IV.

2. Garimberto's *De regimenti* brings us to the second half of the sixteenth century, to the period when the Council of Trent was laying the foundations of the far-reaching reforms that had such a major impact on the religious and moral life of the Italian people. The following chapter provides an in-depth examination of the economic morals that the Council imposed to guide the faithful in their commercial pursuits towards the spiritual aims that were beginning to be neglected in favour of wealth acquisition. The paragraphs below describe the economic aspirations embodied in the social doctrine of the Church, and the attitudes it condemned as contrary to the spirit of Christianity.

It is important to bear in mind that while the Reformists claimed to refer directly to the Old and New Testaments, dispensing with the authority of tradition, the Catholic Counter Reformists returned to the original sources of Chistianity, to which they remained faithful in clarifying dogma and re-establishing practices. This explains the plethora of commentaries to the Holy Books consulted directly by those who spread evangelical principles on wealth. One work that remained virtually unknown, despite its value in documenting the endeavours of the Churchmen of the Counter Reformation to Christianize economic life, was the *Institutionis Oeconomicae*[40] of Stefano Menochio presented below.

Garimberti was contemptuous of men who, after living a virtuous life in the city, went to toil in the fields. Menochio, on the other hand, was a staunch proponent of rural life and farming. Life in the fields, he argued, was not only merry and pleasurable, but altogether practical, useful and honest. Who could deny the joy of the endless plains, the rolling hills, the menacing yet beautiful aspect of the high mountains, the lakes, the rivers, the winding streams and the herds wandering through green pastures?[41] The countryside offered everything necessary for human life, and it was all free, without the need

---

[40] G.S. MENOCHIO, *Institutionis oeconomicae ex Sacris litteris depromptae*, Lugduni, ex officina Rovilliana, 1627. Apart from a mention by the man from Perugia Lancellotti (S. LANCELLOTTI, *L'hoggidi overo il mondo non peggiore, ne più calamitoso del passato*, Venetia, Guerigli, 1658, Disinganno XIX, pp. 396-397) and some brief remarks by U. GOBBI (p. 126 and p. 39 in *L'economia politica negli scrittori italiani del secolo XVI-XVII*, cit.) no other authors appear to have known him. This text is not even mentioned in the brief entry on Menochio in the *Enciclopedia italiana*. The reader should refer to *Bibliothèque de la Compagnie de Jésus*, ed. by C. Sommervogel, Bruxelles-Paris, Schepens-Picard, 1894, t. V, p. 948. Also of interest is the *Dizionario biografico universale: contenente le notizie più importanti sulla vita e sullo opere degli uomini celebri*, ed. by F. Scifoni, Firenze, Passigli, 1844, p. 1086. Note that Menochio himself translated the *Institutionis* into Italian: G.S. MENOCHIO, *Economica Christiana*, Venetia, Per il Baba, 1656. The Italian translation contains several additions and important references to other authors, including some laymen.

[41] MENOCHIO, *op. cit.*, p. 156.

for farmers to mistreat their neighbours «quod de mercatura, aliisque non nullis quaestuosis artibus dici facile non potest, quae rem familiarem ampliorem quidem faciunt, sed alios quibuscum commercia exercentur, quodammodo depeculantur, et spoliant».[42] Menochio acknowledged the joyful purposefulness and upright honesty of labouring in the fields, and marvelled that «nostro aevo cum oppida plerumque domini habitent, et agricolationem sordidam putent, villicis fundo, mercenariisque praeponunt, qui in dominorum locum substituti munus patris familias et partes impleant».[43]

While Menochio frowned upon the nobility that left their fertile estates uncared for, loathe to touch a spade or a plough,[44] he did not condemn trade: on the contrary, trade made it possible to export goods in abundance and import those in short supply. He scorned the petty trading of men who bought and immediately sold on for a profit,[45] a Ciceronian ideal echoed by many other Italian scholars of the Modern Age, as seen below.

Agriculture and trade were important concepts in Menochio's economic theory, and represented the principal means of acquiring wealth. Agriculture was an ideal of life and and trade a legitimate activity provided it did not harm others through fraud. Did Menochio apply the same criterion of sufficiency that had inspired doctrine and practices in earlier centuries? In other words, were men allowed to become rich and, through economic activity, climb the social ladder? The response of Scholastic theologians from the thirteenth to the fifteenth centuries was a resounding no. Most Churchmen shared this opinion, including one of Menochio's contemporaries who wrote that every man should accept «his state, conferred upon him by God, whether rich or poor, thanking his divine Majesty».[46] De Vio was of a different view: he considered the accumulation of wealth legitimate only if an individual was fit for a higher social standing. Menochio followed in De Vio's footsteps: though mindful of St. John's warning against riches,[47] he asserted that the head of the household

---

[42] [A merchant's activities involve many risks]. *Ibid.*, p. 161.

[43] [Many disdain life in the country and leave their lands to the management of employees]. *Ibid.*, p. 184.

[44] *Ibid.*, p. 154. «Sane de agricoltura, ut hinc ordiamur, publice concepta et confirmata est vulgaris existimatio rem rusticam sordidam esse negotium, quod ingenuis inhonestum sit, ac pudendum, ac proinde falcibus et aratris relictis omnes fere nobiles viri dudum intra murum correspserunt, et iam rura colere, aut colonorum opera administrare, aut illis praeesse pudor est».

[45] *Ibid.*, p. 218.

[46] C. Bascapè, *Scritti pubblicati da mons. reverendiss. d. Carlo vescovo di Novara, nel governo del suo vescovato dall'anno 1593 fino al 1609: ridotti in volume per commodità de' cleri, e popoli della sua chiesa*, Milano, per Ambrogio Ramellati, 1660, p. 185.

[47] John, *Apocalisse*, XVIII, 19. «Vae vae civitas illa magna, in qua divites facti sunt omnes, qui habebant naves in mari, de pretiis eius, quoniam una hora desolata est».

should not only preserve his wealth but even increase it, especially when the Lord had blessed him with a large family. Naturally, in the process of acquiring goods Christians were not to become victims of blind greed, a vice more harmful to the soul than poverty to the body.[48] Here, once again, the Churchmen came to the same conclusions about economic motivation as men of practical life.

While Menochio and De Vio before him distanced themselves in certain respects from Scholastic economic thought, most other scholars of the Counter Reformation embraced these ideals. Of specific interest here are preachers, whose homilies had the power to influence the customs and everyday life of people. In particular, those of the venerable Bartolomeo da Salutio[49] are a valuable source for the history of thought.

The economic ideals of Padre Castiglione da Genova, who in 1583 dedicated a series of sermons to the great Archbishop of Milan[50] are of particular relevance here. Those familiar with the pomp and luxury of the Italian people at the end of the sixteenth century[51] will understand why he condemned men who did nothing but «give their bodies all ease, comfort, delight and pleasures, in eating and drinking, in clothing, and making palaces not for ordinary citizens but fitting for a king».[52] Castiglione warned that: «we refuse such delights and superfluity as today are common, and in sobriety, not like the Megarians: of whom it was said proverbially *aedificant sicut semper victuri, et comedunt, quasi cras morituri*».[53] He preached sobriety to the Megarians of his day, that could be achieved only by men content with «the necessities of life and dress» who gave «all that is in excess of this to the poor».[54] Castiglione did not just recommend moderation, he considered it a rule of life, and one not to be brushed aside by men on their way up the social ladder. Unlike De Vio and Menochio, Castiglione considered those «not content with their condition and state who aspire to greater riches and comfort» mortal sin-

---

[48] MENOCHIO, *op. cit.*, p. 206.

[49] Cf. F. SARRI, *Il venerabile Bartolomeo Cambi da Salutio: (1557-1617) oratore, mistico, poeta*, Firenze, Bemporad, 1925. A selection of the works of this well-known preacher can be found in the volume ed. by ID., *Ven. Bartolomeo da Salutio*, Firenze, libr. Ed. Fior., 1924.

[50] A. CASTIGLIONE, *Homelie del reverendo padre A. Castiglione Carmelitano da Genova*, Milano, appresso Pacifico Pontio, 1584.

[51] B. CROCE, *La Spagna nella vita italiana durante la Rinascenza*, n.t.n.; F. NICOLINI, *Aspetti della vita italo-spagnuola nel Cinque e Seicento*, Napoli, Guida, 1934.

[52] CASTIGLIONE, *op. cit.*, part I, p. 32.

[53] *Ibid.*, part I, p. 10.

[54] *Ibid.*, part I, p. 9. «Those do not live well who become wealthy through robbery, usury, fraud and deceit, murdering poor widows and taking bread from the hand of orphans».

ners.[55] That is why he condemned the «greedy and avaricious», who, in their lust for money «expose themselves to a thousand dangers, by water, fire, on land, at sea, to earn and acquire wealth». Continuing in his description of men eager to rise in society at any cost, Castiglione noted: «not everyone is desirous to double their wealth and to accumulate *scudo* upon *scudo*; and they go fearful that their goods may shipwreck or a debtor may go bankrupt and not pay».[56] The type of merchant he described corresponds to the unscrupulous capitalists of today. Castiglione thus confirmed the traditional, static conception of social class professed with few exceptions by Churchmen throughout the sixteenth and seventeenth centuries.

Castiglione thought it sinful to aspire to greatness and importance, and despicable to become rich by harming one's neighbour.[57] Merchants were not to hide defects in their goods, to swindle the buyer, and so on.[58] Inevitably, interest-bearing loans, robbery and fraud[59] were mentioned frequently in the works of Churchmen, being common means of acquiring wealth in those centuries. Castiglione was emphatic in his condemnation of gambling or games of fortune, and indeed any form of pastime involving gaming rather than simple amusement.

Gambling was not a passion only for men: women played with dice, gathering with cards in hand around tables to play. Card games ceased to be an innocent pastime when merchants started to bet not just a few pennies but 25, 50 or as much as 100 *scudi*.[60]

Merchants were enjoined to abstain from gambling, prohibited under both civil and Church laws,[61] and likewise from unrestrained and aggressive commercial dealings. While merchants, like all tradesmen, were prohibited

---

[55] *Ibid.*, part II, p. 415.

[56] *Ibid.*, p. 471.

[57] *Ibid.*, p. 415.

[58] *Ibid.*, pp. 415-416.

[59] Those who expect to get rich through robbery, fraud and deceit, who assassinate ill-fated widows, and take away bread from orphans, do not live a just life. *Ibid.*, part I, p. 10.

[60] CASTIGLIONE, *op. cit.*, part II, pp. 472-475. Those who gamble, observed Castiglione, cannot claim that they are playing for enjoyment. Only a prince or a king can claim this. «But that a gentleman, a citizen, a merchant and a lady bet ten, twenty-five, fifty and one hundred scudi not for avarice or gain, but to pass the time, who will believe such a thing?» MENOCHIO (*op. cit.*, p. 526) also condemned gambling, because it distracted men from their family affairs and had infinite and disastrous moral consequences. In Savonarola's Confessionale, published by Sauli after the Council of Trent with certain additions (G. SAVONAROLA, *Confessionale reveren. fratris Hieronymi Savonarolae ordinis praedicatorum... per Reverendum D. Alexandrum Saulium Theologum, collectis et revisis*, Pavia, apud Hieronymum Bartholum, 1571, p. 72), it states: «Porro qui faciunt chartas, et taxillos, non debent absolvi antequam desistant ab hoc opere».

[61] CASTIGLIONE, *op. cit.*, part II.

from working on rest days, tailors, cobblers and shoemakers flouted the ban and, to avoid losing trade, worked all Sunday morning. In reality, holy days were not observed by the merchants either; to expedite business on workdays they checked their books and did their accounts on rest days.[62]

The purpose of the ban, Castiglione explained, was not to make it a sin to work; on the contrary, work served to ward off sloth, the root of all evil: «it is a good thing to avoid idleness, cause of every vice». «But God prohibits on rest days servile work so that we may rest from the affairs of the world and earthly occupations and dedicate ourselves to the good of our souls».[63]

Castiglione's economic ethics reflected the traditional spirit of Churchmen in their writings and preaching; above all, they advocated faith in divine providence, and discouraged excessive concern with accumulating wealth rather than honest and diligent labour. The Churchmen's ideal of economic life contrasted with the thinking on wealth of Leon Battista Alberti, one century earlier.

However, one Churchman did derive his economic principles from this fifteenth century humanist. In the *Chronicles*, written between 1638 and 1671[64] Gregorio Gattioli, a Cappucine monk from Ala, was principally concerned with the proper means of acquiring wealth. «Do not allow another living creature to know how much money or goods you keep in the house, act like a poor man, because that way you will live more safely, and no-one will ask for a loan. To be safe – continued the bizarre seventeenth century Churchman – you can claim you are up to your neck in debts and you can arrange with God not to be considered a liar».[65] The final and ironic recommendation not to lie is of no concern here. What is interesting is the evident similarity the warning not to lend and Alberti's identical suggestion two centuries earlier.[66] Alberti prudently advised against lending, particularly to friends or nobles. Gattioli was not the only scholar to follow Alberti's cautious approach. «Do business with those who are poorer than you – warned Gattioli – because you will have expertise they do not have and if you deal with them prudently you will earn something, because the poor make homes rich. But if you wish to do business with those who are richer than you and to make merry with them and be en-

---

[62] *Ibid.*, part I, p. 87.

[63] *Ibid.*, part I, p. 91.

[64] Partially ed. by A. DE CESARE, *Un massimario di economia sociale del seicento nel Trentino*, «Nuova Antologia», 1917.

[65] *Ibid.*, p. 170.

[66] FANFANI, *Le origini*, cit., p. 146.

tertained, they will snap at you with harsh words and if you show resentment they will call you a base villain; leave off such company».[67]

Gattioli was concerned to avoid swindling others in the acquisition of wealth; he condemned efforts to improve one's standard of living, advising men to engage in business with persons of a similar rank to make a safe profit. Fame and honour, considered by the humanists to be the ultimate goals of economic life, became secondary: Gattioli focused on the purely miserly intent of earning a calculated profit. Prudence taken one step further became wealth earned by wordly means for wordly purposes, as Alberti defined it, and thus became a means unto itself, condemning those who pursued wealth to a life void of pleasure or satisfaction. Gattioli went on to perfect his economic moral thought, delving into the subtlest nuances: «Do not trust servants and housekeepers because many have been found who steal a little at a time, and then marry among themselves. Keep your eyes open against thievery; I recall a housekeeper in love with a steward who not only treated him to all manner of delicacies but gave him the most excellent wine in the household and also handkerchiefs she told the masters had been lost by the children».[68] Gattioli recommended the same prudence in household management as in the purchase of essential goods: «If you wish to acquire some item with advantage, do so in good time. If it is wine you desire to purchase, do so at the harvest, or oil when it is made, or grain when it is separated. Because those who sell at such times do not think on't. For summer dress, purchase in winter, and buy warm clothing in summer».[69]

Alberti's principle of prudence is also evident in Gattioli's warning: «Above all, take care not to fall into security, the cause of the ruin of many households».[70] The same is true of the following advice: «During summer, when things are harvested, set store for the winter, which is long, and in the cold everything turns to good. Take lesson from the ants».[71] Similar was Gattioli's advice to take wife, who should be not only be virtuous, but also adept at household chores.[72] Gattioli summed up his moral philosophy as follows: «Wish to become wealthy, commence in youth, work and set aside

---

[67] DE CESARE, *op. cit.*, p. 172.

[68] *Ibid.*

[69] *Ibid.*, p. 171.

[70] *Ibid.*, p. 172. By surety perhaps what is meant here is: a signature of approval for credit extended to a third person.

[71] *Ibid.*

[72] *Ibid.*, p. 171. Alberti also stated that a wife should be a good housewife. Cf. FANFANI, *Le origini*, cit., p. 139.

the fruits of your labours, and keep vigil on your appetites, keep off taverns, dress according to your state and do not waste time, and you will prosper».[73]

Gattioli's reference to spending in proportion to social status apparently echoes a Scholastic precept. In reality, it was dictated by the principle of prudence. He did not merely justify saving, he demanded it: for reasons of prudence, and no other, it was vital to curb unproductive expenses. No concept could have been in sharper contrast with economic ideals of the Middle Ages, or closer to the economic spirit of Alberti, though Gattioli's ultimate goal was not fame or honour, as it was for the humanists. In his book, he dealt with a very limited economic world, without capitalist concerns. Gattioli's followers were rather shallow figures, men who sacrificed everything to wealth, to amassing goods, almost to the point of overlooking the very needs that wealth should serve to satisfy. If a man had to quell his every aspiration[74] to accumulate more and more wealth, what scope was left, in his pratical ideal of life, for charity and the social function of wealth? Here, individualism, first seen in Alberti's thought, was taken to the extreme, conveying a vision of wealth and of life itself similar to that of Molière's Harpagon, and a wretched view of economic activity. This conflicted with the Christian ideals spread by the Churchmen, who dismissed Gattioli as a voice out of tune with the Church's unified social doctrine.

3. A representative example of Church social doctrine during the Counter Reformation can be found in the works of Segneri, the best known seventeenth century orator.[75] His lessons on economics are of remarkable historical value. The social principles he propounded in his works were not the ideals of an individual; they enshrined the rules of economic ethics that he preached to

---

[73] DE CESARE, *op. cit.*, p. 171.

[74] «Of all things to guard yourself against, the first is not to offend God, next do not waste time with games, women and horses, or else you shall not become wealthy and shall lose what wealth you have». *Ibid.*

[75] For more on Segneri's life cf.: F. RANALLI, *Vita di Paolo Segneri*, in P. SEGNERI, *Quaresimale del Padre Paolo Segneri*, ed. by F. Ranalli, Prato, Dalla Tipografia Guasti, 1841; A.G. TONONI, *Il Padre Segneri nei ducati di Parma e Piacenza*, «Rassegna Nazionale», IV, 1895. As well as the works of M. Ziino, the following are important sources on sixteenth century sacred eloquence: S. VENTO, *Le condizioni della oratoria sacra del Seicento: ricerche e critica*, Milano, Dante Alighieri di Albrighi Segati, 1916 and the review by A. BELLONI, *Sebastiano Vento, le condizioni dell'oratoria sacra del Seicento. Ricerche e critica*, «Giornale Storico della Letteratura Italiana», LXX, 1917, pp. 188-195; E. SANTINI, *L'eloquenza italiana dal Concilio Tridentino ai nostri giorni*, Palermo, Sandron, 1923. See also G. BARBIERI, *La funzione dei beni economici secondo Paolo Segneri*, «Convivium», 6, XIV, 1935.

innumerable crowds of followers thoughout Italy for many long years, his aim being to promote the moral renewal of society.[76]

Following in the tradition of Apostolic teaching of Bartolomeo Cambi, Segneri became familiar with the politely attentive congregations in great cathedrals, and the chaotic enthusiasm of the country folk who followed him during his missions. Such direct contact with the spiritual and material needs people from walks of life urged him to preach the principles of Faith and the Christian precepts of the social order of wealth. As Segneri became ever more aware of the profound conflicts emerging in society,[77] he focused increasingly on questions of business, aiming to improve the distribution of goods by re-asserting the instrumental nature of wealth, a concept he took pains to define and disseminate within the Church's tradition of economic thought, as discussed below.

Segneri claimed that worldly goods were bestowed upon men by God as a ladder to heaven.[78] Wealth was to be be valued like any other means that facilitated the ascent to God. Of all means, however, wealth was the most insidious, not in itself, but owing to the particular nature of men who were inclined to make inappropriate use of it.[79] What was relevant was not how much or how little men possessed, but what they did with their wealth. «Evil does not consist in possessing such things, but in the attitude to possessing these things. They may be possessed by Arrigo, the most saintly of Emperors, by Gregorio, Carlo, Casimiro, Louis King of France, and none were ruined, because they were mindful to put them to God's uses. Evil consists in believing such things sufficient for a blessed life, and the more possessions the higher blessing».[80]

Belief in the heavenly powers of wordly goods made men slaves. Segneri warned men to remain aware of their fragility and to treat economic goods with circumspection[81] and a degree of scorn.[82] All too often, rather than being a path to Heaven, worldly goods kept men from it.[83]

---

[76] A. BELLONI, *Il Seicento*, Milano, Vallardi, 1930, p. 512.

[77] P. SEGNERI, *Il Cristiano istruito nella sua legge*, in *Opere del Padre Paolo Segneri*, Venezia, Stamperia Baglioni, 1773, t. III, p. 239; ID., *Quaresimale*, in *Opere del Padre Paolo Segneri*, cit., t. II, p. 202. See the vivid description of the crimes committed by men who financed their lives of pomp and luxury by tricking and swindling the weak and the poor (*ibid.*, t. II, p. 200).

[78] ID., *Il Cristiano istruito*, cit., t. III, part II, R. 19, no. 4, p. 174.

[79] ID., *La manna dell'anima*, in *Opere del Padre Paolo Segneri*, cit., t. I, p. 19, 20 January.

[80] *Ibid.*, t. I, p. 370, 23 August.

[81] *Ibid.*, t. I, p. 372, 23 August.

[82] *Ibid.*, t. I, p. 14 (10 January); p. 19 (20 January); p. 32 (1 February); p. 43 (12 February); p. 75 (13 March); p. 78 (16 March); p. 164 (4 May); p. 168 (7 May); p. 351 (12 August).

[83] *Ibid.*, t. I, p. 14 (10 January).

3

Despite the temptations of economic goods and the diffidence men were supposed to show towards them, Christians could not avoid contact with material wealth. In the natural and inevitable relations between Christians and worldly goods, it was important not to overlook the fundamental truth that all earthly riches, as well as those of the heavens, belonged to God, «and those who possess them are not independent; they dispense, distribute and administer them».[84]

The notion that the possessor of economic goods was not the owner, but rather acted as an administrator on behalf of God undermined the concept of private property: ownership became a diminished right, or even a duty towards God, the provider of economic goods. Nevertheless, Segneri justified the right to own property: economic goods were instrumental to a virtuous life, allowing men to feed themselves, help their neighbours and ascend to heaven.

Segneri's ideas on acquiring wealth followed a similar vein. From a Godly perspective, accumulating riches was not only legitimate, it was a duty,[85] though not all means were equally proper. Ideally, wealth was to be acquired through labour: toil entitled the worker to the fruits of his labour. As well as work, Segneri condoned all other acquisitive activities, provided they did not violate the rights of others or the spiritual life of the labourer; in other words, on condition that economic activity respected the principles of commutative justice and did not distract men from their ultimate goal. Everthing men did was to serve as a means to God.[86]

This explains Segneri's distrust of certain payment deferrals granted by merchants, who justified the higher prices they charged by claiming loss of expected profit, consequential damages or capital risk. Such transactions were ill-disguised instances of usury that yielded to the voracious lender illegitimate profits from the sale of time, which belonged not to man but to God.[87] Em-

---

[84] SEGNERI, *Il Cristiano istruito*, cit., t. III, p. 154, part I, R. 17, no. 6; ID., *Quaresimale*, cit., t. II, p. 193, Predica 22.

[85] Cf. FANFANI, *Le origini*, cit., p. 25.

[86] SEGNERI, *Il Cristiano istruito*, cit., p. 51, part I, R. 6, no. 16. The acquisition of goods through gambling was condemned, both for the moral dangers and because it discouraged men from hard work (*ibid.*, t. III, p. 313, part III, R. 32, no. 10). On the distastrous consequences of a passion for gambling, the following episode is interesting: «A young man, in the city of Milan, had nought but a house in the country, and wished to sell even this to go gaming, but because the house was rustic and without land, it was left to ruin. But this did not dissuade him from his purpose. So he took off the roof and tiles and sold them, living in the house with the cold, damp, worse than any wolf in its den» (*ibid.*, p. 312, part III, R. 32, no. 9).

[87] *Ibid.*, pp. 240-241, part I, R. 26, no. 6. In these cases Segneri admitted that the creditor was not asking for a price above the fair price, but only the highest in the range of fair prices. Given that

ployers who paid their workers in kind were equally deplorable and violated justice by overrating the goods given to the workers and undervaluing the goods the employers received.[88] Segneri also censured buyers who offered a less than fair price or paid with debased currency, and shopkeepers who didn't provide lighting to conceal the defects in their wares.[89]

We could continue the long list of instances of improper conduct. Though the principles of commutative justice legitimized all commercial transactions, they were largely ignored in the hustle and bustle of trade and commerce.[90] Considering the risk of neglecting justice in business matters, Segneri recommended that «people who negotiatiate, before stipulating any kind of agreement, should go to a learned confessor and understand what is lawful and what is not».[91] A man who had stolen from his neighbour was duty bound to return the ill-gotten gains, or face eternal damnation.[92] In effect, economic expansion was thus constrained by ethics and religion, and economic interests were subordinate to, and even overridden by, moral and spiritual considerations. Readers who have followed the argument up to this point may well be concerned that though perfect justice in economic relations was desirable, in everyday life it could not be enforced; and even if it were, justice hindered the expansion of economic life and progress.

Such a concern is misplaced and derives from confusing the needs of justice with the static ideal of a life of peace and quiet. This is altogether different from Segneri's ideal of economic life that imposed upon rich and poor alike the duty to lead an active life of hard work. Even so, this duty did not justify a life entirely dedicated to work. Eager to enjoy the fruits of their labour, men forgot that it was divine providence that blessed those who «do their utmost, without idleness».[93] Hard work and efforts to acquire goods were legitimate and dutiful, but the relentless pursuit of material wealth ran counter to divine providence, as the evangelical motto stated: *nolite solliciti esse*.[94]

---

the fair price cannot be precisely determined (SANCTI THOMAE DE AQUINO, *Summa Theologiae*, II-IIae, q. 77, art. 1 ad 1. um) there is a range of legitimate prices with two extremes, the lowest and the highest.

[88] SEGNERI, *Il Cristiano istruito*, cit., p. 240, 1, part I, R. 26, no. 6.

[89] *Ibid.*, part I, R. 26, no. 6, p. 241.

[90] *Ibid.*, part I, R. 26, no. 6, p. 242.

[91] *Ibid.*, part I, R. 26, no. 6, p. 241.

[92] *Ibid.*, part I, R. 26, no. 6, p. 249.

[93] *Ibid.*, part I, R. 27, no. 1, p. 31.

[94] MATTHEW, VI, 35. Segneri thought that, considering the injustices often committed in the headlong acquisition of wealth, Christians should scorn excessive prosperity (SEGNERI, *Il Cristiano istruito*, cit., part I, R. 26, no. 9, p. 243).

The prohibition of work on holy days was perfectly coherent with Segneri's economic principles: by distracting mind and body from the worship of God, such activity distorted the instrumental nature of goods that, in the Christian view of things outlined briefly above, were the true means to heaven.[95]

Segneri's ideas on the acquisition of wealth were significant; a few words on the use men made of goods complete the framework of economic activity he provides. In this respect also, the earthly nature of wealth had a fundamental role. While economic goods nurtured body and spirit, Segneri warned Christians, in their personal consumption, not to seek the satisfaction of their passions but rather to exercise Christian sobriety and moderation[96] in all things. It was a duty for rich and poor alike to be content with their lot,[97] the latter humbly bearing the suffering of deprivation, the former duty bound to exercise charity and to donate their surplus to the poor.

This brings us to the crucial question of alms-giving *quod superest, date eleemosynam*.[98] Segneri was eager to identify a solution in a century characterized by the craving for pomp and noble status, achieved through economic power and grandeur.[99] And this was the case even if a coat-of-arms was tainted with the blood of injustice and misery.[100] *Quod superest* was not derived from the Gospels; according to Segneri was a principle that imposed a grave duty on the rich.[101] Divine justice could not allow that among men «some have no food

---

[95] SEGNERI, *Il Cristiano istruito*, cit., part I, R. 11, no. 27, p. 101. On rest days, servile activities were prohibited (working the land, manual, mechanical and illiberal trades), as were quasi servile trades (money changing, buying and selling unnecessary goods, pleading in the courts). The first type of activity, involving physical labour, prevented men from communicating with God; the second, though not involving hard physical labour, distracted men from divine worship (*ibid.*, part I, R. 11, no. 5).

[96] *Ibid.*, part III, R. 32, no. 4. «The sobriety of a Christian stands in weighing the pleasures of this life and the virtue, in its broadest sense, of living with measure in all things». Note that Segneri was not the only author to preach sobriety in a century of pomp, banqueting and luxury, and not even the first. A century earlier, in fact, Luigi Cornaro wrote *Il Trattato sulla Vita Sobria* and Speroni two long letters on the same topic, against sobriety in the first, and for it in the second in which he described its beneficial moral and physical effects (S. SPERONI DEGLI ALVAROTTI, *Opere di M. Sperone Speroni degli Alvarotti tratte da mss. originali*, Venezia, Appresso D. Occhi, 1740, vol. III, pp. 414 e 421. See also vol. II, p. 515, no. 1).

[97] SEGNERI, *La manna dell'anima*, cit., t. I, p. 238 (15 June).

[98] LUKE, XI, 41.

[99] SEGNERI, *Quaresimale*, cit., Pred. 22, p. 195. «The world has progressed in such splendid clothes, jewels, banquets, carriages, ornaments, furnishings and silverware that we would need to double our income and would barely suffice "to make show of our state" with the decorum consequent on our honour».

[100] Remember the rule in Gattioli's Chronicle: «Do business with those who are poorer than you – warned Gattioli – because you will have expertise they do not have and if you deal with them prudently you will earn something, because the poor make homes rich» (DE CESARE, *op. cit.*, p. 171).

[101] SEGNERI, *Quaresimale*, cit., t. II, Pred. 22, p. 194. SANCTI THOMAE DE AQUINO (*Summa* IIa,

to eat, whilst others feast themselves,» one «no clothes to cover himself, whilst others are covered in luxury».[102] To ensure a more equitable and humane distribution of wealth, men were to give away in alms all goods in excess of those required to honorably maintain their social status with dignity.[103]

Once Segneri had defined the principle of alms giving, the next step was to determine what constituted superfluous wealth.[104] *Quod superest* could not be identified in general terms, but only in specific cases: an individual was the sole judge of his own needs and hence of what was superfluous. Quod superest was a subjective assessment, so two individuals with identical wealth could give different amounts. This subjectivity, however, could not be justified in the face of excessive luxury, pomp and waste impartially judged to be rank abuse.[105] Segneri solved the problem of individual conscience as follows: an individual could not escape his duty to discern what was superfluous; nor could he claim needs relating to his status beyond good measure; nor should he overestimate his future needs, following the Gospel warning not to be overly concerned with food and attire.

This ideal of economic life that Segneri preached in Italian towns and villages over the years was not intended to inhibit the desire to enjoy wellbeing and prosperity; rather it aimed to restore dignity to material reckonings, to dispense with injustice and to redress the profound imbalances that arose when men considered wealth a means of fulfilling their passions and dominating others rather God-given for superior ends: «You may continue to take care of your family and with your crafts and sell and purchase and exchange provided this is done for the salvation of your souls and not through avarice, and your labours are directed to maintaining the life God gave gave you».[106]

IIae, q. 87, art. 1 ad 4 um) in his comment to this passage wrote: «Omnia superflua Dominus iubet pauperibus exhiberi».

[102] SEGNERI, *Quaresimale*, cit., t. II, Pred. 22, p. 194.

[103] The duty to donate surplus goods was closely related to the concept of contentment with one's lot. In relation to social status, Segneri added that it was men's duty to achieve spiritual, intellectual and moral elevation; on the other hand he deplored men's desire to change their social status on account of pride and ambition (*ibid.*, t. II, Pred. 22, p. 196).

[104] Leaving aside the subtle distinction between «superfluous by nature» and «superfluous in relation to the situation» there was a clear different between laymen and men of the church in relation to this duty. Laymen with wealth, as Segneri called private individuals, were bound to donate their surplus only when they came across someone in need; men of the Church had a duty to seek out the poor and needy (SEGNERI, *Il Cristiano istruito*, cit., part I, R. 17, no. 9, p. 155; ID., *Quaresimale*, cit., t. II, pred. 22, pp. 194 e 198. Vedi anche ID., *Prediche dette nel Palazzo apostolico, e dedicate alla santità di nostro signore papa Innocenzo duodecimo*, in *Opere del Padre Paolo Segneri*, cit., t. II, p. 441).

[105] ID., *Quaresimale*, cit., t. II, Pred. 22, pp. 195-196.

[106] ID., *Il Cristiano istruito*, cit., part I, R. 6, no. 16, pp. 51-52.

4. In his approach to wealth, Segneri spared no criticism for employers who paid their workers in kind rather than in money, and in so doing overvalued the goods that the workers produced and eroded the agreed wage.[107] The problem that Segneri outlined received more thorough treatment in the work of a virtually unknown early seventeenth century Francescan, Illuminato Moroni,[108] whose *Responsum de controversia mercatorum cum operariis*[109] on the one hand revealed the importance in his day of wage disputes, and on the other hand offered insight into the mentality of workers and employers and the conflicting interests that were beginning to emerge. Given the importance of the *Responsum*, it is useful to summarize the main arguments here.

Moroni briefly outlined the grounds for dispute at the beginning of the *Responsum*: «Quidem mercatores conduncunt (*sic*) operarios pacta mercede in numerata pecunia, qui postea tempore solutionis non pecuniam, sed frumentum, vinum, et alia huiusmodi tradunt in solutionem, quae, cum, ut plurimum operariis non sint necessaria, coguntur ea vendere magno damno, quia, cum a mercatoribus carissima emant, vili postea pretio vendunt, et multoties iisdem mercatoribus».[110] He questioned whether payment in kind was legitimate or whether it constituted one of the many examples of illegal contract so painstakingly analyzed in medieval and modern studies. Before pronouncing judgement, Moroni cited the arguments put forward by workers and by employers respectively to refute or to justify the legitimacy of this form of payment.

The workers claimed that once a wage had been agreed *in numerata pecunia*, it should be paid in money and not in kind. Such a claim was rejected by the workshop owners, who, whilst admitting that they had agreed to pay a

---

[107] *Ibid.*, t. III, pp. 240-241, part I, R. 26, no. 6.

[108] Moroni († 1659) was initially a Theatine. He joined the Friars Minori in 1635 and in 1658 was elected theologian by Cardinal Alderani Cybo. A year later he died «parum, ut ferunt, feliciter». He left a number of works, including: I. MORONI, *Centum responsa centum quaesitis*, Venetiis, Combi, 1645. Another edition was printed in Milan in 1682, in two volumes:
Risposte alli quesiti etc. sopra il legato del sig. Marieni per la terra di Palazzuolo, Bergamo, 1657.
Specchio piccolo, ma fedele, che rappresenta alcuni difetti emendati nella frequenza della confessione, e comunione, Bergamo, 1658.
Cf. FR. L. WADDING, *Scriptores ordinis minorum*, Roma, apud Linum Contedini, 1806, pp. 381-383 (entry: Illuminatus Moronus).
In his excellent works, U. Gobbi makes no mention of Moroni, in *La concorrenza estera e gli antichi economisti italiani* (Milano, Hoepli, 1884) and *L'economia politica negli scrittori italiani del secolo XVI-XVII* (cit.).

[109] The *Responsum* to which we refer in these pages is the XXII contained in I. MORONI, *Centum responsa*, cit., pp. 90-94 (Venetian edition).

[110] ID., *Centum responsa*, cit., XXII, no. 1, p. 90.

certain number of coins, no undertaking had been made to pay the sum in gold or silver. And since the goods offered in payment were basic necessities that the workers would in any case have to buy at the market, the owners could not understand the workers' complaints. They justified their behavior as follows. Firstly, if they did not offer employment, the workers would starve to death on such barren land and with no other industry to occupy them. Secondly, the owners often kept labourers on, giving them an opportunity to earn their daily bread, even when they had no need for them and the goods they produced lay unsold in storehouses, immobilizing capital that otherwise invested could have yielded a profit. So it seemed reasonable for the workers to buy food directly from their employers, giving them the profits that they would in any case have paid to other merchants. Furthermore, the employers claimed, this was an ancient and widely used practice that was approved even by the religious authorities.[111] The justifications put forward by the employers, despite having a certain probative value, failed to take into account the contractual obligations cited by the workers. In other words, though the arguments put forward by the owners higlighted the advantages to them of wage payments in kind as a form of compensation for losses incurred in organizing business activities, they failed to demonstrate that the owners respected the labour contract.

Naturally, the workers' responded by reiterating their demands for payment in monetary form and not in kind, and then touched on a broader set of grievances towards their masters, and it is these that truly interest the historian today. The workers came to accept that wages could be paid in goods rather than *numerata pecunia*, provided that the value of such goods was calculated at a fair, rather than an inflated, price. Otherwise, it was a form of usury and not the charity that employers claimed to be exercising.

The workers acknowledged that payment in kind was an ancient and widely used practice. However, at all times and in all places it was considered a form of usury. And the claim that payment in kind was legitimized by the Church was false: parish priests and preachers had always spoken out against it. In conclusion, the workers asserted, if a wage of 50 *soldi* a day had been agreed, it should not be reduced to 40 through payment in kind with overpriced goods.[112]

The issue was perfectly clear: the workers were not demanding one system of payment or another: they simply wanted the money or the value of goods

---

[111] *Ibid.*, XXII, no. 2-3, p. 90.
[112] *Ibid.*, no. 4, p. 90.

they received to tally with what had been agreed. The employers' response was interesting in terms of what it revealed about the organization of production. They admitted that the agreed wage of 50 *soldi* was equivalent, in goods, to 40 but claimed to have agreed a wage of 50 *soldi supposito modo solutionis*. The reduction in wages – insisted the employers – was justified for two reasons. Firstly, they paid the wage in advance, and to do so they were often forced to resort to usurers, paying hefty interest. In addition to the loss of profit and loss of future income, employers were also exposed to the risk that the workers might run off, with the additional loss of the raw materials entrusted to them. As for the «high» or «very high» prices of the goods given in payment to the workers, the masters pointed out that price was partly determined by costs. The workers should not forget that to transport grain, wine and other goods to poor regions, merchants bore the cost of feeding men and mules, with an inevitable impact on prices.[113]

The workers were not convinced. Above all, they questioned the legitimacy of secret agreements among employers to ensure that none increased wages or used a different system of payment. Payment in advance, claimed the workers, was a consequence of the appalling wages that drove them into hardship and debt and prevented them from offering their labour to others. As for the risk of workers running off, this would not exist if decent wages were paid in the first place. It was true that the workers implored the employers to hire them, but they did so honestly, and this did not justify payment in overrated goods. The workers argued that the economic order stipulated only the lowest price, the average price and the highest price, and any other price above the highest price was unjust.[114] The expenses the masters incurred to import goods from distant lands did not justify the higher prices, since «haec necessario insunt lucro mercaturae».[115]

From the tone of the debate it is not hard to guess which solution Moroni proposed. In his broad defence of the workers' demands, he attempted to understand price variations and their causes. He observed that differences in prices depended on the multiplicity of buyers, the abundance of money and the shortage of goods: «Hunc ad caussas ob quas potest augeri pretium etiam supra rigorosum. Prima est multitudo emptorum, et copia pecuniae, et

---

[113] *Ibid.*, no. 5, p. 90.

[114] Nec quidquam valet ratio mercaturae quae nunquam dat ius augendi pretium supra rigorosum, nisi alia ratio accedat, quia mercatura ut sic habet tantum tria pretia, videlicet, infimum, medium, et supremum, vel rigorosum, nec aliud pretium cognoscit mercatura. Cf. *ibid.*, no. 5, p. 91.

[115] *Ibid.*

mercis penuria». Even special preferences for certain items, such as gems, ancient statues and the like, could modify prices to a greater or lesser extent. Other factors that caused price variations were the seller's loss of profit and loss of future earnings. In the latter case, Moroni cited examples, such as: an individual decides to sell his grain in May, when prices are highest. As a favour to a friend, he in fact sells the goods in November, when the market price is much lower. The seller is entitled to charge the price he had hoped to obtain, adjusted to take into account the immediate sale of the goods, the averted risk of the goods deteriorating in his warehouse, and the uncertainty of the price actually reaching the desired level. Consequently, the price had to be significantly lowered to a level near the high price, somewhere in the region of the *intra latitudinem iusti*. The same applied when goods were sold on credit, in which case the seller could charge the highest price, within the range of fair prices.

Moroni used these theoretical examples to analyze labour disputes. He immediately rejected the arguments put forward by the employers, who justified the lower than agreed wage paid in advance by the fact that they were entitled to offer and pay the minimum price, but not below. Moroni likened the payment of wages in advance to a form of credit, in which case it was not permissable to charge anything other than a fair price without committing the crime of usury. Merchants who secretly agreed among themselves not to pay a higher wage nor to use a different system of payment were guilty of monopoly.[116] Moroni was more clement towards the masters in his analysis of the stocks of goods that piled up in warehouses. Once it was established that the masters continued production for the benefit of their employees, even in the absence of any demand for their goods, he agreed that it was reasonable to reduce wages, but not without informing the workers. As for the higher prices charged on the goods used to pay the workers Moroni demonstrated that transport costs did not justify any variation in the market price, since this type of expense was typical of any mercantile activity.[117] And neither was the fact

---

[116] For a better understanding of the scope of the crime of monopoly at the start of the Modern Age, see G. BARBIERI, *Spunti di naturalismo economico in un giurista italiano del '500: Tiberio Deciani*, Milano, Giuffrè, 1939, and chapter V of the present volume.

[117] «Item pretium mercium potest augeri ratione mercaturae, potest enim res vendi a mercatore pluris, quam vendatur a non mercatore..., ratio est, quia officium mercaturae est pretio aestimabile. Ex eo autem, quod mercator tenetur alere equos conducere operarios, et famulos pro advehendis frumento, et vino, non licet augere pretium; si enim mercator vult vendere huiusmodi merces pretio currenti in aliquo loco, tenetur illas advehere illuc, et ideo necessariae erunt predictae expensae, quod, si computantur, erit iniusta computatio, et pretium non rerit iustum, *nam iustum pretium est, quod in tali loco currit*, at quod in tali loco currit, involvit illas expensas». I. MORONI, *Centum responsa*, cit., XXII, 77-78, p. 93.

that it was the workers who offered their services to the employers a valid reason for reducing their wages.

Moroni concluded that the payment system used by the employers was illicit; he recommended transparency and good faith in drawing up and respecting labour contracts: «Mercatores debent cum operariis pacisci aperte, et, si in aliquo repugnant, non possunt id, contra eorum mentem ad praxim deducere, quia cum ultro citroque debeant obligari, et debent etiam omnes scire, ad quid obligentur, neque maior potest induci obligatio, quam a partibus intendatur». Therefore, if it had been agreed that wages would be paid in monetary form, then so they should be. If payment in monetary form was agreed, but both parties assented to payment in kind, then fair prices should be applied. If payment in advance caused a loss to the employer, this should be taken into account when setting the wage.[118] These were Moroni's conclusions concerning the labour dispute described briefly above.

The reader will immediately be tempted to ask what penalties applied to offenders. At the end of the *Responsum* Moroni urged parish priests not to administer Easter communion to those who resorted to the payment methods described above, and preachers to denounce them publicly. However, it is likely that all this fell on deaf ears. In earlier centuries, Church penalties were effective in reducing or preventing breaches of economic ethics; the majority of men abided by these rules spontaneously, since they fulfilled their spiritual needs, and relatively few problems of an economic nature actually existed. But when the economic system evolved, the economic mindset changed with it, distancing itself increasingly from the theocentric vision of life of the Middle Ages, so the words of a preacher or the denial of sacrament became of little effect. The only solution was a greater awareness of the problems of the workers and greater participation by the workers. Two more centuries were to pass before the working class movement gained sufficient momentum and power to rise against the capitalist class, which by then dominated the state.

Segneri's defence of the working classes was just one of the many expressions of Church social thought, at all times acutely concerned with the material wellbeing of the faithful. However, by the seventeenth century, political and economic considerations had undermined the Church's social doctrine.

---

[118] [Agreements with workers should be applied to the letter and nobody should be obliged to accept what he has not underwritten]. *Ibid.*, XXII, no. 79-80, p. 93. The question discussed here can also be found in a pamphlet by C.M. DA CASLINO (*L'usuraro convinto con la ragione: opera utilissima*, s.n.t., pp. 44-45), who considered the payment of wages in kind in overrated goods a form of veiled usury. «If a thing is worth ten, they seek for it fourteen or sixteen».

5. The concept of fair price, mentioned briefly above, is discussed at greater length in a confessional by Sauli following the Council of Trent. It is useful to summarize the main points here, to see how some of the Churchmen analyzed prices and the value of goods, without reference to economic ethics.

Following Scholastic tradition, Sauli defined a fairly wide range for fluctuations in the fair price. «Rebus communiter quinque pretia statuuntur, scilicet, primum deficiens, secundum mediocre, tertium summum, quod est quasi punctuale, quod licite excedi non potest, quartum excedens, id est quod excedit terminum, quintum et ultimum superexcedens, id est, illud quod superexcedit notabiliteir pretium summum».[119] In sales contracts, the seller could legitimately sell his goods at a modest or even an inadequate price, when the buyer paid in cash. Conversely, if the sale was on credit, the goods could be sold *pro pretio summo et quasi punctuali, quod autem est in termino, qui excedi non debet nec licite potest secundum iudicium prudentium hominum.*[120]

Even from this brief example, it can be seen how the price scale of *deficiens*, *mediocre* and *summum* were fair depending on the circumstances, whereas *excedens* and *superexcedens* were always unfair, in absolute terms.

So what was a fair price? One that included the first three price categories described by Sauli? It was a price «statutum a lege, vel a consuetudine, vel a iudicio prudentium, quod tamen pretium non est punctuale, quia parvus excessus, et parvus defectus non tollit iustitiam, parvum enim pro nihilo reputatur».[121] Saint Thomas Aquinas had already asserted that a fair price could not be determined with precision,[122] so Sauli's theory was far from original. However, allowing in the case of sales on credit a *pretium summum* and on cash sales a *deficiens* denoted some sort of compromise, in the first case with respect to an interest bearing loan and in the second case with respect to the competition. The difference between the *summum pretium* and the *deficiens* prices was considerable. As the Confessional stated *parvus excessus, et parvus defectus non tollit iustitiam, parum enim pro nihilo reputatur.* What is significant is that the principle of fair price allowed for some discretion that businessmen could exercise in the course of their everyday dealings.[123]

---

[119] SAVONAROLA, *op. cit.*, pp. 69-70.

[120] [Goods may be sold at the maximum price, without however exceeding the opinion of wise men]. *Ibid.*, p. 70.

[121] [The right price is the price established by the law, or by common practice or in the judgement of wise men and may vary slightly]. *Ibid.*, p. 69. Note the discretionality of the seller in setting the deficiens price «Non autem potest alicui vendere pro aliis pretiis, id est, excedenti vel superexcedenti» (*op. cit.*, p. 70).

[122] SANCTI THOMAE DE AQUINO, *Summa Theologiae*, II, IIae, q. 77, art. 1 ad 1.um.

[123] We are not concerned here with the problems solved in the *Confessionale* relating to usury,

Fewer concerns of a moral nature, and a more practical understanding of the market, emerge from certain passages in Mercanti's *Institutione de' Mercanti*, published with Father Fabiano's *Trattato del Cambio* in 1561.[124] A fair price was defined as: «the common price in that place and at the time of the contract, considering the particular circumstances and the method of sale and purchase and the abundance of merchandise and the abundance of money, and the multiplicity of purchasers and vendors, and the comfort that the goods provide, and their usefulness according to a 'just man', without malice or deceit».[125] Apart from the concluding observation on unjustified price manouvres that were to be avoided even when prices failed to repay the toil of producers and merchants,[126] the *Institutione* sought to resolve the complex problem of which factors determined prices. However, the reader might wonder whether the author was familiar with the theory of supply and demand. The *Institutione* reduced the numerous determinants to two fundamental factors: «I said abundance of merchandise or money; because this in truth is the reason for the price of the goods, to which the reasons of time and place and method are subordinate. Only the abundance or lack of goods decreases or increases the price: as experience in the Fairs may demonstrate». It was clearly stated that price depended on both supply and demand.

In relation to supply and demand, the next paragraph was even clearer: «if something was worth more at one time than another, or in one place than another, or could be sold only by imploring buyers, or by imploring sellers, this was due to a glut or scarcity of goods, merchants and money: if a thing has more value at one time than another, or in one place rather than another, or is sold because it is needed and to satisfy the need, it is at a price determined by the abundance or the lack of the merchandise, the merchants with the merchandise and money».[127]

---

interest, and forms of partnership, particularly a livestock company and so on. Finally, note that the *communis aestimatio*, or the rule of the fair price for the earlier Scholastics (see FANFANI, *Le origini*, cit., p. 13) here becomes the *bonus vir* o dei *viri prudentes*, cited many times in the *Confessionale*, p. 67, *passim*.

[124] This belongs VENUSTI, *Compendio*, cit. For more on the probable author of the *Institutione de' Mercanti* cf. A. MONTANARI, *Contributo alla storia della teoria del valore negli scrittori italiani*, Milano, Hoepli, 1889, pp. 6-7.

[125] *Institutione de' Mercanti*, in VENUSTI, *Compendio utilissimo di quelle cose*, cit.

[126] The author of the *Institutione* does not allow producers to resort to forms of monopoly to raise prices, even when justified by the need to earn a legitimate profit. In fact, merchants did not necessarily have to earn a profit, *Institutione*, cit., pp. 30-32. This claim is well-known, because it demonstrates that, according to the *Institutione*, the market is beyond the control, and must be beyond the control, of the actions of one or more merchants. Only in this case is the market fair and for the common good of all.

[127] *Ibid.*, cit., pp. 29-30.

Having established that a decrease in price was caused by an increase in supply, the *Institutione* cited the case of a decrease in price following a fall in demand: «We see that houses and possessions are worth less after wars and pestilence than before, because the number of purchasers has fallen, and this without the houses or possessions falling into a deteriorated state».[128]

This translates as: *rebus sic stantibus*, an expression that was to become typical of modern scientific thought. The use of such an expression in economics marked the start of an empirical approach to the question of wealth, by now excluding all ethical considerations. This was true of both the method and content of Cardinal De Luca's seventeenth century analysis of value and price.[129] Though recently republished in an article,[130] the author fails to discuss the questions raised, so it is useful to summarize De Luca's ideas here.

De Luca started by identifying three price categories, conventional, natural and mixed, and then focused his attention on the natural price: «This happens mostly with properties, i.e. country and urban houses, the price of which is absolutely undetermined because it depends partly on the yield of the house and partly on its better or worse location...».[131] It would be an error to treat this as a thorough discussion of the theory of rent, beyond the scope of De Luca, who was more concerned with demonstrating that the price of land should be established through a process of formal price determination. Nevertheless, this passage does contain a description of the elements upon which Ricardian theory was based. When De Luca referred to the quantity of rent he was not alluding to parcels of land of different size; in this case, price uncertainty and price variations were irrelevant, since the price was natural. He was therefore referring to parcels of land of the same size, whose value could vary in relation to differences in productivity, a basic assumption of the theory of economic rent. There is no doubt about the other aspect De Luca discussed, namely the superior or inferior location of the land or the building.

De Luca's observations on the determinants of the real estate market led him to question the practice of establishing a fixed capital value of land, since it excluded the impact on price of variable factors.[132] De Luca focused on

---

128 *Ibid.*, p. 30.

129 Cf. G.B. De Luca, *Theatrum veritatis et iustitiae sive decisivi et ad veritatem editi in forensibus controversiis canonicis et civilibus*, Venetiis, apud Paulum Balleonium, 1698, book XV, part I, disc. 33, no. 40-66, pp. 103-105.

130 C. Astori, *Un'analisi del valore nell'opera del Card. De Luca*, «Economia», 1938.

131 This excerpt from De Luca, like those cited above, are taken from the article published by Astori, see the previous note.

132 *Ibid.* «It is an evident mistake – De Luca writes – to proceed by such generalizations, when

market fluctuations, and noted the influence of place, time and the type of sale – wholesale or retail – with respectively lower or higher prices. The most interesting aspect was his analysis of supply and demand volumes: «and, without incidents, with the same tranquillity as before, there is still a great variation due to other factors, such as the abundance of liquidity at a given time or the lack of buyers at another or of other investment opportunities, and at other times there may be many sellers and opportunies to invest and few buyers».

Note that the expression: with the same tranquillity corresponds exactly to *rebus sic stantibus*. Far more interesting than De Luca's conclusions was his analysis of different market situations: he held certain factors constant and others, whose influence he wished to investigate, variable.

Once De Luca had demonstrated that the value of goods varied from place to place, he went on to assert that: «the value of single goods in a given place varies according to the circumstances of the moment». In his endeavours to examine all possible price equilibria, could he have also been concerned with the legitimacy of the phenomena he observed?

On just one occasion, unless we are mistaken, De Luca referred to usurers and moralists, merely noting how both sales in cash and sales on credit raised or lowered prices respectively. He discussed this issue with the same objectivity he used to observe market fluctuations, following the empirical and scientific approach that was becoming established in the field of economic theory also.

6. The beginning of this chapter emphasized the need to distinguish between past heritage and new ideas, particularly in historical periods of transition such as the sixteenth century in Italy.

The dominant influence of Scholastic social doctrine on the economic ideals of modern Churchmen was noted. Both renowned theologians and preachers, including De Vio and Segneri, and lesser known figures such as Padre Fabiano and Illuminato Moroni assessed economic phenomena in the light of Thomistic principles. The importance of Thomistic doctrine in modern social thought is far greater than commonly acknowledged. The so-

---

practically nothing has a fixed rule applicable to all cases, but everything depends on specific circumstances and individual cases, according to the different quality of places and regions; because in some province or region there may be more merchandise but also more liquidity, or more people and less territory; or in the same province there are differences between the capital city and other cities and between these cities and other towns and villages, and in one place a property for sale with at a 7 or 8 per cent rate of interest and in others no sellers at a 3% rate of interest or even less».

cial function of wealth, the duty to donate surpluses to the poor, moderation in the use of goods, the ban on lending money for interest and, generally, the subordination of commercial activities to the moral and spiritual needs of Christians were principles upheld by the Churchmen from the Reformation to the Counter Reformation, inspired by the economic precepts of the Scholastic tradition.

Though they remained faithful to the Thomistic doctrine of wealth, the sixteenth century Churchmen sought to propose solutions suited to the practical needs of their time, and defended as far as their principles would allow certain new phenomena. A layman, Davanzati, praised De Vio's legitimization of money changing. The sheer number of Monti di Pietà located all over Italy, and the importance of the Christian spirit of charity proved the need for these institutions. Despite De Vio's criticism, they were approved by the seventeenth century Churchmen, who offered a new interpretation of the precept of *mutuum date* that in theory was violated by the marginal rate of interest charged by money lending institutions. What is more – and perhaps this is the most significant innovation – De Vio and Menochio both defended social mobility, though De Vio made the accumulation of wealth conditional upon the possession of certain attributes, and Menochio upon having a large family. However, once this principle had been established, men were quick to disregard such prerequisites: in that day and age most wanted to climb the social ladder. What is important here is that the economic ideals of Menochio and De Vio, despite their endorsement of social mobility, closely followed the medieval tradition of donating surpluses to the poor.

Garimberto's ideas, inevitably grounded on the social principles of Christianity, were nevertheless inspired by the classics: Plato's influence is evident in his disdain of trade and economic life in general. In this sense, Garimberto stood apart from his fellow Churchmen, who never established a hierarchy of means for acquiring wealth; they were suspicious of activities in which men were most likely to commit an injustice towards their neighbours. Only Menochio, to the best of our knowledge, considered agriculture a means of wealth acquisition available to all Christians; neither did he condemn trade, provided it was conducted with legitimate means and without deceit.

With the exception of Garimberti, all the other Churchmen followed tradition when attempting to solve problems unknown in the Middle Ages. In seeking a solution to disputes between workers and employers, Moroni referred to price theory, loss of profit and loss of future income, concepts familiar three centuries earlier. However, Moroni was also familiar with market phenomena, and despite being a moralist and a theologian, he was able to observe these in detail. Before him, the author of the *Institutione de' Mercanti* and after him Cardinal De Luca abandoned all considerations of a moral nature and analyzed the phenomena of price and value as a modern scientist would.

These were limited examples of naturalism in contrast to the economic voluntarism of the sixteenth century Churchmen, whose rules reflected their lack of faith in a world in which without moral and religious laws, men's unfettered instincts would take over. Having inherited the notion of wealth from the Middle Ages, and with the new guidelines dictated by the Council of Trent, the Churchmen essentially echoed the ideal of economic life that had passed down unchanged through the centuries.

At this point the reader might object that if the economic ethics of the Church really had remain unchanged through the centuries, it would be pointless to reconstruct the lessons learnt in the course of history. And the response might be that Churchmen were not fixated with one concept of economic life; on the contrary, they strove to adapt to new needs as events unfolded. Certainly, the Church and its ministers remained faithful to certain concepts (the subordination of material life and economic activity to spiritual needs) over the centuries. Not surprisingly: «oak trees do not fall at the first blow and an elephant does not bend a stone in passing over it but many ants returning endlessly do make it curved». Deeply entrenched in Church thought, its saints, preachers, confessors, and sacred authors was the conviction that in a moral world, of which economic principles were a part, «always fitting and beneficial it is to impress a truth upon the heart».[133]

---

[133] SEGNERI, *Il cristiano istruito*, cit., *Prefazione*.

CHAPTER TWO

PAPAL COUNCIL AND EPISCOPAL LEGISLATION
REGARDING ECONOMIC LIFE

1. Reconstructing the economic thought of Churchmen certainly helps to understand aspects of social life inspired by the teachings of the Gospels and their continued interpretation through the centuries. The same is true of the many Church laws, partly inspired by the Gospels, that include regulations governing the conduct of business.

Sprinkled here and there among rules of quite a different nature enshrined in numerous Council Decrees, Episcopal Dispositions, Breviaries and Papal Bulls, these economic regulations – far more than the thinking of private Churchmen – undeniably weighed on consciences and influenced the practical lives of people. Whereas the writings of an elite group of Churchmen – irrelevant for the population as a whole – illuminate for the historian a conception of the economy, Church rules represented ideals and a practical framework that people followed in their everyday lives, all the more so because these rules considerably influenced the spirit and letter of statutes and laws adopted by the state.[1]

---

[1] Cf. A. SOLMI, *Storia del diritto italiano*, Milano, Società editrice libraria, 1908, p. 604 and G. SALVIOLI, *Storia del diritto italiano*, Torino, UTET, 1921, p. 101. The influence of Church regulations on civil legislation does not finish with the Middle Ages or the Modern Age, but persists in much more recent times. The principles of the *Rerum Novarum* considerably influenced social legislation immediately before and after the Great War. Pope Pius XI, in his solemn commemoration of the Encyclical of Pope Leo XIII, recalled that its benefits included the unmistakable influence on the spirit and terms of the Peace Treaty in relation to the regulations governing labour according to fairness and justice (cf. *Le encicliche sociali di Leone XIII e Pio XI*: Latin text and Italian translation of "Rerum novarum" and "Quadragesimo anno" with references to other Papal documents, Milano, Vita e Pensiero, 1933, pp. 77-79). A.D. SERTILLANGES, in *La doctrine catholique et les clauses du travail dans le Traité de paix*, «Revue des Jeunes», Chronique sociale de France, 1919, commented on the clauses regarding labour established in the Treaty of Versailles, identifying the clear derivation from the social principles of Pope Leo XIII. For the importance and vitality of the economic and social regulations contained in the Encyclical see, among others, the numerous papers collected in the volume: *Il XL anniversario della Enciclica "Rerum Novarum"*, Milano, Vita e Pensiero, 1931;

4

It is not surprising that over the centuries the Church abandoned the purely spiritual sphere and began to legislate on economic matters. In their actions and economic choices legislators were continuously called upon to address a variety of questions,[2] so it is clear why the Church, both in the past and more recently,[3] decided to promulgate regulations of economic ethics, in the conviction that this was the undeniable right and, indeed, duty – however delicate – of the Church. Nonetheless, Church legislation does not represent a systematic whole, a cogent body of regulations governing business life. This is because Church teachings, and still more regulations governing practical life enshrined in legislation through the centuries, were always prompted by specific historical events and the need to take action in one direction or another, beyond the spiritual sphere. Hence the reader should not expect the following pages to illustrate an organic body of law regarding employment, the relations between entrepreneurs and employees, the sale of goods with credit, trading in securities and commercial companies.

We may need to draw together from different sources a multiplicity of Church regulations, but we should not lose sight of the concrete nature of the economic measures they contain, each rule a reaction to a certain occasion or event. So, for example, when reference is made to a Council or Synod Decree regarding dry exchanges, all other aspects not strictly related to the subject of this book are left aside; however, a Decree was an integral part of dispositions of a spiritual nature requiring the Church to regulate, among other things, aspects of economic life. One such disposition concerned the practice of charging interest on loans, regarded by the Church as evidence of greed and a thirst for money that undermined faith and weakened the spiritual search for the supreme good.

Given this premise, a review of Church laws will not only illuminate specific aspects of the moralizing activities of the Church; it will also shed light – via economic regulations – on the business practices and ambitions that led men to acquire and use goods.

M. Turmann, *Léon XIII, les catholiques sociaux et les origines de la legislation internationale du travail*, Milano, Vita e Pensiero, 1931 e A. Valensin, *L'encyclique Rerum Novarum et les clauses ouvrières du pacte de la société des nations*, Milano, Vita e Pensiero, 1931.

[2] Cf.: G. Toniolo, *L'elemento etico nelle leggi economiche*, in *Scritti scelti di Giuseppe Toniolo*, ed. by F. Meda, Milano, Vita e Pensiero, 1921; J. Mazzei, *Principi etici ed economia*, in *Il XL Anniversario Della Enciclica "Rerum Novarum"*, pp. 304-375.

[3] In dictating their social and economic teachings, Popes Leo XIII and Pius XI explicitly affirmed their duty and right to intervene in questions of this order, whenever the spiritual interests of the faithful required it (see *Le encicliche sociali di Leone XIII e Pio XI*, cit., no. 13 of Rerum Novarum and p. II of Quadragesimo Anno, pp. 15-17 and 91-93).

2. In the sixteenth century, the Church did not distinguish between greater or lesser nobility in acquiring wealth, all means depending on one sole duty: work.

At precisely the moment that Italians began to look on economic activity with a certain disdain, almost as though the sweat of the brow could tarnish their recently acquired, gilded coats-of-arms, the Church began to consider work – whether manual or intellectual – as the means for obtaining spiritual salvation and the only legitimate way of making a living. «Beware of idleness» wrote Carlo Borromeo.[4] This rule was based on the spiritual danger of conducting a life of idleness. And the Archbishop of Milan, one of the leading figures of the Counter Reformation,[5] completed the rule, as follows: «Beware of being idle, like a poison of the soul» Hence Borromeo considered work not only a necessary guarantee of spiritual salvation, but also a duty, applicable also to the hoarders and paupers of life.

This principle can be seen in a Council Edict of 1571,[6] which prohibited hospices and charity shelters from providing hospitality to beggars able to work, citing the well-known admonishment of the Apostle to the Gentiles: «Si quis non vult operari, nec manducet».[7] A decree of the Roman Catechism also made it clear that dedicating one's energies to work was the only proper means of obtaining sustenance: «sunt igitur Fures etiam, qui Furto sublatas res emunt, vela aliquo modo inventas, occupatas, aut ademptas retinent. Ait enim sanctus Augustinus: *si invenisti, et non reddidisti, rapuisti*. Quod si re-

---

[4] C. BORROMEO, *Litterae Pastorales*, in *Acta Ecclesiae mediolanensis ab eius initiis usque ad nostram aetatem*, opera et studio presb. Achillis Ratti, Mediolani, apud Raphaelem Ferraris edit (ex typographia pontificia sancti Iosephi), 1892, vol. III, p. 651.
See also G. BARBIERI, *Norme di morale economica dettate da S. Carlo Borromeo*, Milano, Giuffrè, 1938, pp. 3-4.

[5] In this chapter a great deal of space is dedicated to the regulations issued by the Church in Milan during the period in which Carlo Borromeo was Cardinal, because – as noted by many commentators – he was the most faithful interpreter and most organic promoter of the principles of the Council of Trent. One of the most profound thinkers on the history of Milan commented: «here the movement was directed by a man of sublime moral conscience and inflexible principles, Carlo Borromeo. If the work of this extraordinary man took on the aspect of a tragic duel between Church and State, and weighed heavily on life in Milan, throwing it into utter confusion, this was because he wished and knew how to coordinate the concepts of the Council of Trent to make an admirable organic whole, and he wished to carry forward that programme unwaveringly, penetrating the meanderings of civil, political and economic life». E. VERGA, *Storia della vita milanese*, Milano, Moneta, 1931, p. 265.

[6] G.D. MANSI, *Sacrorum conciliorum nova et amplissima collectio*, Florentiae, expensis Antonii Zatta, 1759, vol. XXXVI bis, col. 72-73. «Sint mendicantibus validis clausa hospitalia. Nam et publice ostiatim mendicare istis est a iure interdictum: Et Apostolus denunciat, quoniam si quis non vult operari, nec manducet». *Concilium bisuntinum*, October 1571.

[7] [If you do not work, refrain from eating]. PAUL, *Epist. II ad Thessalonicens*, III, 10.

rum dominus nulla ratione inveniri potest, illa sunt bona in usus pauperum conferenda».[8]

The rationale behind these dispositions was certainly the idea that work was necessary to justify the acquisition and ownership of goods. However, this should not lead us to the erroneous belief that the Church regarded labour as simply a means of acquiring wealth: not at all. It considered work above all as a means of spiritual elevation. Work in the fields and craft workshops should be carried out in a healthy Christian atmosphere, and wasting the fruits of one's labour in inns or other ways that ran counter to the teachings of the Church was not tolerated. «Let the master craftsman or workman – Cardinal Borromeo admonished – keep no minister, worker or apprentice who is unconfessed and has not communicated in the year, at the Easter of the Resurrection. Nor blasphemer, person with concubine or other scandalous figure, or person who partakes of the revelries of taverns and spends there his earnings, bringing suffering upon his family, unless duly amended of his ways and corrected by brotherly ministration. Nor any that play forbidden games, often conjoined with blasphemy, theft and other evils».[9] From this it followed that work should not procure the means for provoking scandal, but should be a virtuous and beneficial activity for the spirit, so that it might be elevated and be borne aloft, above the hubbub of the workshop and the sun-drenched field, on the wings of prayer.[10]

Naturally, the master craftsman had other duties in addition to expelling from the workshop dishonest and assiduous frequenters of taverns; he was also under a clear obligation, expressed by the Cardinal of Milan: «Let him treat his ministers, workers and apprentices with charity and pay the appropriate sum at the time the payment is due».[11]

The payment of a proper wage by the entrepreneur was fitting to the labours of the workman, who committed a theft if he demanded payment for shoddy work or shirked his duties.[12]

---

[8] [Also to be considered theft are cases in which goods are not returned, over which for various reasons no rights subsist from work and where no owner can be found, the goods should be given to the poor]. *Catechismus Romanus ex Decreto Concilii Tridentini*, Patavia, Typis Seminarii, 1714, p. 454 (*de septimo praecepto*, c. 9).

[9] Borromeo, *Litterae Pastorales*, cit., vol. III, p. 666.

[10] *Ibid.*, p. 667. See some interesting warnings on the need to pray in the shop, workshop and other workplaces.

[11] *Ibid.* «Qui debitam operariis mercedem non persolvunt sunt rapaces». «Quod genus rapinarum in Levitico, in Deuteronomio, apud Malachiam, apud Tobiam vehementer improbatur» (*Catechismus romanus*, cit., p. 455, *de septimo praecepto*, c. 10. Cf.: *Levitico*, XIX, 13; *Deuteronomio*, XXIV, 14; *Malachia*, III, 5; *Tobia*, IV, 15).

[12] *Catechismus romanus*, cit., p. 454, *de septimo*, c. 9. «Furtum etiam apertum est operariorum,

There is no evidence of any other rules governing the relations between master craftsman and apprentice, entrepreneur and workman. But it is clear that these few principles were sufficient to settle any dispute, or – better still – to avoid conflicts between employers and employees. There was not only a need to pay a proper wage and the duty of the workman to provide genuinely productive labour, but also the ethical-religious meaning attributed by the Church to daily labour and to the place, the workshop, where this toil generally took place. The logical conclusion of these considerations on the acquisition of wealth is that only work and productive toil legitimized earnings, which were clearly improper where a workman deliberately reduced his productivity or where the entrepreneur unfairly lowered his wage or failed to pay promptly.

3. After producing goods required by men in the workshop, the problem arose of making them accessible to the consumer.

Inevitably, a key figure was the merchant or dealer in commodities and goods, who may also have been a producer or solely a merchant; their services were required for the common good, because they made available the products of the ploughed field and the beating of the hammer, to satisfy the needs of men and women.

The Church rules of the sixteenth century do not disparage merchants. Whether this was because few Italians were merchants or whether there was a change of thinking by those whose ideas inspired Church laws, it is a fact that in sixteenth century Church legislation there is no trace of the diffidence shown by Churchmen towards merchants (a characteristic of previous centuries). This sheds some light on the considerations set out above.

In the conception of sixteenth century Church laws, earnings were justified by the expense of energy – and the toil of the brow – to increase the public utility of things. For a merchant to be considered to be carrying out a socially useful function, the Church would need to place him alongside the farmer and craftsman in a workshop. In the sixteenth century, the Church did not deny that the age-old suspicion concerning the merchant's role was the result of the dangers of easy earnings and that these easy earnings were a feature of the market. However, rather than seek to attenuate the activity of merchants on account of this danger, the Church preferred to regulate

---

et artificum, qui totam, et integram mercedem ab iis exigunt, quibus ipsi iustam, ac debitam operam non dederunt. Nec vero distinguuntur a Furibus servi dominorum, rerumque custodies infidi: quin etiam eo sunt detestabiliores, quam reliqui Fures, qui clavibus excluduntur, quod feraci servo nihil domi obsignatum, aut occlusum esse potest».

and legitimize trading activity with a series of norms to make the profession as respectable as the others.

The earnings of merchants were justified if the profession was carried out in the spirit and with the ideals of the Church and were a just reward for the work required to act in the market and for the public utility of trade. The truth of the latter becomes clear after reading the copious Church dispositions on the subject. «When trading, selling and buying, do not indulge in deception, falsity, lies and oaths, and do not desire what is not yours».[13] Thus the Archbishop of Milan pointed out somewhat laconically the negative duties of a Christian merchant. No different from this was the spirit of another principle Borromeo announced to govern the behaviour of businessmen: «They shall not deceive anyone in weights, samples and measures, or by other means; they shall write for themselves and for others what is true and have dealings with others as they would wish others to have dealings with them».[14]

Alongside dishonest merchants, who kept false accounting records, or sought illicit earnings by falsifying weights and measures, hoarders of grain at a time of famine were also considered rapacious,[15] as were those who artificially caused prices to rise: «Ex numero eorum, qui raptores dicuntur a sanctis patribus, sunt, qui in frugum inopia comprimunt frumentum; faciuntque, ut sua culpa carior, ac durior sit annona: quod etiam valet in rebus omnibus ad victum, et ad vitam necessariis».[16] The final sentence might be thought to justify price speculation on items not directly consumed by men, but a phrase

---

[13] BORROMEO, *Litterae Pastorales*, cit., vol. III, p. 651.

[14] *Ibid.*, p. 668. «Iniquiores in hoc furtorum genere sunt ii, qui fallaces et corruptas merces vendunt pro veris, et integris; quive pondere, mensura, numero, et regula decipiunt» (*Catechismus Romanus*, cit., p. 454, *de septimo praecepto*, c. 9).
In the Bible similar regulations feature in *Deutoronomy* (25. «Non habebis in saeculo diversa pondera»); nel *Levitico* (XIX, 35. «Nolite facere iniquum aliquid, in iudicio, in regula, pondere, in mensura; statera iusta et aequa sint pondera, iustus modius, aequusque sextarius»).

[15] Popes often declared storing grain illegal where it was done with the evident intent of establishing an advantageous price for the merchant. In 1565 Pope Paul IV (*Magnum Bullarium Romanum Augustae Taurinorum editum*, Sumptibus Seb. Franco et Henrici Dalmazzo, 1860, t. VII, p. 377) dealt with this matter and the following year his successor returned to it, also condemning those who prevented farmers from bringing their grain to town (*op. cit.*, t. VII, pp. 484-485). More organic were the regulations of Pope Gregory XIII, who in 1583 severely prohibited any action aimed at monopolizing grain. He damned above all the usurers who lent money to the producers of grain requiring repayment, ever after years, in grain and not cash. In this way they gained control of merchandise of prime necessity, increasing the price beyond measure. This was punished by the laws governing the crime of creating a monopoly (*op. cit.*, t. VIII, p. 420 and following).

[16] [Those who accumulate grain and prevent it from being sold should be considered thieves, and so also for any other necessity]. *Catechismus Romanus*, cit., p. 457, *De septimo praecepto*, c. 14. Cf. p. 487 (*De Nono et Decimo Praecepto*, c. 23). A Biblical example of this prohibition can be found in *Proverbs* (no. 11): «Qui abscondit frumenta, maledicetur in populis».

of Carlo Borromeo helps to clarify: he clearly prohibited such speculation and even establisheed rules to determine the correct price, resembling the pheno-menon of the *taccamento dei panni* (price stamping on imported cloth) illu-strated so brilliantly by Sapori.[17] Speaking to the merchants, Borromeo esta-blished that «they should not sell except at the proper price, and the revenue comply with the quality of the merchandise, and its cost; and if the purchaser is deceived or by error offers too much, the seller should take only the honest amount. They should make no illicit contracts or sell at disadvantageous terms: they should sell honestly and declare what they earn».[18]

Nobody can fail to see the difference between the economic spirit inspir-ing these regulations and the spirit found in the works of Alberti, for the fif-teenth century, or in the already-mentioned *Chronicle* by Padre Gattioli, who followed Alberti in insisting on the principle of prudence, and advised: «Do not allow another living creature to know how much money or goods you keep in the house, act like a poor man, because that way you will live more safely, and no-one will ask for a loan. To be safe – continued the bizarre se-venteenth century Churchman – you can claim you are up to your neck in debts and you can arrange with God not to be considered a liar».[19]

In the light of the admonishments of Carlo Borromeo, who recommended that merchants declare their profits, some might be tempted to think that the advice of Padre Gattioli was more sensible. Indeed so, but in a century in which bewildering pleasures, luxury and pomp led men all too often to seek easy and often unjust earnings, these Church regulations could not have been otherwise. When noblemen believed that any means, lawful or unlawful, were justified in maintaining the greatness and splendour of their lineage, how could the Church be indifferent to such a view?[20] During that century, some believed themselves justified in, or at least excused of, the crime of theft even when the illegal dealings were not motivated by defence of their lineage but the desire for a better life and a more evident display of refinement and ele-gance.[21] So, it is easy to understand why the Church felt the need to take a

---

[17] A. SAPORI, *Il taccamento dei panni franceschi a Firenze nel '300*, in *In onore e ricordo di Giu-seppe Prato*, Torino, R. Istituto Sup. di Scienze Econ. e Comm., 1931.

[18] BORROMEO, *Litterae Pastorales*, cit., vol. III, p. 668.

[19] *Cronaca tra il 1638 e 1671*, written by P. GATTIOLI, in DE CESARE, *Un massimario d'economia sociale del Seicento nel Trentino*, cit. Cf. chapter I in this volume.

[20] *Catechismus Romanus*, cit., pp. 460-461, *De septimo praecepto*, c. 21. «Ecce nobilium homi-num non ferendae deliciae, qui culpam extenuare sibi videntur, si se affirmarint, non cupiditate, aut avaritia ad detrahendum alteri sua descendere, sed tuendae causa amplitudinis familiae, et maiorum suorum, quorum existimatio, et dignitas rueret, nisi rerum alienarum accessione fulciretur».

[21] *Ibid.*, pp. 461-462, *De septimo praecepto*, c. 22.

stance on economic activity, not only with regulations of a general nature, to ensure fairness and honesty in business dealings, but also with specific dispositions about the numerous ways goods were bought and sold.

Commercial companies[22] already thrived in the fifteenth century, culminating in the joint stock company.[23] We have found no record of this type of company in the copies of Church dispositions but there certainly were dispositions regarding companies based on capital and on labour, in which it is clear that the Church wished to eliminate any form of preferential treatment for the capitalist: «Ne in societate, in quam alter pecuniam confert, alter operas, lucri distributio constituatur, nisi per quotas partes. Nec ultra eas, certa pecuniarum summa, vel quid aliud conferenti pecuniam persolvatur. Neque fiat pactio, ut sors salva sit, fructus vero communiter dividantur».[24] The reason for this regulation – banishing usury from the alliance between capital and labour – was evident. The same concern was expressed in the regulations concerning the loan of animals: «In societate animalium, quae inaestimata alicui dantur ad custodiam, sive ut operas praestet, omnes casus, etiam fortuiti, semper sint periculo eius qui dederit; nisi id alterius socii dolo, vel magna negligentia accidisse constiterit. Ne fiat pactum, ut sors sit semper salva, etiam ex primis faetibus».[25]

Livestock companies were widespread in and around Siena, where it was common practice to charge usury for the loan of animals without taking part in the risk of the enterprise. In 1599, the first Council of Siena sought to correct the abuse with regulations governing companies of this type, more extensive than those of the *First Provincial Council* of Milan: «Quandocumque animalia nullo certo praetio aestimata cuipiam, societatis nomine, vel ut is danti

---

[22] FANFANI, *Le origini*, cit., p. 84.

[23] F. SCHUPFER, *Il diritto delle obbligazioni in Italia nell'età del risorgimento*, Torino, Bocca, 1921, vol. III, pp. 158-161.

[24] *First Provincial Council of Milan*, in *Acta Ecclesiae mediolanensis*, cit., vol. II, p. 122. The Council of Sorrento of 1584 echoed the dispositions of the Council of Milan: «In societate, in qua pecuniam alter, alter operas confert, lucri distributio non aliter constituatur quam per quotas partes, nec ultra eas certa pecuniarum summa, vel aliquid aliud pecuniam conferenti persolvatur; neque pactio fiat, ut sors sive principale salvum sit, fructus vero communiter dividantur». MANSI, *op. cit.*, vol. XXXVI bis, col. 302.

[25] [Profit for companies based on capital must be divided according to ownership, and none should be paid except for this reason, and agreements shall not made which in some manner surreptitiously reward capital]. *First Provincial Council of Milan*, cit., vol., II, p. 122. Pope Sisto V generally condemned transactions in which capital was guaranteed and profits were certain. Cf. CASLINO, *op. cit.* This Council established regulations for renting the use of animals at a given price: «Neve quidpiam certum, praeter sortem, ex fructibus animalium, quae fiunt certo pretio, si illa absque dolo, aut negligentia eius, qui conduxit, deteriora fiant, id semper sit damno eius, qui locarit».

operas praestet, custodienda traduntur, quidquid ex iis casu perierit, id totum periisse domino intelligatur, modo eum, qui in societatem accepit, dolo malo fecisse non constet, ea conditione, ut sors eadem semper maneat, certumve aliquod ex fructibus animalium, praeter sortem ipsam, quiquid acciderit, persolvatur; vel ut, eadem sorte incolum, animalium fructus aequis inter se portionibus dividantur, societates huiusmondi non contrahantur». The regulations referred to companies using animals where no price was established for the animal. «Si animalia certo pretio aestimata cuiquam in custodiam ita dentur, nihil ut sors minuatur, is, qui dedit, nihil praeterea a socio exigat».[26] The regulations would certainly be an interesting research subject for an expert in the history of private law. Here it is sufficient to note that the Church regulations regarding companies based on capital, labour and animals acknowledged the productivity of capital but sought to ensure that capital was not the dominant factor: this was in the name of fairness and the general principle already highlighted according to which the acquisition of goods was justified and the earnings derived from them were fair only when based on the expenditure of energy and the acceptance of risk.

4. The above remarks lead to an important and thorny question, one dealt with frequently – in the treatises and pamphlets of Churchmen, but also the subject of clarification and numerous regulations promulgated by the Councils and Synods of the sixteenth century: the question of usury and money changing.

Starting with the most ancient of the two phenomena, in the Roman Cathechism men «qui miseram plebem compilant, ac trucidant usuris»[27] were considered thieves. Carlo Borromeo was an unstinting opponent of usury. During and after the first Provincial Council he noted the frequency of usury in commercial dealing in Lombardy and recommended eradicating the practice of lending for interest «ad perniciem populorum latius manantem».[28] He prohibited payment for the loan of any fungible goods such as oil, wine and grain: «Ne frumentum, vinum, oleum, aliudve detur, ut eo, quod datum est, aliquid amplius exigatur, sive eiusdem generis sive alterius quomodocumque, etiam si operae sint». He also forbade the loan of comestibles where repay-

---

[26] [In companies where animals are kept the risk cannot be excluded and no reward shall be derived from capital alone]. MANSI, op. cit., vol. XXXVI bis, col. 560, Concilium senense, I, 1599, 19 December.

[27] Catechismus Romanus, cit., pp. 455-456, de septimo, c. 11.

[28] First Provincial Council, cit., col. 121.

ment was with comestibles of a higher quality: «Ne qui mutuo det frumentum, vel id genus aliud corruptum, ut tantumdem integri carioris reddatur, etiam si restitutio differatur in quodcumque tempus debitori commodum».[29] He applied the same prohibition to money lending. «Ex mutuo, vel depositis, etiam apud Judaeum factis, nihil praeter sortem a quovis homine percipi ex convento, vel principaliter sperari possit».[30] It should not surprise the reader that this regulation also applied to people who entrusted their wealth to Jews for a profit. Recently a scholar has documented the shift away from mercantile activities to the safety of «annuities» in the sixteenth century and found numerous inhabitants of Milan who «gave money to the Jews for profit».[31]

Some transactions concealed interest payments by allowing for a charge on overdue repayments, which of course were prearranged. Carlo Borromeo severely prohibited anyone from making money *praeter sortem* in the name of consequential damages or loss of expected profit.[32]

Borromeo did not only attack evident and open usury itself but all practices that involved usury, however disguised or veiled. This included people who demanded repayment in cash for loans that were made only partly in cash, and partly in bills of exchange that were difficult to enforce, or goods estimated at a higher than fair value. Also condemned was the practice of increasing the price beyond the fair amount, due to payment in installments or discounting a price for immediate payment in cash.[33]

---

[29] [Also in cases such as wheat, oil, wine and others, it is legitimate to ask for the return of more than the original value added to work, even if this occurs at a later time]. *First Provincial Council*, cit., col. 122. In the second half of the sixteenth century, the Milanese economy must have been dominated by Jews, if Cardinal Alessandrini could write in 1566 to the Papal Envoy in Madrid: «We beg you to ask His Majesty in his name that in his State of Milan he order the Jews not to weigh beyond measure on the population, His Holiness having been informed once again by the noblemen of that city of the damage caused by usury, which, if continued in the future, shall in all probability lead to utter ruination, which could not occur without great prejudice to His Majesty and above all to his subjects». L. SERRANO, *Correspondencia diplomática entre España y la Santa Sede durante el pontificado de S. Pio V*, Madrid, 1914, t. I, p. 318.

[30] *First Provincial Council*, cit., col. 121.

[31] F. CHABOD, *Lo Stato di Milano nell'impero di Carlo V*, Roma, Istituto romano di arti grafiche di Tumminelli & c., 1934, p. 298, no. 20. This system was well-known the century before, as shown by the research of G.B. PICOTTI (*D'una questione tra Pio II e Francesco Sforza per la ventesima sui beni degli Ebrei*, «Giornale della Società Storica Lombarda - Archivio Storico Lombardo», Vol. XX, S. IV, Fasc. 39, 1913, pp. 191-194. See also a study of mine: G. BARBIERI, *Economia e politica nel ducato di Milano: 1386-1535*, Milano, Vita e Pensiero, 1938, p. 124) and continued throughout the seventeenth century, as can be seen from CASLINO, *op. cit.*, pp. 3-4.

[32] «Si quis oblatas re ipsa, loco et tempore pecunias, etiam dotales, sibi debitas accipere recusaverit; nihil praeter sortem, etiam ratione damni emergentis, vel lucri cessantis, vel ex quacumque alia causa accipere possit». *First Provincial Council*, cit., col. 121.

[33] *Ibid.*, col. 121-122.

More serious, damaging and iniquitous in terms of commercial practice was what went by the name of *stocchi* i.e. false sales with credit and the resale in cash to the seller for a lower price than was originally paid. This pratice was very widespread in Lombardy for the purchase and sale of horses, and was a speciality of the Swiss at the Fairs of Dergano and Derganello. The same kind of transaction was also carried out in Broletto, for all sorts of merchandise, leading to the ruin – so Bandello says – of many noble families in Milan.[34] This contract «wicked, highly iniquitous and utterly unjust» as it was called by Caslino,[35] was considered by Borromeo one of the most illicit means of obtaining wealth: «Ne cui praesentem pecuniam quaerenti quidquam carius vendatur, ut statim ab venditore per se, vel per interpositam personam vilius ematur».[36] But the instrument that was used most commonly to evade the condemnation of the Church was the bill of exchange. The need for the Church to take action in this area can be seen in the 1573 report of Leonardo Donati, who told the Serenissima Republic of the money being made in Genoa through granting credit to the Spanish, to the extent that in that city it was considered shameful «to put money to any other use than to lend it» and «the most honourable sort of negotiation and merchanting consists in exchanging money whereas selling, buying and moving goods are considered things for marketeers and people of lower status».[37] Towards the end of the sixteenth century, the interest charged by the capitalist money lenders of Genoa to the Spanish Crown amounted to 25,000,000 ducats. Such a huge amount was bound to attract the attention of the Church and the question about the legitimacy of these earnings was certain to be raised. It was in connection

---

[34] «Twice a year the Germans from the Alps came to Lombardy bringing horses to sell in Milan in great number but now they go no further than Derghene, or Derganello or sometimes Cagnola, places of greater propinquity than the city of Milan. And it has been long practice of the merchants and the gentlemen of the country, knowing the value of each, that the buyer promise by letter in his hand to make full payment after a certain time, and hence receive the horses. It is also a custom of those who finding themselves in need of money, take horses on belief and as soon as they are taken, sell them for a lower price than the cost. Which also occurs in the market of Broletto for the goods of merchants handled by unscrupulous agents. And this buying and selling is done by «stochi», the reason for which many a gentleman slowly loses his means and substance and barely notices it, becoming poor». M. BANDELLO, *Le novelle*, Bari, Laterza, 1912, vol. II, p. 319.

[35] CASLINO, *op. cit.*, pp. 41-42. Boccaccio de Cingulo (V. BOCCACCI, *Tractatus de interdicto uti possidetis*, Venezia, apud Ioannem Gymnicum, 1582, cap. XVIII) defines *stochi* or *stoccoli*: «contractus qui fiunt ab indigente pecunia, cui venditur res cariori pretio, et statim ab eo viliori pretio reemitur».

[36] [You cannot ask for a greater sum for goods just purchased at a lower sum]. *First Provincial Council*, cit., col. 121-122.

[37] E. ALBÈRI, *Relazioni degli Ambasciatori Veneti al Senato durante il secolo XVI*, Firenze, Tipografia all'insegna di Clio, 1839-1863, S. I, vol. VI, p. 361 (*Report by Leonardo Donato*, year 1573).

with this practice that in the mid-sixteenth century the Church began to set out a corpus of regulations, which were both extensive and insistent: proof not so much of the phenomenon reported by the Ambassador of the Venetian Republic as to the widespread use of the practice of charging interest.

Several decades before the Council of Trent, some dispositions were adopted with regard to bills of exchange but they were of little importance compared to the thinking of Churchmen about the declared practice of usury. When the instruments of credit became more refined, progressing from their original function of exchanging money and transmitting letters of commitment for transactions carried out at the Fair, and began to cover all possible credit operations, the Church noticed that its centuries-old vigilance over, and prohibition of, interest on loans was being undermined. This is how the new credit instrument was described by Bartolomeo Guidiccioni,[38] one of the speakers at the Council of Trent: «Pecuniam indigenti sub spe lucri alio loco alterius forme ab alia persona recipienti plerumque ignota certo tempore sibi restituendam numerant, cum tamen vere agant et intendant, ut in eodem loco in quo data est, ab eadem persona, que accipit, in eadem forma cum lucro ex loco et moneta fictis proveniente et tempore statuto declarato restituatur. Pro lucro illicito et turpi fingitur locus persona, moneta loci illius sub nomine contractus, qui vere cum recipiente pecuniam non initur nec iniri potest, et tot fraudes tot conventa sub una littera cambii a recipiente pecuniam subscripta et penes dantem retenta exercentur et tolerantur».[39]

---

[38] In 1538, Bartolomeo Guidicione wrote: «Quamvis Lateranense, Lugdunense Viennenseque concilia multa contra usurarios statuta ediderunt pro tollendis extirpandisque usuris pagina utriusque testamenti detestatis, quarum vorago exhaurit pauperes et divitum animas devorat, que in tantum invaluerant, ut licitis et honestis negotiis praetermissis pro licitis et iustis passim haberentur exercerenturque, adhuc tamen e Christiana republica eradicare non valuerunt. Inimicus quipe homo, bono semini zizania superseminat ac sedens in insidiis cum divitibus fraudes excogitat, laqueos tendit, involucra parat, ut pauperum rapiat et perplexis testiculorum suorum nervis divites implicet, suggerens eis, usuram peccatum non esse nec inde quesita restituenda esse, in pestiferum Catharorum et Paterinorum errorem eos involvens et demergens divites affectantes ex pecunia, que natura sterilis pecuniam non generat, fructum et utilitatem percipere et pauperibus pecunia indigentibus veluti pascuis uti novum contrahendi genus edocuit, in quo sub nummorum, locorum, personarum et nominum involucro omne genus fraudis conclusit et mutatione nominis mutui in nomine cambii, ut ipsi nuncupantur, marche veluti quodam velamine crimen obtexit». *Concilii Tridentini diariorum*, Friburgi-Brisgoviae, Herder, v.d., t. XII, p. 254.

[39] [With the hope of making a gain, some calculate money for the needy as if it had been paid in other forms, in other places and in other currencies, and in this way feign an illicit contract, which the other must agree to and this fraudulent agreement is practiced and accepted under the form of bill of exchange]. *Ibid.*, t. XII, p. 254. See an instruction by Card. Guidiccioni himself (*ibid.*, t. IV, p. 271): «Et quia detestanda pravitas usuraria adeo per omnes Christianorum civitates invaluit, quod licitis negotiis dimissis quasi licita exercetur, et genus quoddam cambii excogitatum est, quod etiam feminae exercere sciunt et in eo modi omnes fraudandi congesti sunt, salubriter de huiusmodi cambiis constitutio promulgaretur».

This lengthy Latin phrase describes the unscrupulous figure of the new economic agent, tired of sending bundles of merchandise from one Fair to another, with the risk of being robbed en route or of being deprived of the expected earnings by a more skilled competitor. In the light of past experience of goods shipwrecked on the way from the East for sale in the West, the modern capitalist settled down to a less risky trade: money changing. The income was no less satisfying and the risks considerably fewer. Although the profession had no name, it was far from new, as Guidiccioni says. There was no longer the shame of constant rumour-mongering about the profession, because the new forms of loans were hidden by bills of exchange or the exchange of modest ducats into large florins or other currencies. If the money changer was somewhat disturbed by the thinking emanating from the Council of Trent, which permitted modest earnings from money lending but called other forms of contractual loan usury,[40] it was sufficient to be more careful when stipulating contracts, in order to continue the lucrative activity undisturbed.

The fact that the profession prospered despite numerous previous rulings is shown by the Papal Bull of Pope Pius V in 1571, entitled: *Cambiorum illicitorum declaratio et prohibitio*. It openly condemned: «Omnia cambia, quae sicca nominantur, et ita confinguntur ut contrahentes ad certas nundinas seu ad alia loca cambia celebrare simulent, ad quae loca ii, qui pecuniam recipiunt, litteras quidem suas cambii tradunt, sed non mittuntur, vel ita mittuntur ut, transacto tempore unde processerant, inanes referantur; aut etiam, nullis huiusmodi litteris traditis, pecunia ibi denique cum interesse reposcitur, ubi

---

[40] With evident reference to the doctrinal solutions relating to money changing adopted by Card. De Vio, Guidiccione wrote: «statuimus, decernimus et declaramus, genus illud, commutationis nummorum sive cambii, quod non affectu et spe lucri sed causa maioris commoditatis inter habentes difformes et dissimiles nummos sive in eodem loco sive in diversis exerceatur, licitum esse, licet ratione temporis, loci et numorum mutatione lucrum honestum magnum vel parvum iuxta regionum, mercatorum et nundinarum consuetudinem ex illo proveniat.

«Similiter genus illud negotiationis numarie, in quo pecunia uno loco numerata vel existens apud mercatorem in remotis agentem traicienda seu trasferenda suscipitur mercede aliqua seu utilitate recepta pro mercatorum consuetudine, pro labore ministrorum, impensis et periculis imminentibus suspicienti pecuniam trasferendam et in alio loco restituendam licitum esse declaramus.

Illud etiam genus minuti cambii, quod exerceri consuevit a numulariis numos aureos vel argenteos pro ereis aute contrario comutantibus recepto aliquo honesto emolumento loci consuetudine inspecta et consideratis ministrorum et officine impensis suoque labore et periculo non improbamus...

Illud vero genus cambii, quod fit cum non habente pecunias seu numos similes aut dissimiles, uniformes aut difformes apud se vel alium in eodem vel alio loco, spe questus et lucri, ut supra dictum est, omnino improbamus et detestamur, *est enim instar hipochrisis*; non apparet quod est, nec est, quod apparet...». Cf. *Concilii tridentini*, cit., t. XII, pp. 254-255.

contractus fuerat celebratus; nam inter dantes et recipientes usque a principio ita convenerat, vel certe talis intentio erat; neque quisquam est qui in nundinis aut locis supradictis, huius modi litteris receptis, solutionem faciat».[41] Apart from dry exchanges as mentioned here, also severely prohibited were all deposit transactions which involved the loan of money with repayment of the sum loaned on the maturity day plus a payment for the loan. Also illicit were loans where interest was tacitly or expressly recognized.

In order to combat evident cases of usury, Pope Pius V prohibited the payment of interest even for overdue repayments. Real exchanges were allowed only at the original Fairs and not subsequently, due to the generally shorter repayment terms, based on the distance or proximity of the location specified for the payment.[42]

Pope Pius V issued another important disposition against monopolists in general, who could dominate the market and raise prices, and against money lenders in particular, who could control the supply of money to their own exclusive advantage. Monopolies were also severely prohibited in civil law.[43] This work of purification of economic life of all activities that were directly or indirectly related to usury was completed by a register of items of taxable wealth promulgated in 1569 by Pope Pius V. Part of the general trend towards fixed incomes, very common was the acquisition of income, by which a capitalist secured an annuity from funds belonging to others, in exchange for a loan to a third party, i.e. the seller of the income.[44] Because this could rapidly degenerate into usury, Pope Pius V recognised these contracts only when the income came from a precisely identified piece of property from which a revenue was obtained that was at least as much as the annuity imposed. Contracts were allowed where the revenue was similar to the income obtained from property and the loss of the income led to a proportionate loss. It was also established that the right to the income could be purchased only by money (and not goods) to be handed over in the presence of a notary public, and the income could only be rescinded by the seller of the

---

[41] *Magnum Bullarium*, cit., t. VII, p. 884. See also H.J.D. DENZINGER, *Enchiridion symbolorum definitionum quae de rebus fidei et morum a concilii oecumenicis et summis pontificibus emanarunt*, Friburgi Brisgoviae, Herder, 1900, p. 249.

[42] *Magnum Bullarium*, cit., t. VII, pp. 884-885.

[43] *Ibid.*, t. VII, p. 885. «Eos vero, qui conspirationes fecerint vel congestam undique pecuniam ita ad se redigerint, ut quasi monopolium pecuniae facere videantur, poenis quae a iure contra exercentes monopolia constitutae sint, retineri sancimus».

[44] Here we have a *censo consignativo* which is «not a purchase of the property but only of the profit that may be made of the property, in which the capital is secure if the property is not destroyed». Cf. CASLINO, *op. cit.*, pp. 70, 71 and following, 66, 67, 69.

income.[45] These conditions and guarantees were set out with the clear intent of opposing usury and dry exchanges.

In the light of these regulations governing loans and the creation of fixed-income annuities it is clear that the Church made relentless efforts to prevent capital from displacing the more noble means of acquiring goods, i.e. work, through its opposition to usury. While the toil of labour was useful for public wellbeing and hence was justly rewarded, a money changer acted only in his own interest and hence offended against the traditional concept of wealth, which though owned by private individuals was intended to be used for the good of the community. This was the real reason Churchmen so fiercely opposed credit. They may have cited the theoretical principle of the inertia of money[46] in order to justify the prohibition, but this was merely another form of the same concept of wealth, otherwise it would not be clear why usury was prohibited in the case of livestock businesses, where the lender was not allowed to take repayment in the form of profit, but only of capital.

The reader may wonder how cases of loss of expected profit, consequential damages and *periculum sortis* were justified, since they allowed for profit from capital. In this guise, nothwithstanding the need to devolve to the poor any material comforts in excess of requirements and the subordination of economic life to higher aims, the Church wished to consacrate the principle by which the owner of property and user of legitimately acquired goods had the right to be compensated for being deprived of the goods, even temporarily.

These observations are equally applicable to the regulations promulgated by the Church both before and during the decades following the Papal Bull of Pope Pius V. Leaving aside the *First Provincial Council* of Milan,[47] the dispositions of the Surrentinum Council of 1548, which condemned usury in both open and veiled form[48] and the regulations of the Council of Benevento in

---

[45] *Magnum Bullarium*, cit., t. VII, p. 737. A similar constitution was issued by S. Carlo, nel First Provincial Council. Cf. *Acta Ecclesiae mediolanensis*, cit., vol. II, p. 123.

The constitution of Pope Pius V, which is proficiently summarized in CASLINO (*op. cit.*, p. 71 and following) is erroneously dated 1568.

[46] *Concilii Tridentini*, cit., pp. 254-255.

[47] *Acta Ecclesiae mediolanensis*, cit., vol. II, p. 121. «Ne fiant cambia, cum literae ad destinatum locum vere non mittuntur, et ibi non fit solutio; sed uno et eodem loco pecunia datur et recipitur; vel quando dantur, et accipiuntur pecuniae cum eo pacto, ut habeatur recursus ad domum vel ad respondentem dantis, aut accipientes (*quod pactum vulgo vocatur la ricorsa*) atque ita impensae, aut alterius rei onus imponitur».

[48] MANSI, *op. cit.*, vol. XXXVI bis, col. 302-306, *Concilium Surrentinum*, 1584. «Cambia quae sicca appellari consueverunt, quoniam ad destinatum locum litterae non mittuntur, neque ibi solutio fit, sed uno et eodem loco datur pecunia et recipitur, reprobamus».

1599,[49] indicate a long period of continuous attention to the problem of usury, which Federico Borromeo was able to draw upon when declaring loan transactions *ad nundinas* illicit.[50]

The famous Cardinal of Milan addressed the city and diocese with these words: «It has come to our notice in this City and Diocese of Bankers and Merchants and private persons, that money is loaned for purchases at the Fair, without observing the conditions required by the Sacred Canons, and established by Pope Pius V of cherished memory, for such contracts: whereby usury is disguised and hidden, unjustly and injuriously to the souls of men, and to the public weal, and to the ruination of poor debtors and their families; and wishing, nay feeling the obligation upon us for the pastoral office held by us, to establish for this City and this Diocese what should be the righteous conduct in relation to such usury and injustice, for the wellbeing of souls under our care and for the honour and in the service of God, we have made a lengthy and mature consideration with some learned and grave men, concerning the doubts that have been expressed and the considerations made in the past on this subject. Recently we have denounced these cases as more frequent and more dangerous than loan agreements *ad nundinas*. These resolutions and deliberations we hereby approve in writing and we desire for the good of this City and this Diocese that they be observed and put into practice».[51] Of the thirty cases of illicit dealings presented in the document prepared by the Cardinal, the fifth states: «Loans are illicit and connote usury also if the person receiving the money at the Fair has no money, credit or rights there, *nec actu, nec habitu, nec potentia*, and all this the Banker well knows and believes when stipulating the contract». Thus this form of exchange was condemned as an interest-bearing loan. The reason set out by the Cardinal in his pamphlet was as follows: «there are many and convincing reasons for this resolution, to wit: the letters are not sent or are returned without effect...; there is no partial exchange of money, so the transaction is not real, and because it is the intention of the parties to the contract to render and pay the money in the same place where it was given; and because interest is charged solely because the payment takes place over time».[52] Which meant that the Banker should desist

---

[49] *Ibid.*, vol. XXXVI bis, col. 449-450 (September 1599).

[50] F. BORROMEO, *Sulle usure del cambio delle monete*, BA, Misc., S.B.S., IV, 31. [This library reference number does not relate to any manuscript].
There is another copy in the same Library, identified as S.I.G., V, 26.

[51] BORROMEO, *op. cit.*, pp. 1-2.

[52] *Ibid.*, pp. 5-6. The sixth case (*op. cit.*, pp. 6-7), rather than dealing with those who receive the exchange, dealt with the campsor, who was not allowed to give money if he knew the recipient had no money or rights at the Fair.

not only when he knew the counter-party had no credit or rights at the Fair but also when he suspected this to be the case.[53]

For Borromeo and the Commission of theologians and experts he created, money changing was legitimate where bills of exchange were actually sent, facilitating commerce by removing the risk of transporting large sums of money. In all other cases it was illicit, because it involved usury, profits received for the sale of time. «Money changing is illicit and connotes usury – the ninth case of the thirty states unambiguously – if it refers only to prolonging the time for payment. The reason being: because in the exchange this time is required to send the letters and prepare the payment and not for the purpose of gain; for a loan, taking more than is lent, because of time, is usury».[54] This meant that for Borromeo and the Church in general, usury and exchange were distinct and separate transactions. In the first case, time was the only reason for applying interest: in the second, where the transaction was legitimate, time was required to send the letters and the economy as a whole benefited. Money earned from exchange without reference to the distance or proximity of the Fair and hence the time required to perfect the transaction, was illicit.[55]

Another fundamental aspect, which emerges from the cases presented by Borromeo, is the prohibition to predetermine the earnings from the transaction, which must be decided exclusively «by the laws of exchange».[56] This expression should not induce the reader into error, suggesting that Borromeo believed in what could be called a natural order in economic life. The Cardinal was referring to the fair price of goods, i.e. the market price without artifice and manoeuvres by one banker or another. This explains the nineteenth case of illicit dealings presented in the pamphlet: «an exchange is unjust if the Banker gives a lower price than is the normal price in the marketplace to a person who has no dealings with the marketplace and therefore is unaware of the normal price».[57] Whereas an exchange «stipulated in the Bankers Market, excluding any fraud»[58] is fair. Fraud was carried out when the money changer increased the price by partially or totally monopolizing the money market.[59]

---

[53] *Ibid.*, pp. 7-8.

[54] *Ibid.*, p. 9.

[55] *Ibid.*

[56] «Exchange is today illicit when the interest is certain and is part of the agreement». «And the reason for this resolution is because the alteration of the interest does not depend on the contractual parties but on the law of exchange». Cf. *ibid.*, p. 10.

[57] *Ibid.*, p. 14.

[58] *Ibid.*, p. 15.

[59] *Ibid.*, p. 16. «Exchange is unjust if the Banker, who gave the money in exchange, has first

5

Also unfair was an exchange where the trader may not have monopolized the market but was certain that the price had been the object of artificial man-oeuvres by someone.[60] Also illicit was a trade in which the Banker paid two parts in cash and one part in goods, increasing the price above the proper amount.[61] The prohibitions in the pamphlet presented by Borromeo also warned against giving money or having dealings with anyone likely to be pro-fligate or to use the money for gambling, lascivious behaviour or illegal invest-ments. Civil law, in fact, excluded such people from administering their assets. But more than for this reason, the prohibition was part of the general interpre-tation and justification given by the Church to money changing, which was le-gitimate «when it is useful for the republic and necessary for the needs of in-dividuals».[62] In all other cases it was condemned.

The reader who is aware of the social and not merely religious significance of the role of the Milanese Cardinal will immediately understand the weight of these dispositions in the commercial activities of the city, dominated for dec-ades by the authoritative figure of the Archbishop. We do not wish to imply that they were the articles of a code on money changing, which a Church com-mission was appointed to oversee and apply to individual cases. But they were a code of conduct to be followed and men could not expect to escape censure or other consequences if they failed to live up to the ideals established by the Church.

The numerous Church sanctions applied to offenders were both econom-ic and spiritual and were not without effect. If the sixteenth century in Italy is considered a murky period, it is not through the religious indifference that characterizes the Modern Age: denying a man the sacraments and a Church burial for illicit economic dealings and the failure to return the revenues de-rived from them, in Verona or elsewhere, placed the offender in ignominy and infamy.[63] And it was not only in Can Grande's Verona that this fate was suf-

---

made a monopoly to compete or reduce the ability of the market to set a price, or used other artifices and collusions. And the reason is this: the variation of prices as a consequence of this fraud offends the public justice of the free market and the natural justice of the true and fair price; and because damage is made to the debtor through this injustice; and because it is against charity, and the equal-ity of justice in exchanges: by which what is taken must be returned».

[60] *Ibid.*, p. 17.

[61] *Ibid.*, p. 13.

[62] *Ibid.*, pp. 17-18.

[63] G.M. GIBERTI, *Opera*, Hostilia, Apud A. Carattonium, 1740, p. 82. «Statuimus ut nullus sa-cerdos usurariis manifestis de usura concedat ecclesiastica sacramenta, aut sepulturam, nisi primo de usuris, et male ablatis, illis ad quos spectant, satisfecerint, vel de satisfaciendo cautionem secundum forman generalis concilii Lugdunensis apud officium nostrum praestiterint, vel praestitisse legitiman fidem fecerint».

fered, because similar penalties were applied in Milan,[64] Benevento,[65] Siena and throughout Italy, where the regenerating winds of the Counter Reformation blew.[66] A further, and more intimate, punishment was to deny the offender absolution, where the confession had shown that the illicitly gained earnings or stolen money had not been returned to the rightful owner. Even in the face of death and when the offender showed penitence, the Church inisisted that the wrongs be made right and the money obtained from usury be returned to the victims of the practice.[67]

These were spiritual punishments, but there were also penalties of a legal and economic nature: a usurious contract, for example, could not be enforced since it was considered *irriti et inanes*.[68]

Were other means necessary to keep men on the virtuous path and away from the practice of usury? The regulations were so stark and clear and the punishment so severe that the affirmation of Gothein can only astonish: «the Catholic Church which had so far always closed the door to credit, but had very willingly left the window open, came to the help of the flagging economy this time too with the spread of the *Monti di Pietà* covering profits

---

[64] The Second Provincial Council of Milan in 1569 established by Decree: «Ne Parochi usurarium manifestum, ut Gregorii X costitutione sancitum est, etiam si in testamento, aliave quadam ultima voluntate ipse mandarit ea restitui, quaecumque usurae nomine acceperit, in sepulturam ecclesiasticam tradant, nisi pro eorum facultatibus, re ipsa illis satisfactum sit, a quibus usuras exegerit, aut si absunt, Episcopo, vicariove eius vel Parocho, intra eius parochiae fines ille dum vixerat, habitarat, vel Notario publico de restituione cautum sit pignoribus, aut idonea sponsione facta». *Acta Ecclesiae mediolanensis*, cit., vol. II, p. 174.

[65] The *Provincial Council of Benevento* on 25 April 1571 not only forbade Church burials for usurers who had failed to return their ill-gotten gains, or failed to promise to return them, but also excommunicated Parish Priests who gave them burial. MANSI, *op. cit.*, t. XXXVI bis, col. 17.

[66] Interesting is the echo of Church sanctions against usurers mentioned by T. GARZONI (*La piazza universale di tutte le professioni del mondo*, Venetia, appresso Gio. Battista Somasco, 1587, p. 550): «The Sacred Doctors say, through greater detestation of usury, that the usurer offends against all creatures because he sells time, which is common to all hours. In addition he offends all Saints because he practices usury on the days set aside of them, and even on the day of the birth of Our Lord, and Easter. And they add, the usurer is unworthy at his funeral to have the requiem aeternam sung, as is the case with other Christians, because in this life he never left debtors in peace, so shall not hear the world of peace in the other life».

[67] MANSI, *op. cit.*, vol. XXXVI bis, col. 17, *Concilium Beneventanum*, 1571; *Catechismus romanus*, cit., p. 455, De Septimo Praecepto, c. 8; *Acta Ecclesiae mediolanensis*, cit., vol. II, p. 1887; GIBERTI, *op. cit.*, p. 82.

[68] *Acta Ecclesiae mediolanensis*, cit., vol. II, p. 123. «Si quis autem in aliquo ex his casibus, aut aliis, qui usuram sapiunt, et a Jure, ut iniqui prohibentur, contraxerint; ipsi contractus, etiam iure iurando muniti, nulli, irriti, et inanes sint». In relation to Rome, we should recall the particular severity with which Pope Pius IV fought against usury and dry exchanges. In 1559, noticing how the art of exchange was practiced assiduously by merchants in the Roman Curia, the Pope enjoined the Governor to establish a fine of 2000 golden ducats for usury in addition to excommunication, as already established. *Magnum Bullarium*, cit., t. VII, pp. 1-4 (year 1599).

with the mantle of charity».[69] The German historian would do well to remember that never did the Church – certainly not in the sixteenth century – make compromises in order to justify credit, and we are more confident than he is, apparently, that the Church allowed commercial companies to be created and other instruments to spread in order to provide the necessary impetus to economic life, which in the sixteenth century was one of the most subtle factors in the decline of Italy. Nor was recognition and the legitimacy afforded to credit via the spread of religiously-inspired lending institutions (*Monti di Pietà*), whose aims were purely charitable, a form of compromise of Church principles, as made clear in the Papal Bull «Inter multeplices» of Pope Leo X. In 1515 he put an end to speculation about the legitimacy of charging a small amount of interest to cover the administrative costs of the Monte, recognizing this work of Christian charity, whereby the poor were freed from the shackles of insatiable usurers. Given its importance we set out the words used in the Bull to express the legitimacy of the pious institutions «declaramus et definimus, montes pietatis antedictos per respublicas institutos, et auctoritate Sedis Apostolicae hactenus probatos et confirmatos, in quibus, pro eorum impensis et indemnitate aliquid moderatum ad solas ministrorum impensas et aliarum rerum ad illorum conservationem, ut praefertur, pertinentium, pro eorum indennitate dumtaxat, ultra sortem, absque lucro eorumdem montium, recipitur, neque ullo pacto improbari, quinimo meritorium esse ac laudari et probari debere tale mutuum et minime usurarium putari».[70] These charitable institutions, widespread before this definition, were promoted by many cities of Italy, thanks in part to the regular appeals made by the Bishops and Councils to Princes, governors and the wealthy.[71]

On the basis of the lengthy prohibition of usury, it could be thought that the Italian economy was held in check and that this paralysis was one of the

---

[69] E. GOTHEIN, *L'età della controriforma: lo stato cristiano-sociale dei gesuiti nel Paraguay*, translated by G. Thiel,Venezia, La Nuova Italia, 1928, p. 185.

[70] [We declare and establish that the Monti di Pietà founded by communities, repeatedly approved by Apostolic Authorities, may collect money only as indemnity for expenses and the costs of its officers and to keep and protect its goods, and may not collect anything in addition to capital or make agreements of any other type]. Cf. *Magnum Bullarium*, cit., t. V, p. 621 and following e MANSI, *op. cit.*, t. XXXII, col. 905. An excerpt can be found in DENZINGER, *op. cit.*, pp. 174-175.

If the theoretical question of the legitimacy of the Monti was settled by the Papal Bull of Pope Leo XIII, even two centuries later some wished to excuse their usury on the basis of the example of the Monti. They were answered by CASLINO (*op. cit.*, p. 17 and following): «The Monti di Pietà earn money legitimately, because they take what is not in excess of capital or to make profit of loans, but simply to pay the Ministrations and expenses involved for the indemnity of the Monte, which however should be moderate according to Justice and in keeping with charity, it being the blood of the poor».

[71] Cf. *Acta Ecclesiae mediolanensis*, cit., vol. II, p. 126; MANSI, *op. cit.*, vol. XXXVI bis, col. 605, *Concilium Genuense* (ante 1574).

reasons for the decline in the economy. Anyone who has this suspicion should be reassured that the Church established regulations and prohibitions to strike against loans which (as shown below) were generally not drivers of the economy; all too often, these loans were either examples of recourse to the least troublesome means of procuring money employed by idle noblemen to fuel their profligacy, or the means for procuring wealth by former merchants no longer willing to make difficult and dangerous journeys to sell their goods or to buy and sell merchandise without the certainty of profit, preferring as they did the tranquility of the exchange, where many were destined to lose their worldly wealth. Where credit was necessary for economic growth, the Church promoted the instruments and institutions which allowed savings to be invested, naturally without permitting capital to become the preponderant factor, in line with Church teachings which emphasized the superiority of work for the acquisition of wealth and economic goods.[72]

5. On the basis of the economic ideal enshrined in the regulations reconstructed up to here, the Church dispositions concerning days of rest are analyzed below.

Previously, during the Middle Ages when economic activity was dictated by sufficiency, the number of days of rest, although abundant (less so than is often affirmed[73]), did not appear excessive. They were determined by regulations and Council statutes. Only when, for a variety of reasons, medieval religious fervour and the need for an intense religious life weakened, did the notion of taking days away from work disturb men, animated by a new economic mentality encouraged by recently experienced material hardship, who attributed to wealth an exclusively earthly function, incompatible with ethical and religious limitations.

Despite the complaints and protests of the authorities of the Milan City Council, at precisely this moment, Borromeo – untiring in his vigilance over

---

[72] We take the opportunity to cite the thinking of Mario Alberti, although different from our own, in relation to the position of the Church on credit. He says that the Church made categorical decisions and issued formal prohibitions only where credit transactions were made for consumer items. «But when, in certain periods, credit became less and less a source of momentary relief for the consumer in need (or for the producer in relation to the consumer), and lost its characteristic, essential in some historic eras, of instrument meeting the needs of consumption... becoming an instrument functioning according to the requirements and desires of those who, through their economic activity, intended to make money from the transaction and build up wealth from it, the moral assessment of credit and the legitimacy of interest also changed, as was inevitable», M. ALBERTI, *La Finanza Moderna*, Milano, Giuffrè, 1934, vol. I, *La evoluzione e la essenza teorica del credito mobiliare*, p. 208.

[73] FANFANI, *Le origini*, cit., p. 62.

the discipline of economic life, as in other matters – set out the regulations governing days of rest, which he expected people to observe and Bishops and parish priests to enforce.[74] Borromeo specified the precept on numerous occasions; it prescribed for the day of rest the prohibition of any material activities carried out for monetary gain, since these activities would distract the Christian from serene and complete dedication to matters of the spirit. Those who were held to strict observance of the regulation included «carters, riders, coachmen, barbers, tailors, cobblers and other workmen, their apprentices, servants and employees, and other people of whatever profession, craft or business». Not only craftsmen had to observe the day of rest, but shopkeepers and merchants as well: all commercial activity was prohibited except the sale of items required for human sustenance. Hence prohibited was the sale of books, paintings, flowers, plants and similar non-essential goods. All the more illicit was the sale of playing cards, dice, masks and clothes for disguises, activities that were permanently prohibited by Carlo Borromeo. He further specified that «observance... of each day of rest shall be for the entire twenty-four hours, from midnight of the day before the rest day until midnight of the following day».[75]

If the Cardinal of Milan was zealous in exforcing the observance of the day of rest, his biographer, the Bishop of Novara, Carlo Bascapè, was no less fervent. In an Edict of 1595 he prohibited, among other things, the holding of Fairs and public markets on rest days, as well as any preparation for them, even where the event was to be held on the following day.[76] He also prohibited «the transportation of things for moving house in the holy day of S. Michele» and any commerce in non-comestibles or for the sustenance of Christians. And even where these vittles were sold, they were not to be displayed in public, so the shop could stay open «but it is allowed only to keep open the door».[77] Similar regulations were established by the Council of Sorrentino in 1584 and of Benevento in 1599. The first also prohibited dances and similar entertainments.[78] The second prohibited any judicial activity, which like any

---

[74] *First Provincial Council*, in *Acta Ecclesiae mediolanensis*, cit., vol. II, col. 40; *Edicta et ordinationes*, in *Acta*, cit., vol. II, col. 1116-1117.

[75] *Third Provincial Council*, in *Acta ecclesiae mediolanensis*, cit., vol. II, col. 230; *Edicta et ordinationes*, in *Acta*, cit., vol. II, col. 1111-1112, BORROMEO, *Litterae Pastorales*, cit., vol. I, p. 667.

[76] In particular, Bascapè mentions the prohibition on Fairs on the day of S. Martino in the city and suburbs of Novara; on the day of S. Bartolomeo in Borgomanero; on the day of S. Giacomo Apostolo in Terra d'Orta; on the day of S. Michele in Pietregemelle, cf. BASCAPÈ, *op. cit.*, p. 620.

[77] *Ibid.*, pp. 620-621.

[78] MANSI, *op. cit.*, t. XXXVI bis, col. 289.

profane occupation would have disturbed the tranquillity of rest and total dedication to the spirit. [79] This Council threatened to impose sanctions on offenders that included «divine retribution» and the confiscation of goods and animals used for transportation as well as fines to be quantified at the discretion of the authorities.

The extent to which these prohibitions were observed, to speak of Milan alone, can be seen by the number of times the City Council sent ambassadors to the Pope in Rome complaining of how the enormous number of holy days was interfering with economic life.[80] The ninety or so days of work lost through the wishes of Borromeo and the approximately eighty days recommended by the Council of Benevento were less numerous than the number observed in previous centuries. Carlo Borromeo certainly did not refuse to grant permission to work where fields had been threshed but the harvest was uncollected, or grapes needed picking and would rot on the vine without work in the fields, damaging the public weal and private resources.[81]

Except for the obligation to observe a day of rest and not to dedicate any time to economic activities on that day, the Church established no regulations which might have attenuated such activities. Most interpreters of Church thinking – Borromeo first and foremost – recognized the utility of commerce and considered the merchant in the same light as a worker of the fields or the workshop. If commercial life presented too many opportunities for illicit and «immediate earnings», rather than smother commerce, the Church – through Borromeo and others – preferred to establish regulations and controls over the operations of the market, as illustrated above.

6. The discussion of the uses to which wealth could be put will not be lengthy, not because moderation in consumption in the sixteenth century was the norm, but because in the face of the pomp and magnificence exhibited in that century, the Church could do little other than suggest to these latter-day Luculli Trimalcioni that there was a just measure to everything and remind them of their Christian duty towards the needy and the poor.

Naturally the Council of Trent reserved the first regulations on luxury to Bishops whose pastoral duty towards men was to set them an example, by displaying an unstinting and evident distaste for worldly goods. «They should

---

[79] *Ibid.*, col. 436. Cf. anche *Concilium Genuense*, in *ibid.*, t. XXXVI bis, col. 602-603.

[80] VERGA, *op. cit.*, p. 270; L. PASTOR, *Storia dei papi*, Roma, Desclée, 1942, vol. VIII, p. 271 and following.

[81] C. BORROMEO, *Libretto dei ricordi, al popolo della città et diocese di Milano*, Milano, Pacifico Pontio, 1578, p. 33 and following; MANSI, *op. cit.*, vol. XXXVI bis, col. 435-36.

live in such a way that others take example from them in frugality, continence and modesty, and with the utmost humility which is greatness in the eyes of God. But the Synod following the Fathers of the Council of Carthage, not only commands that Bishops should content themselves with parsimonious commodities, nourishment and fare; but they should ensure that their homes do not contain anything that does not exhibit saintly simplicity, a zealous and devout love of God and utter disdain for vanity». These regulations were among the twenty-one decrees of general Refoundation, which also stamped out the bad practice of diverting Church assets to relatives. Forbidden was «the attempt to enrich relatives and members of one's family with the revenues of the Church; this being prohibited by the canons of the Apostles. But if these relatives are poor, they shall receive these revenues as do others in need». This warning was addressed not only to the lower ranks of the Church but also to «Cardinals, upon whose councils with the Pontiff the administration of the Universal Church depends; it would be a grave defect if they were not to be shining examples of virtue and discipline in their lives, since the eyes of the world are upon them».[82] Another constitution of the Council of Trent forbade laymen and Churchmen alike from exhibiting sumptuous pomp especially on the occasions of births and weddings, in the form of rich clothing, luxurious banquets and illicit games.[83]

In his own diocese, Carlo Borromeo applied the same prohibitions to Bishops. They were not to use balm, buckles and gilded items of clothing. They were not to possess wealth, furnishings or live in magnificent homes, or be seen in public with horses beyond the necessary, because pomp and magnificence – the Cardinal of Milan pointed out – do not establish authority over the faithful, which can be achieved solely through faith and the restraint show in one's personal habits.[84] Carlo Borromeo had a thorough understanding of his time and certainly was aware that the civil authorities likewise prohibited luxury and excessive displays of wealth, without success. In the light of the failings of these laws he invited the Princes to set a similar example of temperance and moderation: «admonemus et enixe hortamur Principes et Magistratus, ut effusam impensam et omnem intemperantiam certis legibus coercentes, modum statuant non solum quotidianis epulis atque conviviis, verum etiam vestibus, equis, rhedis, famulis, aliisque non necessariis apparatibus; et denique omni et domestico et externo ornamento et instrumento moderationem ad hibeant: qua pecuniae

---

[82] P. Sforza Pallavicino, *Istoria del Concilio di Trento*, Roma, per Biagio Diversin, e Felice Cesaretti librari all'insegna della Regina, 1663, part III, pp. 823-824.

[83] *Concilium Tridentinum*, cit., XII, p. 418.

[84] *First Provincial Council*, in *Acta Ecclesiae mediolanensis*, cit., vol. II, col. 65-66.

effusione sublata, innumerabilibus malis, quae inde ortum habent, occurretur. Quod facilius etiam fiet, si Principe ipsi, quorum mores, et vivendi rationem populi plerumque imitari solent, non modo leges proposuerint sed etiam, quemadmodum legibus parendum sit, exemplo docuerint».[85]

After exhorting Bishops and Princes to moderation, Borromeo addressed the heads of households thus: «Let them keep only what is deserving of those who serve and their families and spend only what they earn without incurring debt». And: «not spend in superfluity and unnecessary lands»[86] But we are in the century of pomp and splendour, maintained at the cost of systematic debt, squandering the wealth gained over centuries of toil. In the Rome of the Popes, it was necessary to appoint twelve Senators to act as busybodies, supervising spendthrifts, who, after ineffectively being warned, were confined to small villages under the vigilant eye of honest trustees.[87] So far had the idea of the rightful use of wealth degenerated that even after public and disastrous calamities, such as the famous sack of Rome in the sixteenth century, luxury and pomp disappeared briefly only to return even more lavishly than before. The ostentation of wealth and the show of pomp irritated the Pope, who appointed four officials to more rigidly apply the restrictions on the constitution of dowries (this made marriages difficult and risked a decline in the population), the excessive amounts spent on funerals, women's clothes, precious necklaces and other objects of vain exhibitionism.[88] The restrictions were not only for the Capital: even the inhabitants of Fulgina received a warning from Pope Sixtus V against creating showy dowries and feminine luxury.[89]

During this period these dispositions were in perfect harmony with the teachings of authoritative laymen such as Guicciardini and Davanzati.[90] Later, the rules against luxury probably were no longer in line with the doctrine of

---

85 [Princes and Magistrates who establish and apply the laws are warned and advised to avoid banquets, clothing, luxuries and decoration, and to practice an outward moderation, abstaining from all that leads to an exaggerated show of money, because it is much easier for the heads of Cities if they follow the example of the laws they pass and imitate the customs and ways of life of those they administer]. *Acta Ecclesiae mediolanensis*, cit., vol. II, p. 121.

86 *Ibid.*, vol. III, pp. 660-662.

87 J. SPIZZICHINO, *Magistrature dello Stato pontificio (476-1870)*, Lanciano, Carabba, 1930, pp. 245-246.

88 *Ibid.*, p. 264. Panigarola, Bishop of Asti, admonished women for «the bracelets and necklaces which cost your houses so dear and you wear on your arms and around your necks». PANIGAROLA, *Prediche*, without the Title page, is located at BA, colloc. V.St.C. VI, 87, p. 40. The same Library also contains: Prediche di Mons. Rever. Panigarola, vescovo d'Asti, in Asti, appresso Virgilio Zangrandi, MDXCI. This edition, with a different format, contains the same sermons as the first.

89 *Magnum Bullarium*, cit., t. IX, p. 339 and following (1589).

90 Cf. chapter III.

wellbeing and the results of economics. Suffice it to say that the dispositions illustrated above were inspired by the higher principles of Christian social doctrine, which attributed to wealth a social role, according to which the owner of worldly wealth was not an absolute master of these resources but merely their administrator on behalf of God. This was the spirit that moved Carlo Borromeo when he warned Christians not to spend money on superfluous things «which could give life to many of Christ's poorest». And he clearly emphasized the social and spiritual function of economic goods, speaking to the head of the family: «Abstain from useless and superfluous expenses, and remember that if you own things you administer them and are accountable in this to God».[91] As if the latter concept were not clear or forceful enough to induce people dutifully to give to the poor, in the first Provincial Council, Carlo Borromeo warned the wealthy and well-off: «Copiosis et locupleti bus illud semper propositum esse debet sancti Joannis (JOHN, III, 17) Apostoli: "Si quis habuerit substantiam mundi huius, et viderit fratrem suum necesse habere, et clauserit viscera sua ab eo; quomodo caritas dei manet in illo?". Unde facile intelligunt quam facultates suas pauperum difficultates et necessitatem sublevandam conferre debeat».[92]

In addition to these regulations, Carlo Borromeo encouraged charitable works as a means of distributing to the poor what was in excess of one's own needs, a duty he regarded as irrefutable: «Do charitable works, give alms, visit hospitals, prisons, the infirm, and in all possible ways help the poor. Help most those who are in greatest need».[93]

Hence, in the doctrine of the Church, the economy was a means of achieving a greater spiritual good, and men needed to pursue this good. Wealth was not the object of man's action but the means for reaching God. «Handle the things of this world as a means to God and not as an absolute owner; and use them out of necessity and need, and not for pleasure; and beware of forsaking the eternal life for the things of this world».[94]

---

[91] BORROMEO, *Litterae Pastorales*, cit., col. 662. The concept that the rich man does not own his wealth but is only its administrator on behalf of God is common to the Catholic writers of the Middle Ages (cf. FANFANI, *Le origini*, cit., cap. I e IV), and was a doctrine disseminated throughout the Counter Reformation. See for example SEGNERI, *Il Cristiano istruito*, cit., p. 154, part I, R. 17, no. 6; ID., *Quaresimale*, cit., t. II, p. 193, sermon 22.

[92] [The wealthy should not forget the precepts of Saint John, according to which charity is the fundamental principle of Christian life and should inspire their behaviour towards the needy]. *First Provincial Council*, cit., col. 120. On page 121 the regulation regarding giving what is in excess of need to the poor is expressed in very moving terms: «magnopere cavendum est, ne sussidia pauperum in supervacuos sumptus, et inanes delicias effundantur».

[93] BORROMEO, *Litterae Pastorales*, cit., col. 659. Cf. also MANSI, *op. cit.*, t. XXXVI bis, col. 298.

[94] BORROMEO, *Litterae Pastorales*, cit., col. 650.

7. What is the basic spirit of the numerous regulations promulgated by the Church in the sixteenth century to govern economic life?

We have seen that work, both manual and intellectual, was the main means for acquiring wealth, whilst the strategems of the idle, who sought earnings from fraud and deception, without expending any energy for the common good, were illicit. And it is the absence of these essential characteristics – work and social utility – that explains the constant opposition of the Church to credit and usury, the exercise of which swelled the ranks of parasites, intent on biding the time during which their ill-gotten gains would mature. If it is remembered that loans were generally made for consumption and not for the purpose of investment or for production, it is clear that combatting credit was beneficial to the economy and not a factor in stagnation or economic paralysis. Pope Pius V was certainly aware of this when he dictated a letter to the King of Spain requesting him to extirpate usury among the Jews in Lombardy, because he believed it would lead to the ruin of a previously industrious and prosperous population.

Where the intent was to invest in productive activities, the Church had no objection to credit, although the Council of Trent certainly restored and extended prohibitions due to the insurmountable difficulties encountered for some time in the alliance between capital and work and other forms of company and business that in the previous centuries had been the normal means of investing savings. The sixteenth century was certainly not a time of capital investments in industry and commerce, because the evidence points more to the frittering away of fortunes and the effort to secure a fixed income from wealth in the form of the ownership of, or jurisdiction over, land and the acquisition of assets or taxable incomes. This was the symptom of an anaemic economic spirit after the triumph over the seas and the markets, sailed and vanquished in other eras. The Church, which intervened in the material aspects of the life of peoples only where there was a spiritual need to do so, indirectly fought against the feebleness of Italians by opposing credit and preaching the importance of work over capital, bringing together rich and poor in a common effort to benefit society as a whole. Added to this were the measures introduced to combat luxury and the frivolous use of wealth, so that Church legislation reflected the needs of the community for economic growth, at a time when the economy itself – for a number of reasons – was falling into decline, as we shall see.

To sum up, the Church ideal as reflected in its laws offered the prospect of a Christian unsullied by the suspicions that were once associated with trading in the market. Provided he was fair in his dealings, a Christian could also change money where it was for the public good, with the approval of the

Church. Naturally, the pursuit of wealth was not supposed to distract him from his religious duties, the spiritual aspects of life and its ultimate goal. Hence the legislation on days of rest and the precept of giving everything in excess to the poor, the unstinting message of the Church from the Evangelists onwards, carried forward over the centuries by Churchmen every time the material needs of man were addressed.

These concepts from the Christian tradition reached the Modern Age unchanged and demonstrate – as stated in the first Chapter – that Church doctrine enshrined basic and unalterable principles. Charity, for example, and its impact on the distribution of wealth, could not be excluded from the economic ideals of the Church down through the ages.

CHAPTER THREE

THE ECONOMIC IDEALS OF HISTORIANS
AND POLITICAL COMMENTATORS

1. In the sixteenth century, some European countries increasingly organized into powerful central states began the economic and commercial development that transformed them in later centuries into the great powers of Europe.

Without presuming that the unifying power of a centralized state was the only explanation for their economic prosperity, unity of political life was undoubtedly a crucial factor in their commercial expansion, and the economic efforts of their citizens were channeled almost exclusively towards creating the nation state.[1] After showing these new powers the way to economic greatness, like an agave which blossoms into a flower that becomes a vigourous new plant only to wither and die, so Italy, in the early sixteenth century, became divided into small warring states whose divisions led inevitably to the political decline which in a few short decades was to reduce the once-glorious and prosperous nation to utter servitude. Machiavelli's description of Italy in the Prince is poignant: «more slavish than the Jews, more servile than the Persians, more dispersed than the Athenians, without leader, order, defecate, denuded, lacerated, overrun».[2] Machiavelli's name brings to mind many other authors who returned to the origins of Greek and Roman thought and in so doing laid the foundations of the political doctrine that inspired thinkers from many countries concerned with questions of the state, its greatness and its prosperity.[3] Though

---

[1] Less reputable historians identify the subordination of a nation's citizens as the essence of mercantilism. J. MAZZEI, *Schema di una storia della politica economica internazionale nel pensiero dei secoli 17, 18 e 19*, Torino, UTET, 1936 and A. FANFANI, *I mutamenti economici nell'Europa moderna e l'evoluzione costituzionalistica delle classi dirigenti*, Milano, Vita e Pensiero, 1936, cap. III, both argued that this was the case of Italy.

[2] N. MACHIAVELLI, *Il Principe*, in *Opere Complete di Niccolò Machiavelli*, Milano, Oliva, 1850, vol. I, chapter XXVI, p. 571.

[3] Garosci documents the Italian origin of French political thought in the sixteenth and early seventeenth centuries (A. GAROSCI, *Jean Bodin: politica e diritto nel rinascimento francese*, Milano, Corticelli, 1934).

an intriguing question, how these political theories could flourish in Italy at a time of relentless political decline should not concern us here. More important is to analyze the works of certain sixteenth century historians and political commentators, and the economic aspirations that transpire from their assessment of the condition of society and the underlying historical forces. The economic arguments of these sixteenth century authors will shed light on some of the more practical aspects of life; any reconstruction of the practical aspects of life should consider the economic ideals of the social classes in Italian society at the beginning of the Modern Age. Since Machiavelli's life straddled two epochs, it is appropriate to start this brief survey from him.

2. Some authors have claimed «that Machiavelli regarded the state as such and as an organ of dominion, as a means of use to the majority of men. Questions concerning the material and moral betterment of the multitudes were not addressed by Machiavelli».[4] Leave aside the first part of this claim, the second part is relevant here, despite being somewhat inaccurate, as selected passages from Machiavelli presented below will demonstrate.

Naturally, Machiavelli did not intend The Prince to be a treatise on household governance; his primary concern was to portray the salient features of state authority.[5] It was for the purposes of state expansion, for example, that he dictated the rules of colonization, in a rather modern spirit. When the Prince conquered a territory in which the language, laws and customs of the conquered differed from those of the conquerors, not only was he concerned with eradicating the bloodstock of the previous invaders and restoring the customs of the conquered[6] but also with ensuring the stability and continuity of the Prince's rule. This would not have been achieved by resorting to militias, the exorbitant cost of which would wiped out any income from the new state and vanified the very reason for conquering the territory.

From the point of view of the state, it was far more economical to entrust the rule of the new territory to small groups of citizens, won over by the possession of houses and land taken from a few of the natives. The trifling numbers of dispossessed were no cause for rebellion; the low cost of these colonies of city dwellers produced a hefty profit for the Prince's treasury.[7]

---

[4] E. DONADONI, *Breve storia della letteratura italiana: dalle origini ai nostri giorni*, s.n.t., pp. 138-139.

[5] HAUSER, *La modernité du XVIe siècle*, Alcan, 1930, p. 61. Machiavelli was considered by a German historian a early proponent of a national economy. Cf. H. v. SCHULLERN-SCHRATTENHOFEN, *Die theoretische Nationalökonomie Italiens in neuester Zeit*, Leipzig, Duncker & Humblot, 1891, p. 7.

[6] MACHIAVELLI, *Il Principe*, cit., vol. I, chapter III, p. 528.

[7] *Ibid.*, vol. I, chapter III, p. 529.

This system of colonization via small or large groups of citizens explains the populationist theory of Machiavelli summarized as follows: «Those who plan for a city to make a great empire should contrive with all industry to make it full of inhabitants, for without this abundance of men one will never succeed in making a city great».[8] That has been predated by several decades the populationist theories formulated from the mid sixteenth century onwards. He theorized a state whose greatness was assured by the economic forces at work within society. However, never did he suggest that the the focus of economic activities and the ideal of citizens should be to acquire wealth for themselves; rather, all efforts shoud be directed towards increasing the power of the state. And in instructing the Prince how a public reputation was to be acquired, Machiavelli warned that he «should inspire his citizens to follow their pursuits quietly, in trade and in agriculture, and in every other pursuit of men, so that one person does not fear to adorn his possessions for fear that they be taken away from him, and another to open up to trade for fear of taxes. But he should prepare rewards for whoever wants to do these things, and for anyone who thinks up any way of expanding his city or his state».[9]

In a later passage, Machiavelli explained to the Prince how to treat a minister and in so doing observed: «so as to keep him good – honouring him, making him rich, obligating him to himself, sharing honours and burdens with him so that he cannot stand without the Prince and so that many honours do not make him desire more honours, and much wealth does not make desire more wealth, and many burdens make him fear change».[10] These excerpts show how the Prince was to avoid all policies that hindered the efforts of citizens to increase their wellbeing, but rather encourage and support their endeavours, if necessary by distributing welfare to foster the stability and pros-

---

[8] Cf. G. ARIAS, *Corso di economia politica corporativa*, Roma, Soc. ed. del «Foro italiano», 1938, p. 174.

[9] MACHIAVELLI, *Il Principe*, cit., vol. I, p. 566.

[10] *Ibid.*, vol. I, p. 567. Scipione di Castro offered rather different advice; he was considered «a bold and profound follower of Machiavelli in the political doctrine of the Catholic Counter Reformation» (cf. C. GIARDINA, *La vita e l'opera politica di Scipione di Castro*, Palermo, tip. Boccone del Povero, 1931, p. 168). S. DE CASTRO, in *Instruttion al Duca di terra Noua nell'entrar al Governo dello Stato di Milano* offered the following warning to the Sicilian politician: «Having eyes upon the hands of Ministers is useful diligence so many are the ways of deceit they practice, and fraud, to the disrepute of those who govern, damaging the Prince and the people: if in that state attention is required, I can only cite the oft repeated proverb: The Minister in Sicily gnaws, in Naples he eats and in Milan he devours». Shortly before, he asserted that superfluous expenses consisted «in excessive salaries for Ministers who are necessary and mediocre salaries for Ministers who are barely or not in the least necessary». In C. VENTURA, *Thesoro Politico ... Raccolto Per Comin Ventura*, Milano, presso Girolamo Bordone, 1600, pp. 325-326.

In the National Library of Milan, a manuscript (AG._X.25) contains in addition to the political pamphlets partially reprinted in the *Thesoro* the *Instruttion al Duca di terra Noua*.

perity of his reign. Machiavelli staunchly defended individual initiative and private property [11] when economic activities were conducted by citizens honestly pursuing their own interests, who in so doing furthered the public good.[12] This applied both to individuals and to guilds, protected, honoured and supported by the head of State.[13] The Prince of the nascent state was to be even more careful not to create financial obstacles to citizens. Machiavelli dealt with finance in passing in his discussion of the freedom and munificence of the Prince. Though freedom and munificence were virtues that enhanced his reputation, there was a danger that the Prince might be tempted, in order to cover the vast expenses incurred in the exercise of these virtues, to resort to private wealth and impose one-off taxes, duties and levies. Since this was a dangerous policy that was directly detrimental to all his citizens, Machiavelli advised the Prince to lead a life of parsimony, in the certainty that he would «come to use generosity with all those from whom he does not take, who are infinite, and meanness with all those to whom he does not give, who are few».[14]

These warnings were inspired by the prudence that Machiavelli, and a few decades after him Bodin, identified as a prerequisite of a stable state.[15] Political prudence in economic life translated into the efforts to be made by the Prince to promote through industry and agriculture the wealth that assured citizens a tranquil and blissful life, and at the same time served to maintain and expand the State. In the same spirit, in the early fifteenth century Alberti had formulated a set of rules for acquiring, maintaining and enhancing the reputation of houses and of men.[16] The authors of the *Libri della Famiglia* and the *Prince* were, in their respective centuries, pioneers of new ideals: the former a theorist of individual capitalism; the latter, assuming citizens driven by a capitalist spirit, the advocate of a strong state to whom the individual was subordinate but was not subjugated.

---

[11] The erroneous claim made by Tangorra (*Il Pensiero economico di Niccolò Machiavelli*, in V. TANGORRA, *Saggi critici di economia politica*, Torino, Fratelli Bocca, 1900, pp. 152-153) was that Machiavelli showed a certain sympathy towards the pre-comunist theories of the *Ciompi* (wool carders) in revolt.

[12] Compare the observations made by Arias in G. ARIAS, *Il pensiero economico di Niccolò Machiavelli*, «Annali di Economia», IV, 1928. By the same author cf. ID., *Politica ed economia nel pensiero di Niccolò Machiavelli*, «Educazione Fascista», 1929, pp. 465-476 e 526-541.

[13] MACHIAVELLI, *Il Principe*, cit., vol. I, chapter XXI, p. 566 «because each city, divided into guides and tribes, should take into account the needs of such associations, and join then in providing an example of humanity and munificence».

[14] *Ibid.*, p. 553.

[15] GAROSCI, *Jean Bodin; politica e diritto nel rinascimento francese*, Milano, Corticelli, cit., p. 192.

[16] Cf. FANFANI, *Le origini*, cit., pp. 148-149.

No other, more specific considerations[17] on questions of wealth emerge in the works of Machiavelli, whose economic ideals have been summarized here from a theoretical perspective. It would be interesting to know which economic norms guided him in his everyday life. In his brief criticism of Machiavelli Ferrari asserts that: «he did not disdain asking for work or offering patronage or providing advice even if not requested and blew with the wind in defence of his theories; he loved gold and did not disdain the vulgar satisfaction of becoming rich».[18] Though Machiavelli's practical approach to life suggested that he had left behind the economic precepts of Scholasticism, he nevertheless returned, consciously or inconsciously, to these principles when, during a meeting of the members of a sacred order he invoked Christian charity to repress «usurers, the infamous and swindlers, who inflicted suffering on their neighbours».[19] Machiavelli was not moved by the occasion to invite the monks to love and succour their neighbours in the name of God; rather, he offered concrete proof of his charitable soul throughout his life.[20] This is evidence of how one of the strongest personalities of the sixteenth century exemplified the many contradictions in economic ideals at that time.

Echoes of sixteenth century economic problems can be found in the *Ricordi* of Francesco Guicciardini, who, as a historian, was only too aware of the economic decadence of his day and warned men of the dangers of wealth.[21] The Florentine writer did not fail to observe the changes in wealth

---

[17] Machiavelli made a rather acute and witty comment on variations in the prices of seeds in his N. MACHIAVELLI, *Descrizione della peste di Firenze dell'anno*, in *Opere Complete Di Niccolò Machiavelli*, cit., p. 760, when he referred to the price of interment «The first example that comes to mind is that of the gravedigger, not those who look after those with the plague, but those who understand that abundance leads to scarsity. And nobody believed that a moment would come in which he would desire the health of the sick because at other times he would profit from their death». The very high mortality in a period of famine increased the demand for funeral services and hence the income of undertakers. In reality and owing to the carelessness of the relatives of the deceased, as well as competition from the *monatti* (those responsible for removing corpses during a plague) the professional undertakers lamented a drop in their income, to the extent that they prayed for the good health of plague sufferers.

[18] Cf. G. FERRARI, *Corso sugli scrittori politici italiani*, Milano, Manini, 1862, p. 264.

[19] «... But we are taken by lust, enveloped by error, and wrapped in the throes of sin, in the hands of the devil we find ourselves; so to escape it is fitting to repent, to do penance and to cry with David *Miserere mei Deus*, and with Peter to sob bitterly and to regret all our sins, to know that what pleases the world is but a brief dream» (*Discorso morale* di N. MACHIAVELLI, in *Opere*, cit., vol. I, p. 772 and following).

[20] See the two testaments written by Machiavelli, on page LIIX and LXII of volume one of *Opere*, cit.

[21] F. GUICCIARDINI, *Scritti politici e ricordi*, ed. by R. Palmarocchi, Bari, Laterza, 1933, p. 245, n. 29. «It is the lot of merchants, more often than not, to go bankrupt».
Cf. E. ZANONI, *La mente di Francesco Guicciardini nelle opere politiche e storiche*, Firenze, Barbèra, 1897. Toniolo's claim seems inaccurate (G. TONIOLO, *Scolastica ed umanesimo*, in *Scritti scelti di*

that came before his eyes and, in particular, the way the merchants of the sixteenth century changed their economic ideals, so much so that Guicciardini was dismayed by the poverty of Florence, whose population nonetheless aspired to great riches.[22] Some ascribed the countless dilapidated fortunes to moral laxity; indeed, certain moralists asserted that «ill-acquired riches do not pass beyond the third generation».[23]

Guicciardini offered a different explanation: the economic life of households, like that of nations, was to a certain extent subject to an inevitable law of history: a period of accumulation of goods, coupled with a life of parsimony, was inevitably followed by a period of weak economic spirits, when the wealth accumulated by the fathers was frittered away. This is no wonder, Guicciardini observed, because it was only too natural that men accustomed to the hard work and toil required to acquire wealth, who had always lived as paupers, should treasure their hard-earned gold. Their heirs, on the other hand, «do not have the same regard for what, without any effort on their part, they find in the home, having been raised as rich men and not having learned the art of earning one's keep; and so it is little wonder that, through over spending or lack of thrift, they let it all slip through their fingers?».[24] Guicciardini's analysis of the immoral nature of economic prosperity in sixteenth century Italy prompted him to seek a remedy, not because he sought econom-

---

Giuseppe Toniolo, cit., p. 100): he stated that Guicciardini was so concerned with narrating the military events and diplomatic affairs of his day that he was unaware of, or took no notice of, life in society.

[22] GUICCIARDINI, *Scritti politici*, cit., p. 244, no. 19 and pp. 291-292, n. 33. «And the people of Florence are commonly poor, and for the quality of our life all men desire wealth; which is ill appointed to sustain the freedom of the city, because this appetite leads to private ambition without respect or consideration whatsoever for public glory and honour».

Cf. also ID., *Dialogo e discorsi del Reggimento di Firenze*, Bari, Laterza, 1932, pp. 277-278.

[23] «It is believed and oft seen in fact that ill-gotten gains rarely pass the third generation. Saint Augustine says God permits enjoyment of such things for some good that has been done; and hence God ordains that what is gotten from ill shall not be enjoyed». ID., *Scritti politici*, cit., p. 253, no. 65.

[24] ID., *Scritti politici*, cit., pp. 291-292, no. 33. In relation to the accumulation and inevitable loss of wealth in individual families, three centuries later Carlo Cattaneo, a rather astute Italian economist, wrote: «Mobile riches, gained from the free activity of arts and commerce, grow with incredible speed even in the most disastrous conditions; dissipated, they are made up, oppressed, they change country, but are not lost except through several generations; or in the total annihiliation of a nation. This growth, surrounding a man and his children, with all manner of comfort and pleasures, slowly extinguishes the flame of ambition and taste for the hardy enterprises required to make up wealth. The risks of an industrious life require a continual tension of thought and deed and as wealth grows, so do the bounds of attention, and this ill accords with the heavy spirit required for enjoyment and which enjoyment inspires». C.G. CATTANEO, *Ricerche economiche sulle interdizioni imposte dalla legge civile agli israeliti*, ed. by G.A. Belloni, Roma, Saturnia, 1932, pp. 70-71.

ic power for the country, far from it, but because a moderate degree of wealth was required to pursue certain moral and political aims.

«More desirable – asserted Guicciardini – than riches are honor and reputation; nowadays; without riches, it is difficult to earn or preserve a reputation. Men of virtue should avoid excessive wealth, possessing just enough to have or to preserve their reputation and authority».[25] In Guiccardini's mind, riches were a desirable means with which to achieve honour and authority, perfectly legitimate aims that an honest citizen could, or rather should, aspire to achieve in the service of his homeland, leaving aside personal ambition.[26] Indeed, personal ambition produced every kind of moral and material decay. Highlighting the weaknesses of his time, Guiccardini observed the greedy desire to consume goods without any concern for acquiring them. He warned that: «The principal thing, in matters of economy, is to cut off all superfluous expenses,»[27] and to spend to the best advantage: «true husbandry, in my mind, doth lie in expending the same money to more advantage than another, and, as the vulgar say, to have four pennies for your groat».[28] Guicciardini went on to clarify that «economic prudence consists not in knowing how to avoid expenditures that more often than not are necessary, but rather how to spend to one's advantage, one grosso (fifteen denari) for 24 florins».[29] Continuing on the theme of how to avoid superfluous expenses, he wrote «I once heard a Friar say, that a man should have more credit from one Ducat kept in his purse than from ten he should spend».[30]

Guicciardini sought to convince the merchants to spend more prudently; only too often, lacking the necessary capital, they borrowed from the money lenders, tempted by the prospect of future gains that frequently failed to materialize. «Lay no plans upon what thou hast not in hand, neither spend upon future gains, because many times they do not ensue, and thou dost find thyself involved. Merchants fails most through this, when, through hop fo future gain, they enter upon exchanges, the multiplications whereof is certain and

---

[25] GUICCIARDINI, *Scritti politici*, cit., p. 244, no. 18. In another of his memoirs (n. 141, p. 269 of *op. cit.*) he wrote: «An appetite for things comes from a lowly or an uncomposed soul, and it would be enough to enjoy the things, but being the world a corrupt place, he who yearns for a reputation desires things because with things the virtues glitter and the price is right».

[26] *Ibid.*, p. 241, no. 1.

[27] *Ibid.*, p. 275, no. 162. A similar principle was cited by Scipione di Castro in relation to the Prince's economy (DE CASTRO, *op. cit.*, p. 325), when he referred to the need to «cut superfluous expenses» in other words «parsimony is a resource to the public coffers».

[28] GUICCIARDINI, *Scritti politici*, cit., p. 275, no. 162.

[29] *Ibid.*, p. 297, no. 56.

[30] *Ibid.*, p. 275, no. 164.

hath determinate time, but the gains often not come, and are delayed longer than designed; thus that enterprise which thou hast entered upon as useful doth prove most hurtful to thee».[31]

Guiccardini's warnings aimed to discourage the frivolous expenses that reduced many a family to a state of destitution; his words were also designed to frighten men and dissuade them from the excessive risks of large-scale trading ventures. He recommended that they live on the more modest profits of less risky activities, relying on the savings made by cutting superfluous expenditure. His advice was taken to the extreme by many, who even withdrew from «business for love of a quiet life».[32] This was a complicated century in which the greed for wealth could not rival the lust for life that obstructed economic development. The authors and political commentators who warned against excessive spending and who attributed to luxury and pomp the economic weakness of the age were themselves a product of this century, contributing paradoxically to a sense of false security and wellbeing that dampened the spirits required for economic growth.

3. Guidiccioni, a man of letters, orator and politician, reminded citizens of the honest principles underlying the social order of wealth and in so doing revealed a life ideal very different from the trades and business activities conducted by the various classes in society in other centuries. In a letter to his nephew, a monk, he asserted that «the desire you have so ardent for my tranquility is no different from my own: and if I were loosed of servitude and infinite obligations with the Pope, we might be free and content and perchance both live a life of rest».[33]

Though Guidiccioni was condemned at birth by poverty to earn his keep, he aspired to lead the idle life of a man of letters, and confessed: «which I shall embrace the more fervently (denied of fatherly fortune) the less I am now allowed to do so».[34] And he went on: «if God wills for me a lengthy life, I hope to avoid this exercise of vice and enjoy the quiet and idleness of letters».[35] The aspiration that transpires from his works becomes even more re-

---

[31] *Ibid.*, p. 251, no. 56.

[32] *Ibid.*, p. 251, no. 57. «Do not believe those who say they have left off dealing for love of the quiet life. Examples abound, because as soon as these men see the opportunity for increasing their faculty, they throw themselves upon it like fire on something dry or greasy».

[33] G. GUIDICCIONI, *Opere di Monsignor Giovanni Guidiccioni Vescovo di Fossombrone*, Genova, Tarigo, 1767, p. 154.

[34] *Ibid.* p. 174.

[35] *Ibid.*

markable when one considers his life of hardship and need. It is interesting at this point to explore his conception of economic life.

Guidiccioni contemplated the activities of citizens in the pursuit of wealth to the limits set by religion, morals and politics.[36] He asserted that morals without religious norms lacked foundation, just as civic life was to be grounded in good habits and proven virtues. Since wealth was an instrument that served to achieve religious, moral and political aims, the rules for acquiring and using wealth were to be compatible with such aims. Wordly goods were to be used to honour God, «so that if a man be found in error, let him at least be free of impiety».[37] And riches were to be given to «feed the poor» and «give relief to friends and those who have lost their way in life».[38] The uses of wealth he condoned included donating freely to the state, within reasonable limits. To this end Guidiccioni wrote: «I do not say how useful it is to dedicate a small part of wealth to the public good».[39]

Guidiccioni was concerned that political life should be conducted in an orderly manner, ideally by wealthy men who had handed down to their offspring and relatives the toils of trade.[40] By taking up unpaid public office,[41] these men derived satisfaction from the honours of political life, and had no need through greedy pilfering to arouse public indignation and popular discontent. Society should not be divided into two rigidly defined classes: the rich and the poor, the strong and the violent in contrast to the weak and the oppressed. This type of social inequality could be eradicated by a thorough review of the iniquitous laws that aimed to prevent «legitimate profits» being made by less powerful and more needy categories of citizens. Guidiccioni asserted that economic and civic progress required a certain measure of freedom in industry and trade. And such freedom was being restricted by the very laws that granted monopolies on this or that good to certain indivi-

---

[36] *Ibid.*, p. 99 e p. 112. Guidiccioni asserted that cities that did not pay due respect to the Lord were destined to die (*op. cit.*, p. 112). «Put your wealth to good use in the name of God» (p. 112).

[37] *Ibid.*, p. 112.

[38] *Ibid.*, p. 174. Referring to the duty to exercise charity towards the needy, Guidiccioni recalled the charitable spirit of the ancient citizens of Lucca who: «not only did not despise them, but considered the need of others their own shame, and kept the city in abundance and provided for the needy, and gave to the poor, and treated what they gave no differently from what they kept, and hence established their wealth in common and aided citizens: as all men of subtle mind should do». *Ibid.*, p. 105.

[39] *Ibid.*, p. 109.

[40] *Ibid.*

[41] *Ibid.*, p. 90. «The things that bring about the public good and glory to those who keep it, are sought not for comfort but are moved by a certain divine spirit». *Ibid.*, p. 124.

duals, only too often men of the government with «no less wealth than pride and power».[42] It would be an irony, he claimed, to invoke laws to safeguard private enterprise when the merchants continued to cut each other's throats with fraudulent practices and swindles.[43]

In conclusion, Guidiccioni perceived economic activity as conducive to moral and political virtue, the supreme aims of life. He disapproved of men who placed no limits on the accumulation of wealth, «in the belief that men reached perfection by trading intelligently in goods, distancing their off-spring from the true disciplines, from honest customs and documents». Such a desire to accumulate boundless wealth, observed Guidiccioni, resulted in «a nobleman who in order to pursue his studies refused to engage in trade al-most being branded as infamous».[44] Here, he was alluding to the love of lit-erature; and through literature a desire for glory and for the tranquility that was so important for ideals in the sixteenth century.

While Guidiccioni was concerned with the moral nature and political function of economic life, in a famous pamphlet Sarpi, a well-known theolo-gian and monk, proposed the apotheosis of the state and the total subordina-tion of economic interests to political needs. While Guidiccioni frequently urged citizens to contribute part of their wealth to the common good of the state,[45] Sarpi was in favour of regulating economic activity only to prevent if from undermining the greatness and political integrity of the Serenissima Republic. While Sarpi[46] never encouraged citizens to donate money to secure the material well-being of Venice,[47] he severely criticized pomp and splendor,

---

[42] *Ibid.*, p. 89. Guicciardini did not allow the rulers of the city to engage in trade, or monopoly, or to compete with citizens. Economic activity, he wrote, referring to the Duke of Ferrara, «is the business of the citizens, not yours». Cf. GUICCIARDINI, *Scritti politici*, cit., p. 259, no. 94.

[43] GUIDICCIONI, *op. cit.*, pp. 96-97. «How oft have we seen one merchant have dealings to de-stroy another?».

[44] *Ibid.*, pp. 97, 111.

[45] *Ibid.*, p. 102. In his oration to the Republic of Lucca, Guidiccioni put the following words into the mouths of the fathers of the Republic: «We, to maintain the sweet name of liberty and to defend ourselves from powerful neighbours of this Republic, make common use of faculty for uni-versal benefit, take up arms and virtuously fight and lay down our lives. Some do not fight in defence in the values of the Republic and merchants, in particular, allow the most atrocious things to be writ-ten into law and that reason be trodden on and subjected to the will of others».

[46] A. ERRERA (*Storia dell'Economia Politica nel secoli XVII e XVIII negli Stati della Repubblica Veneta*, Venezia, Antonelli, 1877, pp. 22-23) asserted that Sarpi had a great personal influence on the government of the Venetian Republic «in economic matters he did not have that expertise demon-strated in Church questions; yet oft was able to guide the state to the rightful path in industry and commerce». The only example Errera cited, though he considered Sarpi the true economist of the Republic's Council, was the opinion that he was invited to express in relation to the delicate issue of the borders of the Po river.

[47] Sarpi non only recommended special taxes to fund the State, but also proposed lowering

which would have been beneficial to the Republic by reducing the wealth of the extremely rich. Such pomp should be banned, he argued, since the spirit of emulation inherent in human nature persuaded less wealthy citizens to resort to illegal means to acquire goods in the desire to equal or even surpass the grandeur of their wealthier counterparts.[48]

Chapter 7 explores in detail the ideals of men of practical life. But we already know, from the various references in earlier chapters, that trade was not considered a fitting life for the noblemen, whose fathers and grandfathers had been the protagonists of mercantile Italy. Naturally there were exceptions: perhaps some still yearned after their wooden boats, laden with goods, that braved treacherous seas, and now lay at rest in boatyards or had been scrapped to eradicate every trace of the lives of their forebears. Nobleman wishing to resurrect these customs were discouraged by Sarpi, who reminded them of the Serenissima Republic's veto on trade by the aristocracy. Merchants were stateless people, aliens, Sarpi claimed; their loyalties lay elsewhere in foreign lands, and these divided loyalties prevented them from defending the Republic with honour in times of war, since to do so would have forced them to give up the fortunes that they had painstakingly accumulated.

Nobleman were to have no loyalties or concerns other than the homeland, whose enemies would increase if one of its loyal subjects were forced, for reasons of personal advantage, to spare among the enemy forces creditors of the State.[49] There was another reason why nobleman were to abstain from trade:

---

taxes on commercial activities «Let arts and commerce that are peculiar to the city be retained and to retain them, let them not be over-burdened, because the profit that drove men to seek new worlds at such risk of life, it if cannot be found by our merchants where they hope, they will seek it elsewhere even in the Antipodes». P. SARPI, *Ricordi del P. Paolo Sarpi... Intorno al modo di regolare il governo della Repubblica*, Friburgo, Stamperia Italiana, 1767, p. 18.

[48] SARPI, *op. cit.*, p. 33. Cf. on the same theme GOBBI, *L'economia politica negli scrittori italiani*, cit., pp. 105-106. Sarpi, speaking of pomp, asserted that «if it were only displayed by the rich», it would «profit the Republic, because it would let the blood of those who have too much of it» thus comparing wealth to a part of an animal's body, just like DAVANZATI in his *Lezione delle monete* (*Le Opere di Bernardo Davanzati*, cit., vol. II, pp. 448-449). This «habit of continually comparing society, its institutions and ills, to the body of an animal, its limbs, its sicknesses» demonstrated, according to FANFANI (*Storia delle dottrine economiche*, cit., pp. 140-141), a first step towards a naturalistic conception of economic life by the voluntarists, such as Davanzati, Mantchrétien and Poullain. The importance of these comparisons, particularly that of Davanzati, was noted in the Leghorn edition of the *Lezione* transcribed here: «This passage by Davanzati was taken into consideration by the famed Florentine man of letters, Abbot Antonio Maria Salvini, who praised in his academic *Lezione* the acute judgement of the writer that compared the circulation of money to the circulation of blood in animals. He learnt this very useful truth from the pious Spanish doctor Michele Servet (burnt at the stake by Calvin in 1553) and later confirmed in the anatomical sections of Acquapendente by Friar Paolo Sarpi, the well-known mediator of disputes». DAVANZATI, *Le opere di Bernardo Davanzati*, cit., vol. II, p. 449, no. 2.

[49] SARPI, *op. cit.*, pp. 21-22. «Nobleman are to have no loyalties or concerns other than the homeland».

the Republic made its living from trade, the city must be without noblemen who trade because foreign tradesmen were afraid of being subjugated by the power of noble citizens.[50] For one reason or the other, Sarpi authoritatively presented a model of Republic in which economic activity was entrusted to the plebeans while the nobles occupied themselves with other matters. Sarpi's economic theory clearly distinguished between the two social classes. He excluded any form of social mobility or mingling of economic and noble powers «unless an advantageous marriage made the century long efforts of plebeans enrich a noble family».[51]

Those familiar with the ancient splendour of Venice, the jewel of the Adriatic, and the mercantile spirit of the Republic's citizens at the height of its prosperity will appreciate the devastating effects on the economy of the life ideal that Sarpi theorized. And this was not the thinking of a hermit lost in meditation and penance in a cold, stark cell. Sarpi's vision of the Republic was by no means unpopular; men respected and embraced his ideals. Lottini, another political commentator of the sixteenth century, observed in the *Avvedimenti Civili* that «noblemen would rather let themselves fall into poverty than take some action, where no impediment stands against them» and «they grow up with such languid souls and bodies that anything they hear or that comes into their feelings causes them only discomfort and distaste».[52] Lottini, who opposed usurious loans,[53] rebuked the unjust, miserly lenders for the interest they charged and dissuaded men from resorting to such means.[54] However, he too was affected by the malaise of his century: following Aristotle, he asserted that the ultimate aim of hard work was leisure. It is true that Lottini was not referring to leisure as something that «sprung from the languor of the soul» but rather as time dedicated to meditation and moral virtues.[55] Never-

---

[50] *Ibid.*, pp. 30-31.

[51] *Ibid.*, p. 19.

[52] G.F. LOTTINI, *Avvedimenti civili*, Firenze, Bartolomeo Sermartelli, 1573, pp. 113-114, Avv. 248, 251.

During the Council of Trent, Paruta was of a different opinion: «The Neapolitans and Lombards consider nothing so contrary to nobility as mercantile exercise, from which they persuade men to desist as tarnishing their nobility. On the contrary, the Venetians, Florentines and Genoese trade in merchandise with indifference, and the noblest of them are the most assiduous merchants» (P. PARUTA, *Opere politiche di Paolo Paruta*, Firenze, Le Monnier, 1852, vol. I, p. 330).

[53] Lottini considered usury unnatural, since money served to buy things, not as a means to become rich. Furthermore, those who became usurers had a natural desire to become infinitely rich and this was contrary to nature that always used finite means. LOTTINI, *op. cit.*, p. 242, avv. 557.

[54] *Ibid.*, p. 242, Avv. 558. Lottini observed that it was preferable for the needy to bear their discomforts and needs with patience, rather than alleviate them by resorting to usury, since their suffering would multiply as soon as the money was lent.

[55] *Ibid.*, p. 19, Avv. 34.

theless, for one reason or another, economic activity was considered an improper way of life that could be restored to normality through peace and virtuous tranquility, literature and meditation which brought happiness to citizens nauseated by trade and industry.

In the *Avvedimenti Civili* Lottini also underlined the central role of saving: «riches are good when used and not in their possession and should not be desired except to use. But it is the case that riches are no less used when they are saved for future needs, and therefore money may be a shield against ill fortune and protect you when otherwise you would be stricken, and so it is good to take care of your riches for their future use».[56] Saving was facilitated by money, in the sense that money was a store of wealth, Lottini argued; however, it was important not to confuse money with wealth, even though money «is good because it may be used for infinite needs, and spent, and is the nerve of war and of the state». In any case, «things were preferable to money, which was created to acquire things».[57] This was Lottini's answer to the question of whether gold or goods were superior, just one of the different solutions proposed in the sixteenth and seventeenth centuries.

Among the many sixteenth century political commentators, the ideas of Giovanni Botero and Antonio Serra are noteworthy. In reality, they were concerned with economics, rather than with the history of ideals; some of their economic theories remained in embryonic form, while others were developed more fully and have been widely discussed in the academic literature.[58]

---

[56] *Ibid.*, p. 105, Avv. 231.

[57] *Ibid.*, pp. 104-105, Avv. 228. The expression money, the nerve of war, originated from Demostene τά χρήματα νεῦρα τοῦ πολέμου. Many sixteenth and seventeenth sources used this phrase, including DAVANZATI, *Lezioni delle monete*, in *Le Opere*, cit., vol. II, pp. 418-419: «Money is the nerve of war and the republic, so say serious and solem authors».

Before Davanzati, an anonymous source that extolled the virtues of money as the most desirable form of wealth used the same expression: «What can money not be used for? It is the instrument of our actions; nerve of war, sustenance of the state, nutrition for the arts, minister of the best creations, giver of pleasures and, finally, testament to nobility». Cf. CUSUMANO, *Saggi d'economia politica*, cit., p. 53.

[58] For Botero see, in addition to Gobbi, Gonnard and Fanfani, also G. TORNARI, *Del pensiero politico e delle dottrine economiche di Giovanni Botero*, Torino, Politecnica, 1907; A. BREGLIA, *A proposito di G. Botero "Economista"*, «Annali di Economia», IV, 1928 and for an excellent bibliography F. CHABOD, *Giovanni Botero*, Roma, Anonima romana editoriale, 1934.

For Serra see, in addition to general works on the history of economic thought, FORNARI (*op. cit.*), and the monographs by R. BENINI, *Sulle dottrine economiche di Antonio Serra*, «Giornale degli Economisti», 1892, A. DE VITI DE MARCO, *Le teorie economiche di Antonio Serra: memoria del prof. A. de Viti de Marco, letta nell'adunanza 27 marzo*, Memorie del R. Istituto Lombardo di Scienze e Lettere, XVII, Milano, 1890, G. ARIAS, *Les idées économiques d'Antonio Serra*, «Journal des Économistes», 1922, and R. MAGGI, *Note all'opera di Antonio Serra*, «Annali di Scienze Politiche», IX, 1936.

Botero and Serra codified the doctrine and mercantilist policy derived from the period of the City States, that was applied abroad in a more organized form and with greater means than in Italy. The concept of population as a source of power for cities and states, the protection of industry to increase wealth, and the question of lower productivity in agriculture than in manufacturing were just some of the problems that Botero and Serra investigated and for which they proposed solutions in line with the volontaristic thought that influenced the economic culture of the sixteenth, seventeenth and much of the eighteenth centuries.

4. In the works of even the most progressive scholars, there are remnants of Scholastic economic thought. Machiavelli deplored men who were willing to contemplate usury, and urged them to donate a part of their possessions to fund good works, relating wealth to the religious and spiritual aims that were regularly overlooked in the acquisition and distribution of goods. A complete review of Thomistic principles, albeit adapted to the needs of the day, can be found in the works of the greatest historian of the second half of the sixteenth century, Paolo Paruta.[59] The persistence of medieval themes in sixteenth century Italy would not have surprised Paruta, in the light of the political and religious force of the Counter Reformation, particularly in Italy. In the sixteenth century, through the virtue of its saints and the intellect of its thinkers, the Catholic Church regained its following and halted the spread of Protestantism, so that religious life flourished as never before.[60] The principles underlying such a vast operation were set forth in the Council of Trent, with the intellectual and spiritual contributions of the most eminent laymen and

---

[59] For the life and works of Paolo Paruta (1540-1598) see E. ZANONI, *Paolo Paruta nella vita e nelle opere*, Livorno, Giusti, 1904; A. POMPEATI, *Per la biografia di Paolo Paruta*, «Giornale Storico della Letteratura Italiana», XLV, 1905; ID., *Le dottrine politiche di Paolo Paruta*, «Giornale Storico della Letteratura Italiana», XLVI, 1905; An examination of a diplomat's conscience in ID., *Saggi critici*, Milano, Società editrice Dante Alighieri, 1916, pp. 129-147.

For an assessment of Paruta's works within the context of the history of political theory see: CURCIO, *op. cit.*, pp. 195-212. The most important and detailed study is by G. CANDELORO, *Paolo Paruta: la formazione spirituale e la dottrina morale*, «Rivista Storica Italiana», vol. I, fasc. III, 1936, vol. I, fasc. III e IV.

[60] Candeloro, after a brief survey of the crisis in political thought and moral life in early sixteenth century Italy wrote: «This crisis favours the rebirth of religious sentiment and the victory of the Church. Souls at a loss, tormented by doubt, without conviction, find once more in the Church a discipline of life and faith which had the strength of tradition. This new religion met the general political pessimism and become one with it. In the years immediately following the Council of Trent religion was at its highest point and politics at its lowest. These were the years in which Pope Pius V wrote *In coena Domini*, reaffirming the supremacy of spiritual over temporal matters, of the Church over the State and religious life over political life». *Ibid.*, fasc. III, p. 81.

Churchmen of the day. The ideas of this group of honoured and learned men were collected a few years later by Paruta in his work *Della perfezione della vita civile*,[61] examined below. Paruta was all too familiar with the spirits that drove men in his day and their impact on economic life. He formulated a theory of the social order of wealth designed to correct the misplaced ideals of his contemporaries. Paruta was well aware that «it is not such time that riches must be praised for fear of the disdain of the people; because all too many have made them their idol and are happier to look upon their wealth in secret than look at the sun in the heavens in the pure light of day».[62] Neither did he overlook the deleterious moral and political consequences of extreme poverty, since poor men «living in discontent and desirous of new things are hopeful that with a new government their fortunes may change».[63] Alongside the poor, anxious to better their lot, Paruta noted how a lifestyle of vanities and delights had taken root among the Italian people «there has begun, mostly among Italian men, a manner of living full of vanity and delights»; some defined and interpreted these as examples of munificence, while Paruta criticized such behavior in the *Perfezione della vita civile*.[64] In the face of these social contrasts[65] some dreamed of a Republic in which all riches were per-

---

[61] PARUTA, *Opere*, cit., vol. I, p. 37. It was published for the first time in 1579.

Monani summarized Paruta's works as follows: «The author establishes first and foremost the perfection of political life in civil happiness; meaning, in the moderate enjoyment of physical, moral and political life, considered in their social relations, against the opinion of the Stoics who eschewed all comforts and goods. And he thought of the acquisition and exercise of virtue as the supreme moral good, and riches and honours in political life, provided these were used with moderation and were the result of meritorious actions inseparable from virtue» (C. MONZANI, *Prefazione*, in *Opere politiche di Paolo Paruta*, p. XXIX).

[62] P. PARUTA, *Della perfezione della vita civile*, in *Opere politiche di Paolo Paruta*, cit., book III, Vol. I, book III, vol. I, p. 340.

[63] *Ibid.*, book III, vol. I, p. 349. Paruta, in his discussion of the consequences of poverty, notes how it clipped the wings of superior minds, forcing men to forego a profitable activity because they lacked the means to prove its worth. After all, excessive wealth «encouraged luxuries and delicacies and effeminated men who shied in the face of danger, being men of leisure and enemies of virtuous toil». It should not be thought, however – Paruta acutely observed – that all social ills derive from the poor distribution of wealth: «Disputes and accusations do not arise for things that are necessary, which oft are not lacking, but for the superfluous for which we have infinite appetite... having acquired faculty sufficient for a modest life, we desire more, and when we have more, our desire continues; so that to fulfil our ambitions we come to rob or take to Court or do what manner of evil we believed produced by poverty, but in truth are produced by riches, of which we are enamoured the more lies in our possession. And noblemen and the powerful enter into dispute not for useful purpose but for reasons of honour, with greater risk to private riches and to the public weal». *Ibid.*, pp. 349-350. Paruta used this analysis of the causes of social discord in his devastating criticism of socialist proposals.

[64] *Ibid.*, book II, vol. I, p. 256.

[65] «Mostly we see that some are abundant in their possession others are lacking even in necessities». *Ibid.*, book III, vol. I, p. 348.

fectly equal, so that men could live in peace at last satisfied at last that they were inferior, to noone.[66]

Paruta challenged this romantic illusion with pyschological acumen and with certain ideas relevant to the modern world. He argued that the distribution of wealth according to a criterion of arithmetic equality would dispense with the virtues of munificence and generosity that were so beneficial to the reputation of givers: this argument paralled the Scholastic view of wealth, as a useful tool that served to succour the needy in the name of God. Paruta's second objection to those who dreamed of an egalitarian society was more modern: a levelling of means removed the incentive to work and fostered, through laziness, all manner of vices: «Men would fall to idleness, the origin of all evil, because not all are capable of the noblest arts and science». By affirming the need to work for the material and moral wellbeing of society, Paruta sought to demonstrate that any measure designed to distribute wealth equally among individuals violated justice and common sense: it allocated the same proportion of wealth to worthy, valorous citizens as to worthless individuals that contributed nothing to the public good.

Even if it had been possible to solve the operational difficulties inherent in such a scheme of wealth distribution, clearly this new state of affairs would not have endured, given the different aptitudes and abilities of citizens to consume, preserve and produce wealth.[67] For these reasons, Paruta argued that private property should be safeguarded[68] since it provided an incentive to work and a means through which to exercise the virtues of munificence and generosity towards friends in need. In this respect, Paruta did not intend to ignore injustices in the distribution of goods, for which he invoked measures designed to even out «according to certain geometric proportion the different condition of people, distributing variously the honours and offices of the city, so that rich and poor, as befits their state, have similar dignity and duties».[69] However, rather than resorting to measures of fiscal justice, Paruta believed the social order should be corrected through a process of spiritual

---

[66] A.F. DONI, in his *Mondi celesti, terrestri, et infernali, degli academici Pellegrini* (Venetia, Appresso N. Moretti, 1583), dreamed of a communist society both in the production and consumption of goods. For more on the social thought of the best known advocate of communism, Campanella, see chapter IV.

[67] PARUTA, *Della perfezione*, cit., book III, vol. I, pp. 348-350.

[68] Scipione Ammirato and Traiano Boccalini specifically defended private property, though Ammirato considered it a convention and Boccalini asserted that private property called for laws and governments. Both considered private property essential for economic progress. C. SUPINO, *La scienza economica in Italia dalla seconda metà del secolo XVI alla prima del XVII*, Torino, Loescher, 1888, pp. 84-85.

[69] PARUTA, *Della perfezione*, cit., book III, vol. I, p. 350.

elevation, eradicating «with good manners, the immoderate desire for possessions from the soul of citizens»,[70] the root of all evil in the life of States. This was not a utopian illusion: Paruta did not deny the love of riches,[71] but sought to redirect desires with precepts inspired by the *aurea mediocritas* that formed the basis of Thomistic economic ethics.[72] He was certain that «those who stray from the righteous path, go from one extreme to another».[73] And so Paruta endeavoured to spread a conception of economic and worldly goods in which men reached «a state of tranquil life but attentive, attention in tranquility, calm in labouring, of laboured calm: not insolent to dignity or vile in idleness but even to itself and far from all extremes».[74]

Paruta offered a tentative definition of goods in the following passage: «riches are to be included among those things that by their nature are not good or evil, but become so according to their use as we decide upon it».[75] He defined the nature of riches more clearly within the broader context of the things men possessed. First and foremost came the the the riches of soul upon which happiness depended. Then came the riches of nature, consisting of the physical perfection that men should aspire to achieve in order to heighten their spiritual virtues. The goods of fortune, or riches, were inappropriately defined as such. Paruta argued that if riches deserved the name of goods, their function was to become one of the first two forms of wealth. In this way, riches were not valued in themselves, but rather to the extent that they served to nourish the body with good food and protect it from harm, just as riches should become instruments of freedom, munificence and other virtues.[76]

In the light of this conception of economic goods, the claims made by Supino are rather surprising. Supino thought he had finally detected in the *Perfezione* a truly systematic interpretation of wealth, an explanation that went beyond the preconceptions of ascetic and purist morality inherited from the

---

[70] *Ibid.*, p. 351.

[71] «The desire to become rich – Paruta observes – is as natural as the desire for life. Nature provides the animals with their needs, but man, born poor, naked and with many needs, was given this desire for wealth and ingenuity and industry to acquire it». *Ibid.*, book III, vol. I, p. 338.

[72] FANFANI, *Le origini*, cit., cap. I. For analogies between Paruta's economic thought and the ideas of the Scholastic theologians see CUSUMANO, *Saggi di economia politica*, cit., p. 44.

[73] PARUTA, *Della perfezione*, cit., book II, vol. I, p. 247.

[74] *Ibid.*, book I, vol. I, pp. 55-56.

[75] *Ibid.*, book III, vol. I, p. 336. Palmieri proposed a similar definition of wealth when he wrote that «possessions are neither good nor infelicitous but are meritorious or roundly to be condemned according to the use put on them». M. PALMIERI, *Della vita civile*, in *Della educazione dell'uomo e del cittadino*, Venezia, Gondoliere, 1841, p. 264, book III.

[76] PARUTA, *Della perfezione*, cit., book III, vol. I, p. 285. See also *op. cit.*, book I, vol. I, pp. 96-97.

Canonists and the Scholastic theologians. If Supino really believed that wealth was unrelated to questions of a moral and religious nature, Paruta was certainly not the right source: not only did Paruta generically assert that economic life should be subordinated to the needs of ethics and politics, but, in specific relation to wealth he shared the preconceptions of ascetic and purist morality cited by Supino.[77] Is his theory Paruta echoed the early Scholastic concerns relating to the moral consequences of abundant wealth in particular: «Sardanpalus is to be seen nowhere except surrounded by the delights and luxuries of wealth»[78] wrote Paruta, condemning immoderate faculty «with its enticements, ease, and certainty of sin and a thousand other ways that overthrow the reason through the senses».[79] Used in this way, economic goods could be good or bad according to the purpose they served, unlike the riches of the soul. Wealth was to be used for the good of the soul, and therefore instead of being an indifferent instrument it became one of virtue.[80] Hence, wealth was desirable when «used to satisfy genuine needs, to make human beings more beautiful, to relieve men from discomfort and to provide the stuff of certain virtues; but any more wealth than this made men greedy».[81] Men who governed their households, educated their children, maintained their servants, and preserved and increased the wealth and dignity of their family deserved praise.[82] Such activities were dutiful and kept men from idleness, since the delights and luxuries of wealth would certainly lead to sin.[83]

Economic activities ceased to fulfil a supreme duty if motivated by greed.[84] Only too often merchants hungry for wealth resorted to usury, theft and injustice,[85] and no riches could satisfy their appetites.[86] It becomes clear, in relation to the distribution of wealth, why Paruta asserted that it was best for citizens to have «mediocre faculty», since «great faculty» led to delights

---

[77] Cf. SUPINO, *La scienza economica*, cit., pp. 15-16.

Zanoni's assessment of Paruta concept of wealth, and the influence of the Scholastic theologians was less precise: ZANONI, *Paolo Paruta*, cit., p. 74. He erroneously asserted that Paruta identified wealth with money, as the economists of the mercantilist school did later (*ibid.*, p. 74). There is nothing in Paruta's work to support this claim.

[78] PARUTA, *Della Perfezione*, cit., libro III, vol. I, p. 341.

[79] *Ibid.*

[80] *Ibid.*, book I, vol. I, p. 48.

[81] *Ibid.*, book III, vol. I, p. 344.

[82] *Ibid.*, book II, vol. I, p. 196.

[83] *Ibid.*, book II, vol. I, p. 341.

[84] *Ibid.*, book III, vol. I, p. 340.

[85] *Ibid.*, book II, vol. I, p. 247.

[86] *Ibid.*, book III, vol. I, p. 340.

and vanities, and modest faculty to weakness and hardship.[87] In conclusion, in Paruta's economic thought a desire for goods was legitimate, indeed necessary: rulers had a duty to foster the development and expansion of wealth in the city.[88] However, citizens were not to be misled by their efforts to acquire goods, and were to cease when they had accumulated just enough to befit their status and local customs.[89] Even on questions of wealth accumulation Paruta drew on Thomistic ideals: this is hardly surprising, given that Paruta and Aquinas derived their theories from the same concept of wealth.

The guiding principle of Paruta's concept of wealth was the just means of the Thomists: economic activity and its ultimate aim of wealth accumulation were neither to be scorned nor worshipped nor pursued with greed. An equivalent principle inspired his ideas on spending wealth. First and foremost, a good economist should know how to adapt expenditure to revenue, times and circumstances.[90] Dalla Croce, the playwright from Bologna, put similar words into the mouth of his character Bertoldo, who with far-sighted popular wisdom informed the king's court that «those who measure their faculty shall never be beggars».[91]

Though some consider these ideas of limited relevance, in fact they are of the utmost importance for the history of ideals of a century in which a desire for pomp and luxury, as Sarpi and Lottini had already warned, had driven many families to a state of destitution (as discussed Chapter VII). «Men were not to spend wealth so lavishly» – continued Paruta – «lest in a short time they come to lack the substance that would have sufficed to mantain them and their families for a lifetime. Let him know that he should not spend on vain things and out of time, and waste gifts on vile and base people: as some rich people often do, who give only to buffoons and flatterers and leave worthy friends in need to suffer».[92] In the same vein, and in relation to the era in question, a satirist from Naples asserted that the traditional conception

---

[87] *Ibid.*, book III, vol. I, p. 347.

[88] Since «merchants and craftsmen albeit not a principal part of the republic, are nonetheless necessary to the city because members of this body who help to provide for it» the State needed to protect commerce and introduce arts and crafts into the city. *Ibid.*, p. 400.

[89] *Ibid.*, book III, vol. I, p. 340.

[90] *Ibid.*, book II, vol. I, p. 248.

[91] G.C. Croce, *Bertoldo, Bertoldino e Cacasenno*, Milano, Cesare Cioffi, n.d., pp. 65-66.

[92] Paruta, *Della perfezione*, cit., book II, vol. I, p. 247. Cf. also p. 248. In relation to useless expenses, as Governor of Brescia Paruta asked his friend Federico Sarego of Verona to purchase for him a horse and carriage to give himself the dignity befitting his high office, but after a while he sent back the horse and carriage and asked his friend to sell them. Cf. Letter dated April 7th 1592 in G. Biadego, *Lettere inedite di Paolo Paruta*, Verona, Goldschagg, 1885; Zanoni, *Paolo Paruta*, cit., pp. 32-33.

of goods (as a means to sustain the body and exercise the virtues) had been lost and they had come to be considered mere instruments of luxury; he scolded the rich and the nobles addled by their wealth:

> *Gold and much*
> *ease you regale upon*
> *the whore and eunuch,*
> *but a man that's gone,*
> *before you, bare, undone,*
> *drooping with hunger*
> *you give him none*[93]

This explains why Paruta warned that riches should principally be dispensed to good people and friends rather than sprinkled hither and thither regardless of the beneficiary.[94] In this way, goods of fortune, as Paruta defined them, became instruments of virtue, and only virtue could bring happiness for an upright and civil way of life.[95] That virtue and happiness were not automatic, but relied on the supreme good becomes clear when Paruta scolds those who pervert the nature of things and know no longer how to rise and the mystery of how they (the goods) are dispensed by the supreme maker and donor.[96] The highest virtues of all came from doing good and helping many others.[97] So citizens had a duty to sacrifice their own interests to the common good of the homeland.[98]

---

[93] S. ROSA, *Satire, odi e lettere di Salvator Rosa*, Firenze, G. Barbèra, 1860, p. 21, Sat. I, versi 382-387.

[94] PARUTA, *Della perfezione*, cit., book II, vol. I, p. 248. Lottini formulated a broader and more precise concept of donating wealth to charity «there is no doubt – he observed – that such donations to the poor made with Christian charity are good, but consideration must be made not to instill idleness in many, who count upon the generosity of some, and join their hands in supplication, and deny themselves industry, which can procure them comforts, and in such public supplication deprive the truly needy of like charity». Cf. LOTTINI, *op. cit.*, p. 110. Avv. 241.

[95] PARUTA, *Della perfezione*, cit., book I, vol. I, p. 105 e *passim*.

[96] ID., *Soliloquio*, in *Opere politiche di Paolo Paruta*, vol. I, p. 9.

[97] ID., *Della perfezione*, cit., book I, vol. I, p. 42.

[98] *Ibid.*, book I, vol. I, p. 55. For more on praise of homeland see cf. book I, vol. I, p. 45. In relation to the love for one's country in the Paruta's works, it is appropriate to cite Di Tocco's assessment: «Although, as we have shown, Paruta spoke with affection of Italy, his most ardent and moving pages are dedicated to his city, Venice, which he admires for its political order, narrating its history with enthusiasm and defending its conduct even where it was selfishly acting in its own interests and against other Italian States». In the *La perfezione della vita civile* he exalts his Homeland, «which made us, raised us, educated and trained us, maintained our riches, relatives, friends, and gave us honour, bobility and glory». Evidently by homeland he meant the city of Venice, rather than Italy. He was not entirely wrong; two more centuries were to pass before the ancient regional sentiment gave way to a national feeling of identity» (V. DI TOCCO, *Ideali d'indipendenza in Italia durante la preponderanza spagnola*, Messina, Principato, 1926, p. 28).

Paruta derived his economic thought essentially from the Scholastic rule of *mediocritas* that inspired all thinking about wealth. His economic ideal was for a temperate life in which men neither lusted after nor repudiated riches, regarding them as means to an honest and civil way of life in the traditional sense. And this was the life that Paruta led, actively participating in political life, commercial dealings[99] and managing his wealth.

It has been said that Paruta's ideas were far removed from the capitalist spirit[100] of sixteenth century Italy, both in theoretical terms and in everyday practice. In reality, Paruta's work reveals a secret desire for peace and quiet. This becomes clear when Paruta, in solitude, wrote a spiritual testament of sorts, an interior biography in which he sang the praises of those fortunate men who lived free of material concerns: «Fathers, my good Fathers, who live in cloistered distance, alone with the thoughts of the soul, and far from the world's affairs, you have the most delightful quiet; affection without affection, envied without sin, as I envy you that sacred idleness...idleness which is the true art of living...You Fathers live with great peace».[101] This excerpt from the *Soliloquio*, written during Paruta's time in Rome, reflected his new mood in the city of the Pope, so starkly in contrast with his previous political ideals. The work was pervaded by a sense of pessimism, as Paruta came to reject the arguments he had presented earlier in the *Perfezione*, going on to glorify religious as against political life, and to advocate contemplation rather than activity. He changed his mind again repudiating the life exemplified in the *Soliloquio*,[102] although Paruta's ideal of peace and serenity reflected a certain disposition of his spirit, and perhaps of the entire era.

5. A recurrent theme in the thought of the historians and political commentators discussed above is the subordination of wealth, and of economic

---

[99] There is evidence of his activity in this field in a letter written to Count Serego of Verona, on 7th February 1568, in which he confirmed that he had put all that was his in a ship that had set sail for Alexandria in Egypt. See CANDELORO, *op. cit.*, fasc. III, p. 75.

[100] *Ibid.*, p. 94 (fasc. III).

[101] PARUTA, *Soliloquio*, cit., p. 11.

[102] Il Soliloquio, observed Candeloro, «is a document that testifies to a crisis of conscience that is resolved before it reaches its extreme consequences. The religious thinking of Paruta was certainly far from deep and does not lead him to give up his previous ways. This is certainly the case psychologically, but is not the case in terms of his theory. More than a crisis of the soul, the Soliloquy is a systemic crisis, a challenge to the moral order he had sought to establish in Perfection. He continues on his way after this loss of courage for entirely sentimental reasons (which, in his youth, had urged him to ponder the value of political life), but he has lost the theoretical basis of his thinking. This is not surprising given that his moral system had such a fragile philosophical underpinning; and it was associated with such a particular political system that he remained fascinated by it, even if it had begun to outlive its time». CANDELORO, *op. cit.*, fasc. IV, pp. 62-64.

7

activity in general, to the needs of the state. This was true not only of Machiavelli, the archetypal proponent of state power and stability, but of other scholars who did not share Machiavelli's political principles. From Guicciardini to Paruta, from Guidiccioni to Sarpi, the concept of the homeland gradually developed through the identification of the spiritual and material interests defended by the state even against individuals, and so the theory of collective interest took shape. While the Scholastic theologians located this principle within the context of society, modern authors were more concerned with the public good as a matter of state, and only a matter of state. Despite the initial similarity, this explains the diverse interpretations of the social order of wealth presented in this chapter.

Naturally, the political nature of economic life was described in various ways. Machiavelli asserted not only that is was important to foster and support the economic life of citizens to assure the power and stability of the Prince's rule, but also that the resources of other countries, whether civilized or not, should contribute to the State's finances through prudent conquest and the economic exploitation of newly acquired territories. In the process of colonisation, a system that Machiavelli theorized with remarkable foresight, the State placed its reliance on a large number of citizens, a need later identified by the political commentators of the sixteenth and seventeenth centuries. Money was one of the factors that contributed to the power of individuals and of state economies alike – remember Machiavelli's need for a treasury. And while not all the political commentators surveyed shared the anonymous writer's love of gold and riches, most were convinced that money was needed to wage war and create a modern state.

On the issue of public finance, opinions varied. While Guidiccioni affirmed that citizens should donate a part of their wealth to the public coffers to satisfy the needs of society, Machiavelli cautioned the Prince not to resort to private funding. Even Sarpi advised against raising taxes, on the grounds that citizens, acting in self-interest, would be quick to leave town if their earnings were seized by the Republic.

Though they were in favour of centralized state power, not all our political commentators embraced the economic policies of their day. Machiavelli – for one – favoured a corporative order protected and encouraged by the Prince, whilst Guidiccioni had little sympathy for forms of monopoly that undermined freedom in trade and industry. Similarly, Guicciardini defended individual rather than state enterprise. The communist and socialist ideals that flourished here and there in the seventeenth and eighteenth centuries were far removed from the ideas of these authors, who aspired to achieve a more equitable distribution of wealth rather than an economy in which private property was suppressed. In this respect, Paruta's poignant criticism of the socialist system is significant. Though he was the staunchest defender of individual property of his day, he nevertheless felt the need to correct the unjust distribution of goods that material and moral disorder produced in society.

Paruta claimed that the *optimum* level of wealth for citizens was what he called modest faculties. Both Paruta and Guidiccioni championed charitable giving to relieve the hardships of poverty that caused crime and rebellion in cities. Their relentless condemnation of luxury and grandeur was intended to prevent a widening of the gap between the rich and the poor. The two historians criticized a lavish lifestyle as one of the principal causes of Italy's political and economic decline. With great historical insight, Guicciardini observed in Italian cities on the one hand a greedy desire to consume wealth, and on the other a systematic reluctance to put in the effort required to produce such wealth. Guicciardini, like Guidiccioni, Sarpi, Lottini and Paruta identified one factor detrimental to the development of sixteenth century economic life in Italy: wealth, generally considered to pave the way to fame and glory,[103] was to be spent in generosity, munificence and to facilitate the study of letters.

Such aims were jeopardized by trade, which these scholars thought best left to the lower classes in society. Some, like Paruta, went so far as to assert that merchants could not join the ranks of nobles, even by abandoning their trade, unless their abundant wealth revitalized an impoverished member of the nobility.

Having briefly surveyed the economic aspirations of historians and political commentators, one question comes to mind: was there anything new in their thought with respect to the Churchmen and to Church legislation in the same period?

With the exception of certain Machiavellian precepts, such as confiscating the possessions of conquered peoples to fund living expenses in the colonies, the ideals of wealth and the norms propounded by the authors examined in this chapter are fairly similar to those presented in previous chapters. The ideas considered here on the acquisition and donation of wealth for the benefit of the State, were not dissimilar to the moral obligations on the wealthy imposed by the Church, including a duty to help the community. Both our

---

[103] Brignole Sale wrote in the first half of the seventeenth century: «wherever I turn my eys from the creation of the world until today, I see no more ardent stimulus than glory in the heart of man».

Cf. *Politici e moralisti del Seicento: Strada, Zuccolo, Settala, Accetto, Brignole Sale, Malvezzi*, ed. by Benedetto Croce and Santino Caramella, Bari, Laterza, 1930, p. 180.

sources, and the Church, advocated moderation in the acquisition and use of wealth and even the otherwise rather unconventional Machiavelli condemned usury and fraud. Guicciardini condemned not only usury, but also money changing as a way to acquire wealth, and in this sense he was even stricter than the Churchmen in upholding the ban on interest-bearing loans. Guicciardini was concerned not so much with the crime of usury as with the borrower's inability to repay the principal when it fell due. This denoted a weak economic spirit, an inability to face with the courage shown in past centuries the risks of trade at a time of rapid economic development.

The sixteenth century was an age in which trade was regarded with disdain and fear. The politicians were no exception, as we have seen; while the majority of Churchmen were suspicious of commercial dealings, their concern was with the instant gains to be had made from trading. Provided there was no injustice in business relations, the Church legitimized and encouraged economic activity as the individual and social duty of the rich and poor alike.

Apart from this difference, the two approaches coincided perfectly. One political commentator, Paruta, formulated an ideal of economic life that mirrored in every respect that of Aquinas four centuries earlier.

CHAPTER FOUR

POETS WRITERS PHILOSOPHERS
AND SOCIAL REFORMERS IN RELATION TO WEALTH

1. In Italy, the sixteenth century was one of many antitheses in politics and philosophy as well as in socio-economic life and customs. With respect to the social order and the distribution of goods, it is no exaggeration to say that many wealthy men idled their time and frittered their considerable incomes away, whilst the great majority of people lived in penury. Whereas Suriano reported to the Serenissima Republic that in the city of Florence Guadagni[1] possessed 400,000 ducats, Paleotti, recorded the heart-rending lamentation of the poor, who «subject to continuous toil, and goaded by the Devil, easily slid into a despairing consideration of providence, feeling themselves abandoned by God's mercy, or treated as illegitimate children, not only because of the necessity to toil and labour, where others in this world live in abundant comfort and are given much rest; but also because they are without reading and writing and science, and without spiritual exercise, and so are precluded from the road that leads to Heaven».[2] This despair perhaps reflected the widespread religious crisis of the time, to a certain extent also felt in Italy.

For the historian of economic thought, the excerpt from Paleotti testifies not only to the increasing inequalities of the sixteenth century[3] and the growing rest-

---

[1] Cf. A. SEGARIZZI, *Relazioni degli ambasciatori veneti al Senato*, Bari, Laterza, 1912-1916, vol. III, p. 112. Report by Suriano.

For Milan only and only for the third decade of the sixteenth century I was able to establish the incomes of 3,229 families, representing all social classes. The degree of concentration in income distribution (0.65) is an eloquent demonstration of the distance between the citizens in Milan at the beginning of the sixteenth century. Alongside families who paid no tax because their earnings were below 100 ducats, there were others, such as the Fregoso family, which earned 126,000 ducats a year, i.e. 1,700 Imperial lire a day. See G. BARBIERI, *I redditi dei milanesi all'inizio della dominazione spagnola*, «Rivista Internazionale di Scienze Sociali», XLV, 1937.

[2] G. PALEOTTI, *Instruttione ... per tutti quelli che havranno licenza di predicare nelle ville e altri luoghi della diocese*, Roma, Moneta, 1678, 1586, pp. 25-26.

[3] M.G. VIDA, *M. Hier. Vidae Cremonen. Albae episc. Dialogi de rei publicae dignitate*, Cremo-

lessnes of those who, cut off from wealth, no longer put their faith in the divine providence which had made their poverty bearable, this passage also demonstrates and points to his clear understanding of these inequalities and the consequent malcontent of the time. In the sixteenth century, all Italian cities were infected by the desire to climb the social ladder and to exhibit luxury and princely pomp; this only increased the discontent of the poor and workmen, drawn together through a sense of sharing the same underprivileged lot in life.

Note that at the beginning of the Modern Age, the workings of the Italian economy gave rise to a number of social conflicts, as recorded not so much by historians as poets and, in particular, by one of the most remarkable and eccentric men of the sixteenth century, Folengo. His poetry, imitating the macaronic verse of Merlin Cocai, is generally regarded by scholars as a detailed and accurate description of life in the sixteenth century,[4] and of economic life in particular. People in both the city and countryside, absorbed in feverish activity and workmanship, were able to live off the products of their labour. Folengo depicts one of the countrymen of his native Cipada, a typical village in sixteenth century rural Italy, joyously praising first the absence of frogs and crickets from the fields, because the vines are planted neat and straight, and then the fact that his house is not made of straw but of terracotta bricks.[5] He says he would not change places with a city-dweller.

Nevertheless, as Folengo writes, the wealth of the city[6] and its vibrant life of work attracted many peasants and country folk, who – by their thousands –

---

nae, in civitatis palatio apud Vincentium Contem, 1556, remarks on the strong desire for riches and on the profound social inequalities, which led some to fritter away their wealth and others to go without prime necessities.

[4] The historical nature of the poem has been remarked since the eighteenth century and was highligthed in the Preface to the third volume of the works of T. FOLENGO (*Theophili Folengi vulgo Merlini Cocaii Opus macaronicum notis illustratum, cui accessit vocabularium vernaculum, etruscum, et latinum*, Amstelodami, Sumptibus Josephi Braglia, 1768), which states: «Nuptias, praelia, apparatus, popinas, tabernas, et quae ubique vigent, consuetudines ita persequitur, ut nemo secundus in moribus pingendis, et in rebus describendis iudicari merito possit».

In this connection, despite its dubious conclusions, see the study by B. ZUMBINI, *Vita paesana e vita cittadina nel poema del Folengo*, in *Raccolta di studi critici dedicati ad Alessandro d'Ancona*, Firenze, Barbèra, 1901, p. 609. Si cf. pure F. DE SANCTIS, Antologia critica sugli scrittori d'Italia, ed. by Luigi Russo, Firenze, Vallecchi, 1924, vol. II, p. 177.

[5] T. FOLENGO, *Le maccheronee*, ed. by Alessandro Luzio, Bari, Laterza, n.d., vol. I, p. 148 [cited in the text as Merlin Cocai ed. note].

[6] *Ibid.*, vol. I, p. 160; vol. II, p. 238.

> Jam sunt in piazza: mercatus ubique patebat:
> Stringas, cordones, borsellos, cingula, guantos,
> Taschellas, scufias, scufiottos, cultra, guainas,
> carneros, fibias, calamos, calamaria, cordas,
> pectina, specchiettos, rubebas atque sonaios,

abandoned the fields for magnificent buildings and smoking chimneys, adjusting their eyes to the new sights and their ears to the new sounds of the city, at first afraid that they would be overwhelmed and the world would topple over onto them.[7] Here is the huge Palace of Justice:[8] its spacious hall full of people shouting, a thousand different matters being discussed all at the same time. Brokers, judges, legal advisors, a turbulent array of businesspeople talking, negotiating, dealing, arguing, settling. Sometimes, in the hubbub, you catch sight of someone you recognize, in the company of a stranger, a consul or *camparus*, called upon to rule on a question involving peasant folk who are on different sides of a dispute.[9]

It is the Renaissance, the age of city splendour and the unbridled aspiration to wealth, which leads men, in the full consciousness of their rights, to plead their cases and oppose the views of others. Such intense life and work could not fail to provide prosperity the length and breadth of the peninsula.

This is certainly the impression given by an initial reading of the verse of Teofilo Folengo, more than any other writer of his time[10] a vivid portrayer of day-to-day life during the Renaissance. But a deeper look into the world described by the poet reveals the tarnished side of the economic coin, and it is this unseemly side of life that really interests him. He describes not only the market square and Palace of Justice, but the Jewish ghetto.[11] The shop of userer Sadocco flourishes whilst those of many needy shopkeepers languish

---

> boccalos, basias, urces, magnosque cadinos,
> cantara, scudellas, piattos, orinalia, testos,
> zuppellos, scarpas, soverettos atque stivallos,
> martellos, falces, diversaque ferra, badilos,
> salsizzas, trippas, plenos de carne budellos,
> verzas, lactucas, ravanellos, porra, scalognas,
> gallinas, ochas, anedrottos atque capones,
> casos, casettos, bottiria fresca, ricottas,
> unguentos, bisulos, petras, dentesque cavatos,
> radices varias, herbas, curvosque bragheros,
> telas, bisettos, fusos, capisteria, roccas,
> atque pivas illas per quas crysteria ponunt.
> Hic nomines tandem venalia quaeque palesant.

[7] *Ibid.*, vol. I, pp. 131 e 160.

[8] *Ibid.*, vol. I, p. 119.

[9] *Ibid.*, vol. I, p. 233.

[10] «Alas today – writes Bandello – nobody takes pleasure in setting down what occurs each day; and so we lose many acute and beautiful sayings, and many general as well as memorable facts are buried in the deepest oblivion» (BANDELLO, *Le novelle*, cit., vol. I, p. 113). The great sixteenth-century story writer, on the other hand, provides «a magnificent mirror reflecting his century and projecting that abundance of particulars and characteristic leading and secondary figures, that you would look in vain for in the works of contemporary historians» (J. DUNLOP, *History of Prose Fiction*, London, Bell, 1896, p. 214 and following).

[11] FOLENGO, *Le maccheronee*, cit., vol. I, p. 174.

or are forced to close.[12] Many Jews (as Contarini reports) feature in Folengo's poems, mostly as usurious lenders. And the poems make clear that the Jews did not lend for industrial investments or to increase productivity or to boost the economy. No, they lent to consumers, to the poor, the famished, those struggling to get by from day to day.[13] If the Jews occasionally showed mercy to someone who, after all, was of a different faith, the advocates, notaries and brokers with whom these poor people had dealings were not of like mind, robbing them of their worldly possessions in protracted suits they continued to promise could be won.

And in the countryside?

Rarely does Folengo describe rural life. In one instance he mentions a farmer who provides hospitality to two hungry, unclothed wayfarers in his humble home.[14] But his verse abounds in ragged, unshod farm workers,[15] hungry, penniless, the dregs of society. And the effects of this widespread poverty – easily captured in the irony and hyperbole of macaronic verse – weighed on the corrupt economic life of the era. One poor woman, the widow of a prisoner, in the darkness of a huge city tower, is robbed of all she has with her. The soul of a friend of her dead husband comes to her aid, to prevent her from falling into dishonesty.[16]

---

[12] *Ibid.*, vol. I, p. 168.

> Plenam varia de merce botegam,
> quam tenet hebraeus, Sadoccum nomine dicunt,
> Qui centum miseros usurae sfecerat arte,
> Vestimentorum pendebat copia grandis...

In 1588, about fifty years after the composition of the poem, of the 40,000 inhabitants of Mantua, one fifth were Jews. At that time, according to Contarini, they were the leading economic actors of the city (SEGARIZZI, *op. cit.*, vol. I, p. 78).

[13] In a letter of 1531, Aretino acknowledges receipt of four shirts, two nightcaps and two berets, sent by Count Massimiano Stampa as a gift. He writes: «my clothes at the time of Carneval certainly have a great toing and froing when they are handled by the Jews who make usury of them and take benefit». P. ARETINO, *Il primo libro delle lettere*, ed. by F. Nicolini, Bari, Laterza, 1913, letter XXIII (1531), pp. 30-31.

[14] FOLENGO, *Le maccheronee*, cit., vol. I, p. 70.

[15] *Ibid.*, vol. I, p. 105. See the account of the poverty and privations of the peasants.

[16] *Ibid.*, vol. I, p. 136.

In the following century, ROSA (*op. cit.*, sat. II, v. 686-690 e 697-699, pp. 78-79) made the following appeal to the poets:

> Accordate la cetra ai pianti ai gridi
> Di tante orfane vedove e mendichi.
> Dite senza timor gli orridi stridi
> Della terra, che invan geme abbattuta
> Spolpata affatto da' tiranni infidi.
> Dite l'usure e tirannie voraci
> Che fa sopra di noi la turba immensa
> De' vivi Faraoni e degli Arsaci.

The description could be continued, further illuminating the economic and moral squalor of the sixteenth century, hidden beneath the surface of Petrarchan beauty[17] and the wealth of the marble buildings. But let these few examples suffice to demonstrate that the writers of the period were well aware of the inequalities and injustices of their age: while the wealthy used their money for their own pleasure and aggrandisement, others charitably dedicated themselves to the wellbeing of the needy, in many cases the very same people who had so selfishly squandered their wealth, falling to the bottom rungs of the social ladder.[18]

2. If poetry reveals some aspects of the economic life of the sixteenth century, the writings of other men of letters and philosophers reveal how the problems of wealth were considered during the Renaissance and the steps that were taken to rectify these problems.

The works of a well-known follower of Pomponazzi, Sperone Speroni, include interesting thoughts on economic life. Speroni was a philosopher, man of letters, politician and businessman,[19] who left his imprint on all areas of life he came into contact with and who is an invaluable source for the historian of the sixteenth century. In the economic sphere, perhaps the most noteworthy contribution of Speroni was his record of the flight of men and savings from the city to the supposed peace and quiet of the country. We have already come across the severe words pronounced by Garimberti against those who abandoned the city to live the ignoble life of the country. Undoubtedly the ideas of the Bishop of Gallese were not shared by all; many preferred the quiet life to the monotonous tumult of the city, and sold their homes and palaces in town to take up residence in the country, coming to the city only for short periods in which they rented modest lodgings.[20] To these wealthy nostalgics of the country, Speroni – a man who had invested his wealth in estates, buildings and villas[21] – addressed these words of reproof: «You leave Venice

---

[17] For the characteristics of Italian literature in the sixteenth century, see the essay by A. GRAF (*Petrarchismo e antipetrarchismo*, in *Attraverso il Cinquecento*, Torino, Chiantore, 1926), which contains many details of Italian life in that century.

[18] Bandello says that many noble and wealthy families, after losing their riches, wandered «throughout Europe begging for bread, and God only knows if they will return in possession of their old faculties» (BANDELLO, *Le novelle*, cit., vol. III, p. 154).

[19] F. CAMMAROSANO, *La vita e le opere di Sperone Speroni*, Empoli, Noccioli, 1920.

[20] S. SPERONI, *Del ritornare alla città*, in *Opere di M. Sperone Speroni degli Alvarotti*, vol. V, p. 413.

[21] The assets of Speroni must have been placed under attachment, as appears from numerous letters of his, in which he complains that, rich as he is, he can count on less than 2000 ducats (*Letter to Paulo Conte de' Conti*, vol. V of: *Opere*, cit., p. 33).

for a villa that is in no way comparable, like leaving a beautiful maiden for a common wench. And if you say: the wench loves me and the maiden spurns me, I reply, the wench loves you not, since she knows nothing of your virtues, nor does the maiden spurn you».[22] It is not difficult to see in this the fact that the rigours of the life of Venice sometimes led the wealthy to lose their love for the Republic, removing them from the centre of political power. Speroni invited all of these men to: «abandon the villa, as you would a concubine, who has distracted you from service to the homeland ... Stay in Venice, and if you have rented lodgings there, purchase a home worthy of your name».[23] This exaltation of city life and the condemnation of those who left the city for the country is due, in Speroni's view of things, to the need to increase the population of the capital city and hence its political power and economic well-being through hard and productive work. Proof of this is that when the Paduan writer wanted to congratulate Paolo Manuzio on his purchase of a villa near Vigodarzere, he recommended using the new estate «since the pleasures afforded by the villa should be wedded to utility».[24]

No less important in the work of Speroni is the echo of the lively disputes over usury that were raging at the time. It has been affirmed that in the sixteenth century, with the exception of a few who sought theological guidance on the conduct of economic life, in order to settle the tormenting scruples of conscience,[25] Italians freely entered into loan agreements with the repayment of interest. This is clear from the reports of Donato to the Serenissima Republic, detailing the fabulous earnings of Genoa from money lending,[26] but also

---

It seems that not always did the administration of his assets produce profits. In a letter to Magn. M. Giulia de' Conti, his daugther, Speroni wrote: «However I wish you to know that my possessions and belongings in Padua have never been in worse state. Three who rented our houses have made away and I know not if they have paid their rent but I am told all the glass is broken and the keys not returned and locks taken, as well as other things, including the large jalousie that was in S. Anna, cannot be found. From my suits in Court I am profitted nothing except to my injury, and nobody pays...». SPERONI, *Lettere*, vol. V of *Opere*, cit., p. 149. Cf. *op. cit.*, p. 150.

M. FORCELLINI, in his interesting *La vita di Sperone Speroni degli Alvarotti* (vol. V of SPERONI, *Opere*, cit., p. XIII), says that the increased wealth of the family was obtained by Speroni «in Padua and Venice through many suits; the farms and houses he possessed he improved greatly, and he often made great acquisitions. And to increase his faculty, he moved from the house in S. Anna, his paternal home, on 17 October 1536 to la Bovetta, another district of Padua, to live with his mother-in-law, assisting her with the careful administration of her faculties, and contributing willingly to the expenses of her family: sure that one day he would obtain the entire inheritance».

[22] SPERONI, *Del ritornare in città*, in *Opere*, cit., p. 414 of volume V.

[23] *Ibid.*, p. 413.

[24] *Lettera a M. Paolo Manuzio*, in *Opere*, cit., vol. V, pp. 34-35.

[25] Cf. chapter I, par. I.

[26] Cf. ALBÈRI, *op. cit.*, s. 1ª, vol. VI, p. 361 (*Relazione di Leonardo Donato*, in the year 1573).

from the copious Church legislation on this new, easy but costly means of purchasing goods.

Although the practice was widespread, it would be a mistake to think that the problem of the legitimacy and morality of interest-bearing loans had been solved. In this connection, Speroni wrote *The Dialogue of Usury*, in which usury itself, in personified form, pleads for its legitimacy, demonstrating the «miracles» it had made possible. Thus Ruzante,[27] the interlocutor of the dialogue, is addressed by Usury: «I have come to show you a new and beautiful art; by which you can become rich so that the Muses will come to live with you and gold and silver will be enamoured of your purse and seek to enter it and fill it, and be reproduced within your fingers, like the fabled King called Midas. But perhaps you do not believe that any art or artifice can make you rich, so that you may dedicate yourself to studies and writing poesie».[28] This apology of usury reveals an idea widespread in the sixteenth century. If, on the one hand, some suffered the pangs of conscience, on the other, many were enthusiastic about this new way to purchase goods since it involved no evident hardship or toil, as in bygone times. If Speroni pretended to imagine that loans would allow him to live in idleness and dedicate himself to writing poetry, others thought it would enable them to purchase well-constructed and beautiful buildings and marry into high-ranking families. In each case, the promptings of conscience seem to have been silenced by the love of literature, of beauty or of status: all of which could be obtained by usury and its easy earnings.

Yet there were some, and Speroni among them, who judged usury so severely that they were less tolerant even than scholars and Churchmen. For example, he compares usury to a woman of ill-repute and, worse still,[29] criticized Pope Pius V because he allowed Jews to lend money in Rome. This art, observes Speroni, the Pope «does not allow Christians to practice: and Jews are so far on the path to Hell that usury adds little to their progress. The hope of converting a Jew to Christianity is weak, and all the weaker if he is not only a Jew but also a userer».[30]

---

[27] Ruzante was called the Paduan gentleman Angelo Beolco, «who in the rustic tale of Padua, written in verse and prose, emulated the glory of Bembo and Speroni». Cf. SPERONI, *Opere*, vol. I, p. 97, note 2.

[28] ID., *Dialogo della usura*, vol. I of: *Opere*, p. 97.

[29] ID., *Orazione contra le Cortigiane*, p. 242, vol. III of *Opere*, cit.

[30] ID., From «Bordello», vol. V of: *Opere*, pp. 439-440. The question of the licence for usury to the Jews was considered by the Dominican priest from the Veneto SISTO MEDICES (*De foenore Judaeorum*, Venetiis, Griffio, 1555), who considered it the lesser evil.

This shows that in the sixteenth century not only Churchmen but also lay-men considered loans for interest and the art of exchange absolutely immoral, even – as was often affirmed – offensive to nature. And in fact, «money», observed Tasso at that time, «is exchanged like things that are exchanged, as if money and things were the same, but they are not the same; money is the measure of prices but not because it is exchanged. Therefore there is no need of money, inasmuch as it is metal; from it no comfort in private or civil life is derived...when money is changed in and of itself and not for another purpose it is misused. The exchange of money is not natural because, like usury, it can infinitely multiply income, and therefore has no determined purpose», which offends against nature where a purpose is always present.[31] The exchange of goods, on the other hand, afforded a concrete benefit to society and rightfully led to earnings because of the toil involved in the trade.[32]

Returning to Speroni, the follower of Pomponazzi, it should be noted that for all his repulsion of usury he certainly did not think of the ideal life as one in which money was not put to work. In administering his funds, he gave ample proof of this. Speroni believed that money should not be kept locked up out of harm's way but used for honest enterprise.[33] Although his ideal State was self-sufficient, the Paduan philosopher approved of international trade via the exchange of foodstuffs and goods produced in the respective cities of the two states. Speaking of agreements between cities and the dominance of one over another, which generally gave rise to the State, Speroni writes: «These alliances are made to take arms or to defend oneself against the insults of outsiders, and this most commonly; or for comfort in life from day to day. For a city may abound in one thing and lack others: I am speaking of things that are pertinent to life and of clothing. So they give to another city that in which they are abundant and receive that in which they are lacking».[34]

Speroni struggled greatly with the Jews in his city. Until 1469 the Monte di Pietà (as in many other cities) had spared the population from recourse to the Jews, although their power had barely diminished, since they had twenty lending banks in Padua, and the cashier of the Monte, with almost no assets, handed over to his successor no more than 500 ducats. To resolve this situation, Speroni went to Venice and, availing himself of his friendship with many men of credit, he persuaded the Doge Francesco Donato through the offices of Bernardo Navagero, Mayor of Padua, and Alvise Donato, Captain, to prohibit usury by the Jews in the city and surrounding territory. The Decree saved the city 30,000 ducats which it paid in annual interest, and the Monte returned to prosperity, so the cashiers were able to pass on to their successors more than 130,000 lire. FORCELLINI, op. cit., pp. XXI-XXII.

[31] T. TASSO, Il padre di famiglia, in Opere di Torquato Tasso, Pisa, Capurro, 1832, p. 43.

[32] Ibid., p. 44.

[33] SPERONI, Lettera al Sig. Angelo Blasio, vol. V of Opere, cit., p. 170.

[34] ID., Trattatello «della Corte», in Opere, cit., vol. V, p. 415.

After justifying international trade, Speroni goes on to indicate his opposition to certain forms of acquiring wealth, such as gambling, which he regarded as a diabolic invention. He observes that through gambling «in the course of time things are lost, and what is most important, precious time is wasted, nor should be consumed in this fruitless matter, but in negotiating things for the wellbeing of humanity».[35] The ideal of life, according to Speroni, is that «every man who is not naturally wealthy as befits his station may, indeed should, take up an honourable industry to increase his wealth».[36] This echoes the thinking of Tomaso De Vio, according to whom – as shown in Chapter I – seeking to climb higher on the social ladder is entirely legitimate where a man is gifted with uncommon qualities. With the exception of this principle, all the other solutions put forward by Speroni concerning the accumulation of wealth are derived from the Scholastic tradition.

Tasso, too, dealt with the problem of obtaining wealth. «Riches – he writes – should be proportional to the head of the household and the family that is maintained and of this substance he should be the heir and no more, sufficient not only to live but to live well according to his condition and the customs of the time». Even clearer in this regard is the following passage. Riches «cannot be determined in quantity, only must be in proportion to their possessor, who shall not toil to increase them when, divided among his children, they are sufficient for a good life in the city».[37] If Tasso condemns too much attention to becoming rich,[38] he nonetheless does not disparage wealth, since he believes «a city shall become the nobler where nature provides the means for increasing its wealth and inhabitants, and become large and famous, more than a city not assisted by nature in this enterprise».[39] Despite

---

[35] SPERONI, *Trattatello del Gioco*, in *Opere*, cit., vol. V, pp. 441-442. With reference to card games, Speroni writes: «They are called in Latin *aleae*, or *ab alienando*, because they alienate wealth, time and the mental faculties, or *ab alendo*, which means nourishment, because they feed us continually with the desire to play and continually tempt us mortals». ID., *Trattatello del gioco*, cit., p. 441.

[36] ID., *Lettera to Sig. Giacomo Critonio Scozese*, in vol. V of: *Opere*, cit. Quite a different solution was given to the problem of accumulating wealth in that era by Paolo Paruta, who appears to have known Speroni personally, perhaps taking lessons from him at home. Cf. CANDELORO, *op. cit.*, fasc. III, p. 71.

[37] TASSO, *Il Padre di Famiglia*, cit., p. 42. The perfect head of a household, Tasso says, «desires riches, because riches are but multitudes of instruments belonging to family and public life; but the art of acquiring these instruments is not infinite, either in number or size» (*ibid.*, p. 42). This work by Tasso: Il Padre di Famiglia, is cited by GOBBI in *L'economia politica*, cit., p. 332, no. 1.

[38] Bandello (BANDELLO, *Le novelle*, cit., vol. II, p. 297) also says that everyone should seek and use riches according to their status. «These goods – he says – which God bestows upon us should be taken and disposed of with measure, according to our rank».

[39] T. TASSO, *Il forno, overo della nobiltà, dialogo del s. Torquato Tasso*, Vinetia, presso Aldo, 1583, pp. 95-96.

this attribution of nobility to the city of abundance, Tasso was secretly inclined to the sweetness of the countryside. It is only in a villa in the country that a man can enjoy peace and quiet and truly relax.[40] There, a man has no worries, because the countryside produces grain, vegetables and fruit abundantly, feeds the herds and flocks with grass and provides man with the enchantment of gardens and many scented flowers.[41]

Beside this ideal, which is at the heart of every sixteenth century aspiration,[42] the image of the head of the household and good family man embodies the virtues and implicit regulations of a healthy and prudent rural life as well as of the economy of farming. The owner of the villa should first and foremost measure his possessions with the utmost accuracy, know the production capacity of each of the estates he owns, and be aware of the current price of goods as established by law or the marketplace.[43] This is advantageous to the head of the household when selling excess fodder and buying the things required for the honourable maintenance of a family. It is part of his skill to sell when the price is high and buy when the price is low.

Hence the head of the house must take part in the economy of the community and not fall victim to the expertise and guile of merchants, whose sole

---

[40] TASSO, *Il Padre di Famiglia*, cit., pp. 7-8. Praising the life of the «villa» Tasso puts these words into the mouth of a landowner: «No need is there ... that I for something necessary or convenient for the life of a poor gentleman, send to the city, because my lands and God give me what I need, and in abundance and so I have divided them and administer them, as they say, in four parts. The largest is ploughed by me and sown with seed and all manner of vegetables; another is left to the trees and plants, which are needed for fire, or for the use of workshops or the instruments of the house, and in this part, which is sown, there are my orders of trees, such as vines, according to the custom of our small villages; the third are the meadows, for cattle and flocks of sheep, such as I possess, for pasture; the fourth I have reserved for herbs and flowers, where there are many hives for bees, and in this garden there are many fruits planted by me, and which are separate from my other possessions in a large orchard».

[41] *Ibid.*, pp. 6-7.

[42] The poetry of Bandello is full of hatred of the city and the love of the fields:
Per non vedermi mille volte l'ora
Morendo non morir, i' son fuggito
Dal fiero albergo d'onde è già partito
Chi abborre il vizio e la virtude onora.
The aspiration of life far from «citizens» inspires Bandello to sing the praises of solitary life:
Alte e frondose quercie che le spalle
A questi colli ombrate, faggi, ed orni,
Genèbri, e lauri, che li bei contorni
Di queste ornate al ciel si cara valle.
Bandello, this strange sixteenth-century man, dies of the desire to
Veder verdi le campagne, e i monti,
e gli arboscelli rinnovar le fronde,
e tra l'erbose già spogliate sponde
correr lucenti i freschi rivi e i fonti.
(M. BANDELLO, *Il canzoniere*, Torino, UTET, 1928, p. 235).

[43] TASSO, *Il Padre di Famiglia*, cit., p. 32. On p. 34, Tasso lists the various things that can increase or decrease revenue from the land.

aim is profit.[44] This observation and recommendation does not justify idleness or lack of productive work, but warns against accumulating wealth for its own sake. The economy is a means, not an end. Proof of this is provided by Tasso's recommendation to women to learn the art of weaving, an honest and profitable labour and hence an aid to the head of the household.[45] This notion of wealth is reminiscent of the Scholastic tradition so dear to men of the sixteenth century. Nor does the poet take exception to this tradition when he advises moderate savings in order to cope with cases of need. Listing these cases, he does not include board and lodging, but the consequences of fire and flooding, for which money should be set aside and not continually placed at risk by being used and only set aside if it has been increased.[46]

A concept relating to economic life less influenced by medieval philosophy comes to the fore in the pages of the writer from Palermo, Paolo Caggio.[47] In *Iconomica*, his most interesting work,[48] he does not question the legitimacy of seeking wealth according to one's social standing, because the economist has two essential duties: first, to retain the wealth he has, «such as Houses, Vines, Fields, Gardens, Possessions, Palaces, Towers, Ships, Arms, Flocks, Clothes, Goods, Money, Servants, Horses and similar things, according to the generous hand of God».

Second is the economic duty of «diligence in acquiring goods and ability to trade with art and through the excellence of invention, so man may increase his substance» so that «he may live in peace», which many are unable to achieve due to the poor use of their wealth.[49] Increasing one's assets is therefore not only legitimate but actually a duty dictated by prudence and the need to be insured against risk, given the accidents that may befall a man who unwisely makes no provision for changes in fortune.[50]

---

[44] *Ibid.*, pp. 34-41.

[45] *Ibid.*, pp. 36-37.

[46] *Ibid.*, p. 32.

[47] P. CAGGIO, *Iconomica del Signor Paolo Caggio ... nella quale s'insegna brevemente per modo di dialogo il governo Famigliare, etc*, Vinegia, al segno del Pozzo, 1553.
The work of Caggio is cited by the Perugian writer LANCELLOTTI (*op. cit.*, pp. 396-397). For his thinking, see the studies of L. NATOLI, *Paolo Caggio prosatore siciliano del secolo XVI*, «Archivio Storico Siciliano», XXI, 1904; ID., *Prosa e prosatori siciliani del secolo XVII*, Palermo, Sandron, 1904, pp. 35-79. GOBBI (*L'economia politica*, cit., pp. 24-26) summarizes the Iconomica by Caggio, showing how useful it is for an understanding of the uses and customs of Sicily at the beginning of the sixteenth century.

[48] Caggio is also of interest to legal historians. One of his works is entitled: P. CAGGIO, *Iura municipalia, seu consuetudines Felicis Urbis Panormi*, Panormi, apud Ioannem Matthaeum Maidam, 1547. Another edition was produced in Venice in 1575.

[49] ID., *Iconomica*, cit., p. 6.

[50] *Ibid.*, pp. 49-50.

Many are the ways – says Caggio – which lead to wealth, but in all of them prudence must be the guide.[51] In marriage a man must not only look for a bride who is honest «more than is superlative», but also possesses «some substance» which may be used to produce «honourable fruit» for the wellbeing of the family.[52] The same Albertian principle guides the businessman when he invests money in one enterprise or another, so that if a cargo is lost at sea to shipwreck, the good result of another business will offset the bad result of this accident.[53] For this reason – as we shall see later – Caggio prefers agriculture to all other economic activities, since it is free of these risks. The same principle induces the good *iconomo* to avoid useless and disadvantageous expenses, cutting his cloth according to his earnings, unlike the Italic custom of families – so says Caggio – who spend all their money on «buildings such as the Princes of beautiful Italy use, outside the city in villas, where for little purpose and at great expense they keep away from the fire of summer». Nor should so much be spent «on these superb shapes, so magnificent that a whole patrimony is all but used up».[54] The same principle leads to the prudence of the merchant in investing capital in commercial enterprises, in shipping goods from overseas and so on.[55] Opposed to this principle is reducing the wages of workmen, since – according to Caggio – it is more useful to increase their wages and thereby their productivity. This is not a moral principle based on justice, but the hard reasoning of an entrepreneur who wants the men in his service well fed and healthy.[56] In a word, a prudent administration

---

[51] *Ibid.*, p. 14.

[52] *Ibid.*, p. 3. «In the meantime seek to win a bride and, above all, seek a woman who is moderately beautiful and honest in the superlative, and through whom (by means of the goodness of he who confers treasures and his impish spirits) you may be sufficiently wealthy, and ensure that the first part of the dowry be her virtue, whose decorum shall give you sempeternal immortality, as the angels. If you can then receive some substance, add it to your own substance; so that together they produce honourable fruit and sufficient to live and provide for your family through your industry».

Despite this recommendation to marry well (similar advice was given by Leon Battisti Alberti. Cf. FANFANI, *Le origini*, cit., p. 137), a little further on, Caggio admonishes his follower «I told you not to count on making riches from her dowry; because through this appetite for munificent dowries they make their own tangles and blessed are they that do not lose themselves in the thickest wood». Cf. CAGGIO, *Iconomica*, cit., p. 7, t. 8. This warning shows that Caggio considered wealth a means for good living and for acquiring fame and a good reputation, and hence in relation to a wife, a dowry could not outweigh virtue, which was the source of honour for the family, this being one of the supreme aims of life.

[53] *Ibid.*, p. 52 e t. «Invest in many things – Alberti wrote – so you do not suffer ruin from one misadventure». Cf. FANFANI, *Origini*, cit., p. 137.

[54] CAGGIO, *Iconomica*, cit., p. 52.

[55] *Ibid.*, pp. 52-52 t. Of the many ways to invest savings, Caggio does not even mention lending.

[56] *Ibid.*, p. 44. In relation to slaves, Caggio speaks of the need to treat them humanely (following Xenophon: see V. BRANTS, *Xénophon économiste*, «La Revue Catholique de Louvain», 1881), since they are from the same strain as free men (pp. 41-43), but he says that slavery is a state that

of earnings and spending is always the basis for maintaining and increasing one's wealth.[57] In this connection Caggio warns the head of a small household not to keep the fruits of his possessions at home but to sell them where best it suits him in order to earn money to purchase what the family needs, thus avoiding the risk of excessive consumption, or saving on the costs of keeping barns, cellars and so on. For large families Caggio recommends setting aside money for the family's needs.[58] The reader may object that Caggio seems not to reckon with the way prices fluctuate or increase. In reality, building barns, the expense of supervising them and wasting things at hand are far more disadvantageous than increases in prices. And even here, Caggio wisely recommends prudence.

If Caggio appears not to be suspicious about the workings of the market, where those involved act prudently, and the market appears to be a good means for increasing wealth, its dangers nonetheless lead him to a preference for working in the fields and the life of the «villa».[59] Above all other activities, Caggio recommends farming, «as natural, right and proper, useful for strength, for the soul and for the body».[60] Like a wife who gives her husband precious children, farming renders the fruits of the earth.[61] It is «as necessary to the life of mortals as what gives breath, providing sustenance from making

---

is derived from nature, which has created a primary society of free men and, beneath them, for their benefit, the slaves (pp. 40 t-42 t). This natural state of affairs condoning slavery is proved – so says Caggio – by somatic features: «In addition, those who are naturally of high intelligence command those of less ingenuity. In sign of which, Nature has given them strength, valour and force, to serve those for whom, to exercise their intellect, delicate bodies have been given, tenderly complexioned, who cannot abide discomfort of any kind, and have always commanded over other nations...» (p. 42 t). In this way the writer from Palermo is a precursor of today's fashionable theories of biotypes, and finds the thickset physique of slaves proof that they are destined by Nature to be slaves. Similarly, Caggio considers the delicate complexion of noblemen and free men a natural manifestation of their calling to rule social life. The idea came form Aristotle: «Nature seems to wish to give free men and slaves differing bodies: the latter strong for rough work and the former upstanding and elegant, unsuited to such labours, but fitted to civil life». ARISTOTELE, *Politica*, traduzione, note e proemio di V. Costanzi, Bari, Laterza, 1925, p. 11, book I, c. 2.
It seems that in Sicilian farming, slaves were indispensable, alongside paid labourers, who sold their labour for goods (pp. 43-43 t).

[57] CAGGIO, *Iconomica*, cit., p. 53.

[58] *Ibid.*, p. 53 t-54, 55-55 t.

[59] *Ibid.*, p. 52 e pp. 11-12. The best activity – says Caggio – is farming, because it makes the house wealthy without dangers. *Ibid.*, p. 52 t.

[60] *Ibid.*, p. 11 e pp. 8-9. Insisting on the reasoning by which farming was considered better than all other activities, Caggio affirms «Is it not known that there is no better profession and no better earning than from the work of the land, where no harm is done to friends? And what injury is done by cultivating the land and how do I stray from the straight and narrow if I obtain the fruit of the earth from those who do not deny it to me?». Cf. *ibid.*, p. 9.

[61] *Ibid.*, p. 7.

provisions now in one place, now another. As can be seen clearly: because such artifice is natural, and teaching for us, and given to us from nature by the Maker of all things».[62] Furthermore, farming provides great advantage to the homeland, because men become used to hard work and to overseeing the endless expanse of fields and ears of grain, wave upon wave, uninterrupted by walls, and this strengthens the spirit and makes them fit for facing the dangers of war, unlike the cowardly, who live in cities of apparent peace.[63]

In the countryside peace is not apparent but real, and the owner of a villa can dedicate himself to studying literature or to meditation.[64] Here, Caggio returns to his love of the countryside, despite a certain dynamism within the economic ideal, which the worries and anxieties of commerce subvert. Not so in the fields, «the most praiseworthy exercise, most worthy toil and honest labour of all the activities of the World».[65]

The preference of Caggio for agriculture does not exclude the utility of other economic activities, provided they are carried out honestly. «If the work of the land does not please you – he says – and you tire of the fields make choice of another means that is honest, apply yourself and cease sleeping for nothing».[66] These words show that, although convinced that agriculture is the best way to acquire wealth, Caggio justifies mercantile activities and any other activity designed to honestly procure one's living, to live decorously and with some comfort. What was important was work rather than idleness, which does not provide the instruments required for decent civil life. Caggio considered wealth a means of living reputably and honourably,[67] as affirmed by Alberti. In order to have these means available, Caggio recommends making a precise calculation of spending,[68] and moderation in procuring items of luxury for the clothing of women, often the cause of the moral and financial ruin of families.[69]

---

[62] *Ibid.*, p. 8.

[63] *Ibid.*, pp. 9-10. Caggio says that the life of the city, where people live to «waste their time away», makes men idle, all intent on woman's work.

[64] *Ibid.*, pp. 62-63.

[65] *Ibid.*, p. 8. Caggio affirms that since adolescence he has dreamt of a leafy meadow, and cattle, orchards and gardens, where life is peaceful and solitary. Cf. *ibid.*, p. 52.

[66] *Ibid.*, p. 50. Earlier, he had said: «However, if you think on it, there are abundant other honest and legitimate tasks to perform, such as trading, or other enterprises conducted in the city» (p. 11 t).

[67] *Ibid.*, p. 51.

[68] *Ibid.*, p. 52.

[69] *Ibid.*, p. 52, 19-19 t. Caggio says the women of his time complained to their husbands «that they cannot appear where other women are present unless dressed to satisfy the vanity of a woman. Whence the disgraced, seeing themselves without substance, the light fails a lantern and is extinguished if it receives no nourishment, unable to continue to support the haughtiness of women, fall into despair ... Do you imagine you can recover the cost of women living at Court? The splendour of

The same idea of wealth is behind the condemnation of greed and those who, in order to accumulate more riches «drink unripe wine because they sell the good variety and live in certain houses that seem fit for mule-drivers because they lease their best premises to others and lack for everything, they who could have all».[70] If wealth is to be enjoyed by the family reputably and honourably, women must dress according to the ways of the city,[71] refraining from any clothing that might detract from their name and reputation, for example by eschewing rouge, other forms of make-up and the like. For his part, the head of the household was to be moderate in spending and provide for the family's needs, including clothing, horses and servants. Nor should he omit to give charitably and to friends, and spend both for public and private things so as to increase the reputation of the house.[72]

One final concept needs to be understood to fully appreciate the economy as seen by Caggio. Only those who have a family – he says – are fit to govern and exercise public office, since managing the affairs of the family is a necessary introduction to managing affairs of State.[73]

This norm, which predates similar measures this day and age, sums up the economic thinking of Paolo Caggio who claimed to have been inspired mainly by Aristotle but actually is closer to the thinking of Alberti, as shown by ample research.[74]

The economic thought of Caggio shows a clear preference for agriculture over commerce. A similar idea is behind the affirmation of Fioravanti: «no greater pleasure can a man obtain» than life in the field, because for both mind and body «nothing is sweeter in this world than living in a villa».[75]

---

dishes, the gentleness of clothing, the abundance of fashionable attire, as is the custom nowadays, would consume the Treasury of Venice».

[70] *Ibid.*, p. 51-51 t.

[71] *Ibid.*, p. 17.

[72] *Ibid.*, pp. 50-51, 21 t.

[73] *Ibid.*, p. 24 t.

[74] Caggio says in Rome he heard numerous discussions of governing households «citing first Hesiod, a grave poet, then Xenophon, who also wrote an Iconomica. But the commonest opinions and most worthy of praise are from Prince Aristotle, so that I sought to learn my part, and finding me in places where such dealings were made, I could take record of them». *Ivi*, pp. 10-12.
Caggio certainly derived his ideas of the naturalness of social life from Aristotle and Thomas Aquinas: P. CAGGIO, *Ragionamenti: ne quali egli introduce tre suoi amici, che naturalmente discorrono intorno à una vaga fontana, in veder se la vita cittadinesca sia più felice, del viver solitario fuor le città, e nelle ville*, Vinegia, al segno del Pozzo, 1551. In the sixteenth century, Vida dealt with a similar question, reaching the same conclusions as, later, Rousseau. Cf. FERRARI, *op. cit.*, p. 289; CURCIO, *op. cit.*, pp. 124-125, 136-138.

[75] L. FIORAVANTI, *Dello specchio di scientia universale, dell'eccellente medico et cirurgico M. Leonardo Fioravanti Bolognese*, Venezia, Andrea Ravenoldo, 1567, p. 6.

Several times in the previous chapters authors have exalted work in the field, the refuge – in the sixteenth century – of those who wished to escape the grey city and the anxieties of commerce, living in peace and quiet and dedicating time to idleness and books. This desire for peace was so intense that all too often (as Menochio says) the lords of the Manor Houses and villas left the cultivation of the land «to yokels and idiots», entirely ignorant of even the most basic laws of agrarian science.[76] Fioravanti complains of this custom, like Menochio before him, whose *Iconomica Cristiana*[77] set out the basic scientific principles of a useful economic life. The learned Jesuit is not the only writer to have written about farming, attempting to establish some rules and regulations. Before him, Giovanni Tatti of Lucca had published *Della Agricoltura* in five volumes[78] and Popoleschi wrote a treatise on the art of planting and looking after trees in a garden, from which «the wage earner» can obtain considerable pleasure and advantage.[79] Davanzati wrote the work entitled *Toscana coltivazione delle viti e delli arbori*.[80] Other books, before and after his, also explained the profit that could be made from this type of cultivation. A few examples will suffice: the work of the nobleman from Brescia Agostino Gallo, entitled: *Le vinti giornate dell'agricoltura et de' piaceri della villa*[81], *Le ricchezze dell'agricoltura*[82] written by Giovanni Maria Bonardo and *l'Economia del cittadino in Villa* by Vincenzo Tanara,[83] and there were many other important works on the subject.[84] This great flourishing of books on agrarian science shows how much the countryside had become an ideal in the aspirations of men in the sixteenth and seventeenth centuries.

Returning to the surgeon from Bologna, it should be noted that if in the *Mirror of Universal Science* agriculture was considered the first true science because indispensable,[85] trading goods also featured, and Fioravanti did

---

[76] *Ibid.*, p. 4.

[77] Cf. chapter I, paragraph 2.

[78] Published in Venice in 1560.

[79] G.A. POPOLESCHI, *Del modo di piantare e custodire una Ragnaia e di uccellare a ragna* (previously erroneously attributed to Davanzati), in DAVANZATI, *Le opere*, cit., vol. II, p. 603. «In my opinion this netting to capture birds is one of the greatest comforts any gentleman may possess, providing beauty to life and ornament to the villa, if placed in the proper location, in addition to the pleasure of many months of hunting birds; and in addition to earning, if you make some expense, you will save for the household».

[80] In volume II of DAVANZATI, *Le opere*, cit., p. 487 and following.

[81] Printed in Venice in 1569.

[82] Printed in Turin in 1590.

[83] Printed in Bologna in 1644.

[84] For other works on agriculture see GOBBI, *L'economia politica*, cit., p. 48 and following.

[85] FIORAVANTI, *op. cit.*, cit., p. 6.

not miss the opportunity to establish some rules for commerce, of a moral nature. If a merchant wishes to gain riches, he says, let him shun «gambling, whoring and gluttony».[86] He should also remember justice, since often «it can be seen from the effects that follow that ill-gotten gains do not willingly stay with the person who has earned them; in gaining them they damn their souls through deceiving God and the world».[87] Whereas trading goods without offending economic justice or exhibiting greed[88] «is gracious to God and profits the world» and all the more worthy of praise when the merchant has earned enough and goes on to invest his wealth in possessions and villas.[89]

While the Bolognese surgeon, albeit with some limitations, justifies commerce, the greatest exponent and supporter of commerce was the physician Antonio Maria Venusti in his *Discorso d'intorno alla Mercantia*.[90] He begins with the idea – very common at the time – that men seek glory «and illustrious and divulged fame for merits and benefits to the homeland or citizens». And since arms and literature, which are the means of acquiring a reputation, cannot be exercised without money, it is necessary to accumulate wealth as easily as possible. Hence the need to trade, the easiest way to make money, which can then be used in order to «best maintain noble families and aid the homeland at times of calamity; innumerable poor are kept alive; Princes and great lords are aided and there are various and innumerable benefits to the world».[91] After listing the righteous aims that wealth can pursue, Venusti goes on to demonstrate the advantages derived from a merchant's life. Contact with people from different countries makes him prudent and increases his ex-

---

[86] Speaking of merchants the surgeon from Bologna says: «let them be just in selling, liberal in purchasing, moderate in gambling, not given to lust, sober in food and drink». *Ibid.*, p. 33.

[87] *Ibid.* Cf. GUICCIARDINI, *Scritti politici*, cit., p. 253, no. 65.

[88] In relation to greed, Bandello affirms that it is sinful because «these goods God gives to us must be taken and dispensed by us according to our rank» (BANDELLO, *Le novelle*, cit., vol. II, p. 297).

[89] FIORAVANTI, *op. cit.*, p. 33. In the sixteenth century the opinion of Cicero was very dear to Italians: «Mercatura, si tenuis est, sordida putanda est; si magna et copiosa, multa undique apportans, multisque sine vanitate impartiens, non est admodum vituperanda, atque etiam si satiata quaestu, vel contenta potius, ut saepe ex alto in portum, ex portu ipso se in agros, possessionesque contulerit, videtur iure optimo posse laudari» (I book of Uffici). Cf. GARZONI, *op. cit.*, p. 543.

[90] From the second half of the sixteenth century. He was a doctor in Trieste. His *Discorso d'intorno alla mercantia* was published in a small volume which also included the *Trattato di cambio* [*A Treatise on Exchanges*] by Padre Fabiano, already mentioned in Chapter I; an *Esortazione a' mercanti*, an *Instituzione de' mercanti*, and a *Trattato de' cambi*, translated from Spanish. The volume is VENUSTI, *Compendio utilissimo di quelle cose, le quali a nobili e cristiani mercanti appartengono*, cit.. Cf. MONTANARI, *op. cit.*, pp. 6-7.

[91] VENUSTI, *Discorso d'intorno alla mercantia*, cit., pp. 4-6.
To further demonstrate the need of riches to achieve glory, by private and public charity, Venusti recalls «that Saint Paul told fathers to gain riches for their sons (PAUL, *Corinthias II*, 12)».

perience, giving him wisdom which can be turned to profit at home and used to provide excellent advice.[92] From a moral standpoint goods are desirable because they cannot be procured through idleness «which is the cause of all wickedness; and keeps us away from thoughts, words, deeds, and activities; to the soul's anguish and the body's sufferance».[93]

According to Venusti there is almost a natural law that makes commodities and goods worth acquiring: «because while some men know some things, many men know many things, and all together know all things; but nobody in bygone days nor anybody today nor anybody to come will know all that can be known: so every place and country produces something, many produce many things and all together they produce everything; no place and no country has produced, produces nor will produce for itself all that is necessary for the life of men».[94] Hence, it is in the natural order of things for countries to dedicate themselves to different economic activities and to trade the products of those activities internationally, increasing the overall wealth of humanity. This thinking is the precursor of economic theory as elaborated only several centuries later.

In relation to international trade one book deserves mention, *Ragionamento sopra il commercio tra i Toscani e i Levantini*, published in 1577 by the Florentine author and merchant Filippo Sassetti, who was «appointed to assist in trading pepper from India on vessels laden for Portugal».[95] He understood the great utility of importing products from the East for the economy of our country, and was well aware of the dangers of shrinking trade. He urged the greatest possible freedom of trade between nations, eliminating its risks and, as far as possible, abolishing import duties on products from the East, as a necessary condition for exporting goods from Tuscany, to the great benefit of a «multitude of peoples».

This was the thinking of an important merchant, well-known in his time for his munificence and generosity. Venusti was certainly thinking of a similar kind of merchant when he expressed his support for trading, affirming: «True merchants and traders are those who from distant countries bring home goods with honest gain and sell for private and public benefit».[96] Honour could not be bestowed upon a merchant «who buys a great quantity of goods

---

[92] VENUSTI, *Discorso d'intorno alla mercantia*, cit., p. 11.

[93] *Ibid.*

[94] *Ibid.*, p. 6.

[95] Cf. F. SASSETTI, *Lettere edite e inedite di Filippo Sassetti*, raccolte e annotate da Ettore Marcucci, Firenze, Le Monnier, 1855, p. XLI.

[96] VENUSTI, *Discorso d'intorno alla mercantia*, cit., p. 8.

from merchants to sell them in a shop» nor upon usurers who should be excluded from the ranks of honourable merchants. Those who bought goods
and «make them into another form, and so sell them» are not merchants
but craftsmen; whilst honour may be accorded to those who, not personally
but through the toil of workmen, agents and messengers, transformed and re-
sold goods, occupying themselves with the accounts and overseeing the various businesses under them.[97]

From these ideas, it is not difficult to understand the basic attitude of Venusti to the acquisition of wealth. Where large quantities of goods were
bought and sold and the merchant merely oversaw the process, this means
of creating abundance was not only desirable, but honourable and noble.
Manufacturing, craftsmanship and the production of goods for consumers
should be left to the poor, whose only means of sustenance was from the
sweat of their brow. In this opinion about the respective duties of the working
man and the merchant, the physician from Trieste was a man of his times.

Chapters VII and VIII return to this topic. The following paragraph deals
with the economic thinking of Tommaso Campanella, whose ideas represent
the most thorough and least fanciful of the proposals for social reform put
forward in the Modern Age.

3. Campanella is a complex figure: a monk, he was obsessed to the point of
torment with the idea of social improvement and like no other thinker before
him concerned himself with how society as a whole could be elevated. Yet he
barely took part in social life at all; a solitary man, he spent most of his life in
contemplation[98] and his works – at first sight – appear to abound in the strangest contradictions, even in the spheres of political and economic thought.

His *Civitas Solis*[99] is too well known for the various thoughts dedicated to
the problem of wealth to be repeated here. Suffice it to say that his entire
thinking on the subject was dictated by his reaction to the evils he had identified in society after conducting a very thorough examination of its characteristics and trends (as we shall see below).

---

[97] *Ibid.*

[98] For some important studies of Tommaso Campanella see: the lengthy Preface of Alessandro
D'Ancona to T. CAMPANELLA, *Opere di Tommaso Campanella*, edited by A. D'Ancona, Torino, Pomba, 1854; P. TREVES, *La filosofia politica di Tommaso Campanella*, Bari, Laterza, 1930; B. CROCE, *Materialismo storico ed economia marxistica*, Bari, Laterza, 1918, pp. 191-239; G.S. FELICI, *Le dottrine
filosofico-religiose di Tommaso Campanella*, Lanciano, Carabba, 1895; F. DE SANCTIS, *Storia della letteratura italiana*, Bari, Laterza, 1912.

[99] T. CAMPANELLA, *F. Thomae Campanellae Civitas solis poetica. Idea reipublicae philosophicae*,
Ultraiecti, apud Ioannem à Waesberge, 1643.

Instead of a society which considered wealth as an individual goal, to satisfy one's own needs and those of the family, Campanella imagined a *Civitas* in which all things were owned collectively. In his political conception, mechanical engineering – not worthy of mention by other thinkers of the time – was the highest art and the most honourable profession. At a time when various currencies were used side by side for trading purposes, leading to the art of exchange and complex price speculation and manipulation, he dreamed of a city without money.[100] In an era in which economic activity ran counter to nobility, Campanella imagined an ideal State, in which ordinary citizens had no esteem for the idle and unproductive lives of the nobility. These elements alone are enough to identify the Calabrian monk as a profound thinker who, together with the construction of other ideal political systems,[101] demonstrated a keen interest in the economic spirit of his age. His ideas were neither vague nor utopian but were based on an acute and relentless criticism of the social institutions of the day, leading him to propound certain fundamental reforms.

For these ideas we need to turn away from his best-known work, where he tends to demolish the existing order in favour of a revolutionary new state of being, and examine his other works that provide a more realistic analysis of his age, in which his criticism is more coherent with the thinking and economic ideals of the period. Having said that, the contradictions which have been observed in the work and social theory of Campanella are more apparent than real, because *Civitas Solis* and his other works on the economy of his age differ in their emphasis rather than in their fundamental approach to institutions or the recommendations he makes for sweeping social reform.

Campanella attributed the evils of his age to the unequal distribution of riches and the erroneous idea of wealth in the minds of men. He knew what ruin could follow from too much wealth and what suffering from the lack of it.[102] He sought to construct an ideal economic system based on equality, «nourishing Republics», abolishing all rank and leveling «consumption».[103]

---

[100] Cf. FANFANI, *Storia delle dottrine economiche*, cit., p. 163.

[101] I cite only VIDA, *op. cit.*, and L. ZUCCOLO, *Dialoghi di Ludovico Zuccolo*, Venetia, Ginammi, 1625.

[102] T. CAMPANELLA, *Aforismi politici*, in *Opere di Tommaso Campanella*, vol. II, cit., no. 135, p. 37. Vedi anche aforisma no. 40-41, *ivi*, pp. 17-18.

Ricchezze, sangue, onor, figli e vassalli
Per ben dà il fato; e pur ruina a molti
Son al nome, alla patria ed al composto,
E fan gli animi ansiosi, vili e stolti.
(*Poesie filosofiche*, in *Opere di Tommaso Campanella*, cit., vol. II, p. 69).

[103] ID., *Aforismi*, cit., no. 40, pp. 17-18.

Before illustrating his system, he described the manifold and manifest ills of the current economic model. He dedicated particular attention to the immoderate love of riches, especially money, the consequent decline of arts and sciences and the continuous rising of prices.

Here, a lengthy quotation is required to shed light on his thinking: «with truth we can say that gold from the New World has in some measure ruined the old world,[104] because it gave us to greed and spent love between men. All put into money what they feel and oft it comes to fraudery and oft to giving up their honour since money reigns on all things and is so admired they put religion and science thereafter, and have left off work on the land or in the workshop, becoming slaves of money and wealthy Lords. In the same guise it hath produced inequality among men who are either rich too far or full of airs or fall to poverty, envy and murder.[105] The prices of grain, wine, oil and meat, and attire, have grown since there is no commerce of them, and money grows bloated beyond the stomachs of the poor, who are slaves or rob from others; or are soldiers for a crust of bread and not for love of the King or charity and oft eat their words, disregard their children and leave off marrying, to save on duties».[106]

The first statement suggests that Campanella might have seen the connection between rising prices and the import of American metal to Europe. Bodin demonstrated that after 1568 price increases, due in part to monopolies, scarcity, fashions and monetary changes, were caused chiefly by the import of precious metals from the New World.[107] However, it is unlikely that Campanella understood this correlation and he limits himself to describing the moral consequences of the increase in money in circulation, i.e. an excessive love of money as the sole means of achieving personal success. Campanella analyzed the decline of the Spanish economy but failed to understand the importance of the discovery of the New World in that decline. «I do not wonder – he observed – that the Spanish Empire did not grow larger with so much money, through this lack; but I wonder how the King with so many taxes did not make provision for his needs, without which he would fall into ruin

---

[104] C.D.S. MONTESQUIEU, De l'esprit des lois, XXI, 22.

[105] The Aphorisms (no. 41, vol. II of Opere, pp. 17-18) include these words: «The too poor are rapacious and envious, the too wealthy arrogant and lustful, the too ignorant ruinous, the too clever fickle. However, Florence was the most changeable Republic in the world, due to its subtlety; Venice the most stable, due to its gravity».

[106] T. CAMPANELLA, Della Monarchia in Spagna, in Opere di Tommaso Campanella, vol. II, cit., pp. 142-143.

[107] Cf. A. FANFANI, Indagini sulla "Rivoluzione dei prezzi", Milano, Vita e Pensiero, 1940, pp. 4-5.

and if for five or six years he had no trade from the ocean and the fleet laden with silver and gold from the New World was intercepted, his Kingdoms would be afflicted and become hateful, the merchants ruined, the soldiers unpaid and lost for the slightest reason; and it is a wonder indeed to see how so much money goes fruitless and the King is in constant need of it and so borrows from others».[108]

Without a clear understanding of the causes of the increase in the circulation of coins, Campanella could do little but repeat the ideas of contemporaries to explain the rise in prices: they were the result of monopolies, hoarding and so on. He noted the frequency of famine and other shortages, as well as the numerous episodes of plague in his age and concluded that they were caused by usurers hoarding grain, stored in barns for up to three or more years until the price rose. Often the grain was sold after it had gone rotten or was putrid, spreading illness.[109] This is one of the saddest aspects of the economy in Naples, as described by Campanella. It led him to his first recommended reform, which was to remove the commerce of grain from private hands and make it a matter for the State, in the figure of the King who would buy all the grain «and none but the King should buy corn or they who buy and sell it should lose money. With good conscience and for providence, the King can sell the corn to lands, ordering that it be stored commonly and not in private, earning but a carlin for a bushel, with good reason, since the usurers earn 10 and 20 for a bushel, and lead to the ruin of the Christian populace. Similarly, all the ships of grain he should order that they come to Naples and to other places in the name of the King and to prevent the traders from making private store to drive the people to famine and sell at double the price, the King can sell the corn immediately to the city and those in need and take a carlin for a bushel and so there would be no more famine».[110] By making the King responsible for storing grain, Campanella hoped to obtain two

---

[108] CAMPANELLA, *Della Monarchia*, cit., p. 141.

[109] ID., *Sopra l'aumento delle entrate del Regno di Napoli*, in *Opere di Tommaso Campanella*, cit. In the second volume (pp. 325-326), he says: «Shortages are the result of exchanges, when merchants and powerful usurers purchsase all the grain in the area and keep it while people starve and then sell at threefold or fourfold the price; and when they cannot earn what their greed dictates to them, they sell to another, and he to another and this man to another, and so on, until they are mixed with other grain, and give off a terrible odour, so people die first of hunger and then of pestilence; and the villages go without people, who have fled from the Kingdom, and those who remain must take to thieving and banditry in order to eat, whilst others eat food that is gone spoilt and herbs that are sick, and are oppressed by usury, hunger, plague and sorrows, and many do not take wife in order not to suffer this misery and they see the daughters and families of others become whores for a crust of bread».

[110] *Ibid.*, p. 326.

results: better prices for necessities and hence better living conditions for the poor, and a source of income for the State, estimated by the philosopher at around 400,000 ducats.[111]

Broadly speaking, these twin aims are at the heart of Campanella's economic system, in which he saw the King or the Revenue Service, acting directly in the marketplace, as a protagonist. Those who objected that it was not fitting for the King to take such a role, were told that cities would benefit from storing and distributing grain in the place of merchants. Others saw no reason for the King to make money from producing nothing and taking no risks. Campanella replied that the King provided services and paid for them, and that payment for the distribution of grain would only go part of the way to recovering those costs.[112] This led Campanella to believe in heavy taxation. «It is necessary – he writes – to establish good repute (because the power of a State is judged today no less from money than from its size) and to keep peace and to wage war, when needed, so the Prince should have a good sum in cash always to hand, because it is dangerous and difficult to wait the time required to raise the money especially for war».[113] For this purpose Campanella recommended some measures to the Monarch in order to increase his financial power. They included obliging bankers and private citizens to keep money which the King could use in the case of need. All the barons in the reign should pay the King a portion of their wealth and, in return, the King would beg indulgences for the Crusade and set aside money for future wars. Similarly, the Pope should be enjoined to impose a temporary tax on churches, monasteries, dioceses and parishes, to be reduced over five years. Above all, the King's treasurers should have a monopoly of trading in some important goods in various regions, such as silk in Calabria, oil in Sicily and so on.[114] This was intended not to add to the coffers of the Crown but to improve living standards by controlling prices and confiscating the properties of userers, the wealth to go to a Compassionate Fund for the benefit of the poor, who would receive ready charitable assistance from the fund.[115]

---

[111] *Ibid.*, pp. 326-327.

[112] *Ibid.*, pp. 327-329.

[113] CAMPANELLA, *Della Monarchia*, cit., p. 141.

[114] *Ibid.*, pp. 143-144.

[115] *Ibid.* In dictating the remedy to protect the State from ruin, Campanella suggests to the King thus: «he should send a commissioner to all his lands and farms, in particular in Naples, accompanied by a priest against the usurers, and with three witnesses prove usury upon them, against the custom of the Kingdom, and take all that they possess and make of it a Monte, and then the King should return to them half of what they possess, so taking ten thousand scudi he shall give back five thousand; because usurers are vile, cowardly and base and are hated, so that

It is not difficult to understand the economic thought of Campanella or the spirit that inspires it. It was certainly influenced by Botero, both in the power of the Treasury and in advocating the growth of individual industries. Although acknowledging the importance of money, unlike many of his contemporaries, he did not exaggerate it: «I do not say – he wrote – that the whole strength of the King lies in his money».[116] He propounded an economic policy by which the State would gradually take over commerce from private individuals and foster work in the fields and other manufacturing activities, as justified by mercantile considerations: «promoting the greater good and the interests of all above those of the few».[117] However, the recommended policy did not include the creation of a nation state, whether strong or weak. Campanella wanted a social order able to keep men from the excessive love of money, the source of all evils; and to achieve a certain balance among economic classes;[118] to defeat the enemies of religion and promote peace and work, good practices and virtue between people.

It was a vision of the economy derived from Thomism, in which economic activity was to serve religious and moral needs.

4. The pages above are a brief survey of the economic thinking of several important writers of the period.

They show that men of letters and philosophers also considered wealth a means and not an end, one able to contribute to the reputation of an individual or family, to fame, virtue, political power and so on. In relation to the purposes to be pursued with the instruments of wealth, no great distinction can be drawn between the thinking of these men and those of an earlier period or of others in the same era but from different backgrounds and cultures.

Some differences emerge in relation to the methods for the accumulation of wealth and the intensity with which they should be used. The majority of the thinkers discussed above continue the Scholastic tradition, affirming that the accumulation of wealth must be appropriate to social standing, and spending must similarly correspond to social status.[119] Idleness was condemned by men of let-

---

he should not fear rebellion from them, since the people have pleasure in seeing them in ruin and do not give them succour, that they shall deem half enough. Use the remainder to make a charitable institution, where the poor may go and obtain relief against a pledge, which they shall forfeit if they cannot return the loan at the time agreed».

[116] *Ibid.*, cit., p. 141.

[117] CAMPANELLA, *Aforismi*, cit., no. 102, p. 30.

[118] ID., *Della Monarchia*, cit., p. 142; *Aforismi*, cit., no. 28, p. 16; no. 135, p. 37; no. 145, p. 38.

[119] In relation to spending riches, Croce (G.C. CROCE, *op. cit.*, pp. 65-66) has the astute char-

ters, as were efforts that were considered too strenuous to accumulate wealth. Certain means of obtaining riches were not to be used, such as usury and all activities involving credit. Speroni and Caggio, for example, were of this opinion, although their thinking went beyond the so-called «deadlock» of the medieval conception of the economy, as enshrined in the philosophy of Thomas Aquinas, which inhibited any and all efforts to improve one's economic power.

If Speroni and Caggio had this in common, they differed in their opinion about city versus country life and consequently in their opinion about the market versus the villa. Whilst Speroni sought to fight the tendency of the Venetians to move away from the city and to invest in funds (i.e. land) and villas in the countryside, exalting city life, Caggio and the majority of writers in the sixteenth and early seventeenth centuries thought of agriculture as the most natural means of producing wealth and consequently of life in the country as the ideal. For the historian, the preference for farming over all other economic activities is the most important feature of these texts. As will be shown in Chapter VII, it corresponded to a certain weakening of the mercantile spirit among the ruling class. Decidedly against the grain was a writer like Venusti, who praised trading and did not share the opinion of his horrified contemporaries concerning its injustices, frauds and risks.[120]

It is significant, however, that Venusti does not praise the workings of commerce and industry where carried out directly but only in relation to the managerial skills of the merchant who dedicated himself to overseeing his affairs and his wealth to the greater glory of his friends, Princes and rulers. The craftsman and small trader reselling goods were unworthy of the same respect. In this, Venusti demonstrates an important trait of economic life in Italy during the sixteenth century, preferring to the life of the country the wealth and luxury of the city, whose purpose was to increase the fame and glory of the individual or family who possessed it. Several literary figures were

---

acter of one of his works, say to Alboino: *Whoever measures his state, shall want for nothing.* A saying truly fit for the sixteenth century, when many families squandered their wealth on excess and extravagance. Cf. DAVANZATI, *Le opere*, cit., vol. I, pp. 91-92 (Note on TACITO, Book II of *Annali*, paragraph XLVIII).

[120] Garzoni notes the risks and dishonesty of trading (GARZONI, *op. cit.*, pp. 546-547, 503) and cites the following verses by Vittoria Colonna:

> Quell'altro ingordo d'acquistar thesori
> Si commette al poter del mare infido,
> E di paura pieno e di dolori
> Trapassa hor questo, hora quell'altro lido;
>   E spesso dell'irate onde i romori
>   Gli fan mercè chiamar con alto grido,
>   E quando ha d'arricchir più certa speme,
>   Perde la vita, e la speranza insieme.

themselves merchants: Filippo Sassetti, who praised the trade between the Tuscans and Levantines, and died in Goa, traded in spices,[121] whilst his contemporary, Bernardo Davanzati, wrote from Lyon to his friend Baccio Valori that he was sickened «of the time spent at the bank and of being so occupied in gaining riches». Returning to Florence, he dedicated himself to studies and considerably reduced his business concerns, entrusting his savings to partnerships, a less dangerous way of using his money, albeit not entirely risk-free.[122]

An intellectual in the sixteenth century was therefore likely to feel the pangs of remorse in relation to dedicating his life to making money. Not so others, if Campanella was right in attributing all social and moral ills to the excessive love of money, to such an extent that he proposed sweeping reforms – some realistic, others less so – as the only means for promoting the well-being of the general populace and the State. Hence his defence of merchants and trading, in line with the policies of European rulers.

Campanella was a strong believer in the virtue of work, against the idleness of noblemen, who considered money-making an unworthy occupation and maintained their wealth with frequent recourse to loans from usurers.

In the sixteenth century this phenomenon must have been extremely widespread, if poets sang the praises of debt and debtors as the only path to true happiness.[123]

---

[121] E. MARCUCCI, *Prefazione*, in SASSETTI, *Lettere edite e inedite di Filippo Sassetti*, p. XLI.

[122] Cf. E. BINDI, *Della vita e delle opere di Bernardo Davanzati*, in *Le opere di Bernardo Davanzati*, vol. 1, 1852, pp. XIII-XIV.

[123] Francesco Berni inspired a chapter of *In lode del debito* (In Praise of Debt) (in F. BERNI, *Rime, poesie latine e lettere edite e inedite*, Firenze, Le Monnier, 1885, pp. 144-151), in which he describes the blessed state of those who live on loans. The chapter ends with this warning:

Fate, parente mio, pur de gli stocchi:
Pigliate spesso a credenza, a 'nteresse,
E lasciate ch'a gli altri il pensier tocchi;
Chè la tela ordisce un, l'altro la tesse.

Although this chapter was published for the first time only in 1548, it is very likely that Rabelais knew the playful composition when he wrote Book III of Pantagruel (published in 1546), in which Panurgo sings the praises of debt and debtors (Chapters III and IV). And undoubtedly Muzio Petroni di Trevi used the composition for *Il debitor felice* (The Happy Debtor). We have included it in Italian in the appendix to this volume, since it has never before been published. About Muzio Petroni, G. MORONI (*Dizionario di erudizione storico-ecclesiastica*, Vol. LXXIX, To – Tr, Venezia, Typ. Emiliana, 1856, voce: Trevi, p. 63) wrote: «ancient and truthful historian and patriot, author of the Cronache and Memorie cronologiche di Trevi, mss., about the life and martyrdom of S. Emiliano and his companions, as well as p. Ventura di Trevi, printed in Perugia in 1592 and the life of b. Chiara da Monte Falco, dedicated in 1607 to Cardinal Erminio Valenti and printed in Perugia in 1609». The complete text is given in Italian in the Appendix to this volume.

CHAPTER FIVE

THE THINKING OF JURISTS
ON QUESTIONS OF BUSINESS

1. It may seem futile to seek original economic ideas in the works of six-teenth century jurists, given the almost perfect congruence between their thought and the norms of Roman law which were applied throughout the Middle Ages[1] and had a significant influence on legal doctrine and jurispru-dence in the Modern Age. Undoubtedly, Italian legal texts in the sixteenth and seventeenth centuries – to remain within the scope of our analysis – were inspired by the tradition of Roman law that was temporarily eclipsed during the period of Barbarian invasions but revived thereafter.

Sixteenth century jurists did not limit themselves to annotating Roman law; prompted by events of the times and new social needs, they strove to adapt these ancient norms to the changing economic and legal environment. Their endeavours paralleled those of the Churchmen, who, as seen in earlier chapters, were inspired by Scholastic norms, both in relation to wealth and other phenomena and institutions unknown in the Middle Ages. A typical ex-ample is the sixteenth century legislation on money changing, based almost exclusively on the canonist theory of loans.

In the process of adapting Roman laws, though they remained faithful to the Code of Justinian, a number of jurists adjusted their interpretations to suit this new reality. In criticizing the institutions of the age more or less explicitly, they revealed their view of economics. A number of criminal law jurists, who found in the eminently private sphere of Roman law very few norms to guide and correct human actions in relation to the public good and to public order, sought to de-lineate the principles of the social order, even in the key sector of economic life.

---

[1] For the limited or even totally lacking economic vision of the glossators and post-glossators see the perhaps excessively negative opinion of H.F.W.J. VON SCHEEL, *I concetti economici fondamen-tali del corpus juris civilis*, in *Biblioteca di Storia economica*, edited by V. Pareto, Milano, Società Edi-trice Libraria, 1907, vol. II, p. 736, no. 3.

Nevertheless, the authoritative opinion of Gobbi[2] on the contribution to economic theory of the criminal jurists was rather critical: «they discuss violations relating to duties and other commercial rules of little interest to us, losing their way in the minute details of practical cases without ever considering questions of principle». Gobbi was right in asserting that generally criminal jurists merely presented and analyzed a loosely defined framework of specific cases of human conduct, without formulating a set of principles or a hierarchy of solutions. However, an attentive analysis of these case studies actually reveals the underlying principles that the jurists tended not to make explicit. It is easier to identify economic thought in sixteenth juridical doctrine in the works of the eminent jurist Tiberio Deciani (1509-1582), whose originality distinguished him from the other jurists. This chapter focuses on his economic theory for the reason that his ideas were widely echoed in the works of his contemporaries and the scholars that followed him.

2. While the question of credit was of interest to both theologians and papal law in the sixteenth century, it also attracted the attention of a large number of jurists, and in particular the *scriptores criminalium*. It is very important to ascertain how legal doctrine in the Modern Age dealt with the centuries-old problem of credit, not only because the jurists were an important body of thinkers but also because the courts often turned to doctrine as a definitive source of law.

«Mutuum debet esse gratuitum – asserted Pietro Cavallo, the criminal jurist from Pontremoli – et quidquid accedit sorti, et ad creditorem ultra capitale pervenit, usura est».[3] This coincided exactly with the Canonist view of money lending. Bombino, a jurist from Cosenza, not only condemned the execution of loan contracts, but also asserted that «sola spes lucri usuram committere facit».[4] Giacomo Menochio began his chapter entitled *Foeneratorum poena* with the following assessment: «Foeneratorum pestis omnium pessima est».[5] Many other authors, too numerous to mention here, were of the same opinion.

Of greater interest here is the thinking of a number of jurists in relation to usury, and their attitude to the traditional ban on lending. Specifically, despite

---

[2] Cf. GOBBI, *La concorrenza estera*, cit., pp. 15-16.

[3] P. CAVALLO, *Resolutionum criminalium*, Florentiae, apud M.A. Sermartellium, 1609, p. 226, no. 14.

[4] B. BOMBINI, *Consilia, Quaestiones atque Conclusiones*, Venetiis, apud Franciscum Franciscium Senensem, 1574, p. 144, cons. XX, no. 16.

[5] J. MENOCHI, *De arbitrariis iudicum quaestionibus et caussis, libri duo*, Florentiae, Pectinarius, 1571. Caso 398, p. 456, no. 1.

their acceptance of the centuries – old condemnation of usury and money lending, did the jurists provide a theoretical justification for this practice which was so deeply rooted in economic life. A further, related question concerns the jurists' solution to the question of whether usury was to be prohibited «omni iure», in natural law, «de iure naturali» in divine law «de iure divino» and in canonical law «de iure canonico», excluding only civil law. Today, this type of research would not tell us much about a scholar's personal opinion because legal systems are now separate and well-defined sources and leave no scope for alternative interpretations. This was not the case in the sixteenth and seventeenth centuries, when different legal systems and activities were often intertwined, at times chaotically, making it difficult to ascertain the origin of specific norms and prohibitions.

As a result of all this, sixteenth century authors condoned credit by relegating the ban on usury to natural and canonical law, excluding any origin in civil law. It was not a question of «virtue»: in the sixteenth century some scholars, without conceding that civil law justified the use of credit in the economy, expressed the opinion that: «de iure civili usurae infra legitimum modum sint permissae».

Opposed to this view was Claro, one of the greatest sixteenth century criminal jurists. After presenting his counter arguments, he asserted unconditionally «quod usura apud omnes reputatur res illicita, et prohibita, et sic delictum: et consequenter propter usuram potest quis etiam criminaliter puniri».[6] Similarly, Pietro Follieri, and with him the most eminent criminal jurists of the Modern Age, opined «Usura iure etiam communi prohibita est».[7] So, despite a few objections, in the sixteenth century legal doctrine on credit was based on canonical law. And even jurists who, like the Churchmen, attempted to accommodate the new reality, essentially remained faithful to canonical law. For example, Cavallo believed that a contract, though formally usurious, if based on on uncertainty or risk, became legitimate, as in the case of insurance contracts covering ships or their cargoes.[8] It was always

---

[6] G. CLARO, *Opera omnia; sive Practica civilis, atque criminalis*, Venetiis, apud Baretium Baretium, 1614, pp. 94-95, book V.

For more on Giulio Claro (1525-1575) cf. E. BESTA, *Fonti: legislazione e scienza giuridica dalla caduta dell'impero romano al secolo XVI*, in *Storia del diritto italiano*, edited by Pasquale Del Giudice, Milano, Hoepli, 1925, pp. 114-115.

[7] P. FOLLERIO, *Practica criminalis ... Petri Follerii ... dialogice contexta, secundum dispositionem capitulorum, constitutionum, pragmaticarum, e rituum regni Neapolitani*, Venetiis, Apud Bartholomaeum Rubinum, 1568, p. 281. On the question of punishments, Follerio wrote: «iure autem novo constitutionum regni (di Napoli) usurariis nova poena imponitur: puniuntur etiam pubblicatione omnium honorum».

[8] CAVALLO, *op. cit.*, p. 226, no. 12.

9

the element of risk that legitimized a certain percentage of interest applied by the guarantor, without whose guarantee a third party would not have obtained money from the bankers. This percentage was legitimately collected, even when no damage or harm arose in connection with the guarantee, as compensation for the risk to which the guarantor had exposed himself by guaranteeing to repay the bankers in the event of default by the debtor.[9]

In their endeavours to clarify and justify what appeared to be the demands of the age, the jurists followed ecclesiastical sources, and adhered strictly to Church doctrine when called upon to examine the numerous instances of veiled usury in mercantile practice. For example, Claro dismissed as usurers individuals who lent money to people in need of wheat: the borrowers used the money to purchase wheat, convinced that they had received wheat rather than money from the lender. Such contracts were usurious, observed Claro, because they invariably contained a provision to repay the equivalent value of the goods in the month of May, immediately before the harvest, when prices were highest.[10]

Another instance of veiled usury was the lending of wheat on condition that it be returned when the price was likely to be highest, and it was not allowed for the goods to be returned before that date.[11] Equally usurious were business ventures in which one partner put up capital and in return received the profits without taking on any capital risk.[12] Even more sinister and usurious was the practice of «lo stocco»: selling, for example, a horse and blanket for one hundred and buying them back immediately from the buyer for ninety.[13] Those who bought up wheat to create a shortage were also breaking the law.[14] An execrable crime was committed by speculators or «dardanarii»

---

[9] CAVALLO, op. cit., p. 255. The contract described above was based on «propter incertitudinem, quae in eo versatur, et ad iustificationem, et validitatem eius sufficit, quod ex eo damnum possit provenire» (ibid., no. 5).

[10] CLARO, op. cit., p. 95 t, book V.

[11] Ibid.

[12] Ibid., Bertazzoli is rather lenient in justifying the following contract forming a company: Isacco invested in the company 6000 gold scudi and wished to receive an annuity of 370 scudi, paid from share capital «nitidos ab omni expens, ordinaria, et extraordinaria in pecunia numerata, sive esset factum lucrum ex societate, sive non. Et deinde divideretur lucrum aequaliter inter ipsas partes». Bertazzoli justified this agreement, because it constituted a normal and legitimate partnership agreement based on capital and labour. B. BERTAZZOLI, Consiliorum seu responsorum iuris in criminalibus, Venetiis, Apud Ioannem Baptistam Somaschum, 1583, pp. 245-247. Cons. CLXXXII.
In reality it was a distorted form of partnership, that required an equal distribution of profits.

[13] CLARO, op. cit., p. 96, book V. Cf. chapter II, paragraph IV of the present volume.

[14] Ibid., p. 319.

who purchased commodities and destroyed them to push up the price.[15] Even without the aggravating factor of destroying the goods, Mozzi censured those who hoarded wheat in order to resell it at an inflated price by establishing a monopoly position: «nam si aliquis solus emeret, ut carius venderet postea frumentum, proprie esset monopolium».[16]

This remark reflected the general condemnation of all forms of monopoly by jurists, in the same manner as the Churchmen. Criminal jurists denounced usurious practices in whatever form because, by placing one party in an unwarranted position of superiority, they violated commutative justice. Similarly, they censured acts designed to set the prices at which goods were bought or sold. Naturally the interpretation of what constitued a monopoly varied from one source to another: some jurists were satisfied with the etymological definition, others included all acts and phenomena intended to disrupt the right of any individual to act freely in econonomic life, as enshrined in the theories of Tiberio Deciani, examined below. What is presented here are the views of some of the many scholars concerned with the crime of usury, not merely from a legal persective but also in terms of the economic consequences of monopolistic practices.

Bartolomeo Bertazzoli, like his contemporaries, considered monopoly a crime; however, he accepted that in some circumstances it was necessary to defend one man's interests from unjust harm caused by another. This was the case of the butchers of Ferrara, who, faced with a hefty duty levied by the communal slaughterhouse, agreed among themselves to reduce the number of cattle slaughtered to lessen the impact of the exhorbitant tax. They were accused of monopoly practices and acquitted, noted Bertazzoli, since «etiam prohibita congregatione, vel unione universitatis per statutum, vel decretum, illa tamen non censetur prohibita quae sit ad bonum finem et ad defensionem suarum rerum».[17] This case demonstrates that although Bertazzoli upheld the butchers' cause, his view of monopoly was much broader than that

---

15 P.N. Mozzi, *Tractatus de contractibus Petri Nicolai Mozzii maceratensis*, Venetiis, ex officina Damiani Zenarii, 1585, p. 72, no. 19-20.

16 *Ibid.*

17 [All association prohibited, it is not rejected where its aim is worthy and safeguards one's goods]. Bertazzoli, *op. cit.*, p. 107 and following. G.D. Gaito (*Tractatus absolutissimus de credito, ex libris, epistolis, cambiis, apocis*, Venetiis, apud Iuntas, 1626, p. 141, no. 2329) includes another instance of legitimate monopoly when it is to defend oneself against illicit agreements stipulated beforehand: «Declaratur tamen haec secunda extensio, ut non procedat, si venditores, et campsores, primo loco fecissent monopolium, et emptores vel campsuarii scirent monopolium factum per venditores, et campsores, quia hoc in casu licitum esset emptoribus, et campsariis contrarium monopolium facere inter se, ut nullus nisi certo preciso emat, aut cambio accipiat, quasi vim vi repellentes».

of other jurists who merely examined the schemes of one or more merchants designed to increase prices.

Cavallo also took a very broad view of monopoly. It is worth commenting on a note he added to a court sentence handed down in Siena in 1581. If a Prince allowed a wool guild to legitimately renew their charter, and the guild included in the new charter a clause forbidding a buyer from taking with him to a cloth shop one or more shearers to verify the quality of the wares, was such a clause in the spirit of monopoly? This was a genuine case, and the clause was found to be legitimate, as the theoretical motivations outlined by Tiberio Deciani reveal. Cavallo was less convinced,[18] though he did not hesitate to recognize the legitimacy of pacts that allowed a merchant to prohibit vendors from selling anything but their cloth in a certain place.[19]

Of far greater interest was Cavallo's highly detailed analysis of the sales cartels among glassmakers established in Siena, and his lengthy discussion of the price rises resulting from such agreements.[20] However, since Cavallo was the ruling magistrate in this case, a more detailed summary is given in the next chapter. Here, suffice it to note how some sixteenth century scholars identified a link between monopoly practices and artifical price rises. To be considered just, such price rises had to reflect the «common estimatio»,[21] rather than the sellers thirst for profit. This explains why the jurists tended to censure all forms of monopoly, extending the original concept of monopoly inherited from Justinian tradition. In his *Tractatus absolutissimus De Credito* Gaito included in his discussion of money changing a common monopolistic practice examined briefly below, since it sheds light on the widening gap between the traditional concept of monopoly and the broader economic concept formulated by Deciani that will be presented in due course.

In his analysis of monopolies, Gian Domenico Gaito discussed various definitions, including that of Deciani: «monopolium est quaelibet conventio illicita ad damnum publicum, et ad quaestum privatum; aut magis specialiter, monopolium est conventio plurium mercatorum, bono publico ad eorum privatum quaestum obvians».[22] However, Gaito discarded this definition in favour of a narrower and more formal version: «singularis, et penes unum ven-

---

[18] CAVALLO, *op. cit.*, p. 22, no. 1.

[19] *Ibid.*, p. 22, no. 5.

[20] *Ibid.*, pp. 22-24, no. 8-32.

[21] P. FARINACCI, *D. Prosperi Farinacii I.C. Romani Sacrae Romanae Rotae Decisionum ab ipso selectarum nec unquam alias impressarum tomi quatuor*, Aurelianae Orléans, Sumptibus Viduae & Haeredum Petri de la Rouiere, 1623, p. 198, dec. 170, no. 2.

[22] GAITO, *op. cit.*, p. 140, no. 2304-2305.

ditio, aut singularis in civitate, loco, seu oppido negociatio».[23] In fact, he asserted that monopoly «dupliciter committi solet, nempe authoritate publica scilicet superioris permissu, et authoritate privata».[24] If Gaito had examined Deciani's definition of monopoly in more detail, he would not have justified so readily the monopolies granted by the Prince,[25] because these, like the secret pacts between the merchants,[26] had the potential to harm the public good. Gaito also commented on the sentences handed down to men convicted of monopolistic practices, ranging from the return of «eius, quod supra iustum pretium exegerunt» to the confiscation of their possessions;[27] to a certain extent these sentences resemembled those recommended by scholars for usurers,[28] who were denied church burials, and were not allowed to write a will unless they had returned to their rightful owners the sums obtained through usury «de restituendo usuris».[29] Some scholars even thought it right to evict from church graveyards the bodies of those found to be usurers «non praestitit cautionem de restituendis usuris».[30] Could there have been more perfect agreement between Church rules and the doctrine of the jurists in relation to credit?

Another interesting theme discussed in the works of the jurists was the relationship between nobility and trade. In the sixteenth century, much of population aspired to rise to noble status, which would have entitled them to rest at last after years of toil and suffering. How did the jurists consider this phenomenon?

Bombino asserted that those engaging in trade «non potest esse nobilis». The following claim confirmed his inflexible viewpoint: «etiam si ex militari sanguine esset ortus, quia tunc nobilitatis privilegium amitteret».[31] On the other hand, Farinacci identified the differing criteria applied in different

---

[23] *Ibid.*, no. 2303.

[24] *Ibid.*, no. 2306.

[25] *Ibid.*, no. 2307.

[26] *Ibid.*, no. 2309 and following.

[27] *Ibid.*, no. 2320 and following.

[28] «Usurarius manifestus dicitur ille, qui palam et publicae foeneraticiam artem exercet, ita ut ipsa facti evidentia excusari non possit». CLARO, *op. cit.*, p. 95, no. 15, libro V.
For proof that a certain individual was a usurer cf. I. MARSILI, *Hippolyti de Marsiliis Bononiensis i.v. splendidissimi doctoris ac criminalium studiorum professoris illustrissimi, Elegans et accuratus in titulum. ff. de quaestionibus compilatus commentarius*, Venetiis, al segno della Fontana, 1564, p. 27, no. 4-5.

[29] Cf. CLARO, *op. cit.*, ex libro tertio sententiarum, testamentum, quaestio XXVI, pp. 10-11; libro IV (donatio), quaestio VII, p. 42; book V, p. 95 (Usura). Cf. P. ANCARANI, *Clarissimi iurisconsulti Petri Jo. Ancharani Regiensis Familiarium iuris quaestionum libri tres*, Venetiis, 1580, p. 98.

[30] MARSILI, *op. cit.*, p. 203, no. 151.

[31] BOMBINI, *op. cit.*, p. 381.

towns. «Caeterum diversitas ratio inter mercatorem Florentinum, vel Genuensem, et Notarium Mediolanensem, est notoria, quia ille saepe est de Primariis civitatis, et apud exteros etiam habetur pro nobili. Iste vero (from Milan) etiam in patria distinguitur a primariis nobilibus; et apud exteros, ut plurimum reputabitur non vere nobilis. Denique in illis civitatibus fere omnes mercaturam exercent».[32] He did not express his personal views, and merely asserted that riches increased and preserved nobility, and were a sign of past nobility.[33]

Such was the respect that Bertazzoli showed for the nobility that in judicial proceedings he assumed that noblemen always acted in good faith,[34] and doubted the probative value of evidence against a nobleman accused of usury.[35] More on this aspect can be found in Gaito, who considered trade an important public duty;[36] he also stressed the utility and necessity of money changing, a profession recognised even by Popes,[37] taking us back to the question of whether the nobility was to abstain from trade. Gaito cited the two most commonly held opinions: firstly, that trade was an unworthy activity for nobles; secondly, the less extreme view that there was a difference between trade on a small or large scale, following Cicero.[38] Yet again Gaito did not make his personal opinion known, though he like Cicero appears to have considered trade on a large scale a noble activity. In fact, in their descriptions of the Neapolitan nobility, some jurists commented on the phlegmatic sloth of the nobles who lived off income from their estates, abstaining from their management in the conviction that economic activity and especially trade tarnished the family name.[39] Otalora concurred with this negative assessment of the Neapolitan economic spirit, and provoked a fierce reaction from Gaito. Though he admitted that in Naples, just like any other town,

---

[32] FARINACCI, *op. cit.*, p. 341, dec. 297, no. 9.

[33] [There is a difference between the merchants of Florence, Genoa and Milan. For example, at home, Milanese merchants are distinct from the leading noble families and for those who come from outside the City they are not to be considered true noblemen. Even if in those cities almost all deal in merchandise]. FARINACCI, *op. cit.*, decis. 504, no. 9.

[34] BERTAZZOLI, *op. cit.*, p. 230.

[35] *Ibid.*, p. 322, no. 37.

[36] GAITO, *op. cit.*, no. 993, p. 59. MENOCHIO (*op. cit.*, p. 167) denied that merchants performed a quasi public duty.

[37] GAITO, *op. cit.*, p. 124, no. 2015-2016. The phrase with which Pope Pius V, according to Gaito, recognized the utility of money changing, can be found in the well-known Constitution: *cambiorum usus, quem necessitas publicaque utilitas induxit*.

[38] *Ibid.*, p. 127, no. 2078.

[39] *Ibid.*, p. 128, no. 2104 and following.

some nobles lived a life of leisure, content with the income from their land, and scorned commercial activities,[40] Gaito noted how trade had permitted many other Neapolitans of noble rank to become gradually richer, without ever stooping so low as to give their daughters' hand in marriage to a man whose life was not devoted to noble deeds, or to a merchant without substantial wealth. It was in his assessment of the economic behaviour of his noble neighbours that Gaito revealed his view of commercial activities. Though he praised the large scale trading activities of certain nobles, he could not endorse the customs of those who, to fund the luxuries that ambition and the desire for fame required, indulged in smaller-scale trading activities and deprived the lower classes of this opportunity.[41] This was sufficent to justify the discontent of the poor, Gaito observed. In their works, the jurists briefly discussed a number of the other important questions, relating to wages,[42] the value of money,[43] and the subordination of private utility to the public good.[44] However, it is the economic thought of Deciani, the most original sixteenth century jurist, that is considered here.

3. Tiberio Deciani's fame as an eminent criminal jurist is a recent phenomenon. Until a few decades ago he was well-known to scholars as the author of a *Tractatus criminalis* and as a professor of criminal law at Padua University. Only recently has a systematic reconstruction of his thought highlighted the remarkable importance of the *Tractatus* in the history of legal theory. Indeed, today it seems entirely justified to consider Tiberio Deciani one of the founders of modern criminal science. Though plenty of other *scriptores criminalium e de maleficiis* came before him, he was the first to unify original ideas into within a systematic approach to this vast discipline, and to present a general theory of crime, rivaled only two centuries later.[45]

---

[40] «nonnulli solum eorum (nobles) introitibus contenti exhorrent mercaturam». *Ibid.*, p. 128, no. 2108.

[41] *Ibid.*

[42] According to G.B. MAGONI (*De recta iudicialiter patrocinandi ratione tractatus*, Ticini, apud Petrum Bartolum, 1609, p. 39, no. 25) wages should increase when the workload of the labourer increases. See MENOCHIO (*op. cit.*, p. 304) on the same issue: «Quomodo augeri, vel minui debeat salarium pro modo aucti, vel diminuti laboris».

[43] See the ideas on money of Alberto Bruni in A. GARINO-CANINA, *Il concetto di valore della moneta in Alberto Bruno*, «Giornale degli Economisti», 1935.

[44] Cf. MAGONI, *op. cit.*, p. 182, no. 8.

[45] See the broad study by A. MARONGIU, *Tiberio Deciani (1509-1582): lettore di diritto, consulente, criminalista*, «Rivista di Storia del Diritto italiano», VII, 1934.

F. SCHAFFSTEIN also commented on Deciani in his work: *Die allgemeinen Lehren vom Verbrechen in ihrer Entwicklung durch die Wissenschaft des gemeinen Strafrechts*, Berlin, Springer, 1930

Deciani's Tractatus dealt with crimes against the public economy. His interesting views on economic problems[46] set him apart from his fellow jurists.[47]

Attentive analysis of the chapters entitled *De Monopoliis* and *De fraudantibus aut onerantibus annonam*[48] reveals a number of economic ideas in fragmentary form that nevertheless confirm the originality of his views on questions of wealth.

Deciani began the chapter entitled *De Monopoliis* with a general comment on craft guilds: «Porro quia in collegiis praecipue artificum saepe solent monopolia, et pactiones illicitae fieri in dispendium republicae, et civitates habitantium, ideo de monopoliis hic tractandum duxi».[49]

The guilds were a form of labour organization which changed significantly two centuries later for various reasons. In the sixteenth century the system of craft guilds had become established in almost all Italian cities and in most European countries.[50] Though their peak had passed and they were declining, in the period between the City States and the eighteenth and early nineteenth centuries, craft guilds played an important role. In later centuries, they hindered the growth of industry and commerce in all categories of society. The rise of the City States and the establishment of a supreme central power

---

and more recently in an article: ID., *Tiberius Decianus und seine Bedeutung fur die Entstehung des Allgemeinen Teils im Gemeinen deutschen Strafrecht*, «Deutsche Rechtwissenschaft», 1938.

[46] There is no mention of Tiberio Deciani in GOBBI's well-researched work, *La concorrenza estera e gli antichi economisti italiani* (cit.) and neither in the equally valid: *L'economia politica negli scrittori italiani del secolo XVI-XVII* (cit.).

[47] MARONGIU (*op. cit.*, p. 137) in a brief discussion of monopoly observed: «The crime of monopolies, like all previous ones, had Roman origin and basis. It is recorded by criminologists of the thirteenth and fourteenth centuries in the immense catalogue of criminal species. It was not until Deciani that monopolies were dealt with in the law, public finance and the field of employment, in a clear vision of the problem and of economic principles».

[48] Chapters XXI and XXII of Book VII of T. DECIANI, *Tractatus criminalis D. Tiberii Deciani Utinensis*, Venetiis, apud haeredes Hieronymi Scoti, 1614. References to the Tractatus are made in the text, indicating the book, chapter and paragraph.

[49] *Ibid.*, 1, VII, XXI.

[50] I say most European countries because in the sixteenth century and even before, some more or less liberal economic policies were introduced, in contrast to the prevailing corporatism. A typical example is Switzerland. It has been shown that the earliest industry in Switzerland towards the end of the sixteenth century developed in a climate of freedom. Foreign trade, and mainly free trade, allowed the industries that produced goods for export to avoid corporatist forms of labour organization. See. B.M. BIUCCHI, *Tendenze liberiste nella storia economica svizzera*, «Rivista Internazionale di Scienze Sociali», XLII, 1934.

For further analysis of liberalism in the economic history of the Middle Ages in general, and theoretical approaches see the interesting work by K. HUBER, *Die Anfänge des Liberalismus im Mittelalter*, Leipzig, Voglrieder, 1936, particularly Chapter II (Die Gegenströmungen im Bezirke der Wirtschaft und der Politik).

in the towns and countryside undermined the political influence that the guilds had enjoyed since their origins.[51] The craft guilds responded by granting exclusive rights to manufacture or sell new or luxury goods and by strengthening their territorial control. In this way, entreprenuers and industrialists seeking to compete with other nations were confronted with monopolies, privileges, and special powers granted to social classes, tribunals and trade associations. When industry expressed the need for freedom, in many towns the guilds reacted by enforcing the rules on manufacturing, prices and raw material sourcing that had been written when technology was much more traditional. «To the broadly felt need for freedom in trade and industry, the guilds responded by tightening their privileges, increasing the rigour with which offenders were punished for breaching the old regulations about the amount of raw materials to be used, the loom to be used, the measurements, etc. making registration more troublesome and arbitrary, increasing poverty with the idle and vagabonds, arguing amongst themselves over ridiculous matters and the preeminence of craftsmen, driving up prices through monopolies».[52] Once the motives for which the guilds had been founded and which contributed to their success in the prosperous centuries of the Middle Ages were superceded, they became exclusive and monopolistic organizations that privileged a minority of men and ultimately contributed to economic decline.

It is interesting to note which aspects of life a sixteenth century observer such as Deciani sought to condemn; indirectly, this sheds light on his view of economic life and the assumptions underlying his theory.

Firstly, Deciani censured the closed-shop nature of the craft guilds. Originally they were open, at least in their home town, to all those who wished to engage in that particular trade or profession; with time, they tended to admit only the sons and grandsons of members. Deciani considered this practice a true form of monopoly: «Item monopolium committunt artifices, si paciscantur inter se, ne quisquam eorum in illa arte alios instruat, praeter filios, vel nepotes eorum».[53] Sometimes the guilds became fraternities open only to brothers in arms, as was the case of the notaries. Deciani condemned such practices

---

[51] For more on the weakening and suppression of the political power of the merchant and craft guilds in the Duchy of Milan during the rule of the Visconti and Sforza families, see our analysis in BARBIERI, *Economia e politica nel ducato di Milano*, cit.

[52] R. CIASCA, *Le ragioni della decadenza delle corporazioni medievali*, «Vita e Pensiero», XXV, fasc.V, 1934. This article provides a dense, well-written summary of this important topic. For the efforts made to prevent monopolies in the Middle Ages see the interesting study by A.C. DELIPERI, *Sulle coalizioni o rasse nell'economia e legislazione medioevale sarda*, Sassari, Gallizzi, 1934.

[53] DECIANI, *op. cit.*, 1, VII, XXI, 14.

severely as examples of monopoly.[54] He also criticized the learned men who excluded from their fraternities all those who were neither nobles nor citizens of the town.[55]

Such prohibitions shed light on Deciani's approach to the concept of labour. He asserted that the decision to pursue an economic activity in one's town should not be determined by status, by being the son, grandson or brother in arms of an existing member, by having a noble title or certain political beliefs: admission to a guild or fraternity should be based exclusively on election by free members. In other words, Deciani advocated freedom of labour, and condemned all obstacles posed by statutory norms. Charging an inflated price to teach a profession, or imposing excessively long apprenticeships, were crimes.[56] So when guild statutes continued to lengthen apprenticeships both to bar entry to a trade[57] and to exploit cheap or free labour, clearly Deciani's stance on economic matters ran counter to the corporatist tendencies of his day. And his opposition to such practices can be seen even more clearly in his recommendation: «sic et artifices lanae non possunt statuere, quod unus sit solus locus in civitate, quo purgentur panni».[58] The wool weavers sought to control the production of cloth by preventing its manifacture by anybody except fully-fledged guild members. Deciani condemned such practices as monopoly, on the grounds that industrial activity should not be the prerogative of a limited number of members of this or that guild but should be open to all. Corporatist theory and practice was thus undermined by two new requirements of economic life: industrial freemdom and freedom of labour. This was the first anti-corporatist ideal to be formulated in the history of economic thought.

Deciani condemned the corporatist system on account of its monopolistic tendencies, just as he opposed every other attempt to create privileges in industry and in commerce. Not even the state, he asserted, was entitled to grant

---

[54] *Ibid.*, 1, VII, XXI, 15.

[55] *Ibid.*, 1, VII, XXI, 25.

[56] *Ibid.*, 1, VII, XXI, 16.

[57] Adam Smith also noted, in his critique of the corporatist system, this intent. «The bye-laws of the corporation – Smith writes – regulate sometimes the number of apprentices which any master is allowed to have, and almost always the number of years which each apprentice is obliged to serve. The intention of both regulations is to restrain the competition to a smaller number than might otherwise be disposed to enter into the trade. The limitation of the number of apprentices restrains it directly. A long term of apprenticeship restrains it more indirectly, but as effectually, by increasing the expence of education». Cf. A. SMITH, *An Inquiry into The Nature and Causes of The Wealth of Nations*, Milano, Cofide, 1998, vol., p. 121.

[58] DECIANI, *op. cit.*, 1, VII, XXI, 30.

monopoly rights.[59] Yet in the sixteenth century, states and cities began to regulate certain industries, both to promote them more efficiently and to secure tax revenues.[60] Deciani was very reluctant to justify these forms of state monopoly which he considered legitimate only in cases of extreme need and when, for a short period of time, they brought benefits to all concerned.[61] Apart from these exceptions, Deciani condemned all schemes designed to alter the *ratio naturalis*.[62] Therefore he considered the rule that obliged citizens to take their grain to one mill rather than another a violation of *publica libertas*.[63] Freedom, jeopardized by all the restrictions discussed above, was also undermined by orders that prohibited goods from being sent to a certain place in order to inflate prices.[64]

The freedom that was essential to economic life was undermined by all the rulers who hoarded the basic necessities their subjects required, forcing them to buy such goods from their ministries to increase their own wealth.[65]

This brings us to the question of prices, a topic dicussed by Churchmen and medieval jurists, each from their respective legal points of view. Deciani was not explicitly concerned with fair price, and merely dismissed as illegal all schemes designed to disrupt the natural order that he considered essential for

---

[59] *Ibid.*, 1, VII, c. XXI, 34. As far as we know, no other writer condemned state monopolies and advocated an individualistic economic system, as Deciani did. After him Cavriana (F. CAVRIANA, *Discorsi del Signor Filippo Cavriana, sopra i primi cinque libri di Cornelio Tacito*, Fiorenza, Giunti, 1597, p. 411) opposed monopolies granted by the state, that enable the princes to demand money from one man but made all those who could no longer carry out that trade poorer. Cavriana made an exception for those who introduced a new trade, who deserved not only privileges but also rewards». Cf. GOBBI, *L'economia politica*, cit., pp. 128-129.

[60] For more on these phenomena see: E.F. HECKSCHER, *Il mercantilismo*, Torino, UTET, 1936; P. BOISSONNADE, *Le socialisme d'état: l'industrie et les classes industrielles en France pendant les deux premiers siècles de l'ére moderne (1453-1661)*, Paris, Champion, 1927; R. GONNARD, *Histoire des doctrines économiques*, Paris, Valois, 1930, p. 52 and following, and among the works of J. MAZZEI, *Politica economica internazionale inglese prima di Adamo Smith*, Milano, Vita e Pensiero, 1924 e ID., *Schema di una storia della politica economica internazionale nel pensiero dei secoli 17, 18 e 19*, cit..

[61] DECIANI, *op. cit.*, 1, VII, XX, 4, 5.

[62] *Ibid.*, 1, VII, XXI, 5.

[63] *Ibid.*, 1, VII, c. XXI, 21. Giulio Claro was of the opinion that God could not «possit cogere subditos suos ad molendum in suis molendinis», unless the feudal lord had ius molendinorum through custom or privilege Cf. CLARO, *op. cit.*, c. 74, book IV (Feudum), quaest. XXX.

In an additional comment (*op. cit.*) Geronimo Giacario asserted that if even since time immemorial this custom or privilege had been in force, a ruler could not force his subjects to go to one bakery or one mill «quia in iis quae sunt facultatis non cadit praescriptio». Giacario thus subscribed to Deciani's view; however, while Giacario justified his claim on the basis of a legal norm, Deciani derived his view on the general principal that formed the basis of his ideal economic system.

[64] DECIANI, *op. cit.*, 1, VII, XXI, 12.

[65] *Ibid.*, 1, VII, XXI, 5.

the good of the community. After hoarding, prices were always higher than market prices in normal conditions. Deciani was convinced that by re-establishing the natural order, hoarders would be forced to lower their artificially inflated prices.[66]

There is an interesting detail in the *Tractatus criminalis* relating to price manouvres. In Deciani's day, cartels set the price of various goods at a level beneficial to producers and traders, who also agreed among themselves not to purchase goods at a price above the natural price. Deciani condemned these manouvres reminiscent of modern day price cartels.[67]

On the subject of cartels in the Middle and Modern Ages, considerable historical interest resides in the analysis of industrial coalitions by Pasquale Del Giudice. The primary source of all ordinances and statutes against the coalitions was the Roman law *de monopolis*, which defined the concept of monopoly in such a broad and flexible way that it was extended even to coalitions of workers, and criminal penalities were applicable as a result. In countries with a tradition of Roman law, such as Italy, there was therefore no need for special provisions to prevent coalitions since the jurists had broadened the ancient definition of monopoly to include implicit or explicit agreements between craftsmen.[68] Del Giudice then commented on a passage from the *Tractatus criminalis* in which Deciani condemned all forms of economic agreements that violated the public good, including pacts that fixed the cost of teaching a trade or the length of an apprenticeship when both could be lower. Del Giudice's claim concerning the influence of Roman law on legal provisions relating to cartels in the Middle and Modern Ages was certainly true. Yet it would be mistaken to assert that the focus of Deciani's thought was the condemnation of agreements between firms, following Roman law. He did not censure this or that form of agreement between firms, but rather private or public initiatives designed to disrupt the natural and indivualistic order of manufacturing or trade. He therefore declared illegitimate not only the intrinsically monopolistic agreements between corporations, but also the infinite variety of privileges that the State felt obliged to grant at the height of mercantilism.

A proponent of freedom in industry, labour and trade, Deciani seems to have justified state intervention in the staple food market, particularly in re-

---

[66] *Ibid.*, 1, VII, c. XXI, 18.

[67] *Ibid.*, 1, VII, XXI, 6, 7, 20.

[68] Cf. P. DEL GIUDICE, *Studi di storia e diritto*, Milano, Hoepli, 1889, pp. 94-95 (*Le coalizioni industriali dirimpetto al progetto del codice penale italiano*).

lation to questions of price. He was well-acquainted with the practice of hoarding, and the terrible famines it caused, so he accepted that those in charge of staple food markets should have the power to oblige the rich to sell a certain quantity of grain at the market price even in the absence of famine. In times of urgent need, those with plentiful supplies of grain should be obliged to sell at below the market price.[69] This assertion is surprising, suggesting that Deciani supported the misguided political policies designed, in times of famine, to lower the price of grain with the utopistic aim of ending the shortage. In reality, Deciani intend simply to normalize the price of grain, inflated by hoarding or famine. None of his other prescriptions concerning the prices of staple foods influenced his framework of economic and commercial freedom.[70]

Deciani's final observation on commerce is worth noting. Merchants who entrusted the sale of their wares to an agent, with an obligation not the sell the goods of others for a certain period of time, were not guilty of monopoly. What is significant about this position is the motivation «quia pactum cum uno tantum factum non tollit libertatem publicam»,[71] which furthers our understanding of Deciani's economic theory. He was persuaded that the best possible economic order was a spontaneous one established in a climate of freedom. He considered all forms of artificial intervention in economic life detrimental to the public good; conversely, the efforts of individuals involved no particular risk, since acting singly they were unable to influence an entire market to their own advantage.

4. Detailed analysis of the cases described by Deciani in the previous paragraph reveal the fundamental principle underlying all his ideas. He departed from a very narrow, technical concept of monopoly (*monopolium dicitur, cum penes unum tantum alicuius rei vendendae potestas est*),[72] and included in this category of crime all actions undertaken by merchants for their own private gain that were detrimental to the public good.[73] In this way, he observed a broad range of economic phenomena with pioneering insight. Deciani noted, as the Ancients had done before him, how monopoly allowed the monopolist to maximize revenue. Typical examples were Thales and the Sicilian hoarder

---

[69] DECIANI, *op. cit.*, 1, VII, c. XXII, 24.

[70] *Ibid.*, 1, VII, XXII, 1, 2, 5, 22, 23, 36, 37.

[71] *Ibid.*, 1, VII, XXI, 27.

[72] *Ibid.*, 1, VII, XXI, 1.

[73] *Ibid.*, 1, VII, XXI, 9. Cf. the value of Deciani's concept in DEL GIUDICE, *op. cit.*, p. 95.

of iron banished by Dionysus.[74] Though the profits of a monopolist were «uberrimus e paratissimus» Deciani argued in favour of the eradication of all forms of monopoly, in employment, industry and commerce.

The principle with which Deciani justified his economic vision was: «Sunt enim monopolia contra rationem naturalem, quia praecludunt viam benefaciendi proximo, cum omnes negociari prohibeantur, et qui illa exercent, non tantum non benefaciunt, sed nocent proximo».[75] In other words, he conceived an economic order in which individuals enjoyed the utmost freedom in employment, in their choice of profession and in the production of goods, on condition that they respected the rights of others. In fact, the creation of a monopoly, in whatever form, increased the profit of one individual at the expense of the freedom and the good of all others. Such a situation of tyranny that disrupted economic life, in which the supply of staple goods depended on the greed and free will of a few men, had to be eradicated.[76]

Deciani also opposed all other artificial intervention in economic life. As an advocate of freedom of labour, he condemned corporatism precisely because it violated such a right. As a proponent of industrial freedom, he declared illegitimate statutes and other rules that undermined it. Not even the state should distort economic life by granting monopolies. In relation to prices, in general Deciani deemed legitimate only those that were not artifi-

---

[74] DECIANI, op. cit., 1, VII, XXI, 2, 3. Tiberio Deciani confirmed his observation on the relationship between supply, demand and price by citing two episodes from Aristotle's Politics (1. I, c. 4). One concerned a Sicilian who having a sum of money put aside, bought up all the iron from the workshops; and then, the merchants came to him, he sold it without raising the price excessively: nevertheless, claimed Aristotle, he earned 100 talents from 50 (Cf. the acute observations on the link between the interests of the monopolist and the price level C. OPERANS, Come nacque e morì la corporazione cittadina, «Rivista di Storia del Pensiero Economico», II, 1935, pp. 73-74).

The second episode is far better known than the first. Deciani recalled, slightly inaccurately, the case of the famous philosopher Thales of Miletus, who on account of his poverty was mocked by the people, who taunted him by asking why his philosophy couldn't come to his aid. Thales predicted a bumper olive crop, and bought all the olive presses in his town and in Chio at a good price, there being no competition. After the harvest, he was able to sell the presses at any price he wanted, there was so much demand. Thales thus came to be considered a forerunner of those who construct and exploit economic barometers today. Cf. FANFANI, Storia delle dottrine economiche, cit., p. 27.

In relation to hales, E. CANNAN (Rassegna della teoria economica, in Storia delle Teorie, Torino, UTET, 1932, p. 2) somewhat inappropriately undermines the importance of this episode in the history of economic thought. After describing the philosophers actions, Cannan concluded: This, however, does not prompt in him any economic reflection about the power of monopolies; he observes only that Thales «demonstrated to the world in this way that philosophers could easily become rich if they so desired, but their leanings lay elsewhere».

This claim was inaccurate considering that four centuries ago Tiberius had cited Thales as an example of the higher profits that a monopolist could earn.

[75] DECIANI, op. cit., 1, VII, XXI, 5.

[76] Ibid., 1, VII, XXI, 3.

cially influenced by groups of merchants or by pacts among them. If a single merchant wished to set a much higher price than his competitors, he was at liberty to do so provided he did not harm the public good.

The public good was a constant in all the norms and observations cited above. Deciani believed that the public good could be achieved only in a climate of freedom. Indeed, in the chapter entitled *De Monopoliis*, he conceived an economic world in which the sole actors were individuals, groups and the state being excluded due to their power to divert the natural economic order.

The importance of Deciani's vision in the history of economic thought and of economic ideals emerges clearly from this brief discussion. Living in the age of mercantilism, when industry and commerce had taken on a political function, he argued that economic life should be based on the actions of individuals who could freely choose and exercise their profession or trade. When monopolies, privileges and closed corporations became the dominant forces in the economy, Deciani denounced all forms of association and agreement. In relation to prices, with very few exceptions, he excluded all forms of government intervention and all cartels or other agreements, in the conviction that the best, most advantageous price was spontaneously determined. Was this vision, in contrast with the theory and practices of his day and age, an embryonic form of the naturalistic theories that were to emerge in the eighteenth century? The author believes that Deciani embraced the principles of economic naturalism, rather than the practice and theory of his day. It is important to clarify the meaning of *ratio naturalis*, a concept Deciani often cited in his *Tractatus*, particularly in the chapters discussed above, to justify his approach to questions of wealth. Deciani's concept of *ratio naturalis* should be compared with that of the Churchmen and the natural law of the Physiocrats. The Scholastic tradition envisaged two economic orders: as it was and as it should be. The latter, which formed the basis of medieval economic theory, was termed «natural» by the Scholastic theologians, in the sense of an ideal order that could be achieved by overcoming the basest instincts of men and adapting the resources of the physical world to the needs of spiritual life. In other words, a voluntaristic econonomic order, exemplified by the rules relating to the question of wealth.[77] Natural law, or the natural order of the Physiocrats, envisaged an economy that was the outcome of the free workings of the forces of nature, and excluded any form of human intervention by autho-

---

[77] Cf. FANFANI, *Storia delle dottrine economiche*, cit., p. 62; ID., *Caratteri delle regole in materia economica dettate dagli scolastici medievali*, «Rivista di Filosofia Neo-scolastica», XXIV, fasc. III, 1932; ID., *Le origini*, cit., chapters I e III.

rities or groups of men. For the Scholastic theologians, just like the Physiocrats, the natural order represented the best possible system. Having said this,
the question is whether Deciani's *ratio naturalis* coincided with the natural order of the Scholastic theologians or the economists, or at least which of the
two it was closer to.

Deciani's natural order did not perfectly match either. In the *Tractatus*
there is no trace of the religious and spiritual elements that shaped the ideal
economic order of the Scholastic theologians, or at least in Deciani's observations and rules relating to economic activity. There is no clear link between
Deciani's natural order and that of the Physiocrats either, given that the latter
based their theory on the certainty that the natural order was not only the
most perfect system that existed, but also one that could not be permanently
changed by men. Conversely, Deciani identified the natural order with the
public good, to achieve which he outlined a set of rules governing economic
life, in what was virtually a positive order.

Though Deciani did not elaborate an explicitly naturalistic principle in the
Tractatus, the economic world he conceived, in contrast to the one in which
he lived, was very close to the economic order of the Physiocrats. Always the
ultimate goal, the public good was best pursued when political intereference
in economic life was minimal. Deciani's criticism of the monopolistic tendencies of the craft guilds and merchant corporations was closer to the proponents of liberalism than the Scholastic theologians, for whom the Church,
the state and the corporations ensured compliance with the rules that made it
possible to arrive at their ideal order of economic life. What is more, the economic rules embodied in the *Tractatus* were almost exclusively negative, both
in their form (given the specific nature of the text), and in their content. In the
construction of his ideal economic world, Deciani did not call for this or that
action in this or that direction: he required men not to act, not to intervene in
economic life, not to manipulate prices and not to hinder the free movement
of labour or goods. This applied to the State, to corporations and to groups of
merchants, all of whom he wished to exclude from economic life, to leave
scope for the efforts of individuals.

No other sixteenth-century or medieval work placed such emphasis on the
individual, specifically in terms of their economic power. Deciani's social
thought combined individualism with freedom, upon which the public good
depended. His apparently fragmented set of economic norms and observations were based on this one principle. His anti-corporatist stance was not dictated by empirical, political and cicumstantial considerations, but rather a
well-defined principle of freedom that, Deciani argued, should regulate all aspects of commercial life.

After Deciani, in France and in other states, and only much later in Italy,[78] the system of corporations came under attack, and ultimately the guilds were abolished. Subsequent criticism, such as Alberti's work on the arts and crafts guilds, *Corporazioni d'Arti e Mestieri*,[79] was far more detailed. What is significant is that Deciani was the first to condemn the corporatist movement, without all the exceptions raised by other authors in the endless disputes over the desirability of craft guilds; Deciani did so in the name of one principle: the public good.

By placing Deciani's ideas within the context of his lifetime and the historical moment, the motives underlying his economic theories can be better understood. He was not only a distinguished professor of law at Padua University; before and after taking up the chair, he participated actively in community life. He was a sought-after lawyer and consultant, and wrote five volumes of *Responsa* a testament to the large variety of circumstances and social relations which, he examined in the light of juridical principles. His experience of life was deepened by his involvement in politics. On several occasions he was sent as ambassador to the Venetian Republic to negotiate and defend the rights of his fellow citizens. On one occasion, faithful to the economic principles he professed, he complained to the Venetian government about the heavy duties imposed on trade in cloth and silk. He was Vicar General in the the towns of Vicenza, Padua and Verona, at the service of Lorenzo and Francesco Veniero, and Bernardo Navagero. Therefore, he was perfectly acquainted with the spirit of his day, its virtues and its shortcomings.[80] These details of Deciani's life justify the following conclusions.

Anyone commenting on social behavior over time, like Deciani in the *Tractatus* and the *Responsa*, would have observed that many men tried to increase their wealth to the detriment of others, by exploiting privileges and monopolistic practices that inflicted great hardship and suffering on the weakest members of society.[81] In the name of justice, a concept that tran-

---

[78] Consider that in 1670 O. MONTALBANI published a work whose title reveals its subject matter: *L'honore dei collegi dell'arti della Città di Bologna, brieve trattato fisicopolitico e legale storico*, Bologna, Benacci, 1670. Not only is there no mention of freedom of labour, but it is also claimed by some that the peaceful and virtuous union of Guilds is far from menacing to others.

[79] The full title of the work by is: G. ALBERTI, *Le corporazioni d'arti e mestieri e la libertà del commercio interno negli antichi economisti italiani*, Milano, Hoepli, 1888.

Note that Alberti discusses at length the ideas of foreign writers on corporations, and cites the most important laws relating to the guilds, up to their abolition.

[80] For a more in-depth discussion, see the study by MARONGIU, *op. cit.*, pp. 5-29.

[81] This phenomenon is mentioned in the *Tractatus* (1, VII, XXI, 3), where Deciani underlines that the life means of entire populations should not depend on the free will and greed of a handful of men. Paolo Segneri expressed the same sentiments: see chapter one, paragraph three and my note. I have discussed the function of economic goods following Paolo Segneri, in «Convivium», no. 6, 1935.

spired from every line of the *Tractatus*, Tiberio Deciani condemned monopolies and corporations, and invoked freedom. Such freedom, however, was to be compatible with the public good and with justice in social life. His concept of individualism was not intended to disaggregate society, but rather to prevent abuses by corporations, merchants and Princes who violated social justice.

5. Just a few comments are necessary to complete this brief analysis of the contribution made by the jurists to economic theory and ideals.

Above all it is important to underline the perfect harmony between the solutions of the Churchmen and those of the jurists in relation to certain key phenomena such as credit and monopoly. The medieval doctrine of fair price was confirmed by the sixteenth century jurists who, like the Churchmen, condemned the efforts of one or more merchants to create conditions or situations of privilege detrimental to the collectivity. This aspect was analyzed in depth by Tiberio Deciani, whose conclusions anticipated the theories of economic liberalism. He criticized the institutions of economic life, and argued that the collectivity would benefit only from an economy based on freedom of labour, industry and commerce. He followed Guidiccioni and Guicciardini in their criticism of monopolies granted by the State, and argued that intervention in economic life should be very limited, justifying monopolies only when they were truly necessary for the public good. For the same reason he distanced himself from the voluntarists, and supported the concept of a natural order of economic life.

The jurists were among the early proponents of economic naturalism. Just like other categories of scholars, they jurists frequently made reference to «rebus sic stantibus», heralding the onset of systematic methods of enquiry. One of the first systematic jurists was Giacomo Menochio,[82] and it is with his view on the compensation due to workers injured or debilitated and thus made unfit for work that we wish to conclude this chapter. Obviously, Menochio stated, workers were entitled to compensation, the question was how much. He maintained that compensation should be based on

---

The disastrous economic and social consequences of monopolies were highligthed by DA CASLINO (*op. cit.*, pp. 43-44). First of all he defined a monopoly as something: «which is done as follows: some Merchants come together and make an agreement not to sell or buy goods and merchandise except at this or that price, as determined by them, against all charitable laws and the public weal». Against such schemes, obseved Caslino «even Human Laws suffer great pains, sicne they are the destroyers of districts and several may destroy a whole city».

[82] MENOCHI, *op. cit.*, p. 198, no. 3.

the economic condition of those who injured the worker, as well as the worker's status and means,[83]

This example would have been more fruitful if Menochio had been able to address the problem of injuries sustained in the workshop. But labour organization in his day did not provide the jurist with sufficient elements to do so. However, it is interesting to note that in his discussion of the general question of compensation, he chose an example of what was later to constitute an industrial accident.

---

[83] *Ibid.*, p. 198.

CHAPTER SIX

THE ECONOMIC SPIRIT OF THE LAWS

1. The previous chapters have touched on the opinions of jurists in relation to wealth and on some laws concerning the problem of wealth creation. This chapter revisits these ideas in depth, due to the light they shed on the ideal economic order in Italy and the compliance of the Italian population.

This chapter on the economic ideals of the sixteenth and seventeenth centuries reinforces what was stated at the beginning of Chapter II in relation to Church laws on business. The economic aspirations of the various categories in Italian society in the Modern Age are certainly of enormous historical interest. Of even greater interest, however, is the thinking behind the laws governing the economy, because these – more than the ideals expressed by individual writers and thinkers – exercised a considerable influence over practical business matters, due to the penalties and sanctions that were inflicted (obviously beyond the powers of writers and thinkers, however important). Even the many statutes and laws in the cities and States into which Italy was at that time divided, indicate an approach to work and idleness that reflected the thinking of practical men. Of specific interest here is the behaviour of these men, in so far as their economic mentality reveals a great deal about the not very prosperous life of industry and commerce from the sixteenth century onwards. This chapter therefore completes the previous chapter on Church regulations on the economy and the economic ideal enshrined in legislation, and further investigates the economic spirit of the period and its repercussions on the acquisition and use of wealth.

Before turning to the laws which enshrine the ideals of economic life that inspired the actions of Italians, it is important to mention the laws issued by the Vatican, focusing specifically on economic laws rather than the regulations governing the life of the Christian tout court, which have already been illustrated. To clarify the section on the position of the Jewish community, it is important to show its role in the provision of credit in the sixteenth and seventeenth centuries, since the practice of loans, as conceived and carried out at the time, is a clear symptom of a sick economy.

2. The idea that work was the proper means for acquiring wealth and simultaneously a moral duty – emphasized throughout these pages – derived from the Church regulations on economic life. Civil laws also considered work an unavoidable duty, and the penalty for idleness was expulsion from the city or the various hospices of the city in which the idle took refuge, simulating illness and infirmity. To counteract this phenomenon, in 1557, the Governor of Rome ordered out of the city all those without stable possessions, work or a profession.[1] In the same year the Prefect responsible for rations in Rome expelled the gypsies, giving them two days to abandon the territory.[2] Similarly, Antonio de Leyva expelled beggars and the unemployed from Milan.[3]

A radical measure was adopted in 1542 in Montepulciano, following provisions introduced by Cosimo I, establishing public charity in order to eliminate the abuses of «those who seek alms to avoid toiling».[4] These brief examples indicate that idleness was not tolerated and that work was considered necessary and virtuous, whilst begging was deemed a form of dishonesty. Theft[5] was unlawful, of course, as was alchemy – severely prohibited in Venice and throughout the State – punished by imprisonment for one year.[6]

Alchemy suggests the idea not so much of making a scientific discovery as of taking a painless short cut to riches. Another such route was gambling, for many a steady source of income. The previous chapters have already shown how widespread gambling was amongst women no less than men. It was another way of making a small fortune without the bother of work. In 1521, in Milan, a measure was introduced to fine gamblers twenty-five gold ducats, plus two lashes. The measure stipulated that no-one was to «dare make bets or play forbidden games or gamble or allow others to do so at home».[7] Just

---

[1] *Regesti di bandi, editti, notificazioni e provvedimenti diversi relativi alla città di Roma ed allo stato pontificio*, Roma, Cuggiani, 1920, p. 26, no. 156.

[2] *Ibid.*, p. 26, no. 161.

[3] ASM, *Panigarola Statuti*, Registro no. 27 (PP), c. 67 t-68t.

[4] Cf. P. TACCHI VENTURI, *Storia della Compagnia di Gesù in Italia*, Roma-Milano, Albrighi-Segati-Civiltà cattolica, 1910-1922, vol. I, p. 360.

[5] Cf. P. MOLMENTI, *La storia di Venezia nella vita privata*, Bergamo, Istituto Italiano di Arti Grafiche, 1926, vol. II, pp. 23, 446.

[6] *Statuti di Peschiera*, ms. della BNM (AD._XIII.44), c. 22 t. 23.
This Codex was handed over to Gerolamo Quirino in 1559 by the Doge of Venice, Lorenzo Priuli, when he was appointed Governor [provveditore] of Peschiera on behalf of the Republic.

[7] ASM, *Panigarola Statuti*, Registro no. 16 (P).

three years later, the provision needed to be revised,[8] not very effectively, it would seem, since in 1530 the penalties were futher increased.[9] In Bologna, too, the passion for gambling was so strong that cards were played and dice thrown not only in private houses but also in the streets. In 1581, the Papal Legate prohibited gambling altogether.[10] In 1588, the Pope imposed a heavy duty on playing cards and prohibited all games involving dice.[11] It wasn't only in the big cities that gambling was a mania, but also in small towns, where fines were introduced, as in Senigallia, where the Captain of the Port was allowed by the local statutes to fine gamblers one florin of new money for playing at *zara* or allowing it to be played in his house.[12]

It was not possible to eradicate the passion for gambling and it proved difficult even to control it. In Rome, for example, people bet on the strangest and most unthinkable things. In the second half of the sixteenth century it must have been very common to bet on the sex of a baby due to be born, since the Governor of Rome imposed a penalty of 100 gold scudi and three lashes for offenders.[13] Eleven years later the Treasurer General prohibited any form of «lottery or game of fortune», except where a special licence was granted.[14] The measure indicates the popularity of lotteries and games.[15] After this, it became necessary to introduce regulations to prohibit another invention of the imaginative population of Rome: betting on the appointments of Cardinals, punishable after 1587 with a fine of 500 scudi in the case of nobility, five years imprisonment for craftsmen, and life imprisonment for Jews.[16] The Governors of Rome[17] were extremely strict in enforcing the law and other regulations prohibiting betting on the life, death and election of Popes.[18] Some tolerance was required in the case of other bets, such as the gender of a child. Finally, Cardinal Camerlengo Enrico Caetani regulated

---

[8] *Ibid.*, Registro no. 16 (P).

[9] *Ibid.*, Registro no. 27 (PP).

[10] Cf. L. Frati, *La vita privata in Bologna dal secolo XIII al XVII*, Bologna, Zanichelli, 1928, p. 110.

[11] *Ibid.*

[12] M. Mariani, *Lo statuto senigalliese dell'anno 1537*, «Le Marche», IV, 1910, p. 175.

[13] *Regesti di bandi*, cit., p. 67, no. 416 (20 March 1578). For betting in the Middle Ages on the sex of children yet to be born cf. Fanfani, *Le origini*, cit., p. 81.

[14] *Regesti di bandi*, cit., p. 79, no. 485 (17 January 1586).

[15] *Ibid.*, p. 83, no. 509 (8 Nov. 1586).

[16] *Ibid.*, p. 87, no. 533 (10 September 1587). A few days later the ban was repeated (*op. cit.*, p. 88; no. 536, 17 September 1587).

[17] *Ibid.*, p. 93, no. 571 (2 September 1588); no. 585, 28 December 1588; p. 102, no. 627, 27 December 1589.

[18] *Ibid.*, p. 104, no. 645 (21 March 1591).

these bets, appointing two agents to receive and make records of the wagers.[19] The reason was to «gratify the populace of Rome», so these bets were certainly very widespread and were considered a quick and easy way of making money.[20] At the same time, the law was evidently deviating from its original function of enshrining an economic ideal.

If gambling was prohibited as corrupting the material, moral and spiritual order, of course the law established even more severe punishments for theft, lying, fraud and so on. Perhaps the most serious crime of this sort was debasing coins, painting them or otherwise falsifying money. Counterfeiting coins was a very serious crime in all Italian cities and regions. In Valtellina, for example, the counterfeiters of gold and silver coins were branded with fire.[21] And this was not the worst penalty, because everywhere – as Cavallo observed «monetam tondens, radens, vel aliter minuens, ut sit minoris ponderis, si liber est, ad bestias damnatur, si servus, ultimo supplitio punitur».[22] He says that the same fate befell «qui monetas tingunt de argento, vel auro, aut quia sint de argento, tingunt de auro, ut appareant argentae vel aurae».[23]

Bearing false testimony was also severely punished. As were «giuntatores euntes per civitates, et terras et diversas mundi partes vendendo gemmas falsas, et minimi valoris magno pretio, fingendo eas fuisse derobatas alicui Principi, vel Nobili, et certo modo ad eorum manus pervenisse» who were handed out more severe punishments than for common thieves.[24] In relation to theft and embezzlement, it appears that the wool workers of Fabriano had the habit of making off with the raw materials entrusted to them by merchants. The Statutes sought in vain to combat this risk.[25] In Valtellina, in addition to heavy fines, many lashes were inflicted for theft.[26] Nor did the Romans have any

---

[19] *Ibid.*, p. 100, no. 615 (31 July 1589).

[20] Cf. CLARO, *op. cit.*, p. 82 and following. Baiardo says to Claro in an aside: «Item adde, quod ludus permittitur tempore pestis, ad effugiendas malenconicas cogitationes». *Ibid.*, p. 83, no. 5.

[21] *Li Statuti di Valtellina riformati*, Poschiavo, B. Massella, 1668, p. 191. See also MARIANI, *op. cit.*, pp. 189-195.

[22] [Those who alter coin, if he is a free man, let him be given to the beasts, and if he is a servant let him suffer the ultimate penalty]. CAVALLO, *op. cit.*, pp. 394-395.

[23] *Ibid.* Naturally, the penalties for counterfeiting money varied according to the currency, the conditions of the falsifier and the customs of the city. Cf. CLARO, *op. cit.*, p. 33, no. 308.
Pope Pius V, for example, upheld the death sentence only for falsifiers of gold and silver coins. Cf. *Regesti di Bandi*, cit., p. 55, no. 343 (25 October 1570).

[24] CAVALLO, *op. cit.*, p. 366.

[25] A. ZONGHI, *Statuta artis lanae terrae Fabrianae (1369-1674)*, in *Documenti storici Fabrianesi*, Roma, Rossi, 1880, p. 82 (in the year 1568). For the flight of workers, see G. BARBIERI, *Controversie del lavoro nel secolo XVII: il pagamento del salario*, «Rivista di Scienze Economiche», 1940.

[26] *Li Statuti di Valtellina*, cit., p. 183.

greater respect for property on the occasion of the illness or death of a Pope, whose possessions, at such times, were regularly plundered. Pope Pius IV sought to end this deplorable custom in 1560 when he ordered everyone who had ransacked the Pope's lodgings to return what they had stolen to Francesco Odiscalchi.[27] Naples was another city where theft was common, so much so that a law stipulated that sales contracts could only be made by parties who knew each other. Florence followed the example in 1562.[28]

But, setting aside theft for a moment, there were other ways of gaining riches without having to endure the hardship of honest work. Bakers in Senigallia were obliged to carry out their profession *bene fideliter et sine fraude*,[29] and shopkeepers dealing in spices in Savona invited the Console to inspect their merchandise to verify its condition and authenticity.[30] Where dishonesty was most manifest in shopkeeping was in the use of weights and measures. Statutes and by-laws the length and breadth of Italy sought to combat abuse in this area, but the sheer number of provisions suggests that it was a losing battle. And in Milan, in 1490 the Vicar of Provisions, in the knowledge that it was often impossible to look into shops because of the use of thick blinds «ita ut facilius decipi possint emptores», ordered that the entrances be kept clear.[31] In subsequent years provisions were made to prevent drapers measuring cloth on benches covered with cloth or other materials, to stop the shopkeeper selling less merchandise than he had claimed to measure off.[32] In 1508, further provisions were introduced in the light of the fact that outsiders often found themselves cheated of the amount of fabric they believed they had bought and were forced to buy still more «to the great shame of the city».[33] Nor did the regulations designed to ensure the honesty of shopkeepers end there, since Milan and other cities introduced new by-laws over the following decades.[34]

---

[27] *Regesti di bandi*, cit., p. 29, 3 April 1560.

[28] Cf. A. PERTILE, *Storia del diritto italiano*, Torino, UTET, 1896-1902, vol. IV, pp. 555-556.

[29] MARIANI, *op. cit.*, pp. 172-173.

[30] G. FILIPPI, *Statuti dell'Arte degli Speziali in Savona del 1592*, Savona, Tip. Bertolotto, 1890, p. 25. See CAVALLO for comments on goods gone bad, *op. cit.*, p. 141.

[31] ASCMi, *Dicasteri*, envelope 219/5, Reg. Provv. (1451-1493), c. 184-185 (24 May 1490).

[32] ASM, *Panigarola Statuti*, Reg. n. 24 (FF), c. 199-200 (24 May 1506).

[33] ASCMi, *Dicasteri*, envelope 220/7, R. Provv. (1505-1513), c. 62 e t (28 February 1508).

[34] Cf. ASM, *Panigarola Statuti*, Registro no. 25 (GG), c. 604 t-608 (20 March 1510); ASCMi, *Dicasteri*, envelope 220/7, R. Provv. (1505-1513), c. 105 t-106, 20 March 1510; *ibid.*, Reg. Provv. (1514-1523), c. 252 e t (23 June 1522); *ibid.* (11 July 1522); MARIANI, *op. cit.*, p. 169; *Statuti del Paratico delli Tessitori di tele de lino della Mag. Ca città et Principato di Pavia*, manuscript of BNM, location AD._XIV.2, chapter 74.

Another way of making money illegitimately was selling at the wrong price. The purchaser would obtain little benefit from the proper use of weights and measures if the price of the cloth was set too high. A number of regulations sought to control the market for and the value of merchandise, salaries and profits. If in Por Santa Maria, a small Adriatic town, the Captain *super vectualibus* tried to ensure that bread, cheese, oil, salted meat and fodder were not sold *ultra debitum*,[35] the town statutes established a maximum fee for commercial agents of one dinar and half a florin, prohibiting any other gift or payment.[36] In Milan, in October 1524, following the outbreak of plague, Francesco II Sforza sought to prevent prices from rising. On that occasion, to safeguard the interests of workers, he ordered merchants and entrepreneurs who «must sell their goods at a just and honest price, and with this edict, all shopkeepers shall reduce the price of their merchandise which shall be sold at the honest price and not a penny more».[37] In some circumstances, given the general increase in prices, the government of the Duchy ordered the increase of salaries in line with the higher price level and controlled them during periods of price stability.[38]

Particular mention should be made of trade in grain, which attracted the attention of speculators and where governments were forced to introduce a series of regulations to ensure fair prices and its continuous supply to subjects. In this connection, the authorities for food rationing oscillated between prohibiting trading in grain and total free trade, which was sometimes considered damaging and disadvantageous to the public good. In Florence, for example, one statute included the provision: *De non emendo granum vel hordeum causa revendendi* prohibiting the resale of grain, with severe penalties for offenders. «Fines and lashes, relegation, confiscation, prison; death and even rewards offered for murdering a hoarder, these are the penalties introduced by the ruling Medici family in 1591 and on 23 September 1625, subsequently repealed

---

The provisions regarding the measuring of cloth were only for retailers: which in 1510 caused some members of the profession to complain. In fact the regulations «do not mention drapists and it is not good that only the retailers need to obey them whilst others have freedom to do as they please». So «to be fair and even all others who have merchandise to sell, particularly silk and so on, should be ordered not to obstruct the vision of these goods». Cf. ASCMi, *Dicasteri*, envelope 220/7, Reg. Provv. (1505-1513), c. 106, 20 March 1510.

[35] MARIANI, *op. cit.*, p. 173.

[36] *Statuti dell'arte di Por Santa Maria del Tempo della Repubblica*, ed. by U. Dorini, Florence, Olschki, 1934, p. 761 (year 1525).

[37] ASCMi, *Dicasteri*, envelope 220, Reg. Provv. (1524-1531), c. 30 (5 October 1524).

[38] In this regard, see our study: BARBIERI, *Economia e politica nel ducato di Milano*, cit., p. 113 and following.

and replaced by others on 17 August 1618, 14 September 1633 and 22 June 1687, establishing a free market in grain».[39] The Statutes of Peschiera prohibited the purchase of grain for the purpose of resale,[40] and the Rector of the small town on Lake Garda had the obligation to inspect grain in the production sites and to notify the government of the Serenissima Republic of the expected quantity.[41]

This demonstrates how fiercely the Serenissima Republic sought to control food rationing. Very different was its attitude in the short period from 1590-91, years of grain scarcity. First, the Government sought to use old systems, but these proved inadequate and «soon it allowed things to go as they pleased, to the benefit of all».[42] The Vatican similarly fluctuated between severe controls and total freedom,[43] whilst in Sicily, despite severe disadvantages, grain was never allowed to be subject to the free market.[44]

It seems the food rationing system adopted in Sicily discouraged the production of grain and therefore damaged agriculture, the principal source of wealth for citizens. Elsewhere, farming was encouraged by the law. For example, the government of the Serenissima Republic prohibited creditors from accepting a pledge on the animals needed for farming.[45] Without mentioning other cities, the example of the agricultural policy of the Papal States, from the Middle Ages through to the sixteenth and seventeenth centuries may suffice: in 1566 the Pope ratified new statutes for farmers,[46] based on an appreciation of work on the land, producing abundant grain, and the reclamation of land from marshes and swamps, increasing the amount of arable land.[47] The condition of farmers in Orvieto, Monteleone, Castel della Pieve and Ficulle attracted the attention of Pope Gregory XIII, who started land reclama-

---

[39] V. Cusumano, *La teoria del commercio dei grani in Italia: studi storici*, Bologna, Tip. Fava e Garagnani, 1877, pp. 13-14.

[40] *Statuti di Peschiera*, ms. cit., c. 2 t.

[41] *Ibid.*, c. 3 t. 4.

[42] *Chronaca Veneta*, ms. della BA [n.s.], p. 756. For how Jacopo Cornaro solved the problem of scarcity of grain, see S. Speroni, *Orazione a Jacopo Cornaro Capitano di Padova*, in *Opere Di M. Sperone Speroni Degli Alvarotti*, vol. III, cit., pp. 175-187.

[43] Cf. *Magnum Bullarium*, cit., vol. 7, p. 377 (year 1565); vol. 7, pp. 484-485 (year 1566); vol. 12, year 1611; vol. 12, p. 718, year 1622; *Regesti di bandi*, cit., pp. 6-7, no. 31 (7 January 1513); p. 34, no. 209 (2 June 1562); p. 138, no. 882 (23 December 1599).

[44] L. Bianchini, *Della storia economico-civile della Sicilia*, Palermo, Lao, 1841, pp. 354-359.

[45] *Statuti di Peschiera*, ms. cit., c. 10 t. 11.

[46] See the remarks in my study: G. Barbieri, *Alcuni statuti di gremi sardi relativi alla agricoltura*, Sassari, Gallizzi, 1938, pp. 6-7.

[47] *Magnum Bullarium*, cit., vol. VII, p. 481 (year 1566).

tion projects, which Pope Sixtus V helped to fund, setting up the so-called Monte d'Orvieto.[48] The support and encouragement given by Popes to agriculture continued after the end of the sixteenth century, with further privileges granted to encourage prosperous farming in the Rome area during the following century.[49]

If this prosperity in farming was fostered partly by laws introduced in the sixteenth and seventeenth centuries, the same was true of commerce and manufacturing. Among the most common systems for promoting trade was the granting of privileges large and small to merchants. Pope Leo X was the most generous of all Popes (and more so than the Princes), granting «wondrous privileges – Venusti observes – for some merchants from Lucca, rendering honourable and saintly testimony to the world by their faith and bounty».[50] In Milan, too, Venusti says, merchants were given particular favours by the Prince.[51] The merchants of Ancona obtained ample concessions from the Pope, which were extended when trade threatened to dwindle.[52] When, in the first decades of the seventeenth century, the Venetians asked for particular protection and privileges, they obtained from the government the fullest understanding and their requests were granted without objection.[53]

Similarly, the laws and regulations of various Italian cities sought to support and promote industry, both by encouraging new activities and by protecting existing activities from the competition of foreign manufacturers and products, demonstrating a tendency to believe in the virtues of autarchy, staunchly upheld by lawmakers at the time of the City States until the creation of the modern State.[54] If the mercantile policies of the governments of various populations in Italy contributed to the creation of new industries in cities and

---

[48] *Regesti di bandi*, cit., p. 84, no. 515 (19 February 1587).

Emilio Maria Manolesso, in his Report on Ferrara presented to the Serenissima in 1575, says that: «recently, towards the sea, an area of fifty miles in length by nearly sixty in breadth has been given over and converted to crops, all of which, including valleys and marshes, may yield greatly to your Excellency». Cf. SEGARIZZI, *op. cit.*, vol. I, p. 28 (year 1575).

[49] *Magnum Bullarium*, cit., vol. 12, p. 15 (year 1611).

[50] VENUSTI, *Discorso d'intorno alla mercantia*, cit., c. 12.

[51] *Ibid.*, c. 11-12.

[52] *Magnum Bullarium*, cit., vol. 10, p. 104 (year 1594); p. 235, year 1595.

[53] ERRERA, *op. cit.*, p. 20.

[54] See my essay, G. BARBIERI, *L'autarchia nel pensiero e nella politica italiana dal Medioevo all'età moderna*, in *Note e documenti di storia economica italiana per l'età medioevale e moderna*, Milano, Giuffrè, 1940.

The volume also reprints a lecture of mine given to the Bologna Congress of S.I.P.S. on the subject: *Tendenze autarchiche nella politica economica del ducato di Milan* [The tendency to self-sufficiency in the economic policy of the Duchy of Milan].

to the expansion of trade, the same cannot be said of the laws introduced to protect corporativism, i.e. certain activities that were reserved for the very few – often without merit or skills – through the hardening of regulations that had outlived their original purpose of promoting production. One example was in Fabriano where a guild of wool makers, by preventing others from using teasels, exercised a monopoly to the detriment of the general population.[55] This hampered the spread of industry which, in the Italy of the seventeenth century and afterwards, was in continuous decline. In other towns a merchant was not allowed to hire an apprentice who was indebted to another merchant or had not completed his apprenticeship.[56] This might seem a reasonable law dictated by justice, but in fact – at that time – was more the result of the high cost of teaching and the over-long periods of apprenticeship.[57] The Statutes of Pavia prevented the reduction of the period of apprenticeship for wool and linen weavers and for helpers in craft workshops. The penalty was a fine of one ducat to be paid to the coffers of the Guild.[58] To prevent the spread of these skills in the districts of Pavia the statutes established a salary of twenty-four Imperial dinars for weavers – men and women – outside the city.[59] For the same reasons traders in spices in Savona needed to pass a very difficult examination and a large payment was required to enter the profession.[60]

Craft guilds had been established to promote work and to hand on skills for the good of the community, but they had become a dead weight[61] on the Italian economy of the seventeenth and subsequent centuries.[62] It was not until the eighteenth century that the negative effect of the guilds was fully appreciated; before then, statutes were regularly upheld and strengthened in defence of one guild or another. Such protectionism was rightly considered negative for the overall economic wellbeing of a community and an obstacle

---

[55] ZONGHI, *op. cit.*, p. 62 (year 1529).

[56] *Ibid.*, p. 58 (year 1516).

[57] Cf. chaptre V, paragraphs III and IV in this volume.

[58] *Statuti del paratico delli tessitori di tele de lino*, cit., chapter 58.

[59] *Ibid.*, chapter 43.

[60] FILIPPI, *op. cit.*, p. 28. Cf. also *Statuti del paratico delli tessitori di tele de lino*, cit., chapter 42.

[61] Cf. CIASCA, *op. cit.*

[62] Manzoni righly observes (A. MANZONI, *I promessi sposi*, ed. P. Bellezza, Milano, Cogliati, 1930, pp. 22-23, chapter I) that the Italian guilds of the seventeeth century had unequal strengths, so that often they were unable to provide mutual aid as the Statutes required. And this was particularly the case in the countryside, where confraternities and craft guilds could do nothing to oppose the power of a wealthy nobleman if given to violence. Cf. C. SUPINO, *Le idee economiche nei "Promessi sposi"*, «Rendiconti dell'Istituto Lombardo», 1923, series II, vol. LVI, folder XII.

to progress and expansion. Similarly, the excessive use of taxation had a negative impact, removing potential sources of investment. Leaving aside documentation that could take us too far afield, evidence of the high level of taxation in the sixteenth and seventeenth centuries is provided by the Marchese Del Vasto, who asked the Emperor to reduce the tax burden on the State of Milan in order to alleviate his conscience over the excessive hardships he had been forced to impose on the city in the form of taxation,[63] an indication of the persistent influence of ethical and religious regulations on the political and economic life of the age.

Up to here, as can be seen in all evidence, the laws of the State and those of the Church regarding the accumulation of wealth went hand in hand. Where the two forms of legislation differed, however, was in their consideration of usury and, in particular, of credit in general. Theoretically, laws prohibited loans with interest,[64] and legal theory – as we have seen – bowed to Church law in banning interest-bearing loans. However, despite this generic and unconditional prohibition, loans were not only made but instruments of credit were continuously being perfected without any serious hindrance. Tolerance of the practice is evident from the non-application of numerous laws in many states.[65]

Whether the failure to apply the law was based on the conviction of the ruling class that no intervention could eradicate the practice of usury or on the belief that the provision of credit benefited society, the fact remains that the practice continued in the teeth of the disapproval of the Church and was tolerated through the failure to apply civil law, which formally prohibited it. A letter from Charles V to the King of Bohemia is evidence of this oscillation between theory and practice, prohibition and tolerance,[66] a characteristic of

---

[63] CHABOD, *Lo Stato di Milano*, cit., p. 170.

[64] Cf. the testimony of CLARO, *op. cit.*, p. 94 t; del FOLLERIO, *op. cit.*, p. 281.

[65] Cf. per Roma *Magnum Bullarium*, cit., t. 7°, pp. 1-4 (the prohibition of usury, exchanges and all types of usurios contract); *Regesti di bandi*, cit., p. 23, no. 136 (27 August 1555); p. 25, no. 152 (15 January 1557); pp. 29-30, no. 180 (17 May 1560); p. 36, no. 221 (17 February 1564); p. 40, no. 229 (1559-1565); p. 53, no. 329 (28 January 1570); p. 83, no. 506 (21 October 1586).
And as in Rome so in other Italian cities, usury was banned.

[66] «Muchas y diversas vezes he sido persuadido por mis confesores que resolutamente mande prohibir y, quitar en nuestros reynos y señorias los interes y cambios, encargandome la conciencia y haziendo instancia en ello, deziendo no ser permitidos ny poderse en ninguna forma permitir. Y aunque desseo remediarlo mas que nadie, si se pudiese hazer, assy por estar fuera d'este escùpulo como por escusar el daño general que se sigue y el mio proprio particular, todavia està tan estendido y se trata tan comunemente en toda la Cristiandad, teniendo las unas provincias correspondencias con las otras por este medio, de onde depende el comercio de las mercadarias, que es mucho de considerar y cosa que en razon paresce casi impossible poderse executar, specialmente que ya que lo man-

periods of transformation and progress in many spheres of life. In the case of loans, progress should be considered as their legitimization after the centuries-old condemnation of the Church and their formal prohibition by civil laws. If Charles V, albeit convinced of the immorality of usury, did not believe it was politically and commercially advisable to attempt to eliminate interest-bearing loans, it should surprise nobody that in the pages of an illustrious historian the Spanish monarchy is described – despite the protests of its citizens – as protecting the Jewish community in Lombardy. Throughout the sixteenth century, the rulers of the region were aware that the declining Duchy was in dire economic straits. Therefore, in the overall policy of the Spanish, the credit provided by the Israelite community was deemed welcome if not actually providential.[67]

The fact that the policy of the Spanish rulers was so favourable to lenders demonstrates that the credit provisions severely prohibited by the Church did not concern productive activities but the unproductive needs for consumption dictated by the diminishing resources of families, reluctant to accept a declining standard of living. The spread of the Monti di Pietà (charitable lending institutions) under the auspices of the religious and civil authorities, is a clear demonstration of the hardships faced by families during the period. These beneficial institutions limited themselves to lending small sums,[68] against which an item was left as a pledge of repayment. Now if the majority of the statutes of these institutions indicate that they were created in order to free the needy from the stranglehold of usurers, above all, the Jews, it means that loans were made not in order to finance production but simply to provide for a family's basic needs.

Further evidence of this will be given below. Suffice it to say here that despite the ineffectiveness of the civil laws against usury, the sixteenth and subsequent centuries maintained the Scholastic tradition and hence the formal

---

dase quitar en mis estados, toda la contratacion se pasaria en Francia y en otras partes, de onde se podria seguir daño e inconvinientes yrreparables y nuestros estrado verrian a padescer». But since exchanges and interest could sometimes be allowed with «ciertas moderaciones», the King passed the question over to the Council of State, in all secrecy, because even the rumour of such a plan would have thrown the commercial world into turmoil. Cf. CHABOD, *Lo Stato di Milano*, cit., pp. 166-167, note.

[67] Cf. E. ROTA, *Gli ebrei e la politica spagnola in Lombardia*, «Bollettino della Società Pavese di Storia Patria», VI, fasc. 3, 1906, pp. 361, 362, 369.

[68] Some Monti did not lend money, only grain, which was returned at harvest time. Cf. ASDMi, Visita Apostolica, Brescia, vol. XL, c. 428 t. During the visit in 1580 by Carlo de Agostini, on a mission from Carlo Borromeo, to the city of Brescia, he reports: «Mons pietatis adest, cuius institutio est mutuo dare blada panperibus», with the obligation to return what had been received at the time of the next harvest.

prohibition of interest. In all other aspects of economic life Church laws and civil laws ran parallel, not only in theory but in practice. Chapter II noted how carefully Church authorities established regulations governing the day of rest. In Senigallia, for example, officials appointed by the City were entrusted with the task of making sure the sabath was properly observed.[69] In Valtellina, complete rest was required for over a hundred holy days and this was written into civil law; contracts signed on these public holidays were deemed null and void.[70]

If Church and civil laws often coincided, the same cannot be said for the sumptuary regulations introduced in the sixteenth century. As stated in Chapter II, through its Bishops and priests, the Church sought to combat the sixteenth century desire for luxury, not only with its sumptuary regulations applicable to both Churchmen and laymen, but also through the example of saints and holy men who eschewed luxury in all its forms. In order to reinforce Church teachings, Bishops often sought the active support of Princes and Magistrates, who were enjoined to pass severe dispositions against luxury and intemperance, inducing the people to limit the show of wealth in their dress and to follow a frugal and parsimonious way of life.[71] The sixteenth century is replete with sumptuary regulations issued by the Church in an attempt to oppose the display of wealth and luxury.

On 4 January 1507, the Senate of Venice noted that the ruin of most fathers and husbands was due «to varying and changing from one force to another».[72] In October of the same year, a letter was addressed to the Doge of Venice accusing three gentlewomen, Lucia Soranzo, Marina Emo and Adriana Cappello, of bringing their families to the verge of ruin.[73] The Serenissima Republic could not stand idly by and watch its best families fall into destitution because of the love of luxury. As a result, the Republic issued a decree according to which «let personal clothing be simple and uncomplicated without any sort of workmanship, neither tinkered about, nor masked, nor cut, without embroidery, braid, ribbons, strips, sequins, gold or silver stars».[74] To limit excessive spending on «wedding feasts and company», the Republic prohibited wedding ceremonies where liqueurs were served inside the wed-

---

[69] MARIANI, *op. cit.*, p. 163.

[70] *Li Statuti di Valtellina*, cit., pp. 70-72.

[71] *Acta Ecclesiae mediolanensis*, cit., vol. II, p. 121, Conc. Prov. Milanese.

[72] G. BISTORT, *Il magistrato alle pompe nella Republica di Venezia: studio storico*, Venezia, Tip. Libreria Emiliana, 1912, p. 129. Cited by MOLMENTI, *op. cit*, vol. II, p. 310.

[73] M. SANUDO, *I diarii*, Venezia, Visentini, 1879, vol. VII, pp. 158-159.

[74] MOLMENTI, *op. cit.*, vol. II, p. 310.

ding cakes».[75] It also prohibited illuminating the wedding banquet with «more than six candles of six liras each» and forbade women from «wearing necklaces with more than one row of gold with a price of no more than 25 ducats or a chain of gold of value no more than 100 ducats».[76] Ladies and damsels who wore clothes with «more than a quarter train» had the offending clothing confiscated and were fined 25 ducats for each offence.[77] In Milan, too, widespread luxury among the social classes, had given rise to the need for the introduction of sumptuary regulations,[78] as was the case in Genoa, where the city exhibited a wealth that Princes and even the most famous Emperors might have envied.[79] One characteristic of the regal life of the city was the pomp and ceremony on show at large banquets, with precious and generous gifts, which families jostled to offer each other on the occasion of leaving for, and returning from, holiday, a custom that prompted the City to adopt sumptuary regulations in December 1506. The citizens were evidently unimpressed since a Pragmatic Sanction of just six years later insisted that «the comings and goings from Genoa to the villas and from villas to the city be without presents and gifts of any kind, or conviviality, because a great abuse has come to be made of this».[80]

In sixteenth century Bologna, in vain Cardinal Bessarione continued to remind citizens of the sumptuary regulations introduced in 1545 and renewed in 1549, 1556 and 1558, which forbade «men and women alike from wearing any kind of clothing or gold or silver accoutrement, or velvet or garment woven or embroidered in gold or silver».[81] The regulations were ineffective partly because they were contradictory and partly because, as Borromeo had complained, those who should have set the example of a frugal and parsimonious style of life, were the first to exhibit all manner of splendour and pomp.[82]

---

[75] A. De Johannis, *Sulle condizioni della economia politica nel Cinquecento e la scoperta d'America*, in *La vita italiana nel Cinquecento*, cit., pp. 120-121.

[76] *Ibid.*

[77] *Ibid.*

[78] Verga, *op. cit.*, p. 251.

[79] L.T. Belgrano, *Della vita privata dei Genovesi*, Genova, T. Istituto Sordo-Muti, 1875, p. 439.

[80] *Ibid.*

[81] Frati, *op. cit*, p. 36 and following.
In 1563, in Rome, too, luxurious clothing had forced the Governor, Mons. Alessandro Pallantieri and the Senator Filippo Rainaldi, to publish a notice relating to the enormous and immoderate expenses of men, and especially women, in Rome for clothes and banqueting. Cf. *Regesti di bandi*, cit., p. 35, no. 220 (8 December 1563).

[82] Many of the Sumptuary Laws in Venice were rejected or repealed by the Senate. It is not

11

This is the essential difference between the sumptuary regulations and Church laws established to combat luxury and the excessive display of wealth.

For the reasons set out above, civil laws were far from effective in reducing the flaunting of wealth and luxury. Nonetheless, as we shall see in the following chapter, they were better able to promote the works of charity institutions and social solidarity. To give only one example, the state of Venice encouraged private initiative in charitable works helping foundlings, the unemployed, the sick, widows and the poor and needy. In 1544 it obliged notaries public to remind those making their wills to give some thought to people less fortunate than themselves. In addition, it obliged public officials, when elected, to pay one ducat to charity.[83] In other cities too the laws encouraged charitable works and donations, often enshrined in statutes in favour of the sick, the needy and the poor.[84] If the show of wealth by Princes, merchants and high-ranking Church officials demonstrated how the many sumptuary regulations introduced in the cities of Italy were continuously flouted, flying in the teeth of the now outmoded notion of moderation in all things, nonetheless many Princes and governors were generous in their donations not only to friends, artists and servants, but also to the poor and needy, in line with the Christian injunction to charity.[85] Hence, in the century of pomp and magnificence, charitable souls lived alongside greedy usurers intent on accumulating ever greater riches by lending to the poor.

---

surprising that a city like Venice should not wish to ban the display of personal luxury, which was also a demonstration of its power (MOLMENTI, *op. cit.*, p. 180 in the second volume). In addition, if citizens disobeyed sumptuary laws and bans, Judges tended to be lenient and this generosity tended to rewrite the laws themselves with a host of concessions, exceptions and instances of restricted application (*ibid.*, vol. II, p. 312).

If the laws had been coherent, it is the behaviour of Princes that limits pomp and luxury, G. SFORZA, *Cronachetta massese del sec. XVI ora per la prima volta stampata*, «Giornale Storico e Letterario della Liguria», III, 1902, p. 45, see year 1563).

[83] MOLMENTI, *op. cit.*, vol. II, p. 53.

[84] *Magnum Bullarium*, cit., vol. 6, pp. 285-286 (year 1540), vol. VIII, p. 284 and following, year 1579; vol. XIV, p. 635, year 1638.

[85] In 1540, Navagero informed the government of the Serenissima, speaking of the Cardinal and Duke of Mantua: «He is abundant in *limosine*: and this past year when men were shadows and simulacra of men due to famine, if it had not been for his barns and *caneve*, which were open to the poor, as many again would have died as perished in fact». Cf. SEGARIZZI, *op. cit.*, vol. I, p. 56.

Again according to Navagero, the Duke was second to none in charity works, and the Duchess: «makes charity and in all generosity and, more importantly, does so in secret and without pomp or wanting others to learn of it; and I have discovered that last year, when men were fighting with hunger and cold, at night she secretly gave *scudi* and half *scudi* and *mocenighi* to many poor people, nor did they ever know who their benefactor was, but it is the opinion of all and sundry that hers was the charitable office». *Ibid*.

For charitable donations, see the balance sheet of the State of Urbino cf. SEGARIZZI, *op. cit.*, vol. II, p. 217.

3. Given the lending activities of the Israelites in the sixteenth and following centuries, it is of interest to examine the role of the Jewish community in the politics, economics and social life of the Modern Age, in order to gain a better understanding of the economic ideals at the most important and complex time. Already present in small numbers in the peninsula, after 1492 the Jewish population in Italy grew rapidly following their expulsion from Spain. It is not known how many settled in Italy or how much of the thirty thousand million ducats exported from Spain were brought to Italy.[86] Certainly, the already evident problems of the Jewish population grew in size and importance. The conventions and agreements that allowed Jews to lend to communities in the Middle Ages[87] became a matter of course in the Modern Age,[88] wherever the scarcity of circulating coins made their presence useful. In previous centuries, [89] their chief economic role had been as lenders, although in some locations they had also become weavers and shopkeepers.[90]

Before going on to discuss the laws and behaviour of the population in relation to the Jewish community, the work of Sombart and those who followed him should be summarized briefly since he is a source of information about the economic function of the Israelites in Europe, in general, and in Italy, in particular. The famous German historian asserts that the role of the Jews in the creation of a modern economy was much more important than is generally believed, so much so that they fostered commerce and trade in the States where they were welcomed, leaving other States,

---

[86] Cf. L.A. SCHIAVI, *Gli Ebrei in Venezia e nelle sue colonie: appunti storici su documenti editi ed inediti*, «Nuova Antologia», III, 1893, p. 316.

[87] Cf. L. ZDEKAUER, *I Capitula hebraeorum di Siena (1477-1526)*, «Archivio giuridico "Filippo Serafini"», 1900, pp. 259-270; SCHIAVI, op. cit., p. 321; F. FOSSATI, *Gli ebrei a Vigevano nel secolo XV*, «Archivio Storico Lombardo», XX, 1903, pp. 199-215; G. TRECCA, *Legnago fino al secolo XX*, Verona, Gurisatti, 1900, p. 69, no. 1; and many other studies.

[88] See among the numerous studies in the «conduct» of the Jews: P. GUERRINI, *Gli ebrei a Verolanuova*, «Archivio Storico Lombardo», s. V, fasc. 3 and 4, 1918, pp. 538-550; G. BARBIERI, *L'industria tessile a Legnago nei secoli XVI e XVII*, in *Note e documenti di storia economica italiana per l'età medioevale e moderna*, Milano, Giuffrè, 1940; G. CAMMEO, *Cenni storici sulla comunità israelitica di Finale (modenese)*, «Vessillo Israelitico», XLII, 1894; U. BALDONI, *Storia di Finale-Emilia. 1190-1927 Capi, Podestà e Vicari*, Bologna, Officina Grafica Combattenti, 1928, pp. 106-107; A. CISCATO, *Gli Ebrei in Este*, Este,Typ. Longo, 1892, p. 12 and *passim*.

[89] To our knowledge, only in the Fortress of Legnago, in the Veneto, were Jews both lenders and industrialists. See our study: BARBIERI, *L'industria tessile a Legnago nei secoli XVI e XVII*, in *Note e documenti di storia economica italiana per l'età medioevale e moderna*, cit.

[90] Cf. R. CESSI, *Di alcuni documenti sugli ebrei nel Polesine durante i secoli XIV e XV*, «Atti e memorie della R. Accademia di Scienze Lettere ed Arti di Padova», XXV, 1908-1909, pp. 57-64; A. CISCATO, *Gli ebrei in Padova: (1300-1800)*, Padova, Soc. Cooperativa Tipografica, 1901, p. 110 and following, 121-123; SCHIAVI, op. cit., p. 507.

where they were not welcome or from which they had been expelled, to rack and ruin.[91]

Kawan agrees with Sombart, without noting any contradiction, when he remarks: «The Jews expelled from one city took refuge in a nearby town and then returned after some time to their native lands».[92] Given their travails, welcomed, expelled, accepted again and expelled again, is it reasonable to think that the prosperity or economic decline of the Italian peninsula depended on their presence or absence?

Even the limited resources of charitable lending institutions (Monti Pii) at the beginning of their activities were sufficient to prohibit usury, traditionally an activity reserved for the Jewish community. Whilst the Jews – often ahead of others in forging a modern economy – were not always weakened by the lending of these institutions,[93] they certainly did their utmost to prevent the Monti from flourishing and fought them tooth and nail.[94]

A Jewish historian has this to say: «The field of activities which was theirs (of the Jews) and especially reserved to them was the small loan with interest or often against a pledge».[95] It is easy to see that only high finance – in the sixteenth century in the hands of Christians – could exercise a strong influence on economic progress, financing important industrial and commercial activities. Small loans for consumption cannot be considered a source of economic growth but were more a symptom of economic decline,[96] all the more so because the high rates of interest[97] aggravated the difficulties of families,

---

[91] W. SOMBART, *Les juifs et la vie économique*, Paris, Payot, 1923, *Preface.*

[92] L. KAWAN, *Gli esodi e le carestie in Europa attraverso il tempo*, Roma, Bardi, 1932, pp. 94-100.

[93] Cf. in this regard G. LUZZATTO, *Storia del commercio*, vol. I, *Dall'antichità al rinascimento*, Firenze, Barbèra, 1914, pp. 398-399.

[94] In Velletri, to cite an example, the *Monte di Pietà* was closed after a series of events at the beginning of the sixteenth century, through the opposiition of the Jews who saw it as competing against their own illicit activities. And soon afterwards, in fact, they returned to the city and set up their business stalls for usury. Cf. A. GABRIELLI, *Alcuni capitoli del 1547 per un banco di prestito a pegno tenuto dagli ebrei in Velletri*, Velletri, Stracca, 1917, p. 10.

[95] LUZZATTO, *Storia del commercio*, cit., p. 395. On the same question, Salvioli says that the Jews, who dedicated themselves to commerce by vocation or necessity, and were especially active in money trades, never rose to the status of «an important bank or became capitalists, in the service of industry and commerce». He continues: «Only in the cities where craft guilds did not develop did the Jews continue to work in some industries». Cf. SALVIOLI, *op. cit.*, p. 380.

[96] Rota demonstrated the pernicious effects of usury by Jews on credit in Milan. Which explained – according to the historian from Pavia – the efforts of Milan to fight these speculators. Cf. ROTA, *op. cit.*, p. 369 and following.

[97] SCHIAVI writes (*op. cit.*, p. 321): «It must have been that the revenues of banks were very high, if the University of Venice attracted the Jewish community from far and wide, to provide subsidies».

whether needy or noble and fallen into ruin. Hence the opinion of Sombart is unfounded and contrary to the facts as objectively observed.

The above explains the periods of protection and the repeated expulsion of the Jews. When the finances of the City States and Duchies were at low ebb, and coins – already scarce before the discovery of America – could not be found, the activity of Jews was tolerated if not welcomed, providing some social relief and helping to curb rebellion and opposition to the Governments of the day, an undercurrent the Princes feared and sought to control by strengthening their power. In such circumstances rulers were practically obliged to protect and favour money lenders[98] and the Jewish community was exceptionally good at sensing when and where the need for their services arose, moving easily from place to place in order to satisfy these needs. This explains why, in Lombardy, the Jews were treated with such tolerance by the Spanish governors, anxious to hide from view the economic decline of a once prosperous Duchy.[99] When the increasingly onerous requirements of Princes and City governors could not be met by taxation, a licence to the Jewish community, for a brief or lengthy period, was the easiest way to raise capital.[100] Other authorities could hardly refuse. In Verola Alghise, today Verolanuova, the Jews were allowed to take up residence because the wife of Niccolò Gambara, unable to solve the thorny problems of household administration, turned to the Jewish communities of Vescovato, Novellara and Ostiano for help.[101]

However, this kind of help was transient and illusory, and the result was that Jewish communities multiplied and prospered, to the extent that in Mantua, in 1558, of the population of forty thousand, eight thousand were Jews.[102] This simply turned one community against another, increasing hostilities, as the Jews who had first limited themselves to charging high rates of

---

The information gathered by Schiavi shows that in the first half of the seventeenth century, there were 2,650 Jews living in Venice, and they had funds amounting to two million ducats, or almost 800 each. Cf. *ibid.*, p. 507.

[98] The leniency and generosity of the measures dedicated to the provisions of the Jews is well-known.

[99] Cf. ROTA, *op. cit.*, pp. 361, 362, 369 and following, 377.

[100] It is known that the Jews were very numerous in Ferrara, Modena, Parma, Urbino and other small City States, whose rulers made frequent recourse to loans from the Israelites. But they did not prosper in the cities that came under the rule of the Pope. When, in 1597 the d'Este family lost its last member, Cardinale Aldobrandini entered Ferrara yelling: *Down with the Jews*. Cf. M.L. MARGOLIS and A. MARX, *Histoire du peuple juif*, Paris, Payot, 1930, pp. 464-465.

[101] Cf. GUERRINI, *op. cit.*

[102] Cf. SEGARIZZI, *op. cit.*, vol. I, p. 78 (*Relazione del Contarini*). See also FOLENGO, *Le Maccheronee*, cit., vol. I, p. 168.

interest, took over commercial and industrial activities.[103] As soon as the Princes and local populations could be rid of them, the Jews were peremptorily expelled.[104] If some towns opposed the expulsion of the Jews, this was because they felt that their function had not been exhausted and loans were still needed to manage day-to-day living expenses.[105]

Before ending this chapter, it is necessary to briefly clarify the widespread claim that Popes were particularly lenient and generous with the sons of Israel. In this regard, it should be noted that until the first half of the sixteenth century the Jewish problem was not of particular relevance to the economy. Hence many Popes tended to pay little attention to it. But as soon as they saw that their policies for economic life, above all in relation to industry and commerce, were threatened by invasive loan activities, the Popes sought to «intellectually and economically paralyze the Jews with laws of the State and the Church which remained in force until the Napoleonic age»[106] Pope Pius V, accused by Speroni of allowing Jews to practice usury,[107] issued a number of restrictive regulations aimed at keeping the Christian and Jewish communities separate, defending the moral and material interests of the faithful against the activities of the Jews.[108]

---

[103] Venice was indulgent with the Jews up to a certain time but felt the need to curb their commercial activities, excluding them from all arts and crafts. ERRERA, op. cit., p. 37. Pope Pius IV, in 1555, limited the activities of the Jews to «rag and bones». Magnum Bullarium, cit., vol. VI, p. 449.

[104] In 1613, the Jews were hounded out of Capodistria «considering the damage and extermination of this magnificent city caused by the usurous earnings of the Hebrews». Cf. PERTILE, op. cit., vol. IV, p. 606, n. 64.

More than a century before, in Belluno, when the city was without a government, «Judei fuerunt totaliter depopulati et nihil eis remansit preter spiritum». PERTILE, op. cit., vol. III, p. 204.

In 1570, the Jews were expelled from Tuscany. Ibid., vol. III, p. 208.

For the struggle against the Jews in Padua, due to their excessive usury, see FORCELLINI, op. cit., pp. XXI-XXII.

The Jews were expelled from Finale di Modena in 1601, following the opposition to usury of P. Bartolomeo Cambi da Salutio, preaching Lent (cf. SARRI, op. cit., pp. 56-64 e passim; CAMMEO, op. cit., p. 224).

The Cardinal of Milan battled with the Jews in Brescia during a pastoral visit. Cf. ASDMi, Visita apostolica, cit., vol. XI, folder V. Many other examples could be given.

[105] In 1540, commendably, the Neapolitans tried to prevent the the expulsion of the Jews from the Kingdom, fearing that there would be no more loans. Cf. PERTILE, op. cit., vol. III, p. 208.

[106] MARGOLIS and MARX, op. cit., p. 468.

[107] SPERONI, Opere, cit., vol. V, pp. 439-444. To Pope Pius V un anonymous letter writer, on 13 August 1566, begged tolerance for the Jews, since God is tolerant with all men. BA, ms. identified with: D 172 inf., c. 2, t. 8.

[108] These documents include: Magnum Bullarium, cit., vol. 7, p. 514; vol. 10, year 1593; vol. 10, year 1596; Regesti di bandi, cit., p. 89, no. 543 (4 January 1588); p. 32, no. 196 (8 August 1561); p. 22, no. 133 (14 July 1555); p. 42, no. 264 (19 April 1566); p. 48, no. 300 (26 February 1568); PERTILE, op. cit., vol. III, p. 204; p. 213.

4. This brief survey of civil laws relating to the problem of wealth enables us first of all to make a a comparison with Church laws. The requirement of work, the regulations introduced to ensure commercial honesty, the prohibition of usury and exchanges, the need to observe rest days, sumptuary regulations and encouraging charitable works and donations were all enshrined in the legislation of the City States in Italy. The laws were evidently influenced by Church leaders and writers dealing with the morals of economic life, which governors continued to heed. However, the influence was not so great as to create an absolute harmony between Church and civil laws on the economy; the State and the Catholic Church adopted different measures and similar measures sometimes differed in their application. Charles V was unable to take one consistent approach to usury, wavering between prohibition and tolerance.

The numerous sumptuary regulations introduced the length and breadth of the peninsula are evidence of the tendency of the age to flaunt wealth and finery against the wishes of the Church. Naturally, the lawmakers were the first to flout the regulations, since a certain show of luxury was deemed a necessary accompaniment to social standing and failure to make a fine display of one's fortunes was considered damaging to one's reputation and the dignity of one's family. Hence the contradictory nature of the sumptuary regulations, which chopped and changed, remaining largely ineffective and often unapplied.

The question could be asked about how effective civil legislation was in promoting economic activity and arresting the expected decline. Some measures were certainly useful, particularly for the spread of industrial activities and the defence of existing practices. However, industrial policy is a good example of the reasons for Italy's economic decline: vested interests and monopolies held sway against initiative and innovation, legislation failing to keep pace with technical change and social developments; the economy was held back, thwarting real change.

In relation to the problem of the Jews, nothing further needs to be said. Far from acting as a spur to industry and commerce, the Israelites limited themselves to making small loans to consumers, further weakening the economy in the face of imminent decline after centuries of prosperity. They lent against small objects pledged as security and charged high rates of interest, so that their activity, if not actually a cause of decline, was certainly a symptom of an undeniable fall in economic wellbeing during the period. The lower classes of the sixteenth and seventeenth centuries certainly resented the Jews and regarded the practice of usury as ruinous. The laws sought to curb their activities, but Governors and Rulers were soon obliged to seek their services, and to protect Jewish communities, in the hope of disguising the true material condition of their subjects.

How utterly mistaken this idea was will be clarified in the next chapter.

CHAPTER SEVEN

THE ECONOMIC IDEALS
OF PRACTICAL MEN

1. A French historian has affirmed that the spirit of an age is not reflected in the ideals of the masses rather the aspirations «de quelques êtres d'élite», «des porteurs de torches qui éclairent les routes de l'avenir».[1]

Like all categorical assertions relating to historical criteria, Hauser's remark is open to criticism, particularly by a researcher intent on investigating the economic spirit of the sixteenth century in Italy, a time when the idealistic and material forces of the Middle Ages persisted despite the increasingly disruptive impact of new institutions and a new mentality. Though it was a period of transition and of transformation, Hauser's remark has certain limitations.

Firstly, it is not always possible to identify the spirit of the times, in other words, the mentality of a people in a given era. Historians are often tempted to choose the thinking of one man as representative of an age and the aspirations, desires and wishes of the masses; but this is generally the result of a lack of source material with which to reconstruct the period and from this reconstruction attempt to the understand the attitudes of the age. Furthermore, there are some centuries in our history that are characterized not by one spirit but by several conflicting trends and ideals, and these cannot be detected from the thought of a single man or group of men. Often it would appear that the spirit of the most noteworthy thinkers, writers and men of letters is, to a greater or lesser extent, in contrast with the mentality and aspirations of the masses, which – even when documentary evidence is scarce – are the driving forces shaping the future. Exemplary thinkers or individuals from this or that walk of life may present to us the spirit of the age if they are truly representative of one aspect of the lives of the people among whom they live and who

---

[1] Cf. H. HAUSER, *op. cit.*, p. 20.

shaped their thinking. It is only by comparing the ideals of solitary thinkers with those motivating people in general that historians can establish which individuals are genuinely representative of the period.

This premise explains the reasoning behind this chapter, that seeks to identify the ideals of economic life in the sixteenth and seventeenth through the testimony of practical men. These men were the true, direct protagonists of economic life in the period and hence their attitude to wealth is fundamental to the historian's understanding of sixteenth century in Italy. Chapter Eight will deal with the many questions facing historians of sixteenth century Italy, while this section presents the economic spirit animating businessmen in this period. This is no small task, given the lack of direct source material. As a result, indirect sources will be used, such as the chronicles, tales and histories contained in literary and other works, which speak of the aspirations of the various cultural groups into which Italian society in the sixteenth and seventeenth centuries was divided.

2. The reader might think that in the sixteenth century, an epoch of unrivalled ostentation and of literary and artistic triumphs, the problems of economic life were of little importance and the desire for «facultà», so characteristic of other ages, relatively weakened. This tricky question will be answered in Chapter Eight, the concluding chapter. Here, the testimony of men of the time will be presented to ascertain how they intended to use old and new means of acquiring wealth.

As we have seen, in the analysis of the *Perfezione della vita civile* by Paruta, the sixteenth century cannot be considered an era in which the love of riches played no part. On the contrary, the Venetian historian says that «all too many made it their idol and took more pleasure in the contemplation of their riches than in the sight of the sun or sky».[2] This affirmation is so true that if one examines, one by one, the means for acquiring wealth, it becomes clear that they included methods of dubious morality and even downright dishonesty. If the printers and jewellers of Rome in the service of the Pope and the Cardinals were by and large honest men, Ceseri Macherone was not, preferring to make false coin rather than pursue an honest living.[3] And the busi-

---

[2] PARUTA, *Della perfezione*, cit., vol. I, book III, p. 340.

[3] B. CELLINI, *La vita di Benvenuto Cellini scritta da lui medesimo*, Firenze, Le Monnier, 1852, pp. 117-118.

Many Milanese goldsmiths worked in other Italian cities (*ibid.*, pp. 88, 99; BANDELLO, *Le novelle*, cit., p. 234).

It must have been easy to become wealthy when a man «took a notable sum from a friend to set

ness partner of Davanzati in a commercial enterprise certainly had no scruples in seeking to ruin his partner, despite the fact that Tacitus, via his translator, had already pointed out that false bookkeeping and bloating costs for one's gain was unlikely to produce the desired result.[4]

Of course, there were honest people. The Venetian Patrician Gerolamo Priuli must have made quite a name for himself, for when his businesses failed he lost none of his honesty and dignity: «Patience! No more of it! My bad fortune, the evil times, the ruin of the Venetian state, were the causes and not my failings». Thus commented the bankrupt, who, having the capital sufficient to pay all his creditors, was a clear and excellent example of commercial honesty. He was also well-known as a man of charitable works, to which he dedicated his life after his business ruin.[5] If the Venetian Patrician set an example of honesty and for holding riches in disregard, not everyone was of the same rectitude: two villains barbarically killed the wife of Marc'Antonio Venier for her gold and jewels.[6] And a young man in Florence spent the daytime staring into the workshop of Benvenuto Cellini, who was making a precious gift for the Pope, only to break into the workshop at night in the hope of making off with «hidden treasure», which, however, he was unable to find.[7]

Any discussion of clearly dishonest and criminal ways of acquiring wealth should include the many laws and severe penalties of the period aimed at thieves, counterfeiters, gamblers and so on.[8] So popular was gambling in the sixteenth century that many regarded it as a more than satisfactory way to acquire wealth quickly and without toil. The «tavolero», as Castiglione called it, attracted bets of 25, 50 or even 100 scudi.[9] And this vice was not only pursued by men: women spent entire days playing with dice and cards.

---

up business and eleven months later, without disadventure or losses, had forty four thousand ducats; and received help, favours, friends and courtesy: and walked out head held high and spent happily, letting it be known he had returned the money received to the friend, in the presence of witnesses, but not a bit of truth was there in it». Cf. DAVANZATI, Le opere, cit., Prefazione, p. XIII.

At the beginning of the seventeenth century, Filippo Guicciardini seems to have tried to cover up his dishonest dealings by hiding his accounting books for the partnershop with Carlo Barberini. Cf. ASV, Fondo Borghese, serie II, 11, c. 143 and following (2 August 1608).

[4] DAVANZATI, Le opere, Prefazione, p. XIV e vol. I, p. 134.

[5] SANUDO, op. cit., XVIII, pp. 354-369.

[6] Ibid., LV, pp. 128, 248, 282.

[7] CELLINI, op. cit., p. 115.

[8] Li Statuti di Valtellina, cit., p. 183; Statuta artis lanae terrae Fabriani, cit., p. 82; Li Statuti di Valtellina, cit., p. 191 e Statuto Senigalliese, cit., pp. 189, 195.

[9] CASTIGLIONE, op. cit., p. II, pp. 473-475.

These were not the only games: lotteries caused a great deal of agitation among the population, with rich and poor alike buying as many «bolettini» as possible in the hope of winning one of the better cash prizes or some precious object. In order to buy a ticket, some people «turned others out of their beds to sell them and buy two tickets. A widow told a priest, all pinched into his tunic: – Take this crown and say for me the Mass of San Gregorio for the blessed soul. – Masses, ah? – he replied – I will have to melt the candles. – And with shuffling steps inside the Church, he explained he was living from the little he made with the lottery». Even more significant for an understanding of the soul of the betting man, were the words of Aretino in a letter to Giovan Manenti: «A peasant, stumbling on a game of lottery, thinking he might win with six coins, he sold his cloak and thinking he had won, he gave up working the land and the the hoe, held by Christ the farmer».[10] Thus, gambling was seen as a way out of work, in the past considered a religious duty.

One of the most famous women gamblers in Italy was Bartolomea Calora, from Modena, who bet large sums whenever she was in town.[11] By now «the game of cards and dice was so abused that not only was gambling common in homes and whore houses but also in the public streets».[12] Is it necessary to continue the list of examples to note that the love of riches had certainly not diminished but, on the contrary, had increased, to such an extent that Church regulations governing the morality of economic life were often ignored?

People from Bergamo sacrificed everything for the shining of gold florins. Bandello says they put up with all manner of insults and coarseness in the pursuit of their aim: money.[13] Some feigned themselves ill or disabled in order to get out of work. These were the so-called Guidoni, who thought it better – says Garzoni – to stay locked up in the Tower rather than perform an art or craft.[14] Without continuing this pitiful list of petty and not so petty dishon-

---

[10] ARETINO, op. cit., p. 323 and following (letter dated 1537 to Messere Giovan Manenti).

[11] BANDELLO, Le novelle, cit., vol. II, p. 130. Another famous gambler was the Neapolitan Antonio Perillo, who enherited great wealth from his father and «took up gambling and soon became known for cheating... He was so fond of gambling that nobody could distract him from it. So in a little time he consumed near all his wealth». Ibid., I, p. 164.

[12] FRATI, op. cit., p. 110.

[13] BANDELLO, Le novelle, cit., II, pp. 22-23.

[14] GARZONI, op. cit., p. 580. «Some are not inoperative or fallen into poverty so much as idle, and abandon arts and sciences and give themselves up to sloth and neglect, and live a life of quiet, or shun all happiness and with utter roguery continually beg for food, and lodgings, reputing this life more sweet and blessed than any other. And their teeth chattering with cold, and screaming in the streets like mad dogs, shivering from the frozen morning, or dying of heat, or walking without boots, or on their knees or with their buttocks in the mud, or being buried in a cart, is considered by them more tolerable than working at an art or craft, as do honest men».

esties, suffice it to say that whilst Garzoni exaggerated the immorality of economic life in his *Piazza Universale*, a survey of the professions, in which he pours scorn on all the arts – exercised deceitfully and to the detriment of one's fellow man, he says – dishonesty was certainly a feature of economic activity in the sixteenth century. The ideal for acquiring riches during the period is well expressed by a merchant from Genoa, who commented: «those in fear of the Devil made nothing since almost nobody becomes rich without deceiving others».[15] Even the immense toil of the alchemists, their anxieties and eternal disappointments, testify to the feverish desire for gold[16] and clarify a critical aspect of the economic ideals of the century: in the aspirations of men of the sixteenth century, whether peasants lamenting the burdens of toil while others rest,[17] as Paleotti says, or the rich merchant,[18] no longer able to tolerate the worries of commerce, there is a kind of weariness in those who have worked for centuries, as if men in the sixteenth century felt the need for respite after so much toil carried out not by them, but by their fathers and forefathers.

Did Italians really scorn the marketplace? Is there any evidence of what activities they carried out?

3. What strikes the researcher most about economic life in the sixteenth century is the steady development of credit activities. Whether in the form of small-time usury or huge loans from a merchant in Genoa to the King of Spain or England, the fact remains that the testimony that has reached us demonstrates just how diffuse lending was in Italy. As seen above, the citizens of Genoa thought it almost shameful to «do ought else with money than lend it» and the «most honourable sort of dealing and making goods was lending

---

[15] *Ibid.*, p. 546.

[16] *Ibid.*, p. 138 and following. Garzoni says this of alchemists: «It is difficult to narrate the hardship and deprivation, the vigils, the purchases, pledges, loans and extravagant expenses, and the poverty and calamities that befall them finally, when they have spent so much time and effort all in vain, and find themselves with nothing and have no more means ... having consumed their wealth searching in books and recipes and secrets...».

[17] For the disconent of poor workers and their struggles with nobility see la *Cronaca di Cremona*, n.t.n., p. 199.

[18] In the *Esortazione a' Mercanti* (in the volume by VENUSTI, *op. cit.*, c. 3) the following is said of the merchant who has made riches: «How arrogant he is, the richer he becomes, and no more deigns to labour except to obtain authorities, because nobody in the Republic is better than he. How curiously he dresses; how gluttunous in his eating, how dissolute in his pleasures...». Further on Venusti writes: «He maintains fools, chatterers, dwarves and madmen, not out of Christian charity but curiosity and pleasure and vainglory, as he keeps falcons, dogs and horses, richly appointed, the ponds filled with fishes, the woods with fowl, houses with servants»: such is the life of the successful merchant.

money since the selling and buying of goods and loading ships with them is for those who go to market and the lower classes».[19]

This ideal of acquiring wealth, so clearly depicted by merchants in Genoa, was left practically unscathed by the efforts of the Church – partly assisted by civil laws – to suppress interest-bearing loans. People were not concerned that the Fraternities so common in the sixteenth century did not allow usurers (or even those suspected of usury) to join.[20] Calling usurers thieves, as did the Catechism of the Roman Catholic Church, contributed little to stamping out the practice.[21] Loans generated revenues and this was reason enough to make them. According to Bandello, Giacomo Scappardone: «lent everything he could convert into money with public usury and at such high rates of interest that having begun at a tender age he became so rich he bought abundant possessions, and lending greatly and spending little, obtained great faculty».[22] Garimberto notes that one usurer had so much devoured his debtors as to vomit not his own things but the bodies of those on whom he had nourished himself daily.[23] Campanella speaks of hoarders of grain who made fortunes through the illicit use of their money.[24] In the city of Genoa, where lending was more common than elsewhere, the Bishop thought it necessary to set up a Committee of theologians to explain the evils of the practice,[25] but merchants were able to get round the moral stigma by inventing forms of credit that even the cleverest theologians and jurists would have found it difficult to censure in terms of evangelical or Thomistic regulations applicable to lending.[26]

And if the regulations ever obstructed lending activities, it was always possible to entrust the money to the Jews, second to none in putting funds to good use.[27] Public opinion (recall Speroni's *Dialogue on Usury*) was less harsh on lenders, though the law formally condemned them. Some noblemen did not consider it beneath them to marry a commoner if she had a large enough dowry, even one procured by her father practicing usury.[28] By now, the eco-

---

[19] Cf. ALBÈRI, *op. cit.*, s. 1ª, VI, p. 361 (*Report by Leonardo Donato* dated 1573).

[20] *Regola della Confraternita dei disciplinati della città di Roma*, n.t.n., p. 5.

[21] *Catechismus Romanus*, cit., *de septimo*, p. 456.

[22] BANDELLO, *Le novelle*, cit., vol. I, p. 58 (nov. IV).

[23] GARIMBERTO, *op. cit.*, p. VIII.

[24] CAMPANELLA, *Aumento delle Entrate*, cit., pp. 325-326.

[25] FABIANO, *op. cit.*, c. 1.

[26] GAITO, *op. cit.*, p. 69, no. 1161-1167.

[27] CHABOD, *Lo Stato di Milano*, cit., p. 198, nota 20.

[28] Cf. BANDELLO, *Le novelle*, cit., vol. I, p. 58.

nomic mentality of the sixteenth century was so different from the ideals of the previous era that the problem of a discrepancy between theory and practice in terms of the legitimacy of lending was unlikely to exercise anyone's conscience, certainly not that of most practical men, who sometimes took steps – if they bothered at all – to bend their way round the letter of the law. In Papal Rome, which – as seen in Chapter Two – prohibited usury and exchanges, dozens of banks were active in making loans in the interests of the Vatican. Among others, these included the Chigi Bank,[29] which prospered from the end of the fifteenth century until the beginning of the sixteenth, the firm known as Filippo Guicciardini and Associates,[30] which looked after the interests of Cardinals and the Pope, the bank known as Mg.ci Sig.ri Bandini, run by Filippo and Vincenzo Ruspogliosi,[31] and many others too numerous to mention. It was not only in Rome that bankers developed their business, because even small towns such as Pontremoli dedicated themselves to trading in the money of a few of their citizens. For example, this was how Michele di Giovanni[32] was able to finance Captain G. Francesco Aldobrandini on his trip to Hungary in 1602 to take over command of the Papal Army deployed against the Turks, to support the Imperial throne.

It should not be forgotten that in the sixteenth century – and to a lesser extent the seventeenth –, Italian bankers invested a great deal of capital in loans abroad, above all to Princes and reigning monarchs. Here, too, a few of the many available examples will suffice: in the last two decades of the sixteenth century, Giovanni Aldobrandini, a relative of Pope Clement VIII, put all his capital into the bank of Lyon.[33] Lyon was a major banking centre where many Italians were active, as *les grands livres* of the Affaitadi family testify by recording their dealings.[34] In London, the Cavalcanti family lent huge sums to the King of England; in 1544, Tomaso Cavalcanti was thought to be the single largest creditor of the Monarch. Twelve years later he had spread the loan around other Italian bankers,[35] including the Giraldi family, associates of

---

[29] See my volume: G. BARBIERI, *Industria e politica mineraria nello stato pontificio dal '400 al '600: lineamenti*, Roma, Cremonese, 1940.

[30] AB, 6212, in ASV (*Giornale di Spese per il viaggio in Ungheria di Gio. Francesco Aldobrandini*).

[31] AB, 4373 (*Spese della Fabbrica del Incurabili del 1587*), in ASV.

[32] AB, 6212 (*Giornale di Spese*, cit.).

[33] ASV, *Fondo Borghese*, serie III, 96 AB[1] ff. 69 and following.

[34] J. DENUCÉ, *Inventaire des Affaitadi: banquiers italiens à Anvers, de l'annèe 1568*, Paris, Leroux, 1934, p. 44.

[35] DENUCÉ, *op. cit.*, p. 48; R. EHRENBERG, *Das Zeitalter der Fugger*, Jena, Fisher, 1922, vol. I, p. 283.

the Affaitadis in the lending business. Their bank became powerful when a member of the Giraldi family, Ambassador of the King of Portugal in London, married Lucrezia degli Affaitadi, uniting the fortunes of the two families.[36]

It has now been shown that the firm run by the Affaitadi family was Italian in origin, from Cremona[37] More will be said in due course on the contribution made by the family to the economy of the sixteenth century; here it is sufficient to note only the role of their bank in the Fair of Medina del Campo, where other important international banking concerns were also present: the Fuggers, the Pallavicini, the Spinolas and Malvendas.[38] Clearly, Italian capital was spread far and wide in Europe, funding the most important trading initiatives of the time, and serving the growing financial needs of Europe's rulers. Often, ambassadors from the King of France were sent to Venice to ask for large loans. In 1568, for example, Venice lent the French monarch 200,000 gold ducats «to sustain the War against the Huguenots, aganst which he pledged much jewelry such as a diamond with a value of 10,000 ducats». To amortize the huge debt the King handed over to the Venetians «a dwelling in Paris worth 30,000 ducats a year».[39] The following year, in January another ambassador sent by the same monarch, Monsignor di Valcoch, asked for a further loan of 200,000 ducats, pledging a diamond worth 60,000 scudi and a cross of similar value.[40] The report concludes: «and it is thought he will have them». So, in a just a few months, 400,000 ducats were transferred from the Venetian economy to a foreign country, with evident repercussions on the industry and trade of the Serenissima Republic. Nor was the King of France, among European rulers, the only borrower of Italian capital. Towards the end of the sixteenth century, Genoa had a credit with Spain of 25 million ducats in interest alone: the loans themselves must have been of almost incalculable amounts.[41]

Of course this means that capital was flowing out of Italy and one can certainly speculate on the consequence of all this lending on the economy of the peninsula. The subject will be dealt with a little later. Suffice it to say here that

---

[36] DENUCÉ, *op. cit.*, p. 48.

[37] Cf. ASCMi, *Codici Trivulziani*, cod. 1817, f. 298 III (1 July 1506); cod 1818, f. 324 I. [These Codexes are no longer available n.d.r.]. At the beginning of the sixteenth Ludovico de Affaitatis was a merchant in Venice. Cf. BARBIERI, *Economia e politica nel ducato di Milano*, cit., p. 216, and n. 3.

[38] DENUCÉ, *op. cit.*, pp. 23-24.

[39] *Chronaca Veneta*, ms. ambrosiano, n.s., c. 681.

[40] BAV, Urb. Lat. 1041, c. 11.
The Guadagni family lent huge sums to Francis I, always in need of finance to pursue his ruinous wars. The Florentine merchants were so famous in Lyon that a street – rue de Guadagne – was named after them. Cf. A. COMBE and G. CHARAVAY, *Guide de l'étranger à Lyon*, Lyon, Charavay, 1847, p. 219.

[41] A. SEGRE, *Storia del commercio*, Torino-Genova, Lattes, 1923, vol. I, p. 519.

Campanella, in his long meditations on the political and economic life of his age, thought that the practice in Genoa of lending large sums contributed to the economic decline of the city.[42] And, indeed, the dissemination of large amounts of capital lent by Genoa to this or that ruler had the undoubted effect of depriving the principal markets for banking activities in the sixteenth century of adequate liquid funds. Mid-way through the century, trade in Antwerp was paralyzed by the lack of money and in 1552 a fleet was sent to Spain to seize huge quantities of silver in order to revive the flagging economy of the mercantile city. The creditors of the Spanish Emperor hoping through this expedition to recover part of their loans included Lionardo Gentili and Jeronimo de Franchi, both from Genoa.[43] The commercial correspondence of the Fugger family – from which these details have been taken – confirms that the credits of the city of Genoa were not only repaid in the following years, but increased to the point that King Philip of Spain, in 1556, repeatedly begged Silvestro Cattaneo to become his agent for credit operations in Italy.[44]

Are other examples necessary to show how much capital was leaving the peninsula? One more: in the first two decades of the sixteenth century, Niccolò Grimaldi, Prince of Salerno, and Antonio Pallavicino were the main suppliers of money to the King of Spain, for amounts in the region of 600,000 and 800,000 ducats.[45]

In the light of this expansion of credit,[46] it is clear that Church regulations aiming to prohibit interest on loans had no effect on the practical side of eco-

---

[42] CAMPANELLA, in *Opere*, cit., *Poesie Filosofiche*, vol. II, sonetto «A Genoa», p. 87.

[43] Cf. EHRENBERG, *op. cit.*, vol. I, p. 345. Gentili is mentioned also by DENUCÉ, *op. cit.*, p. 36.

[44] Cf. EHRENBERG, *op. cit.*, vol. I, p. 345; BA, *Pergamena* 5209 bis, 7 September 1557 (Antonio Fuchar and the nephews of Augusta ordered the company of Silvestro Cattaneo and Giovanni Battista Spinola in Antwerp to pay a sum to Bartolomeo Jenis. 24 days later, to be precise on 30 September 1557, the notary public Giovanni Keller, representing Antonio Fuggero and nephews, protested against Lazaro de Grimaldo, administrator of the company owned by Silvestro Cattaneo and Giovan Battista Spinola, for failure to pay a promissory note to Bartolomeo Jenis. BA, *Pergamena* 5209, 30 September 1557. The importance of Cattaneo in commerce is also noted by BANDELLO, *Le novelle*, cit., vol. II, 277-78.

[45] Cf. EHRENBERG, *op. cit.*, vol. I, p. 345.

[46] Cf. in BA, le *Pergamene* 7461 (on 18 January 1580, Giovanni Battista de Persico received a loan of nine hundred gold ducats from Marco and Giovanni Fuggeri, brothers and Barons of Kirchberg and Weissenborn), 5218 bis (7 September 1557, Antonio Fuchar and nephews wrote to Tomasio Frescho and Bartolomeo Doria, in Antwerp, for a payment to be made to Giorgio Stecher), 5218 (30 September 1557, protest by Giovanni Keller, on behalf of Antonio Fuggero and nephews, for failure to make payment to Giorgio Strecher by Pietro Francesco Sampsone, administrator and Director of trade for the Tomaso Flisco and Bartolomeo Doria Company), 5238 bis (14 September 1557, bill of exchange of Antonio Fuchar and nephews to Andrea Lixals and Tomaso Hechamer, for a payment to Antonio Spinula and Giovanni Battista Lomelino), 5238 (on 6 October 1557 the notary public notified expiry of the promissory note).

nomic life. Leaving aside questions of morality, to which businessmen were impervious, the historian is left wondering what drove Italians in the sixteenth century to use capital for this form of investment. To understand this, it is first necessary to investigate all the other aspects of the Italian economy at the time.

4. The brief examination of the spread of credit in the economy of the sixteenth century has, among other things, revealed a great deal about the protagonists of the mercantile world in Italy during that period. Now, the time has come to examine the economic behaviour of practical men to understand the spirit that motivated them.

In the Middle Ages, the famous mercantile families were the Datini, Bardi, Peruzzi and others; in the sixteenth century other families rose to importance in commercial life. Most important of all perhaps was the Affaitadi family, whose agents were present not only at the Fairs in Europe, but in Africa, Asia and America. Gian Carlo Affaitadi was a dominant figure for forty years, rivalling in economic and financial power the illustrious Habsburg Fugger family, considered at their height the richest traders in Europe.[47]

Now that the inventories of the Affaitadi have been published by Denucé, it is clear that the bankers from Cremona, whose wealth was consecrated in a magnificent building in Cremona in 1561, traded with other important families in Italy.[48] In Venice,[49] they had business dealings with Atavanti, Badoer, Boson, Bragadini, Cappello, Corallo, Corraco, Corchinelli, Cocumella, Cornaro, Correr, Cusano, Foscarini, Turga, Gabiano, Gionti, Giustiniano, Larchari, Marandella, Marini, Priuli, Vignola and others. In Milan the Affaitadi did business with Dugnano, Foppa, Litta, de Marchi, de Marini, Salice, Scarione, Trinchero, Vitalle and Vixino.[50] In Naples, the leading family was

---

[47] Denucé, *op. cit.*, p. 7. Gian Carlo Affaitadi, «supremi nominis inter negotiatores», was praised by men of letters of the time, including Aretino, who – in return for a large fee – dedicated the fourth volume of his correspondence to him.

[48] *La Cronaca di Cremona* (n.t.n., p. 259) records under the month of August 1523 the death of Martoro Affaitato in Venice «he was one of the first merchants in Italy, a gentleman and merchant from Cremona».

[49] In the early decades of the sixteenth century, Venice was not yet in decline. «City – an observer remarked – of marvels and true wonders to be admired, given the site, the marble and superb palaces, the precious merchandise, so rich and continuously coming and going, the variety of the many nations that trade, and where no food can be grown or animals pastured, there is all manner of things to eat». Cf. Bandello, *Le novelle*, cit., II, p. 271.

[50] During the Empire of Charles V, the d'Adda family dominated the industrial and commercial activities of the Lombard city. In 1548, for example, the Chamber of Merchants included three members of the family, Pagano, Erasmo and Ottaviano. Cf. Chabod, *Lo Stato di Milano*, cit., p. 200, note 23. The inventory of Denucé, *op. cit.* (p. 40) mentions Erasmo.

Giraldi, in Palermo the largest traders were Manson, Mansbel, de Nobili and Tarongi, whilst in Messina the important trading families included Camarena, Cigalla, Corsi, Giustiniano and others.

In other words, all Italian cities[51] appear in the inventories of the Affaitadi family and business relations took place with many other families.[52] Not all of these families limited themselves to trading in Italy. Cavalcanti – as seen above – was busy in Antwerp, but also in London, Portugal and even Brazil, where the family was remembered for its honesty and straightforward dealings.[53] Many Italian emigrants – especially Tuscans and the Milanese – did business in mercantile Lyon.[54] According to Bandello, businessmen from Bergamo could be found the world over.[55] Many merchants from Genoa had dealings in Oran, so much so that one of the districts of the city was called the Lodge of the Genoese.[56] The widespread study of accounting and reckoning as well as the number of teachers of these skills is evidence of the importance of trading; treaties between different powers always including commercial agreements.[57]

However, the mercantile world of the sixteenth century had none of the power and prosperity of the previous centuries. The Affaitadi, the richest merchants of their time, had left their homeland and focused their business on a country more suited to capitalist expansion.[58] The few merchants in the city of Guidobaldo II della Rovere[59] were foreigners. Siena loved agricul-

---

[51] In Ancona Pandolfo Biliotti, Annibale Carenzone, Lorenzo Civi, Tomaso Corbinelli, Giovan Angiello Garibaldo, Prospero Lampugnano and Fedrigo Lanfranchi were well-known merchants.

In Bologna traded the heirs of Carlo Ardizone: Giovan Gabrielli, Bartolomeo Canobio, Stefano e Bonifacio Dessiderii, Annibal Gindalotto, Cornelio de Malvagia, Orsini and Orsi, Galeza Paselli, Pietro Maria Scappi, Alberto Sigicello and Nicolò Villanova.

[52] These lists were taken from the *Grands Livres* and *Inventaire* degli Affaitadi. See Denucé, *op. cit.*, p. 39 and following. See also Garzoni, *op. cit.*, p. 547.

[53] P. Peragallo, *Cenni intorno alla colonia italiana in Portogallo nei secoli XIV, XV e XVI*, n.t.n., p. 56.

[54] Bandello, *Le novelle*, cit., II, p. 222. Tra i milanesi primeggiava Teodoro Triulzo.

[55] *Ibid.*, II, p. 22.

[56] *Ibid.*, *Le novelle*, cit., II, pp. 277-278.

[57] A. Casanova, *Modi ed ordini di scrittura da usare nei negoziamenti della mercanzia*, 1558, in *Opere antiche di ragioneria*, p. 250.

See L. Paciolo, *Trattato de' computi e delle scritture*, 1494; D. Manzoni di Oderzo, *Quaderno doppio col suo giornale secondo il costume di Venezia*, 1540; Alvise Casanova, *op. cit.*; A. Pietra, *Indirizzo degli economi*, 1558, all in *Opere Antiche di Ragioneria*, Milan, Monitore dei Ragionieri, 1911.

These were not the only treatises of the time. See Ragioneria generale dello Stato, *Elenco cronologico delle opere di computisteria e ragioneria venute alla luce in Italia dal 1202 sino al presente*, Roma, Tip. Nazionale Reggiani, 1886.

[58] Cf. Denucé, *op. cit.*, pp. 7-8.

[59] Segarizzi, *op. cit.*, vol. II, p. 200.

ture and industry but repudiated trading.[60] And Florence was losing its characteristic as a trading city by the end of the century, as Francesco Contarini reported to the government of the Serenissima Republic in 1589.[61] Commerce in Milan was less actively pursued than earlier, with revenues of 170,000 ducats in duties on provisions and goods, against nearly 400,000 ducats in the past.[62] In Piedmont, the decline was even more evident: «the more they live comfortably the more they neglect industry so the rivers, the Po and others, are not used for navigation, abundance leads to no exchanges, transit in different part of the world produces no commerce. Everybody nourishes himself and enjoys the present, without a thought for tomorrow».[63] In Florence, universally praised for its mercantile spirit, despite what Paruta thought,[64] some merchants were growing tired of their trade. In fact «the young in cities are delighted by its pleasures and follow the customs of the Court rather than busying themselves in workshops and attending to merchandise».[65] In the city of the Gonzagas, several merchants – convinced of the unworthiness of commerce for men of their standing – abandoned their activities to the many Jews willing to take them over.[66] Even Venice, which had thrived on trading with the East, by 1535 was full of a new generation of men described by the Senate as unwilling to «do commerce with the city or navigate or be active in any other laudable industry».[67]

Hence the leading cities in Italy, once drivers of economic expansion throughout the world, saw their trade diminish and with it their prosperity, not only because of growing difficulties,[68] but above all because Italian merchants began to give up their trade, tired of long voyages and accounting

---

[60] *Ibid.*, vol. I, p. 210 e p. 131.

[61] *Ibid.*, vol. III, part II, Relazione del 1589.

[62] *Ibid.*, vol. II, pp. 41-42.

[63] BAROZZI and BERCHET, *Relazioni degli Stati Europei letti al Senato dagli Ambasciatori Veneziani nel secolo XVII*, Venezia, Naratovich, 1856, serie III, I, 20.

[64] PARUTA, *Della perfezione*, cit., vol. I, p. 330.

[65] SEGARIZZI, *op. cit.*, vol. III, part I, p. 186.

[66] *Ibid.*, vol. I, p. 78.

[67] R. FULIN, *Breve sommario di storia Veneta*, Venezia, Visentini, 1873, p. 47 (cited by MOLMENTI, *op. cit.*, p. 12 of vol. II).

Molmenti says that after the decline of trading in Venice, the Serenisssima was forced to turn to other sources of wealth and new businesses. The lesser arts, providing decorations to the houses and ornamental apparel, were a good source of wealth. However Venice – the historian continues – never became an industrial city. «The grandchildren of merchant Patricians and navigators, who had shared the dangers and fortunes of voyages with the common people, were able to become landowners but not to direct the work of factories or manufacturers». Cf. MOLMENTI, *op. cit.*, p. 137 in volume II.

[68] See the Chapter VIII of this volume.

books, in order to take up more sedentary occupations. Not a businessman, but a man of letters, Annibal Caro, captured the spirit of the age when he expressed the wish to retire with a small pension, «so stable that I know not where I could obtain a better post».[69] Towards the end of this chapter, it will be easier to understand the meaning of this desire for a small but secure income within the overall context of the economic ideals of the age.

The time has come to examine the spiritual and social origins of the decline of mercantile energy in Italy during the sixteenth and seventeenth centuries.

5. It is well-known that the sixteenth century in Italy – a time of infinite complexity from all points of view – saw a profound transformation in society, perhaps the most radical in our history. In the Middle Ages, the merchant class earned a great deal from its industrial and trading activities and during the fifteenth century achieved economic and political power, progressively raising merchants above the class of craftsmen and workmen. This division was first economic but then became social, when the merchant class felt the need to put themselves beyond the reach of former colleagues and others less fortunate than themselves. In other words, they wanted to be seen to possess an uncommon social status through the display of wealth accumulated in the past. In the fifteenth century, men climbed the social ladder, aspiring to the ranks of nobility without abandoning their activities or depleting their wealth. They rose up but continued their industrial and commercial enterprises, contributing to the growth of the economy.

The history of the Duchy of Milan is a typical example. From the mid fifteenth century onwards, a very powerful mercantile class was formed, initially far from ashamed of the means it had used to acquire its wealth – manufacturing and trading. The Borromeo family and many other families in Milan became rich and powerful, but continued to promote industry and commerce in the city.[70]

In the sixteenth century this ceased to be the case. An examination of an important Codex in the Historic Archives of Milan shows how the capital accumulated in industry and trading was increasingly used for the purchase of

---

[69] Cf. A. CARO, *Lettere inedite*, con annotazioni di Pietro Mazzucchelli, Milano, Pogliani, 1827-1830, vol. II, p. 119.

The opinion of this man of letters regarding a secure income was shared by many other writers in the sixteeenth century who «were professional literary men», i.e. made their livings from writing. See the observations of DE SANCTIS, *Storia della letteratura italiana*, cit., vol. I, pp. 329-330.

[70] See my volume BARBIERI, *Economia e politica nel ducato di Milano*, cit. (The analytic index includes the names of mercantile families in Milan who continued to work throughout the second half of the fifteenth century even after the were elevated to the nobility).

land and other forms of fixed income, starving industry and trade of capital (as discussed in further detail in the next section). When the richest merchants in the city began to invest in land and properties, the noblemen who had contributed to economic expansion and wellbeing ceased to drive the economy forward, and industry and trade suffered as a consequence.[71]

Something must have happened. The reader might suppose that the crisis of the textile industry in Italy from the fifteenth century onwards penalized economic actors who were unable to reproduce the huge revenues of the previous period. Accordingly, these difficulties then forced noblemen in the sixteenth century to seek forms of fixed income and security, in view of the precariousness of trading and all its ups and downs. And this despite the evident wealth they had accumulated precisely through industrial activity and trading.

Undoubtedly the difficulties of the Italian economy in the sixteenth century contributed to this change. Certainly, the conditions for accumulating wealth were different. But this cannot explain why the most important merchant families of the fifteenth century, having achieved the status of nobility, promptly abandoned industry and commerce in the following century, turning their backs on the very activities that had made them wealthy and enabled them to rise above the masses. The difficulties of the economy, though real, were not sufficient to justify such a change of attitude and the new recourse to fixed incomes from duties, taxation, assets and properties. Something more dramatic must have taken place to determine the lack of economic progress in Italy over the next two centuries.

The evidence gathered in the course of research points to a psychological and spiritual change among the members of the ruling class in the sixteenth century.

Virtually every document uncovered speaks of a distaste and repugnance for trade. «Most of the nobility – wrote the Ambassador of Lucca to Florence – disdains the market, wears a sword, and the few who deal with it, consider it beneath their dignity to have direct contact with it and send their ministers, so the utility is diminished and the costs increased out of all proportion».[72] Bandello speaks of a widowed noblewoman who cannot have had much respect for the marketplace since she persuaded her son not to follow in his merchant father's footsteps «intent on withdrawing all the merchandise her husband had in Italy, Flanders, France, Spain and Syria, in order to buy possessions

---

[71] See my essay: Barbieri, *I redditi dei milanesi all'inizio della dominazione spagnola*, pp. 773-774; Id., *Economia e politica nel ducato di Milano*, cit., p. 224.

[72] N. Rodolico, *Il ritorno alla terra nella storia degli italiani*, «Atti della Reale Accademia dei Georgofili di Firenze», 1933, p. 33.

for her son».[73] Another contemporary observed that the nobility: «do not follow the example of their fathers and live in idleness and grow up with such
languid souls and bodies that anything they hear or that comes into their feelings causes them only discomfort and distaste».[74] If we turn to the noblemen
of Naples, the historian detects not only profound nausea for the market but
also for anything that directly or indirectly smacked of economic life. Otalora
– criticized by Gaito for his opinion – writes that the noblemen of Naples
made their livelihoods from property but kept well away from agriculture,
considering such activity unworthy of their noble status. They fled the market
(mercaturam ut rem turpissimam vilissimamque exhorrent) and from those
who had dealings there. Proof of this is the fact that Neapolitan nobles were
willing to die of hunger rather than allow a daughter to marry a rich merchant.[75] In other regions of Italy this disregard for work was less accentuated,
but noblemen elsewhere were no longer animated by the economic ideals of
the past age. In Venice, the market was considered unworthy of a politician,
suited to the riff-raff, «so only rarely was a Patrician seen with his goods on
the Rialto».[76] In the city of trade par excellence «there are no longer any merchants who sail to the East, traders and soldiers of a bygone time; the market
is considered base; ships are leased and crews engaged not in Venice but the
colonies».[77] In Milan, too, perhaps the city that held out longest against the
creeping economic decline of Italy, the ruling class considered nothing «less
worthy of nobility than mercantile activities».[78] In Genoa, praised – as we
have seen – by Venusti for its nobility and mercantile tradition,[79] those
who still pursued economic interests lent money in Italy and abroad. If a nobleman believed that trading was not unworthy of him, his sons soon dis-
abused him of the notion and ushered in the new economic climate of the sixteenth century through the exercise of idleness.[80]

---

[73] BANDELLO, *Le novelle*, cit., vol. I, p. 254.

[74] LOTTINI, *op. cit.*, p. 114, Avv. 251. Just before, Lottini had written: «seemingly noblemen
prefer to fall into poverty than take up some work, so they are not prevented in their intention»
(*op. cit.*, p. 113. Avv. 248).

[75] GAITO, *op. cit.*, p. 128, no. 2104 and following.

[76] MOLMENTI, *op. cit.*, vol. II, p. 11.

[77] SCHIAVI, *op. cit.*, pp. 492-493. See the erroneous opinion of VENUSTI (*op. cit.*, c. 12) concerning the mercantile spirit of Venetian nobility. PARUTA (*Della perfezione*, cit., vol. I, p. 330) believed in
the mercantile ideals of the Venetian Patricians.

[78] PARUTA, *op. cit.*, vol. I, p. 330. Cf. F. CALVI, *Il patriziato milanese*, «Archivio Storico Lombardo», 1874, t. I, p. 116, t. II, p. 416.

[79] VENUSTI, *Discorso d'intorno alla mercantia*, cit., c. 11.

[80] To cite just one example, while the father of Gian Vincenzo Pinelli left Genoa for Naples

If this feeling of nausea and distaste for trading in the sixteenth century impacted negatively on industry and commerce, how were the huge sums accumulated in the previous era invested? And what use of capital was considered worthy of the ruling class and in line with its new economic ideals?

6. If a historian wished to research the transition of Italian families from the Middle Ages to the Modern Age, he would be able not only to bring to light very curious information about the customs and ideals of the time, but also to explain the phenomenon of the decline of the economy in the latter period, which still puzzles many.

Pending detailed research and analyses, the present discussion is limited to the information it has been possible to uncover, here and there, concerning the affairs of some powerful mercantile families in the fifteenth century, and how these families faced (or failed to face) the problems of the coming Modern Age. The Borromeo family, whose commercial and financial power rivalled that of the most famous European merchants in the fifteenth century, was mentioned above. These merchants of S. Miniato must have accumulated so much wealth at that time that by the third decade of the sixteenth century one of their descendants, Count Giovanni, was considered one of the most important rentiers in Milan, with an annual revenue of 73,000 ducats. The importance of the sum and of this piece of information comes from the profession of the Count: he had no dealings in London, none in wool at Borgogna or S. Matteo; he was a soldier who entrusted his riches to the land after considerably multiplying them with the dowry of his wife, Cornelia Rho.[81] The heirs of the Borromeo family took up various business activities, professions and callings, but none were merchants.

The same can be said of an albeit slightly less powerful family, the Panigarola,[82] who left Genoa for Milan during the period of dominance of their native city by the Duchy of Milan. After dedicating themselves to trading,

---

«magnam ibi copiosamque mercaturam facturo», his son had no intention of following in his father's footsteps, preferring to spend his considerable fortune on cultural initiatives, some of which bore his name. Cf. G. BARBIERI, *Un'inchiesta cinquecentesca sui Fugger*, «Rivista Internazionale di Scienze Sociali», 1936.

[81] Cf. ASCMi, *Serie Famiglie*, folder 1629, codex entitled: *Rubrica de' S.S. Abitanti nelle Parrocchie di Milan e loro entrata in ragione di ducati annui*, carta 86; ASM, *Panigarola Statuti*, Registro no. 19 (T), c. 64 and following (The precious documentary material for Conte Borromeo includes the list of objects and properties in the dowry of his wife).

Cf. F. CALVI, *Famiglie notabili milanesi*, Milano, Vallardi, 1881, vol. II, table VII of Vitaliani-Borromei family.

[82] See my study: G. BARBIERI, *Gottardo Panigarola mercante e spenditore sforzesco alla luce di nuovi documenti*, in *Atti e memorie del Terzo Congresso Storico Lombardo*, Milano, Giuffrè, 1939.

they became important state bureaucrats. The family coat of arms had long stood above the door of these officials in Milan when one of them, Gottardo, tried to increase the family fortunes in the textile industry and in commerce. Despite his trading ventures, he did not give up his modest but safe and dignified income as a public servant. He passed on this somewhat wary mercantile spirit to his sons and grandsons. His heir Alessandro worked with him in his industrial enterprises but showed less interest in the risky profits of commercial activities than in the secure revenue he obtained administering the lands of the Church and in the pleasures of his Vaprio estate, acquired by marriage.

The other sons of Gottardo Panigarola were even further from the entrepreneurial spirit of a now bygone age. They were content to administer the tender awarded to them for the collection of customs duties in Milan and for the Duchy. Some of the direct descendents of Alesandro Panigarola became legal counsel and politicians, others went into the Church. From the beginning of the sixteenth century onwards, none became merchants and none carried on the family's industrial activities, founded by the most famous and prestigious member of the Panigarola family.[83]

These two examples exemplify what befell the energetic mercantile class of the fourteenth and fifteenth centuries after building up their fortunes in industry and trading; they entered the nobility and abandoned undignified work in favour of the liberal professions, politics and careers in the Church, where there were no riches to be gained, just a steady income. In the light of the view that trading and working in industry brought the reputation of the family into disrepute, it is easy to understand why former mercantile families shunned the sources of their own wealth, preferring instead an untroubled life and a fixed income from property. Significant in this regard is a passage by Garzoni, who ridicules the fad for nobility and describes one of its characteristic traits, so feverishly coveted: «Nobility today consists in having a little land and a hut to be idle in; a farm with farmhouse made of straw or wood and an

---

[83] In relation to Milan, the history of a well-known family of gunsmiths is interesting: the Negroni de Ello aka Missaglia. The head of the family, parhaps a weapons maker, died in 1428. His sons began the highly profitable industry that enabled them in less than a century to build up an immense fortune. The most famous of the Negroni, Antonio Missaglia, headed the family enterprise for decades. Princes came to them for huge quantities of arms. To ensure that the workshops did not run out of steel, Missaglia extracted iron in the territory of Canzo, and created a company with Filippo Erba to smelt iron in the same locality. At the height of their power, towards the end of the century, the family had a Count's coat of arms. After this, they disappeared from the industrial and commercial world of Milan. Cf. BARBIERI, *Economia e politica nel ducato di Milano*, cit., pp. 183-184.

orchard of lettuce or cabbages called a garden...».[84] Leaving this irony aside for a moment, it should be said that in the sixteenth century the custom of putting capital into land and estates was very widespread; indeed, it was effectively proof that the status of nobility have been achieved.

In 1561, a Venetian Ambassador reported on the prosperity of Siena, based not on industry but on agriculture. The report includes a passage that demonstrates the love of the land and land-owning: «The people of Siena are very accommodating and have all they need».[85] Five years later, another Ambassador explained the city's disregard for commerce in terms of the wealth generated by agriculture for the noblemen of Siena: «gentlemen living from their abundant revenues».[86] A further ten years on and Andrea Gussoni speaks of Siena in similar terms, noting the wealth of the noblemen and their lack of mercantile spirit.[87] No more mercantile was the nobility of Urbino, for whom «two things almost universally are in their liking: arms which they exercise as young men, and the the discipline of study and agriculture, where they are greatly diligent».[88] Now, it is well-known that Siena and Urbino had a history of intense trading. So, clearly, the two cities had turned their backs on the sources of their previous wealth and the entrepreneurial spirit had vanished there as well. In Venice, deposits of money were increasingly short, since the wealthy, no longer attracted by mercantile enterprises, preferred to acquire estates.[89] And if someone from Padua, enthusing about the political life in Venice, should rant and rave about those who abandoned the city for the land and for the quiet life of the villa, he was likely to be given a deaf ear – a lot of deaf ears – considering that the Venetians had transferred their wealth to the land, becoming the owners of large estates.[90]

Returning to Milan once more, the phenomenon of the «involution of commercial and manufacturing activity» was particularly striking, given the former mercantile power of the great families who now decided to turn over their wealth to property.[91] The exacting archival research conducted by Cha-

---

[84] Garzoni, *op. cit.*, pp. 176-177.

[85] Segarizzi, *op. cit.*, vol. III, p. I, p. 131 (1561).

[86] *Ibid.*, vol. III, p. I, pp. 185-186 (year 1566).

[87] *Ibid.*, vol. III, p. I, p. 210 (year 1576).

[88] *Ibid.*, vol. II, p. 202 (1575). A similar observation was made in 1547. Cf. *ibid.*, vol. II, p. 171.

[89] Molmenti, *op. cit.*, vol. II, p. 38.

[90] Cf. Speroni, *Opere*, cit., vol. V, p. 33.

[91] In relation to fixed assets, Luzzatto observes: «The tendency to invest in funds is as old as the existence of middle class enriched from commerce: in Venice in the thirteenth century, when the territory did not extend beyond the lagoon, there was a race to buy lands on the mainland, despite the dangers to which the owner of lands abroad were exposed; and just a few decades later, at the

bod is of fundamental importance. The Milanese historian describes the dual process of acquisition of real estate by city dwellers to the detriment of country dwellers, and the buying up of small and medium-sized properties by the great landowners, whether city or country folk.[92] In Milan, this phenomenon became very common. Much rarer was «the example of those who left the quiet life of the landowner and who did no other than lend money through an intermediary, in order to return to the lively and insecure life of the merchant with dealings far and wide».[93] Generally, the preference was for moving capital away from risk and hence from the market, towards investments «increasingly in the acquisition of land, of legal rights, of annuities from land and income from the Chamber of Milan, in feudal arrangements, or lending to the Chamber, obtaining in return revenues from this or that asset, or to great financiers, such as Marino, who gave sufficient guarantees of solvency».[94]

At this point the reader will have noted the new orientation in economic life of the Italians and the growing importance of credit, described in the third section of this chapter. At first sight it might be thought that the tendency to invest capital in property was motivated by quite a different spirit from that of the merchants seeking to lend money in Italy and abroad. In reality the two processes were both driven by a common desire to accumulate wealth without excessive toil and worry. These investment tendencies also had similarly ruinous negative effects on the Italian economy in the sixteenth and seventeenth centuries.

It would be superfluous to restate the spirit and motivations underlying these typical phenomena in sixteenth century economic life in Italy. Country estates were far more sought after than damp and crowded merchant warehouses by the newly ennobled who perceived land as a symbol of their wealth and status, as in feudal times.[95]

7. The new economic spirit of not only the ruling class but also other classes in Italy in the sixteenth century went hand in hand with a widespread love of

---

time of the tragic bankruptcy of the Bardi and Peruzzi and many other banks, depositors and other creditors could obtain quite a high percentage of their credits because of their property funds in which the partners of those companies had quickly invested part of their commercial profits». Cf. G. LUZZATTO, *Storia economica. L'età moderna*, Padova, Cedam, 1934, p. 99.

These examples, taken from the Middle Ages, of the race to buy land and invest in property do not detract from the importance of the phenomenon, in Italy in the sixteenth century, when it became widespread.

[92] Cf. CHABOD, *Lo Stato di Milano*, cit., pp. 198-199.

[93] *Ibid.*

[94] *Ibid.*

[95] Cf. J. AYNARD, *La bourgeoisie française: essai de psychologie*, Paris, Librairie Académique Perrin, 1934, p. 37 and following.

the countryside[96] which absorbed not only a great deal of capital but also a large part of the population previously employed in the industry and commerce of the bustling cities. In the third decade of the sixteenth century, as one Florentine observer commented: «The hills around are all fertile, cultivated, pleasant, full of beauteous and bountiful villas, built with an excess of spending and with all imaginable delights: gardens and woodlands with fountains, baths and all other types of delight, with views that look like paintings».[97]

A few decades later, Gussoni was able to tell the government in Venice about the sumptuous villas the Florentines had built for themselves at huge expense in the hillsides around the city,[98] including the famous Villa Poggio, unrivalled at the time, which struck even Charles V with wonder.[99] The huge sums sunk into properties not only made no money but involved massive further costs for upkeep. In this regard, a Venetian commented in 1588: «The hills are covered with buildings and palaces, whose number, quality and cost, are truly magnificent; all the more wondrous because the fields are of no utility, on the contrary are merely an expense, and serve only the pleasure of the villas built with so much expense».[100] Of course, it wasn't rural life or agriculture that attracted capital from noblemen in the city – and some writers and moralists complained about the way farms were abandoned to ignorant administrators and farmhands – it was the idea of building villas on huge estates to glorify the name of the family and to broadcast far and wide the status of the owner. It should be remembered here – insofar as it is a related phenomenon – that as in the Middle Ages, and even more in the sixteenth century, the population fled the heat of the cities for several months, taking refuge in the countryside. «Come summer and nobody wished to remain in the city; they jigged their duties, deserted their offices, bade farewell to merchandise, and took to the country with all its corrupt luxuries and idleness».[101] This was not a matter of a few days away from work in the countryside, but of a period from mid August to mid November.[102]

Not only the wealthy and noblemen, but also workmen and craftsmen, escaped from the the heat of summer to the country. On 24 July 1502, a Flor-

---

[96] CHABOD (*Lo Stato di Milano*, p. 201) says that ownership of land was sought, because it could be «place of rest and delight and the villa dedicated to the humanistic dream of idleness...».

[97] SEGARIZZI, *op. cit.*, vol. III, part I, p. 8 (1527).

[98] *Ibid.*, vol. III, part I, p. 211 (1576).

[99] *Ibid.*, vol. III, part I, p. 246 (1579).

[100] RODOLICO, *op. cit.*, pp. 330-331.

[101] BELGRANO, *op. cit.*, p. 439.

[102] *Ibid.*, pp. 443-444.

entine dealer in second-hand goods, Bernardo di Cenni, hosted a group of friends in his villa. One of them, the boilermaker Bartolomeo Masi, says his friends were restless and wanted to visit some nearby cities. Their pleasant holidays lasted only thirteen days and ended with a banquet. Significantly, Masi says: «And this was the first time any one of us had left the district and the country of Florence». But not the last time, since from 18 to 26 September of the same year the boilermaker and his friends made any number of trips to the country.[103] We are at the beginning of the sixteenth century and craftsmen and workmen are aware of something different in their private and social lives. The monotony of a dark house in the city could finally be broken by a trip to the countryside and some educational excursions. If the lower classes had this idea of the peace and quiet of the countryside, its freshness and the relaxation it afforded, it is not difficult to imagine how the wealthy thought the same on a grander scale.

The Genoese began and ended the holiday season with rich banquets and the exchanging of gifts,[104] in which they frittered away some of their wealth. The multifarious sumptuary laws were of little effect in attempting to combat this profligacy and were entirely unable to restore the sense of value in work over the new value of exhibiting magnificence and pomp: this had become the lifestyle of the wealthy in Italy in the Modern Age.

8. A Venetian historian of the second half of the sixteenth century was struck by the enormous waste of money associated with the magnificent works his fellow citizens felt obliged to create, and by the overall profligacy of the nation. Given his own economic ideal, inspired by moderation, he could not but condemn the show of wealth, often accompanied by a decline in honesty and customs. «Alas, in our times there is a habit of living among us Italians that is full of vanity and delights, and hence even this is sign of magnificence it would be better to give up such virtues».[105] But the cries of an isolated nostalgic were not about to reverse the trend of the Modern Age, increasingly intent on displaying its riches and refinement. Paruta was particularly critical of Venice in his considerations of political and economic ideals,

---

[103] B. MASI, *Ricordanze di Bartolomeo Masi Calderaio Fiorentino dal 1478 al 1526*, Florence, Sansoni, 1906, pp. 52-56.

[104] BELGRANO, *op. cit.*, p. 444.

[105] PARUTA, *Della perfezione*, cit., vol. I, p. 256 «in our homes and households what can be added to our finery these days? There is no city in Italy without beautiful and noble palaces and villas, and other modern constructions with luxurious gardens, a sign of the greatness of these families and more serviceable to pleasures and exhibition than to usefulness» (*op. cit.*, pp. 255-256).

perhaps unsurprisingly given that it was a city of splendour, refined customs, elegant buildings and high fashion, none of which it was reluctant to show. Suffice it to say that the Venetians found nothing strange one fine August, when the Fugger family, considered the wealthiest merchants in the world, sent a family member to live in Venice, where he built an entire district, admired for its magnificence by Henry III[106] who immediately wanted to see what had been done. In the sixteenth century, the inhabitants of the lagoon reached the highest levels of luxury in art, in their homes, their buildings and their villas. Marin Sanudo said there were «an infinity of houses with gilded chambers of 800 ducats or more».[107] In the fifteenth century only a few famous men had their portraits painted; now an entire school of painters grew up in the service of the vainglory of men and women – vying for the best artists – eager to hand down their image to posterity.[108] The food and drink served at Venetian banquets included the most unimaginable extravagances and strangest dishes.[109] In terms of fashion, it is well known how the century invented the most sumptuous garments,[110] sewed by master tailors who made their fortunes, as depicted in the art works adorning the sartorial schools named after Sant'Omobono and Santa Barbara.[111]

The sixteenth century was no less full of pomp and ceremony in Milan. The most famous artists of the day were treated in the capital of Lombardy to the generosity of Princes and Patricians, who called to their service painters, sculptors and architects from all over Italy.[112] It was also the century of singing, dancing and theatrical productions.[113] In 1574, a master of ballet, Cesare Negri, organized one of the most magnificent celebrations of the per-

---

[106] MOLMENTI, *op. cit.*, vol. II, p. 183.

[107] *Ibid.*, vol. II, p. 174.

[108] *Ibid.*, vol. II, p. 263 and following.

[109] *Ibid.*, vol. II, p. 493 and following.

[110] In that century, gloves became very common, those for women beautiful and scented, made of lace and embroidered silk and dyed leather (*ibid.*, vol. II, p. 287). Metal corsets also came into fashion, closed over the chest with a key, and with springs that snapped shut, a torture device, changed at the end of the sixteenth century with fabric and whalebone corsets (*ibid.*, vol. II, pp. 283-285).

«All manner of clothing was adorned with the most complicated artifice. The use of belts and buckles became so common that it became a new and special art». *Ibid.*, vol. II, p. 283.

«The colours of the most precious fabrics, purple, Shamite and silk, were used to adorn some of those clothes, like gold and jewels resplendent as sumptuous buildings, or shining under the sun on the marble walkways of Piazza S. Marco, campo di Santo Stefano, Santa Maria Formosa, San Paolo». *Ibid.*, vol. II, pp. 276-277.

[111] *Ibid.*, vol. II, p. 308.

[112] Cf. VERGA, *op. cit.*, pp. 240-242.

[113] Cf. A. BIAGI, *La Musica nel secolo XVI*, in *La vita italiana nel Cinquecento*, pp. 387-410.

iod, unrivalled in its elegance and show of luxury, for the hero of Lepanto.[114] If, at other times during the rule of the Sforza family, there was a hustle and bustle of merchants in the city, arriving from, or leaving for, various European cities, now the «masters of genteel rites» came and went, teaching the art of dance to courtiers in Italy and the rest of Europe.[115] Everything men and women of good taste could possibly desire was available in Milan, a city anxious to gain the admiration of visitors. «Where but here – wrote a contemporary man of letters – do the carriages have fixtures of gold and are finely engraved, pulled by four fine steeds? Where are sixty such carriages pulled by four houses, and countless pulled by two, with blankets of silk and indented with gold, of such variety, that when the ladies ride in their carriages through the town it seems they are showing off a trophy».[116] The sixteenth century commentator was struck perhaps even more by the tasty banquets of the Milanese. He wrote: «the abundance and delicacy of the food is so singular and splendid in all conviviality, and its seems they cannot live if they do not eat and drink in great company».[117] The citizens of Milan were well known for their good taste and healthy appetites, especially for sugars, stews and cakes. «They sprinkled sugar on roasts – says Verga – on fowl, on fish, over their soup and maccheroni, and their hors d'ouevres included truffles, oysters, lettuce and so on».[118]

When the life of Patricians, noblemen and a new class of wealthy men consisted in going from one gathering to another, from the theatre to a banquet or vice versa, could the sumptuary laws of the day – unsupported by the example of legislators – change their ways? In Ferrara, if a rich man thought it better not to make too much show of his wealth, the Duke took it upon himself to show him how to dress for social gatherings, how many servants to have and what their livery should be.[119] In nearby Bologna, there was a certain reluctance to exercise moderation in spending, as the fabulously embellished home of Alessandra Carminali shows. So much did she spend on the house that she had difficulty getting rid of an uninterrupted flow of visitors.[120]

Luxury and opulence were similarly put on show in other Italian cities, too numerous to document in detail. However, note that this lifestyle was of-

---

[114] VERGA, *op. cit.*, p. 260.

[115] *Ibid.*, p. 261.

[116] BANDELLO, *Le novelle*, cit., vol. I, p. 124.

[117] *Ibid.*, vol. I, p. 123.

[118] VERGA, *op. cit.*, pp. 256-257.

[119] SEGARIZZI, *op. cit.*, vol. I, p. 6 (anno 1565). See p. 7 for a description of the magnificent festivities that took place in Ferrara.

[120] FRATI, *op. cit.*, p. 19.

ten maintained by amassing debt and the slow, inevitable, squandering of the wealth another generation had made sacrifices to acquire. Not surprisingly Davanzati furiously criticized the «founders of their faculties», whose «excess of luxury» led to the economic ruin of their homeland.[121] Some, indeed, «to pump themselves up outdoors» made economies at home, depriving themselves even of bare necessities, as a play by Maggi makes clear, in which a nobleman of good sense lets off steam with his mother, who will not allow her daughter to marry a wealthy man, because he is not a titled aristocrat:

> Five children you brought

The son tells his rebellious and perplexed mother:

> Into this world, three maidens
> To give in marriage and keep us
> From the lash of law
> To pay away our debts. Our wealth is
> Squandered and our nobility
> Falls heavy over us;
> Among our peers we should
> Strut as equals, imitate their luxury,
> Yet pomp is but abuse
> And ambition's use
> For fancy and fond foolery,
> Fools and madmen we must rival
> And with ingenuity strive
> To keep apace with those
> Who puff out their finery as our clothes
> Run bare of thread
> And we are barely fed.[122]

Spanish arrogance thus accompanied diminishing resources, ruining an increasing number of families, all intent on squandering the wealth accumulated by their ancestors. This was the century of love for «faculties»; yet more than by a love of money Italians were motivated by pleasure, the desire for an honourable name, pomp and and the ostentation of wealth, all of which cost money and brought none in.[123] It seems almost that Italians believed their

---

[121] DAVANZATI, *Le opere*, cit., vol. I, pp. 91-92, postscript TACITO, *op. cit.*, cap. XLVIII.

[122] Transcribed by VERGA, *op. cit.*, pp. 284-285.

[123] Even when there were abundant resources, they were never enough. The six-monthly balance sheet of Cardinal Salviati, for example, in 1595 showed a revenue of 4776 scudi and expenses of 5011, a loss of 200 scudi. Cf. AB, 4374, c. 2. In ASV.

wealth could never run out, precisely when their disregard for work and their habitual squandering was taking them deeper and deeper into ruinous debt. «Yet the ruin could not have been either immediate or complete: the great wealth accumulated at better times, the knowledge gained and the organization of technical instruments for industry and trade, enabled the economy to hold on tenaciously. This also explains why art, literature and thought continued to flourish».[124]

9. Though it has been seen that Italian society took refuge from work and frittered away its wealth, in the sixteenth and seventeenth centuries Italians followed their forefathers in their charitable works. Charities grew in number and type[125] in every city and region of Italy, following the examples of the Saints and, no less important, of men of government.

The Doge, Cristoforo Moro, died stipulating in his will that a row of houses be built in the S. Giobbe district and be given to the poor for the love of God.[126] This authoritative example was not lost on others, since charity institutions benefited from many private donations and bequests, including perhaps most importantly the hospice for the needy and homeless built in 1527 from the generosity of a lawyer, a haberdasher and other benefactors.[127] In 1522, Gaetano Thiene of Vicenza opened a new hospital in Venice for people suffering from incurable diseases (mainly venereal disease), who at that time largely attracted scorn and contempt. The hospital became well-known throughout Christendom on account of the working contributions of Gerolamo Miani, Ignatius of Loyola and Francesco Saverio.[128] Not a saint, but a good timber merchant, in 1535 Bartolomeo Nordio of Bergamo set up in his home town a pious institution distributing money and bread to noblemen fallen into ruin and to poor girls. A little more than twenty years later, it also helped women keep to the straight and narrow.[129] In the same century a keen sense of morals and charity inspired Isabella d'Aragona to house vulnerable, homeless and converted girls in Milan;[130] in the same city, the S. Giovanni Fraternity set up by merchants and commoners assisted prisoners.[131] In Mi-

---

[124] SOLMI, *op. cit.*, pp. 639-640.

[125] Cf. TACCHI-VENTURI, *op. cit.*, vol. I, p. 352.

[126] MOLMENTI, *op. cit.*, vol. II, p. 454.

[127] *Ibid.*, vol. II, p. 53.

[128] *Ibid.*

[129] *Ibid.*

[130] VERGA, *op. cit.*, p. 278.

[131] *Ibid.*, p. 277.

13

lan, there was a long tradition of charitable works among the merchant class. Venusti writes: «privately and publicly infinite profit they bring to this country and to Christianity, marrying poor and honest daughters, maintaining poor gentlemen, helping chaste and needy men of religion and donating to places of piety, liberating with great sums many Christians enslaved by the Moors»[132] Further evidence of this charitable spirit is provided by the agreements between shareholders in commercial enterprises, which often destined part of the profits to alms for the poor and needy.[133] A great deal of the merit for these charitable works undoubtedly rests with the very important figure of Carlo Borromeo, who in the middle of a terrible famine in 1570 – causing thousands of peasants to come to town in search of food – appealed to the hearts and minds of the wealthy, after himself giving everything he possessed to the starving.[134] And this is only one of the examples of the efforts made by the Cardinal of Milan to correct the uneven distribution of wealth and the causes of serious hardship.[135]

Despite the economic decline of Florence throughout the sixteenth century, the city's merchants also had a tradition in giving alms. An enthusiastic Ambassador from the Venetian Republic, resident in Florence, wrote: «There are near 40 hospitals in the city, which have, in my understanding, 60,000 ducats in revenue, and are built magnificently and most excellently governed; one hospital, of which the city is rightfully proud, is Santa Maria Nova, which has between 15 and 60,000 ducats of revenue, and accepts all those who are infirm. God willing, this city may become as rich in hospitals and pious places as Florence! But our gentlemen who make such efforts to build and construct new hospitals for the incurable, and other places of devotion, are greatly to be praised, because it is be their means that they procure the grace of God for our State».[136] This was written in 1527, when Venice had already shown the world what charity could do for the needy in society. Rome followed the example, building the hospital of S. Giacomo,[137] enlarged through the donations of benefactors throughout the sixteenth century.[138]

---

[132] VENUSTI, *op. cit.*, p. 13.

[133] Cf. ACCM, Cartella 363.

[134] Cf. S. Carlo Borromeo nel terzo centenario della Canonizzazione, Periodico mensile, July 1909, p. 137.

[135] See the lengthy description of the activities of San Carlo with regard to helping the poor, by G. RATZINGER, *Geschichte der kirchlichen Armenpflege*, Freiburg, Herder, 1868, pp. 335-339.

[136] SEGARIZZI, *op. cit.*, vol. III, part I, p. 23 (year 1527).

[137] TACCHI – VENTURI, *op. cit.*, vol. I, p. 356.

[138] AB, 4373, folder entitled: «Spese della Fabbrica del Incurabili del 1587». See also AV.

The passage above from the Ambassador of Venice leaves no doubt about the motives behind charitable works and donations, which in the sixteenth century made it possible to create some of the most worthy institutions. In an era when ostentation and pomp were a rule of life, certain initiatives cannot be explained by sentiments of humanity and solidarity, as some have unhappily attempted to show, but only by faith, animating in men, above all in sinners, the desire to seek – through giving alms to the poor and needy – the blessing and forgiveness of God. The Venetian Ambassador says so explicitly, seeing in the charitable works of Venice the means for attracting the benevolence of God. If in other aspects of the economic and social life of the Italians in the Modern Age, what emerges is a gradual weakening of faith and hence the loosening of the relations between economic activity and moral or Christian aims, in charity the evangelical spirit had not been quenched despite all the deviations in norms and customs in the course of Italian history.

10. Ultimately, what does all this copious testimony on the conduct of practical men reveal about the economic spirit of the times?

Above all, the researcher cannot fail to acknowledge the great love of money that drove Italians in the Modern Age in their pursuit of wealth through legitimate and illegitimate means, often in open conflict with the ecclesiastical tradition and with civil laws. Whether this was due to a weakening of faith or to the greater economic difficulties of the time that people faced in their search for wealth, the fact is that only a few men in the Modern Age who pursued riches and felt the torment of conflicting views on its acquisition, actually allowed themselves to be directed by ethical considerations. However, it would be wrong to assume that, because of this, Italians were guided in their economic choices solely by their own material interests. The aims they sought to achieve through their activities will be considered shortly. Undoubtedly, the sixteenth century saw an entirely new moral code replace the traditional codes of practice that had hitherto assisted men in their dealings with each other.

The aim of economic activity in the sixteenth century was essentially to achieve glory, honour and power. This was true not only of the nobility but also of the lower classes, anxious to climb the social ladder as they observed those above them acquiring more and more power. Naturally, this volume focuses its attention on the economic activities of the nobility, families whose enormous capital, built up in the Middle Ages and the fifteenth century, derived from trade and industry. The nobility was the ruling class and their attitude to wealth and the means of acquiring it determined in which direction the economy in Italy moved as the peninsula approached the Modern Age, both in terms of the capital used by noblemen and the positions its members occupied in political life. How did these families conduct their affairs and shape the economic life of those beneath them?

Unlike their forefathers, who had built up their wealth through hard work and trading – in situations of hardship and difficulty – the nobility of the sixteenth century had no regard for trade or industry. This is not a new historical finding and if this volume has presented umpteen instances of conduct based on the aristocratic disregard for work it is because the economic decline in Italy during the second half of the sixteenth century can be ascribed largely to this attitude. Noblemen withdrew their labour and their capital from productive enterprises and adopted indirect forms of involvement in the economy. The spread of credit is one symptom of this tendency, lending being considered an untroubling form of capital investment, ensuring a fixed income without undue effort.

CHAPTER EIGHT

CONCLUSIONS

1. When a building has been completed, the scaffolding is pulled down so everyone can see what has been built and admire or criticize the architectural form. Similarly, after the copious documentation provided by historical research, the time comes to summarize the results so they can be placed alongside other considerations about the era under investigation.

It is not easy to reduce to a few lines the thinking of Churchmen, poets, jurists, philosophers, social reformers and businessmen of the sixteenth and seventeenth centuries or the laws that governed economic life in the period. Each cultural grouping and social class saw things from their own point of view, putting forward an ideal of economic life coherent with its political, moral and religious convictions. There were even differences of opinion within the same groups, to which the reader's attention has been drawn during the course of the research presented here.

The complexity and variety of thought in relation to wealth at the onset of the Modern Age, as traced back to theorists, writers, theologians, lawmakers and practical men, can be broken down into two basic currents, one embodying the principles and doctrine of the Middle Ages,[1] and the other new ideas more suited to the modern period.

The thinking of the Church belongs to the first current and its regulations regarding the acquisition of wealth and its use were inspired by consolidated principles and values. In the sixteenth and seventeenth centuries, as in the past, riches were thought of by the Church as a means and not an end, with a social and religious function, as God-given and hence to be distributed through charity to the poor and needy, in pursuit of a supreme good. Moderation was urged for Christians in seeking wealth and its comforts, this being

---

[1] All references in this chapter to the Middle Ages in relation to wealth and business are derived from FANFANI, *Le origini*, cit.

coherent with the mission of every man in life and with his duty to promote social wellbeing.

It is not difficult to see that the economic spirit which inspired the Church laws of the sixteenth and seventeenth centuries was the logical continuation of Thomistic thinking in relation to business. Nor did the clarifications provided by some thinkers within the Church radically alter its position, while establishing important moral precepts for economic life. The justification given by De Vio and Menochio to social climbing, generally considered illegitimate and against the principal of accepting one's social standing in life, was insufficient to break with the Church tradition of economic ethics, both because social ambition was the privilege of only a few exceptional individuals or those who created large families, and because – in relation to the acquisition of wealth and its use – these two Church thinkers were careful to support the most faithful interpreters of evangelical social thought in their teachings and preaching. All this appears more an effort by the Church to adapt to the economic practice of the sixteenth century than a radical break with tradition.

This includes the attitude of the Church to credit and the compromises it reached in the sixteenth century in the form of loss of expected profits, consequential damages and so on. Despite this, it would be wrong to think that the Church condoned the payment of interest: any payment for the use of money over time was consistently and roundly condemned by the Church and Church writers, both within the Scholastic tradition, and through the continuation of the thinking of Thomas Aquinas during the Reformation and Catholic Counter Reformation. Even the endless series of laws established for exchanges shows that the medieval tradition continued and the new laws were made necessary by the increasingly sophisticated ways to circumvent the prohibition through the invention of new forms of contract veiling the underlying usury. The cases of damages for loss of income and of *periculum sortis* show the attitude of the Church during the period, entirely consistent with its previous teachings related to economic effort and the fruits of labour. Since men should naturally seek their subsistence through the sweat of their brow, the Church allowed money they had earned honestly through their labours to be lent and for recompense to be given for this use not as interest but as an indemnity against the risk of failure to return the loan, for the privation of the money and the fact that the lender, who might have invested the money in a profitable commercial or industrial enterprise, had opted instead to help a friend or person in need. It should be noted that these cases were, of course, rare. Just how rare is difficult to say, but certainly the Church justified these loans only where the lender was disadvantaged by his decision to deprive himself of his money for a certain period.

As stated above, Churchmen and the laws of the Church considered work the only honest means of making a living and providing for one's family: an affirmation of great importance in a century, such as the sixteenth in Italy, in which practical men, with the support of learned contemporaries and men of letters, gradually withdrew from hard physical labour, viewing work and economic activities on the whole as damaging to the honour, reputation and nobility of their station. This is what distinguished some classes from others and separated them from the traditional social thinking of the Church. Whilst in terms of economic morals in relation to money changing and loans, no class took a different position from that of the Church, whose principles were upheld and often applied very strictly, in the case of work some entirely new attitudes emerged in certain classes, in clear contrast with the teachings of the Church. Men of letters, politicians, philosophers and jurists were not entirely unaffected by the fascinations offered by the period, in which social classes had gradually emerged, with a wealthy nobility patronizing the learned, who otherwise might have had less fortune in their intellectual pursuits. The generous patronage of the time served to enrol artists and thinkers into the life of noble families, generally only recently elevated to such exalted ranks through the commerce and business of the preceding period. This new tenor of life, which consciously or unconsciously took possession of the ruling class, not without the influence of the enlightened thinking and ideals of the fifteenth century, exercised considerable sway over the writers of the time within the various cultural fields examined in this volume. And these writers helped to create an atmosphere in the sixteenth century in which men and women of the nobility disparaged toil and the sweat of the brow – previously deemed entirely virtuous – as unworthy of their standing in society. The new virtues were reputation and honour, which the exercise of arms, the study of letters and the pleasures of a bountiful life could procure for individuals and their families. Such virtues were undermined by the practice of a trade or the conduct of commerce, which took the nobleman far afield, to foreign countries, where he risked life and limb and, perhaps worse, came into contact with people of less than adequate standing and without learning. The rediscovery of Platonic thought – unknown in the Middle Ages – renewed the idea of a society in which arts and crafts were carried out by the lower classes whilst noblemen dedicated themselves to the life of the mind and to conducting affairs of state. Among literary men, a certain number extolled the virtues of the «villa» and the countryside, praised for its fertility and honesty, and for the pleasantries of a life of ease.

These opinions are expressed about economic life – sometimes strongly, sometimes obliquely – by writers from various cultural backgrounds in the sixteenth and seventeenth centuries. Given their affinities and their attitude to morals in economic life, it can be said that they continued the medieval tradition. Yet these poets, men of letters, philosophers and political theorists also viewed intense economic activity as unworthy of nobility and the life of the spirit, and hence gave some support to the economic ambitions of practical men, or to be precise to the landed gentry and class of noblemen which dominated political and social life in the sixteenth century. This was the class whose attitude to work and the proper means of accumulating wealth was to determine the economic future of Italy.

There is no reason here to repeat what has already been said about the practices of businessmen in the period. Suffice it to say that perhaps at no other time, in Italy and Europe as a whole, was credit so widespread. Loans from Jews were generally of a small amount and were made against the pledge of an item of some value, and hence had no influence on production but ruined the needy and fed the insatiable greed of the lenders. What became of the wealth accumulated by families through trade and commerce in the fourteenth and fifteenth centuries? Motivated by an ideal of life in which work was denigrated as unworthy (although it was precisely this that had elevated merchants and traders to nobility), many saw no reason why their wealth should not be entrusted to bankers in return for a steady, risk-free income and a quiet life. A quiet life meant a life of luxury dedicated to the display of rank and riches, procured by using property for a fixed income rather than having to endure the hustle and bustle of commerce. And what quieter and more peaceful life than that of the country and the villa, as frivolous men of letters in the sixteenth century began to urge upon them? Often, the villa was not built in order to superintend the cultivation of the land but the cultivation of the land served no other purpose than to provide for the villa and the hunting expeditions of the noblemen, a favourite pastime in the sixteenth century. After abandoning industry and commerce, the huge sums accumulated by ennobled families were entrusted to bankers and given over to the life of the country. And never mind if these activities were not as profitable as the commerce and industry of olden times, the noblemen and wealthy of the sixteenth century hardly gave it thought. If the need arose, they could always sell off part of their properties.

In our opinion, this approach to economic life in the sixteenth century was the result of the work and industriousness that had been put into the previous period, during which a life of ease in one's old age was seen as a fitting conclusion to life's many travails. The ambition of the mercantile class began to come to the fore in the fifteenth century and was transformed in the following century into the wish to conduct a life of ease, dedicated to the untroubled display of the status acquired in the previous period. It is not difficult to understand the effect this new style of life had on the economy of the peninsula. Could it be that the decline of the Italian economy in the second half of the sixteenth century was due, in part, to this new unproductive lifestyle?

Before answering this question, we should turn our attention, however briefly, to the form, scale and consequences of this decline and the explanations historians have put forward up to now to account for it.

2. Many famous historians have investigated the economic decline of the Italian peninsula during the sixteenth century. Tamassia says that what strikes the researcher of the period most acutely and feelingly is «the economic distress, both public and private, which the image of a scintillating and lavish society cannot conceal».[2] The history of commerce written by Segre gives a concrete account of the economic decline of Italy at the beginning of the Modern Age. He writes: «whilst large and small European States, almost all focusing on the life within their borders, made progress in various forms and saw their public economies flourish, Italy with the splendour of its Medieval period, conquered by foreign powers and divided into small City States, dragged itself forward pettily and painfully, without means of its own, the doormat of France, Spain and Austria».[3]

More recently, a researcher into economic history, albeit warning against the facile conclusion that «the Italian economy of the Renaissance period should be considered an economy in evident and full decline,» says that in the sixteenth century «the period was long gone when the fleets of Pisa, Genoa and Venice allowed themselves to contend supremacy in the Mediterranean without concerning themselves with how this might advantage other, far from fearsome competitors; long gone was the time in which Italian merchants had a monopoly of exchanges and banking in France, England, the Low Countries, and used their financial dominance to obtain favours at the most important Fairs and in the export of precious raw materials».[4] This suggests not so much that the economy of Italy was declining in absolute terms, but that growth had come to a standstill. Others believe that the period after the City States was one of absolute decline.[5] Contemporaries in the sixteenth

---

[2] N. TAMASSIA, *La famiglia italiana nei secoli decimoquinto e decimosesto*, Palermo, Sandron, 1910, p. 3.

[3] SEGRE, *op. cit.*, p. 456.

[4] LUZZATTO, *Storia economica*, cit., pp. 81-82.

[5] MOLMENTI, *op. cit.*, vol. II, p. 12.

century and early seventeenth century felt the decline, unfavourably comparing the wealth of their period with that of the previous age.

The reports to the Government of the Serenissima from its ambassadors to various Courts throughout Italy speak of the luxury and wealth on display, for example, in the palaces and villas in and around mercantile Florence, the banquets at Court in Ferrara, the magnificence and generous hospitality of Princes everywhere. But they also spoke of an undoubted decline in prosperity throughout the peninsula. Only a few years after the Sack of Rome, Suriano informed the Serenissima that in beautiful Fiorenza (Florence) eight or more families possessed the considerable sum of one hundred thousand ducats, including Guadagni with four hundred thousand and Albizzi two hundred thousand. But Suriano adds that «better means they had to make great expense, if this were not followed by hardship and too much spending: first the House of Medici that so medicated its dominance that the skin has been stripped away: wars, captivity and expenses of the Christian Weal and its possessions: the sack of Rome, the ruin of Naples». It is easy to understand how the increasing financial needs of the Medici negatively affected a city of merchants such as Florence, not to mention the loss of important clients. The Sack of Rome had cancelled or severely diminished the earnings of eight thousand ducats a week in trade with Rome. At the same time the cruelty of war and the ruin of the Kingdom of Naples led to a further loss of three thousand ducats a week.[6] A few decades later, according to the custom of the Ambassadors of Venice to Florence, Vincenzo Fedeli sang the praises of the city's beauty, its climate and the hard work of its citizens, but said the city had «once been more florid and populous».[7]

Priuli also reports on the unfavourable conditions in Florence. Several years after Fedeli, he had this to say: «Reasoning myself with a practical person, I was told the riches of citizens had been reduced almost to poverty, because their faculty consists in the arts, and trade and surpluses, the traditional earnings of the Florentines, by nature very sparing in their lives; and now, (in addition to the profit of the Prince) the young in cities are delighted by its pleasures and follow the customs of the Court rather than busy themselves in workshops and attend to merchandise: so, for the excessive expenses and lack of revenues, few in Florence want to marry in order that their children be not left poor and in dependence».[8]

---

[6] *Relazione di Antonio Suriano* in 1533. SEGARIZZI, *op. cit.*, vol. III, part I, p. 112. V. on p. 106 and following pages of the same Report for the immense, extraordinary war taxes.

[7] *Relazione di Vincenzo Fedeli* in 1561. Cf. SEGARIZZI, *op. cit.*, vol. III, part I, pp. 126 e 128.

[8] *Relazione di Lorenzo Priuli* in 1566. Cf. *ibid.*, vol. III, part I, p. 186.

Apart from demographic considerations, which can be found in the lesser writings of the sixteenth century, indicating the aspirations of the centuries of the Renaissance, the reports of the Ambassadors to Florence describe a once prosperous city now in decline. In 1576, Andrea Gussoni wrote of Florence that «riches have weakened, lacking trade, and the situation has become grave».[9] The same was true of other cities in Italy. In Milan, for example, it can be said – on the basis of similar reports – that the city had fallen into a state of poverty in the first two decades of the sixteenth century, and this situation was not temporary, if Basadona was moved to write that its «poverty cannot be repaired in a short space or time since the workshops are in ruin and the craftsmen dead so industry and public revenues and particulars are all lacking».[10] The revenues of the city also indicate its economic decline, with a fall from almost 400,000 ducats to 170,000 in 1533, for duties on supplies and merchandise.[11]

Exactly one hundred years later, the economy of the city had declined still further, as Bertuccio Valier wrote to the Government of the Serenissima in 1633: «As I was able with certitude to establish, the Duchy of Milan, once florid and full of men, with soft countryside and the affluence of abundance and merchandise, is now anguished and continues to cry out and has been taken to calamity and despair. Those disconsolate citizens, in their continuous and affectionate visiting of my house, each with an office to perform, confess the mediocre have no livelihood, because the soldiers take all; the wealthy earn one third of what they once enjoyed; the poor perish of famine and distress; and Milan, a capital once with 300,000 inhabitants, now has barely 80,000; luxury and pomp has turned to misery and want».[12] In the final decades of the sixteenth century, the city cannot have been in such economic straits if De Castro was able to report good revenues from the markets around 1580, the result of a period of lengthy peace, which fostered «trade and mercantile industry».[13] In the same manuscript,[14] De Castro also writes of fierce competition among lenders with a fall in interest rates, indicating a less than prosperous economy.[15] In Mantua the nobility disparaged this and all

---

[9] *Relazione di Andrea Gussoni* in 1576. Cf. *ibid.*, vol. III, part I, p. 211.

[10] *Relazione di Giovanni Basadona* in 1533. Cf. *ibid.*, vol. II, p. 38.

[11] *Relazione di Giovanni Basadona* in 1533. Cf. *ibid.*, vol. III, pp. 41-42.

[12] *Relazione di Bertuccio Valier* in 1633. Cf. *ibid.*, vol. II, p. 86.

[13] DE CASTRO, *op. cit.*, c. 32.

[14] *Avvertimenti dati al Sr. Marc'Antonio Colonna quando andò vicerè di Sicilia*, of RICCI, in VENTURA, *Thesoro Politico*, cit., part II.

[15] DE CASTRO, *op. cit.*, c. 32.

other economic activities, leaving the business of lending to Jews,[16] and in Urbino, the city of Guidobaldo II della Rovere, this custom was promoted by men of letters and the law, leading to its adoption «in numerous localities in Italy».[17]

As we have seen, the sixteenth century was a period during which noble families allowed themselves to fall into economic distress rather than «taking up an occupation that nought prevented».[18] If a Venetian merchant, breaking with the by now consolidated tradition of the nobility to snub commerce and trade, had set sail with a cargo of wood, left in storehouses in the City Arsenal for over a century, the example of Paolo Sarpi, born into a family of merchants but with the vocation of monk in the Servite order, wounded in service to the city, would have dissuaded him.[19]

The above does not mean that all of a sudden the economy of Italy had ground to a halt like the apprentices in a workshop dropping their tools at the sound of the siren. In the sixteenth century still «Bologna produces hemp, tow, finery and all kinds of work and silk, gypsum and marble». Modena had not stopped supplying «velvet, cotton finery, delicate wines, wheels, mascara and other goods,» and throughout Italy «the miraculous cheeses of Parma and Piacenza are appreciated,» and «in Brescia iron is worked in all manner, and hackbuts, and all kinds of arms». Puglia continued to export «grain, broad beans, chickpeas, oils, wines, olives, oranges, lemons and great quantities of corn, as from Friuli «flour, vegetables and fruit of all kinds».[20]

So it would be a mistake to think that in the sixteenth century the Italian economy was unproductive, but it would be equally mistaken to ignore the testimony of contemporaries, who describe an economy in severe decline. In this connection, the position of Luzzatto appears unacceptable where he claims that the decline was entirely due to the loss of a monopoly position, and not to «a genuine reduction in the volume and value of production and trade and as a consequence a deterioration in the standard of living and potential productivity».[21] However, in our opinion, a contemporary described the problem more accurately when he affirmed that in economic mat-

---

[16] *Relazione di Francesco Contarini* in 1588; in SEGARIZZI, *op. cit.*, vol. I, p. 78.
[17] *Relazione di Federico Badoer* in 1547; in *ivi*, vol. II, p. 170-171.
[18] LOTTINI, *op. cit.*, p. 113, avv. 248.
[19] P. SARPI, *op. cit.*, pp. 30-31 and *passim*.
[20] FIORAVANTI, *op. cit.*, c. 32.
[21] LUZZATTO, *Storia economica*, cit., p. 84.

ters «no progress was made, but a going back, and not moving forward and advancing is like losing and going backward».[22]

But whether or not an absolute decline, as we believe it should be described, or a relative decline, the fact remains that the economy of Italy no longer grew in the sixteenth century and this has puzzled historians and been the cause of much controversy. In relation to this problem, Molmenti cites the discovery of the Americas, the sea route to the Indies, and the loss of Eastern markets due to the influence of the Turks, who prevented Italian cities from continuing the prosperous trade with the Levantine region, as the causes for the decline of the wealth of Venice, whose annual symbolic wedding to the sea by the Bucintoro[23] must have begun to feel rather inappropriate. The geographical explanations of the decline of Italy's economic fortunes appeared plausible – as one historian puts it – «until it was observed that the discovery of the East Indies, where Portugal had a virtual monopoly, does not explain the decline of Portugal, just as «the discovery of the West Indies, where Spain dominated, does not explain its decline».[24] Critical was the explanation given for the decline of the Kingdom of Naples by Antonio Serra, who considered the geographical position of southern Italy, without a genuine trade in transit from one region to another, as one of the causes of the weakness of the Neapolitan economy.[25] Yet Naples had not moved, so the explanation seems untenable.

Religious reasons, essentially associated with the Reformation and Counter Reformation, have also been cited for the decline of the Italian economy.[26] A great deal has been written on the subject, including the theory of Weber,[27]

---

[22] GARZONI, op. cit., p. 225, disc. 26.

[23] MOLMENTI, op. cit., vol. II, p. 12. The symbolic wedding of Venice and the sea, once evidence of domination and power, inspired the ferocious sarcasm of a French poet, who wrote the following lines about the ceremony:
> «ces vieux cocus vont espouser la Mer,
> Dont ils sont les marits, et le Turc l'adulter».

(J. DU BELLAY, in a sonnet on p. 96 of the first volume: *Recueil des plus belles pièces des poètes françois: depuis Villon jusqu'à Benserade*, Paris, Par la Compagnie des Libraires, 1752, VI, Paris, Par la Compagnie des Libraires, 1752).

[24] A. FANFANI, *I mutamenti economici nell'Europa moderna e l'evoluzione costituzionalistica delle classi dirigenti*, Milano, Vita e Pensiero, 1936, p. 139.

[25] A. SERRA, *Breve trattato delle cause, che possono far abbondar li regni d'oro et d'argento dove non sono miniere*, Milano, Destefanis, 1803. Cf. G. ARIAS, *Les idées économique d'Antonio Serra*, pp. 275-276.

[26] For an ample bibliography on the subject, see A. FANFANI, *Riforma e capitalismo moderno nella recente letteratura*, «Rivista Internazionale di Scienze Sociali», 1930. See also ID., *Cattolicesimo e protestantesimo nella formazione storica del capitalismo*, «Rivista Internazionale di Scienze Sociali», 1934, chapters I, II and VII.

[27] M. WEBER, *Die protestantische Ethik und der Geist des Kapitalismus*, Tubingen, Mohr, 1920.

«who attributed to Calvinism the merit of introducing to the world the sense of a vocation which today, albeit decoupled from its original religious inspiration, is the driving force of modern capitalism».[28] However, this does not explain why Reformed England made economic progress, while Protestant Germany did not, nor why Catholic Spain lost ground at the same time that equally Catholic France began its economic advance.[29] Although these phenomena induce Fanfani to dedicate a great deal of space in his work to Catholicism and Protestantism and their role in the historical formation of capitalism, the literature which associates the economic growth of modern States to religious influences, is unconvincing. Sombart[30] believes that the growth of some States was due to the presence of a Jewish community in those States and that the decline of other regions in the sixteenth century was due to their expulsion.[31] However, in Italy at least, as we have seen, the presence of Jews was not a factor in the development of the economy, but quite the opposite, since loans were made for consumption and not production, leading to a gradual impoverishment of whole classes, encouraged by the desire to display wealth and luxury beyond the means of the families who thus desired to affirm their status in society and whose declining wealth was hidden by loans from the Jews.[32]

Some historians believe the cause of the economic decline of the Italian peninsula was war, the continuous series of military conflicts that ruined not only towns but the fertile countryside. Similar attention has been dedicated to political fragmentation as a possible cause of economic decline, with small City States unable to compete with emerging nations in terms of the sponsorship and protection of industry and trade.

In the face of these explanations and theories (and there are many more), a researcher into the spirit of the economic ideals that informed the enterprises and endeavours of men of the sixteenth and seventeenth centuries is tempted to give his own view and his own explanation of the economic decline of Italy during the period under examination.

3. It is known that during the prosperous Middle Ages, Italy's economic role was that of intermediary between East and West. If the relations between

---

[28] FANFANI, *Cattolicesimo e Protestantesimo*, cit., p. 11.

[29] ID., *I mutamenti economici*, cit., pp. 140-144.

[30] W. SOMBART, *Die Juden und das Wirtschaftsleben*, Leipzig, Duncker & Humblot, 1911.

[31] FANFANI, *I mutamenti economici*, cit., p. 141 and following.

[32] See paragraph 3 of Chapter VI.

corporations and political power in the hundred cities of Italy are analyzed, it is clear that merchants and their trades were given pride of place. Without going into a large number of examples, suffice it to mention the enormous power of the *mercatores magni* in Milan, especially during the domination of the Visconti family. All economic power in Milan was subordinate to them. And even under the subsequent reign of the Sforza family, when an effort was made to rebalance the autonomy and power of production and commercial categories, the powers of the merchants remained, their control over the prosperity of the city deriving from trade with other European markets. Merchants worked through «consuls» or agents, who were the fulcrum and promotors of economic activity with Milanese settlers elsewhere. Manufacturing in the city depended on the work of these merchants and their ability to sell its products. Added to this, the role of Milan as a transit point for goods increased its earnings from duties and hence the prosperity of the city. This was the case throughout the period the Milanese, and Italians in general, were willing to take on the risks and dangers of trading with other nations, often less than honest in their dealings.

What happened when this entrepreneurial spirit gave way to the wish for a quiet life? The reaction against trading just as the world was moving from the Middle Ages into the Modern Age penalized the economy of the peninsula and its dedication to work, on which its prosperity had been based throughout the medieval period. Just as Italy was facing strong competition from other nations in its traditional role as intermediary, the newly elevated nobility of the peninsula turned its attention to the ideal of ease and social status. Instead of continuing to build up wealth, the time had come for the gradual consumption of capital in a display of luxury and pomp, leading ultimately to the loss of those fortunes upon which the prosperity of the peninsula depended.

Without Italian merchants, international trade diminished, making a reorganization of the economy based on industry necessary. There was a considerable manufacturing base to build on but the transformation was bound to be slow and industry was not entirely free of the infectious spirit of ease that had taken its hold on the Italian nobility. Added to this was the fact that the vehicles for the investment of the huge sums accumulated in the past did not provide investors with the kind of revenues they expected. Most of the capital was entrusted to bankers for various forms of fixed income based on property. In other words, the ruling class turned away from direct economic activity, preferring a regular income without risk or the expense of energy, through loans via intermediaries for the purchase of rights under various jurisdictions. Rulers abroad saw the opportunity to obtain loans from Italian bankers in order to solve their financial problems. For example the King of France borrowed as much as 400,000 ducats from Venice. At the same time, a rise in prices eroded the fixed incomes of the nobility leading to the emergence of a new class, whose earnings were mobile. Historians have demonstrated[33] how negatively affected by the revolution in prices the aristocracy in Italy was during the sixteenth century, precisely when it had turned its attention to investments.

In our opinion, this is the chief reason for the economic decline of Italy in the sixteenth and seventeenth centuries and for the disappearance of the nobility from the peninsula, with the sad consequences of this decline. It took two more centuries for a new ruling class to emerge and for the economy to resume growth, in the eighteenth and nineteenth centuries.

---

[33] FANFANI, *Indagini sulla "Rivoluzione dei prezzi"*, cit., pp. 177-179.

IL DEBITOR FELICE

(*Discorso accademico del Sr. Muzio Petroni da Trevi*)

<small>Biblioteca Vaticana, Ms. Vat. Lat. 11761, ff. 233r-238v</small>

Tutte le felicità, che per sentimento di tanti fra di loro discordanti filosofi disunite si ritrovano, unitamente concorrono a felicitare un huomo, che non havendo del proprio, sa vivere con l'altrui. E vaglia il vero, o Signori, se riguardiamo all'opinione d'Epicuro, che ne' piaceri, che di presente si godono, ripose il sommo della beatitudine, non vi ha chi si possa chiamar più beato del nostro debitore, vive egli così felice, che non invidiando le dispense dei più svogliati Apicii, che nel corso di ben pochi anni assorbirono dui millioni, e cinquecento mila scudi, obligandosi con poche parole con una forma di Camera riempie di materia una Cucina, e dice con Epicuro, Ede; sempre intento all'intiera sodisfazione del corpo, non vi è chi più spensierato beva, se procacciandosi tutto di nuovi creditori sta sempre nella credenza Bibe; la sua vita non è che un continuo giuoco con la sicurezza di sempre vincere, che sebene è fallito, non fa mai fallo, ma fa ben spesso fallire il compagno, e vince ogni partita lude; vive sempre lontano da ogni pensiero, che possa intorbidargli con la consideratione delle miserie future le delitie presenti, et ogni qualvolta considera il fin de debitori, che suole per lo più terminare in una Carcere, ha sempre in pronto il rimedio del Petrarca: la morte è fin d'una prigione oscura Post mortem nulla voluptas.

Hor niegatemi, se potete, o Signori, che la vita di un debitore non sia ripiena d'ogni felicità, se la felicità della vita humana può confinarsi dentro termini così vili: ede, bibe, lude, post mortem nulla volutaptas!

Se riponiamo la beatitudine di questa vita nell'opinione de Peripatetici, che de commodi del Corpo si contentarono, corporis commodis compleri beatam vitam, non so vedere chi più del nostro debitore sia felice: e per procedere distintamente tutti i commodi del corpo (prescindendo dalla salute) dependono dalla fortuna, che per non cagionar confusione con la particolar denominazione di ciascheduno, è necessario ridurli tutti alla materia prima del danaro, che vien comunemente confessata con Plauto per l'origine dell'allegrezza, laetitia hominis aurum. Se dunque ponderiamo i commodi del corpo in riguardo alla salute, come quella che immediatamente depende dalla mano dell'Onnipotente, può credersi perfettamente goduta

14

dal nostro debitore, se non vi è chi non gli desideri lunga vita per essere a qualche tempo sodisfatto, e non porga incessanti preghiere a S. Div.tà per la conservazione di quella Testa, che più vale di quel che pesi; se li consideriamo in riguardo del denaro, non vi è chi con maggior felicità li possieda del nostro debitore, posciache uscendogli di bocca l'accidente di quel verbo latino oro e vedendosi riempire la borsa della sostanza di quel nome volgare oro, si fa conoscere che ha in casa la gallina d'Esopo, e mena così delitiosa la vita, che anche ad onta del più freddo rovaio allora che nel colmo del verno non lascia sopra gli alberi per renderne testimonianza una foglia, si vede già maturati i frutti, né io saprei più degnamente paragonarlo che a quell'Arbore di fico nel giardino d'Armida, di cui disse Tasso:

> *Sopra il fico cadente invecchia il fico*
> *Coi fiori eterni eterno il frutto dura,*
> *e mentre spunta l'un altro matura.*

Ma se finalmente vogliamo fondare la beatitudine della vita nell'opinione di Xenocrate veramente più d'ognaltra probabile, in virtute non beatam modo vitam, sed etiam beatissimam, come non vi ha chi sia più virtuoso di un debitore, così viene in conseguenza non potersi dare in questa vita felicità maggiore, che haver de debiti; e negatemi, se vi dà l'animo, che questa, che a prima faccia vi rassembra avaritia non sia la madre di tutte l'arti liberali. Poniamo un debitore che fra l'altro non habbia havuta mai cognizione di lettere humane; et eccovelo dai debiti insensibilmente erudito, apparisce primieramente buonissimo grammatico, poiché appena vi conosce, perché vi insegna a vostre spese qual sia la declinatione, e portandovi di un salto ai Latini, non vi parrà di haver consumati gli attivi, che vi vedrete in volto nei passivi, et confondendosi l'attione contro il debitore con la passione del creditore impara con poco divario a confessar col Caporali:

> *Ma se l'attivo in me si fa passivo*
> *Ahi che son pur congiunti agere e pati,*
> *Aristotil non sa dunque s'è vivo.*

E se per avventura vi accorgete haver commesso in questo latino un error da Cavallo, che perciò voleste procurare l'emenda col farvi mettere in pratica dal nostro debitore un deponente, deponendo questi la significazione passiva, come quegli l'attiva, trovasi in mano il povero Creditore il più difficil neutro che s'insegnasse giamai nelle scuole de Pedanti, e avanzandosi con la prattica della scienza a conoscere quanto possedete, vi lascia con un participio assoluto, per farVi a Vostro malgrado confessare, che havete apprese tutte le regole del Donato.

Né qui si fermano i progressi del nostro debitore, imperciocché non può esservi chi seco trattando, non lo confessi per bravissimo rettorico, che non fa, che non opra per persuaderti! Le metafore più vaghe, l'allegorie più chiare sono le più domestiche figure, che adornino la di costui Rettorica; se vuole, fa figura d'iperbole, se deve, è un'ombra di diminutione, e a guisa di quelle donne d'Egitto, che all'hor che vi empivano di parole l'orecchie, vi vuotavano di danari la borsa, vi accorgete esser così fina la sua rettorica, che è necessario dire, che il nostro debitore:

> *Ha nelle mani, e nella lingua unita*
> *Per trarre a se quel che da te desia*
> *La forza occulta della calamita.*

Vi descrive il suo stato quasi fusse un delizioso giardino, né molto si dilunga dal vero il suo sentimento, perché sempre sta in terra di promissione, che ripieno da pertutto di fiori, vi assicura la maturità di quei frutti, che vi deve

> *E quel ch'è il bello, el caro accresce l'opre*
> *l'arte, che tutto fa nulla ti scuopre.*

Né mai arriverete conoscere di haver coltivato un Prato Rettorico, se non nel punto della raccolta, che vi scoverete haver fatto una maledetta sinedoche. Pars pro toto. Et in fatti è così spiritosa la Rettorica di un debitore, che basta per ammaestrare chi che sia che vi tratti, se dopo una vaghissima unione delle più belle figure, ed una graziosissima sincope, che tollit aliquid de medio, lascia i creditori eruditi come tanti cipriani.

Se poi pretendete agitare contro il nostro debitore lo sperimentate un perfettissimo logico, poiché prendendo un termine cathegorematico *unius mentis* va slogandolo con tanti, non gravetur, e tante dilationi, che non facer dovesse veder mai fine. Passa il nostro debitore alla fisica, e par che voglia provarvi l'infinito a parte rei, e non riuscendoli appagarvi in questa guisa, o con un segno verde al Cappello, che lo chiameremo significativo ad placitum a differenza di quegli, che prendono il soccorso dei Testi canonici per farsi lecito possedere l'altrui, con maggiore civiltà, o veramente con un argomento in celarent, vi esclude affatto da ogni pretensione.

E per non uscir dall'arti liberali, eccovi il nostro debitore diventato musico, comincia appena a far de debiti, che lo vedete carico di cento istrumenti, che riconoscendo per maestro un notaro, sono tutti composti a forma di cetera, canta all'hor che si vede bisognoso, et alterando la voce per persuadervi con la sua umiltà di essere un Basso, ottenuto ciò che desia, varia nel tuono, e quasi stridula canna strepitando il concerto, vi riesce il più bizzarro falsetto, che giamai praticaste. Canta, ma sempre sopra la parte degli altri, né canta per dilettarvi, ma per allegrezza di havervi incantato, e con una gentilissima maniera sa cavarti in un modo punto danari dalla borsa, e lagrime dagli occhi, et allor che lo vedete soggetto all'altrui battuta, terminando il canto in una fuga, vi lascia in mano la deffinitione della musica: sonus, aura, nihil.

S'avanza nelle scienze il nostro debitore, et eccotelo Aritmetico, sta sempre nel numerare, sempre sul far de conti, e o che sommi, multiplichi, o parta, sempre vi fa partite, e per tenere in bilancio l'entrata con l'uscita, vi riduce i frutti, che vi deve alla ragione di quattro per cento, e vi dà ad intendere, che il numero di quattro è numero perfetto appresso i Pittagorici, e cominciando a numerare uno, due o tre, e quattro, entra con la regola di Tritenio nel principio della sua Poligrafia, siste gradun, habes navique decem, e ritornando a numerare al contrario Vi fa toccar con mano, che nel quattro havete il diece, ma nel punto che pensate di possedere il numero denario, entra il nostro Aritmetico a partire, e salvandosi per se l'unità, o vi lascia col numero di dentro, che non può darvi che nove, o vi esclude con quel di fuora, che non vi frutterà mai più di un zero. Et è così fina l'aritmetica del nostro debitore, che partendo il nostro, e moltiplicando il proprio all'hor che fallisse, si mette in capitale. Ma in tuono per gratia o debitori, né vi scordate al maggior uomo delle Vostre più ordinate regole:

> *Perché tra Voi questa ragione è vera*
> *Che chi suol far su quel degli altri il conto*
> *Parte poi per colonna, e per galera.*

Passa il nostro debitore all'Astrologia, e mostra un contrassegno evidentissimo della sua dottrina in quel divulgatissimo detto, Sapiens dominabitur astris perché nel concorso de creditori, che lo tormentano come che il debitore habbia in mano le stelle, e la fortuna, ciascheduno li domanda la sua sorte principale, ed egli, che si avvede non poter sodisfare a richieste così alte, ricorre all'astrologia, e a tutto di facendo lunarii. Vi vede abbondante di ricchezze, et egli alzandovi una figura di natività, già vi incomincia a fare sopra il calcolo, et il giuditio, qui si che direi, che il povero debitore stasse male assai, perché chi fa de calcoli patisce di pietra, se questa pietra non concorresse a fabbricare di quei Castelli in Aria, che non il maggior capitale de' poveri rovinati, e trovandovi in ascendente un Giove se ne ripromette ogni giovamento; ma perché il suo giovamento va unito al vostro danno, vi accorgerete in fine di esser soggetti ad un Pianeta così combusto, che par che al suo arbitro sian soggette le stelle; imperciochè confinando in un angolo la nostra luna col suo maledetto Saturno, e mettendo sopra la vostra robba le sue mani, che giurareste havere tutta la forza della coda del Dragone, e vi fa confessar per vero quell'Aforismo formidabile ricevuto da tutta la scuola degli Arabi Luna in angulo cum Saturno unita cauda Draconis facit inopes etiam Reges né partendosi mai il nostro debitore con la consideratione dall'horoscopo, perché d'ogni suo motivo l'oro è scopo, è astrologo tanto più stimabile, quanto che disprezzando e trini, e quadrati, sol va dietro a quadrini, che non riuscendogli ottenerli da chi può darglili, canta con quel moderno

> *Se quadrin non mi date*
> *Prego il ciel quanto posso*
> *Ch'abbiate un di mezzo zodiaco adosso,*
> *Prego abbiate nel petto un sagittario*
> *E negli occhi un Acquario.*
> *Che per donna infedele habbiate un giorno*
> *Di dentro un pesce, e fuori il Capricorno*
> *E per fin de guadagni*
> *Leone al fianco, e 'l cancro che vi magni.*

Hor negatemi, Signore, che l'aver de debiti non sia la maggior felicità, che possa godersi in questa vita, mentre a felicitare un debitore concorrono tutte quelle qualità, che vi sapessero mai desiderare i più svegliati huomini del mondo? E che l'haver de' debiti è una felicità tanto più stimabile, quanto men conosciuta. A questo solo è permesso ammaestrar gli huomini in tutte le scienze, la maggior parte delle quali, per non tediarvi, tralascio, ma non parendomi conveniente, che in un congresso di virtuosi non habbi da comparirvi il nostro debitore compiacetevi di vederlo anche poeta; e sentite per cortesia come canta:

Canto al vostro suonar, ne fia stupore
che dove gnun va delle lire in busca,
Tiri di contrappunto un debitore.
> *Già mi picco ancor io di lingua etrusca,*
> *e se debiti fo, cercando il pane,*
> *accademico anch'io son della Crusca.*
Così varian qua giù le cose humane,
E se furon nemici a gran ragione
Trovansi in me congiunti Apollo, e Pane.
> *Entrambi erano mercanti, et a tenzone*
> *li spinse l'avaritia d'una lira,*
> *Considerate s'era d'un Testone.*
Tra lor perdente il vincitor si mira,
Resta Febo con l'acqua, e Pan col vino,
Pan all'arrosto, e Febo al fumo aspira.
> *Dunque è legge crudel d'empio destino,*
> *che sempre il dio dell'huomo sapiente*
> *Chieda al nume de Satiri un quadrino;*
Ma si canti pur sempre allegramente,
Scagli fulmini il cielo, avventi strali,
Morda la lingua, se non rode il dente,
> *L'altra necessità de' nostri mali*
> *A fare il calzolar par che ti spinga,*
> *Già che solo hanno spaccio li stivali.*
Se la zampogna mia non vi lusinga,
Nol dite almen, perché da dir non s'habbia
Far male al dio degli Orti una siringa.
> *Canto ma non d'amor, canto di rabbia,*
> *Se un creditor, che non mi crede a pieno*
> *Voglia sentirmi di cantare in gabbia.*
Che perciò tirarò i giorni meno,
Se qual olimpia vien per minchionarmi
Il traditore, e perfido Bireno.
> *Et io se non potrò col suon de carmi*
> *Fugar simil canaglia in conclusione*
> *Mi fa soldato, e do di mano all'armi.*
Ed ecco, che per prima inventione
Di gente, che già fecemi servitio,
formo di Compagnia uno Squadrone.
> *Et si prattico son nell'esercitio,*
> *Che già mi fanno official maggiore,*
> *perché son tutte Compagnie d'offitio.*

Per imprimermi al cuor fiero timore
Già minaccia prigion, fumi apparecchia
L'incredulo, e creduto creditore.
  Prendi un Curial di quella razza vecchia
  Di Can Corsi digiuna arrabbiata
  E mi metta alle corte un mozza orecchia,
Io che temo di qui qualche imboscata,
solo al Salvum me fac aprendo gli occhi,
faccio con l'honor mio la ritirata.
  Quando perché a temer più non mi tocchi
  Veggo venir pront'il bisogno humano
  Cento usurarî a proveder di stocchi.
All'hora il Creditor adopra invano
le scomuniche sue per farmi avante
con le censure diventar pagano;
  Ch'io, ch'appresi a mio costo esser furfante,
  schermendolo ad ogn'hor con le proteste,
  Mi fo pria che pagano, Protestante.
M'al fin ceder bisogna a questa peste,
Che per ribatter sol colpi si crudi,
se si trova tra voi che me l'impreste
  Havrei necessità di mille scudi.

AFTERWORD

When, presumably between 1932 and 1933, Gino Barbieri began to work on what was to become *Gli Ideali Economici degli Italiani all'inizio dell'Età Moderna* – initially in the form of an undergraduate dissertation supervised by Professor Amintore Fanfani at the Catholic University of the Sacred Heart in Milan – he could certainly not have imagined that events in Italy would unfold as they did. The economic and political context, the cultural milieu and the habits of university life with which he was accustomed probably appeared to Barbieri as the normal condition of his country. Italy was then – and remains today – rather provincial, though not lacking in men of great cultural and historical standing. One such example was Father Gemelli, the Franciscan monk leading the Catholic University in its struggle to survive in a society that tolerated no dissent even within the seemingly innocuous context of the history of thought in the sixteenth and seventeenth century. The apparent normality of all this was the outcome of a unique moment in Italian intellectual life, both in relation to the recent past and to subsequent developments.

Gino Barbieri grew up in the countryside south of Verona, near Legnago, certainly not the poorest town in the province but one that had yet to achieve the prosperity of the 1960s. His family was hardly affluent, and Gino was the only one of his siblings to complete his classical education – on account of his academic brilliance as well as the generosity of the charitable institution founded by Don Nicola Mazza – and to enroll at the newly established Catholic University in Milan, founded and led by Father Agostino Gemelli. For Barbieri, a Catholic upbringing meant far more than sacred texts and doctrine.

In the 1930s, the official economic doctrine espoused by economists that shaped Italian economic policies went under the name of "corporatism",[1] a set of principles that left an indelible mark on Italian society then, now,

---

[1] It is not insignificant in the sections of the book in which Barbieri presents criticism of the direction taken by the corporatist organization of the Italian economy in the Sixteenth and Eighteenth centuries, he uses the term "corporazionista" (c.f. p. 146, 154 onwards), denoting a reluctance to find fault even with earlier forms of what became Italian edition official economic doctrine of the 1930s.

and perhaps always. Intellectuals, not just in Italy, rarely sacrifice their professional aspirations and career prospects to fight injustice and prevarication. So it came as no surprise that Italian universities vigorously supported the general consensus of fascism; only at the end of the war, with Mussolini dead, did the country take stock of its limits and the full extent of such superficiality. Of over twelve hundred University teachers, from the time of the Government Decree of 1931 championed by Balbino Giuliano onwards, only nineteen refused to swear allegiance to the Regime, surrendering their posts. The others, Catholics, liberals and even Communists found, as intellectuals invariably do, all manner of justifications, an early indication of the culpable apathy – with very few exceptions – of Italian academia in the face of the expulsion of Jewish teachers from 1938 onwards.

The conformism of the vast majority of Italian intellectuals in many cases exceeded even the hopes of the Regime, anticipating the liberticidal intentions of fascism; paradoxically, at times the attitude of intellectuals even fostered new expectations. From 1935 until the outbreak of World War Two, among the very few critics of the Regime were some of the earliest fascists – including highly influential men such as Alberto de' Stefani – who ran the risk of *confino* (forced exile), averted only by their unblemished professional records and their personal connections at the highest levels.

Fascist corporatism thus conditioned the study of economics in Italy, with considerable ease. From the 1929 crisis onwards, nationalism, protectionism and state management became typical features of Western economies, to the extent that very few academic economists in the world refrained from harshly criticizing the capitalist system based on a competitive market; some advocated planning, others proposed various corrective measures, whether of a monetary or organizational nature. Even beyond Italy, economists presented alternative models to capitalism designed to allay fears of communism and with it the suppression of private property and entrepreneurial freedom. In the Western bloc in the 1930s, a decade in which a book published in Paris by Mihail Manoilesco,[2] the former Rumanian Minister of Labour, was highly acclaimed despite its title, it was hardly surprising that in Italy, a country that had established its first corporatist institution in the form of the 1927 Charter of Labour, the study of economics and political economy was concerned principally with corporatism. On the contrary, and with the benefit of hindsight, the efforts made for several decades in the postwar period to discredit the

---

[2] M. MANOÏLESCO, *Le siècle du corporatisme: doctrine du corporatisme intégral et pur*, París, Libraire Félix Alcan, 1938.

conversion of the Italian economy to a corporatist system as a superficial and unexpected phenomenon appear at best naïve: rather it was part of a wider global movement with broad foundations and enduring effects.

Far from being merely a question of lexis, Christian social thought from Pope Leo XII onwards had many points of contact with corporatist theories and certainly the leading exponents of the Catholic corporatist revival of the 1920s were inspired by medieval systems of economic organization, one of the most important influences of which was considered to be the Catholic religion. More than any other scholar, Heinrich Pesch provided the theoretical tools that made it possible to reconcile Thomistic economic ideals with the search for a third way between capitalism and socialism propounded in the encyclical *Rerum Novarum*, as well as the rejection of modernism, a phenomenon that had alarmed the Popes in the early twentieth century.[3] In the same vein, Giuseppe Toniolo, the sociologist from the Veneto region greatly influenced the material and ideological construction of the Catholic university, inspiring many very different men, from Amintore Fanfani to Alberto de' Stefani, who contributed with Toniolo's heirs to the publication of his Complete Works.[4]

Even in America, the home of competition and the free market, the 1930s saw a revival of Catholic corporatism, with the emergence of a school of corporatist studies; its best known exponent was Father Bernard Dempsey S.J., then a doctoral student at Harvard supervised by Joseph Schumpeter. Particularly in the later stages of his career as a pioneering economist and theorist of capitalism, Dempsey supported the principles of Catholic corporatism expressed in the encyclical *Quadragesimo Anno*.[5]

Even this brief survey confirms that the Institute of Economics at the Catholic University, where both Amintore Fanfani and his precocious student

---

[3] See in particular H. PESCH, *Lehrbuch der Nationalökonomie*, Freiburg im Breisgau, Herder, 1905; recently translated into English, H. PESCH e R.J. EDERER, *Lehrbuch der Nationalökonomie = Teaching guide to economics*, Lewiston, N.Y., Edwin Mellen Press, 2002; also of considerable importance is, H. PESCH, *Ethik und Volkswirtschaft*, Freiburg im Breisgau, Herder, 1918; among recent studies, see at least E. O'BOYLE, *Contributions of German and American Jesuits to economics: The last 100 years*, «Forum for Social Economics», 31, no. 2 (2002), pp. 25-43.

[4] G. TONIOLO, *Opera omnia di Giuseppe Toniolo*, Città del Vaticano, Comitato Opera Omnia di G. Toniolo, 1947.

[5] B.W. DEMPSEY, *Interest and Usury. With an introduction by Joseph A. Schumpeter*, Washington, American Council on Public Affairs, 1943; J. SOLTERER, *Quadragesimo Anno: Schumpeter's alternative to the omnipotent state*, «Review of Social Economy», 63, no. 3, (2005), pp. 357-368; J.A. SCHUMPETER, *Il futuro dell'impresa privata di fronte alle tendenze socialiste moderne*, in *L'imprenditore e la storia dell'impresa scritti 1927-1949*, ed. by A. Salsano, Torino, Bollati Boringhieri, 1993, pp. 91-96.

Gino Barbieri trained, belonged to the mainstream of 1930s Italian corporatism. Inspired by the Catholic socialist principles of Toniolo, very little opposition to the economic and political cornerstones of the dictatorship was voiced in university lecture halls Though the theme is too vast to deal with adequately here, the works of Francesco Vito provide an excellent overview; appointed Professor in 1935, Dean of the Institute of Economics and Rector of the University from 1959 to 1965, Vito was arguably the most influential Catholic economist of his day.

It is important to note certain key elements of Vito's economic thought. 1. The cultural influence of the German academic environment in which he completed his post-graduate studies; 2. His tendency to develop an economic vision in harmony with Christian thought, albeit with entirely independent, solid theoretical foundations; 3. In the 1930s at least, his unfailing support of corporatism, confirmed in many of his works.[6]

The Institute of Economics of the Catholic University was not renowned for its pro-capitalist sentiment; despite a lack of overt support for alternative economic models, no shortage of appropriate – and in some cases inappropriate – criticism was directed at the self-regulatory capacity of markets. The debate on the business cycle raging on the global stage dominated the study of economics in the 1930s; several Italian economists intervened with growing authority, one of the most eminent being Luigi Amoroso. Francesco Vito also made a number of significant contributions, challenging the weaknesses of Hayek's model in particular[7] and showing off his keen analytical skills.

Anti-capitalism, the Roman Catholic Church's proposals for an alternative economic model, and support for corporatism were the currents of thought that shaped the cultural environment of the Catholic University where Gino Barbieri took the first steps in his academic career. Despite the real need of

---

[6] Cf. F. DUCHINI, *Francesco Vito. Cenni biografici*, «Rivista Internazionale di Scienze Sociali», 101, no. 4, (1993), pp. 579-582; among the works of those years, for a thorough assessment of Vito's ideas on corporatism see: F. VITO, *Le basi teoriche dell'economia corporativa*, «Giornale degli Economisti e Rivista di Statistica», 74 (Anno 49), no. 7, (1934), pp. 467-547; ID., *Sui caratteri dell'economia corporativa*, «Giornale degli Economisti e Rivista di Statistica», 74 (Anno 49), no. 10 (1934), pp. 704-771; ID., *Economia corporativa, contributi dell'Istituto di scienze economiche. Serie prima*, Società editrice "Vita e pensiero", 1935; ID., *Sui fini dell'economia corporativa*, «Giornale degli Economisti e Rivista di Statistica», 75 (Anno 50), no. 5 (1935), pp. 429-443; ID., *Politica economica e sociale corporativa*, «Rivista Internazionale di Scienze Sociali», 8 (Anno 45), no. 4, (1937), pp. 569-658; ID., *Politica economica e sociale corporativa*, «Rivista Internazionale di Scienze Sociali», 10 (Anno 47), no. 3 (1939), pp. 461-480.

[7] Cf. ID., *Il risparmio forzato e la teoria dei cicli economici*, «Rivista Internazionale di Scienze Sociali», 5 (Anno 42), no. 1, (1934), pp. 3-46. Vito's review in 1949 of Hayek's *The Road to Serfdom*, was extremely negative: by failing to grasp its true enence, he dismissed Hayek's work as an insignificant sociological analysis.

the Catholic economists led by Father Gemelli to ingratiate themselves with the Fascist Regime, rarely did they openly advocate fascism, either in their house organ *"Rivista Internazionale di Scienze Economiche ed Ausiliarie"* or in other publications such as *"Vita e Pensiero"*, concerned principally with current affairs and controversial issues. There were of course certain exceptions.

One exception – worthy of mention here on account of its connection with Barbieri – was an article by Amintore Fanfani, Barbieri's mentor and, at the time of publication, a young scholar climbing the academic hierarchy. In a brief but memorable article in the *"Rivista Internazionale di Scienze Sociali"* – of which he was editor – Fanfani unequivocally praised Italian imperialist policies.[8]

More than four thousand miles from Rome, as a result of bloody battle and lightning marches, half a million legionaries thrashed the hordes from Shewa. From October to May Italy conquered her Empire. The Negus is on the retreat. His former subjects offer the Roman salute to the victorious liberators who bring schools and hospitals. The laws of Rome have unshackled millions of slaves ... forty-three million Italians at home and ten million abroad have triumphed in the subtle battle imposed by fifty two states, resisting the odious pressure... following Unification, this is surely the greatest event in the history of Italy over the last fourteen centuries... in the war in Africa not only did we defeat a barbaric ruler, we broke a tradition that made us beholden to the advice and protection of others... Our people took but fourteen years to go down the path to the Empire where others took centuries. Political pacification, reorganization of economic and social life, greater military power, conciliation with the Church, a Roman Catholic and fascist education for the young: these are the achievements that created the will to succeed and paved the way to victory.[9]

Obviously, what we wish to underline here is the cultural environment of the Catholic University in Barbieri's time. It is not our intention to express any form of inappropriate moral assessment: there is one Day of judgment, and these men need not account for their actions to intellectual colleagues who came after them and were and are so often misguided. Furthermore, the work of historians of economic thought, including Fanfani who had recently received critical acclaim for his work on Protestant ethics, and shortly

---

[8] Fanfani's unequivocal links with fascism did not end here. He was a regular contributor to the fascist review «Dottrina Fascista», and also one of the 330 signatories to the anti-semitic Manifesto of Race (*Manifesto della Razza*) in 1938. Nevertheless, he later became one of the "fathers" of the new Italian Constitution that was issued in the postwar years.

[9] A. FANFANI, *Da soli!*, *ibid.*, 7 (Year 44), no. 3, (1936), pp. 229-231.

after him Barbieri, should be assessed in the light of the political inudvement demanded of university teachers, who in addition to teaching were obliged to promote the State's economic policies.

In such a context, the history of Italian economic thought underwent a renaissance, spurred on by the prospect of offering an authoritative contribution to questions of considerable general interest. In terms of academic merit, it was a relatively new discipline in contrast to the tradition of political history, one that was encouraged by the success in Germany of the Historical School which once found fertile ground in Italy. Italian scholars were especially interested in the research that from Max Weber [10] onwards linked the development of capitalism and the modern economy with aspects of religion, relegating the Catholic tradition to a role of secondary importance. Themes relating to national identity and the power of the State awakened the interests of a nation led by a government with a strong cultural policy – largely inspired by Giovanni Gentile – that made the spirit and idea of the nation state the two fundamental pillars of its academic research policy, and not only in the field of history.

Armando Sapori had already investigated these themes from the mid nineteen twenties onwards: by researching archive sources for the events involving Bardi and Peruzzi (1925), and later Florence's international wool trade (1932), he had indirectly provided a historical explanation by documenting Italian capitalist practices prior to the Modern Age and the Lutheran reforms.[11] Nevertheless, in the cultural environment of 1930s Italy, the analysis of the capitalist phenomenon by Werner Sombart (1863-1941) was better received than Weber; though written along the same lines and at the same time, Sombart's interpretation more closely reflected the sensitivities of Italian scholars, and Fanfani's in particular.[12]

In 1934, at the tender age of twenty-five, while employed as a lecturer at the Catholic University and already supervising Barbieri's dissertation, Fanfani published "*Cattolicesimo e protestantesimo nella formazione storica del capitalismo*". Though his work was mainly theoretical, it also analyzed economic

---

[10] The original edition of *Etica Protestante* was printed in Germany during 1904-1905, followed by the Italian translation edited by Piero Burresi and the late edition by Ernesto Sestan in 1945.

[11] A. SAPORI, *La crisi delle compagnie mercantili dei Bardi e dei Peruzzi*, Firenze, L.S. Olschki, 1926; A. SAPORI, *Una compagnia di Calimala ai primi del Trecento*, Firenze, L.S. Olschki, 1932; A. SAPORI, *La cultura del mercante medievale italiano*, Torino, Einaudi, 1937.

[12] See, G. BARBIERI - A. BERTOLINO - A.M. CAROSELLI - H. KELLENBENZ - G. LUZZATTO - F. MELIS - G. MIRA, *L'opera di Werner Sombart nel Centenario della nascita*, Milano, Giuffrè Editore, 1964.

phenomena, introducing the dual approach that was similarly to become a distinctive feature of Barbieri's work. Fanfani's article, of undisputed academic merit and republished recently, sought to demonstrate the inadequacy of Weber's model in interpreting events in Italy.[13] Shortly after, Gino Barbieri wrote *"Gli ideali economici degli italiani"*, extending Fanfani's research.

We have attempted to portray the cultural environment in which Barbieri wrote "The Economic Ideals of Italians at the beginning of the Modern Age". It was an era of cultural vivacity, not without tensions caused by the political pressures exerted by an undemocratic Regime on university institutions, particularly those of Catholic inspiration. The period nevertheless fostered a remarkable level of academic activity that lasted beyond the demise of fascism. Barbieri, who maintained close ties with the Catholic University and with Milan where for many post-war years he was Vice President of the *Banca del Monte*, learnt from Fanfani a method of historical and economic inquiry that was far from simple but extremely effective: research and editing of archive material; particular caution in the use of sources and literature, without excluding any form of documentary evidence. Certainly – but who are we to judge? – Barbieri was far from adverse to a Catholic, ideological interpretation of cultural and economic events; all told, it afforded him a breadth of vision of economic phenomena that remains unparalleled even today.

SERGIO NOTO
Università di Verona

---

[13] A. FANFANI, *Le origini dello spirito capitalistico in Italia*, Milano, Vita e Pensiero, 1933; A. FANFANI, *Cattolicesimo e protestantesimo nella formazione storica del capitalismo*, Milano, Vita e Pensiero, 1944. The last one was printed as English edition in 1939 in New York, by Sheed and Ward, a Catholic publisher.

NOTES ON THE TRANSLATION

> *... translation does not find itself in the centre of the
> language forest but on the outside facing the wooded
> ridge; it calls into it without entering, aiming at the
> single spot where the echo is able to give, in its own
> language, the reverberation of the work in the alien
> one.*[1]

The first time we looked at Barbieri's work through the translator's lens,
we came to the conclusion that Barbieri's book was 'untranslatable'. Indeed,
Barbieri's *Ideali economici degli italiani all'inizio dell'età moderna* is a complex
book. Linguistically, this complexity is visible in both the lexicogrammar and
the semantics as well as in the author's style and rhetorical choices, which reflect, as Colander highlights in his Introduction, the classical knowledge of an
intellectual and social historian rather than the mind of an economist.

Against this backdrop, the translation of Barbieri's work is an ambitious
task that requires linguistic sensitivity, flexibility and knowledge of the dia-
chronic changes that affect the styles and lexicon of a language. Arguably,
the task of the translator is to render an accurate and readable text while remaining true to the author's thought and, as far as possible, style. With this in
mind, certain criteria were adopted in dealing with both content-related and
formal issues, which determined the approach to the translation.

Regarding the former, the semantic markedness of Barbieri's text is apparent in the use of lexical items considered obsolete or belonging to specialized
vocabularies such as the institutional, the religious, the economic, etc. Thus
particular attention was paid to the translation of those terms and definitions,
which are actually relevant to the understanding of Barbieri's argument.

In order to respect the historical character of the text, literary or obsolete
lexical items have been kept in the original language, when their meaning was

---

[1] W. BENJAMIN, *Illuminations*, New York, Shockenbooks, 1968, p. 76.

inferable from the context; in other cases, an English version is given in the footnotes. Similarly, while the Latin quotations are maintained in the original language, a summary of the content in English is supplied in square brackets.

The same principle is applied to Italian words bearing obsolete meanings or the many quotations from authors of the scholastic tradition such as St. Thomas Aquinas, or economists and scholars of the Italian Cinquecento. Furthermore, it was decided to translate the citations in Latin or Renaissance Italian directly from the original Barbieri text, even though English translations are sometimes available.

As Samulesson-Brown argues, «style is the greatest bone of contention and the benchmark»[2] when it comes to discussions of translation methods.

Clearly, Barbieri's wording reflects the ornate literary style of his time. This is particularly evident in the choice of words and the syntactic structure of sentences that are often 'unknown' to the modern translator, or at least sound quite unfamiliar. Many words used in the book retain their original meaning. For instance, the term *villa* means a 'rural estate', in Barbieri's quotations from authors of the XVI century. In the author's citations from medieval texts, *villa* bears the meaning attributed by medieval choreography of 'a small rural centre encompassing a few agricultural activities'; in other words, 'a village'. However, in some other instances and within more modern contexts, it is used to mean 'a large country house having an estate and consisting of farm and residential buildings arranged around a courtyard'; that is, 'a house', 'a villa in the country' as opposed to 'an urban house'. Hence, the corresponding terms of 'village', 'house' or 'villa' were used according to the meaning of the word within its context.

Barbieri's style is redundant. Concepts and words are often repeated within the same sentence. In order to simplify the reading for the contemporary translation recipient, we opted for converting the original intricacy of parts of the text into a more agile version without distorting Barbieri's meaning, or unjustifiably dissociating him from his own time.

Another feature of Barbieri's style, which contributes to rendering the text complicated for a contemporary reader is the frequent use of an old-fashioned lexicon and register. To some extent, this feature reflects a natural process of language change, which has taken place over the years, especially as concerns

---

[2] G. SAMUELSSON-BROWN, *Managing Translation Services*, Clevedon, Multilingual Matters, 2006, p. 42.

Italian literary language. Yet it was also typical of the author's personal way of writing such as the predilection for elaborate hypotactical constructions. For example, the following sentence from Chapter 4 contains thirteen subordinate and embedded clauses, which clearly make the logical construction of the sentence extremely complex:

Se infatti il Suriano può scrivere alla Serenissima che nella città di Firenze 400.000 ducati possiede il Guadagni, il Paleotti – che già conosciamo – ricorda gli accorati lamenti dei poveri, «i quali sottoposti alle continue fatiche, facilmente si lasciano, per suggestione del demonio, indurre in certa titubazione della provvidenza di Dio, parendoli d'essere come dalla sua pietà abbandonati, overo tratati come figlioli illegittimi, non solo perché si vedono esposti alli travagli e sudori, dove molti altri in questo mondo abbondano di commodità, e riposo; ma anco perché essendo privi di lettere, e di scienze, e modo di darsi a li esercizi santi, par'a' medesimi che li fia come preclusa la strada di salir al Paradiso».

The version provided in the translated text respects stylistic intricacy in so far as it does not affect comprehension; thus hypotactical constructions are only partially removed:

Whereas Suriano reported to the Serenissima Republic that in the city of Florence Guadagni possessed 400,000 ducats, Paleotti recorded the heart-rending lamentation of the poor, who «subject to continuous toil, and goaded by the Devil, easily slid into a despairing consideration of providence, feeling themselves abandoned by his mercy, or treated as illegitimate children, not only because of the necessity to toil and labour, where others in this world live in abundant comfort and are given much rest; but also because they are without reading and writing and science, and without spiritual exercise, and so are precluded from the road that leads to Heaven».

Instead, the following excerpt from the second paragraph of Chapter 1 shows an instance of how such pleonastic style has been simplified by splitting one sentence into two or more sentences, which also involved a process of rewriting:

A tale criterio attenendoci lungo il corso delle nostre ricerche, in questo primo capitolo ci proponiamo di ricostruire le soluzioni, che ai problemi della ricchezza hanno dato alcuni fra i più rappresentativi degli ecclesiastici del Cinquecento e del primo Seicento, senza dimenticare, per rendersi conto dell'origine, dell'evoluzione e del significato del loro pensiero, che negli ultimi secoli del medioevo tutta una teoria di regole di etica economica era stata elaborata da teologi e moralisti, fra i quali primeggia di gran lunga l'Angelico.
With this precaution in mind, Chapter 1 examines how the most eminent Churchmen of the sixteenth and early seventeenth centuries approached the problem of wealth.

15

To understand the origin, development and meaning of their ideas, it is important to realize that in the closing centuries of the Middle Ages, theologians and moral philosophers had already postulated principles of economic ethics. The most important of these men was Dr. Angelicus.

The reflections thus far testify to the fact that translating Barbieri's writing style was arduous work, not least because the text had to be made 'translatable', an operation that contributed to a certain extent to its survival. As Derrida writes:[3] «a text lives only if it lives on, and it lives on only if it is at once translatable and untranslatable. [...] Totally translatable, it disappears as a text [...] Totally untranslatable, even within what is believed to be a language, it dies immediately».

Every translation is partial because faithfulness in translation concerns rather the choice of *what* to translate of the source text than *how* to translate it. The partiality of translation lies in the decision how to present a foreign text and the culture that it represents. In discussing translator's choices of *what* to translate, we probably need to connect those choices to the social, political and economic situation; in other words, the cultural environment in which the translators live and work. This is the nexus for a deeper understanding of translation, rather than concentrating on comparing linguistic differences between the source and target texts.

On this point, Venuti reflects on how theorists like Derrida question the concepts of semantic unity and authorial originality that continue to subordinate the translated to the original text when they argue that «both texts [...] are derivative and heterogeneous, consisting of diverse linguistic and cultural materials which destabilize the work of signification, making meaning plural and divided, exceeding and possibly conflicting with the intentions of the foreign writer and the translator. Translation is doomed to inadequacy because of irreducible differences, not just between languages and cultures, but also within them».[4]

Maria Cristina Gatti
Università degli Studi di Milano

---

[3] J. Derrida, *Living on Borderlines*, in H. Bloom et al. *Deconstruction and Criticism*, New York, Seabury Press, 1979, pp. 102-103.

[4] L. Venuti, *The Translation Reader*, London and New York, London, Routledge, 2000, p. 218.

ABBREVIATIONS

AB   = Archivio Borghese
ACCM = Archivio della Camera di Commercio di Milano
ASCMi = Archivio Storico Civico di Milano
ASDMi = Archivio Storico Diocesano di Milano
ASM   = Archivio di Stato di Milano
BA   = Biblioteca Ambrosiana
BAV   = Biblioteca Apostolica Vaticana
BNM   = Biblioteca Nazionale di Milano

REFERENCES*

Acta Ecclesiae mediolanensis ab eius initiis usque ad nostram aetatem, opera et studio presb. Achillis Ratti, Mediolani, apud Raphaelem Ferraris edit (ex typographia pontificia sancti Iosephi), 1892.

ALBÈRI E., *Relazioni degli Ambasciatori Veneti al Senato durante il secolo XVI*, Firenze, Tipografia all'insegna di Clio, 1839-1863.

ALBERTI G., *Le corporazioni d'arti e mestieri e la libertà del commercio interno negli antichi economisti italiani*, Milano, Hoepli, 1888.

ALBERTI M., *La finanza moderna: La evoluzione e la essenza tecnica del credito mobiliare*, vol. I, Milano, Giuffrè, 1934.

ANCARANI P., *Clarissimi iurisconsulti Petri Jo. Ancharani Regiensis Familiarium iuris quaestionum*, Venetiis, Zenari, 1580.

ARETINO P., *Il primo libro delle lettere*, edited by F. Nicolini, Bari, Laterza, 1913.

ARIAS G., *Les idées économiques d'Antonio Serra*, «Journal des Économistes», s. 6, fasc. 73, year 81, 1922.

— *Il pensiero economico di Niccolò Machiavelli*, «Annali di Economia», IV, 1928.

— *Politica ed economia nel pensiero di Niccolò Machiavelli*, «Educazione Fascista», VII, no. 7, 1929.

— *Corso di economia politica corporativa*, Roma, Foro italiano, 1938.

ARISTOTELE, *Politica*, traduzione, note e proemio di V. Costanzi, Bari, Laterza, 1925.

ASTORI C., *Un'analisi del valore nell'opera del Card. De Luca*, «Economia», May 1938.

AYNARD J., *La bourgeoisie française: essai de psychologie*, Paris, Librairie Académique Perrin, 1934.

BALDONI U., *Storia di Finale-Emilia, 1190-1927, Capi, Podestà e Vicari*, Bologna, Officina Grafica Combattenti, 1928.

BANDELLO M., *Le novelle*, edited by G. Brignoligo, Bari, Laterza, 1910-1912.

— *Il canzoniere*, Torino, UTET, 1928.

BARBIERI G., *La funzione dei beni economici secondo Paolo Segneri*, «Convivium», 6, XIV, 1935.

— *Un'inchiesta cinquecentesca sui Fugger*, «Rivista Internazionale di Scienze Sociali», XLIV, 1936.

— *I redditi dei milanesi all'inizio della dominazione spagnola*, «Rivista Internazionale di Scienze Sociali», XLV, 1937.

---

* The following list is based only on Barbieri's text.

— *Alcuni statuti di gremi sardi relativi alla agricoltura*, in *Testi e documenti per la storia del diritto agrario in Sardegna*, published and edited with notes by Gino Barbieri [et al.], under the supervision of Antonio Era, Sassari, Gallizzi, 1938.

— *Economia e politica nel ducato di Milano: 1386-1535*, Milano, Vita e Pensiero, 1938.

— *Norme di morale economica dettate da S. Carlo Borromeo*, Milano, Giuffrè, 1938.

— *Gottardo Panigarola mercante e spenditore sforzesco alla luce di nuovi documenti*, in *Atti e Memorie del Terzo Congresso Storico Lombardo*, Milano, Giuffrè, 1939.

— *Spunti di naturalismo economico in un giurista italiano del '500: Tiberio Deciani*, Milano, Giuffrè, 1939.

— *Industria e politica mineraria nello stato pontificio dal '400 al '600. Lineamenti*, Roma, Cremonese, 1940. [The publication originally cited by the author was *Linee storiche della politica e industria mineraria nello Stato Pontificio dal Quattro al Seicento*, Roma, Signorelli, 1940, editor's note].

— *Note e documenti di storia economica italiana per l'età medioevale e moderna*, Milano, Giuffrè, 1940.

— *L'autarchia nel pensiero e nella politica italiana dal medioevo all'età moderna*, in *Note e documenti di storia economica italiana per l'età medioevale e moderna*.

— *Tendenze autarchiche nella politica economica del ducato di Milano*, in *Note e documenti di storia economica italiana per l'età medioevale e moderna*.

— *L'industria tessile a Legnago nei secoli XVI e XVII*, in *Note e documenti di storia economica italiana per l'età medioevale e moderna*.

— *Controversie del lavoro nel secolo XVII: il pagamento del salario*, «Rivista Italiana di Scienze Economiche», XII, 1940.

BAROZZI N. – BERCHET G., *Relazioni degli stati europei lette al Senato dagli Ambasciatori Veneti nel secolo decimosettimo*, Venezia, Naratovich, 1856-1877.

BASCAPÈ C., *Scritti pubblicati da mons. reverendiss. d. Carlo vescovo di Novara, nel governo del suo vescovato dall'anno 1593 fino al 1609: ridotti in volume per commodità de' cleri, & popoli della sua chiesa*, Milano, per Ambrogio Ramellati, 1660.

BELGRANO L.T., *Della vita privata dei Genovesi*, Genova, Tip. del R. Istituto Sordo-muti, 1875.

BELLONI A., *Sebastiano Vento, le condizioni dell'oratoria sacra del Seicento. Ricerche e critica*, «Giornale Storico della Letteratura Italiana», LXX, 1917.

— *Il Seicento*, Milano, Vallardi, 1930.

BENINI R., *Sulle dottrine economiche di Antonio Serra: appunti critici*, «Giornale degli Economisti», III, 1892, pp. 222-248.

BERNI F., *Rime, poesie latine e lettere edite e inedite*, Firenze, Le Monnier, 1885.

BERTAZZOLI B., *Consiliorum seu responsorum iuris in criminalibus & poenalibus controversiis emissorum*, edited by C. Bertazzoli, Venetiis, Apud Ioannem Baptistam Somaschum, 1583.

BESTA E., *Fonti: legislazione e scienza giuridica dalla caduta dell'impero romano al secolo XVI*, in *Storia del diritto italiano*, edited by Pasquale Del Giudice, Milano, Hoepli, 1925.

BIADEGO G., *Lettere inedite di Paolo Paruta*, Verona, Goldschagg, 1885.

BIAGI A., *La Musica nel secolo XVI*, in *La vita italiana nel Cinquecento*, Milano, Treves, 1919.

BIANCHINI L., *Della storia economico-civile della Sicilia*, Palermo, Lao, 1841.

Biblioteca di Storia economica, edited by V. Pareto, Milano, Società Editrice Libraria, 1907.

BINDI E., *Della vita e delle opere di Bernardo Davanzati*, in DAVANZATI, *Le opere di Bernardo Davanzati*, vol. I.

BISTORT G., *Il magistrato alle pompe nella Republica di Venezia: studio storico*, Venezia, Tip. Libreria Emiliana, 1912.

BIUCCHI B.M., *Tendenze liberiste nella storia economica svizzera*, «Rivista Internazionale di Scienze Sociali», XLII, 1934.

BOCCACCI V. [de Cingulo], *Tractatus de interdicto uti possidetis, sive de manutentione in possessionem: continens quaestiones vtiles in praxi & theorica, quae versis paginis indicantur*, Venezia, apud Ioannem Gymnicum, 1582.

BOISSONNADE P., *Le socialisme d'état: l'industrie et les classes industrielles en France pendant les deux premiers siècles de l'ère moderne (1453-1661)*, Paris, Champion, 1927.

BOMBINI B., *Consilia, quaestiones, atque conclusiones clarissimi iuriscon. d. Bernardini Bombini Cosentini, ad diversas causas, atque frequentiores, quae in foro versantur, materia edita. Quibus praeter argumenta*, Venetiis, apud Franciscum Franciscium Senensem, 1574.

BORROMEO C., *Libretto de i ricordi, al popolo della citta et diocese di Milano, dati dall'Illustriss. Card. di S. Prassede, Arcivescovo per il vivere christiano, communemente à ogni stato di persone, et particolarmente a Padri, et Madri di fameglia, Mastri, ò capi di boteghe, et lavoranti*, Milano, Pacifico Pontio, 1578.

— *Litterae Pastorales*, in *Acta Ecclesiae mediolanensis ab eius initiis usque ad nostram aetatem*.

BORROMEO F., *Sulle usure del cambio delle monete*, BA, Misc. S.I.G.V. 26.

BRANTS V., *Xénophon économiste*, «La Revue Catholique de Louvain», p. 4, 1881.

— *L'économie politique au moyen-âge: esquisse des théories économiques professées par les écrivains des XIIIe et XIVe siècles*, Louvain, Peeters, 1895.

BREGLIA A., *A proposito di G. Botero "Economista"*, «Annali di Economia», IV, 1928.

BREY H., *Hochscholastik und "Geist" des Kapitalismus*, Borna-Leipzig, Noske, 1927.

BUONINSEGNI T., *Tractatus ad iustas negociationes inter homines fieri consuetas summe necessarij: videlicet De venditione ad tempus, De diminutione praetij, ob anticipatam solutionem, De cambiis, De censibus, De ludo, et De montibus*, Florentiae, in officina Sermatelliana,1587.

CAGGIO P., *Iura Municipalia, seu consuetudines Felicis Urbis Panormi*, Panormi, apud Ioannem Matthaeum Maidam, 1547.

— *Ragionamenti: ne quali egli introduce tre suoi amici, che naturalmente discorrono intorno à una vaga fontana, in veder se la vita cittadinesca sia più felice, del viver solitario fuor le città, e nelle ville*, Vinegia, al segno del Pozzo, 1551.

— *Iconomica del signor Paolo Caggio gentil'huomo di Palermo. Nella quale s'insegna brevemente per modo di dialogo il governo famigliare, come di se stesso, della moglie, de' figliuoli, de' servidori, e schiavi, delle case, delle robbe, et d'ogn'altra cosa a quella appartenente*, Vinegia, al segno del Pozzo, 1553.

CALVI F., *Il patriziato milanese*, «Archivio Storico Lombardo», I, fasc(s) 1-4, 1874.

— *Famiglie notabili milanesi*, Milano, Vallardi, 1881.

CAMMAROSANO F., *La vita e le opere di Sperone Speroni*, Empoli, Noccioli, 1920.

CAMMEO G., *Cenni storici sulla comunità israelitica di Finale (Modenese)*, «Vessillo Israelitico», XLII, 1894.

CAMPANELLA T., *Civitas solis poetica. Idea reipublicae philosophicae*, Ultraiecti, apud Ioannem à Waesberge, 1643.

— *Opere di Tommaso Campanella*, chosen and edited with notes by A. D'Ancona, Torino, Pomba, 1854.

— *Aforismi politici*, in *Opere di Tommaso Campanella*, vol. II.

— *Della Monarchia in Spagna*, in *Opere di Tommaso Campanella*, vol. II.

— *Sopra l'aumento delle entrate del Regno di Napoli*, in *Opere di Tommaso Campanella*, vol. II.

CANDELORO G., *Paolo Paruta: la formazione spirituale e la dottrina morale*, «Rivista Storica Italiana», vol. I, fasc. III, 1936.

CANNAN E., *Rassegna della teoria economica*, in *Storia delle Teorie*, Torino, UTET, 1932.

CARO A., *Lettere inedite*, with notes by Pietro Mazzucchelli, Milano, Pogliani, 1827.

CASANOVA A., *Specchio lucidissimo nel quale si vedeno essere diffinito tutti i modi & ordini de scrittura che si dive menare nelli negotiamenti della mercantia, cambii, recambii: con li loro corrispondentie, disgarbugliando & illucinando l'inteletto a negozianti*, 1558, in *Opere antiche di ragioneria*, Milano, Monitore dei Ragionieri, 1911.

CASTIGLIONE A., *Homelie del reverendo padre f. Angelo Castiglione Carmelitano da Genova, per le domeniche, et tutte le feste principali*, Milano, appresso Pacifico Pontio, 1584.

Catechismus romanus ex decreto sacrosancti Concilii Tridentini, Patavia, Typis Seminarii, 1714.

CATTANEO C., *Ricerche economiche sulle interdizioni imposte dalla legge civile agli israeliti*, edited by G.A. Belloni, Roma, Saturnia, 1932.

CAVALLO P., *Resolutionum criminalium Petri Caballi I. C. Pontremulensis*, Florentiae, apud M.A. Sermartellium, 1609.

CAVRIANA F., *Discorsi del Signor Filippo Cavriana, cav. di S. Stefano, sopra i primi cinque libri di Cornelio Tacito*, Fiorenza, Giunti, 1597.

CELLINI B., *La vita di Benvenuto Cellini scritta da lui medesimo*, Firenze, Le Monnier, 1852.

CESSI R., *Di alcuni documenti sugli ebrei nel Polesine durante i secoli XIV e XV*, «Atti e Memorie della R. Accademia di Scienze Lettere ed Arti di Padova», XXV, 1908-1909.

CHABOD F., *Giovanni Botero*, Roma, Anonima Romana editoriale, 1934.

— *Lo Stato di Milano nell'impero di Carlo V*, Roma, Istituto romano di arti grafiche di Tumminelli & c., 1934.

CIASCA R., *Le ragioni della decadenza delle corporazioni medievali*, «Vita e Pensiero», XXV, fasc. V, 1934.

CISCATO A., *Gli Ebrei in Este, 1406-1665*, Este, Typ. Longo, 1892.

— *Gli ebrei in Padova: (1300-1800)*, Padova, Soc. Cooperativa Tipografica, 1901.

CLARO G., *Iulii Clari Alexandrini ... Opera omnia; sive Practica civilis, atque criminalis*, Venetiis, apud Baretium Baretium, 1614.

COMBE A. – CHARAVAY G., *Guide de l'étranger à Lyon, contenant la description des monuments, des curiosités et des lieux publics remarquables, accompagné d'un plan de la Ville gravé sur acier*, Lyon, Charavay, 1847.

Concilii Tridentini diariorum, Friburgi-Brisgoviae, Herder, v.d.

CROCE B., *Materialismo storico ed economia marxistica*, Bari, Laterza, 1918.

— *La Spagna nella vita italiana durante la Rinascenza*, n.t.n.

CROCE G.C., *Bertoldo, Bertoldino e Cacasenno*, Milano, Cesare Cioffi, n.d.

CROSARA A., *Sovranità dello Stato e prepotere del denaro*, «Rivista di Storia del Pensiero Economico», VI, 1937.

CURCIO C., *Dal rinascimento alla controriforma: contributo alla storia del pensiero politico italiano da Guicciardini a Botero*, Roma, Colombo, 1934.

CUSUMANO V., *Saggi di economia politica e di scienza delle finanze*, Palermo, Tip. dello Statuto, 1887.

— *La teoria del commercio dei grani in Italia: studi storici*, Bologna, Tip. Fava e Garagnani, 1877.

DA CASLINO C.M., *L'usuraro convinto con la ragione: opera utilissima*, n.t.n.

DAVANZATI B., *Le opere di Bernardo Davanzati ridotte a corretta lezione coll'aiuto de' manoscritti e delle migliori stampe e annotate per cura di E. Bindi*, Firenze, Le Monnier, 1853.

DE CASTRO S., *Instruttion di Don Scipio de Castro al Duca di Terranova, nell'entrare al governo dello Stato di Milano*, in VENTURA, *La prima (-seconda) parte del Thesoro Politico*.

DE CESARE A., *Un massimario di economia sociale del Seicento nel Trentino*, «Nuova Antologia», vol(s) 275-276, 1917.

DE JOHANNIS A., *Sulle condizioni della economia politica nel Cinquecento e la scoperta d'America*, in *La vita italiana nel Cinquecento*, Milano, Treves, 1919.

DE LUCA G.B., *Theatrum veritatis, et justitiae, sive decisivi discursus per materias, seu titulos distincti, & ad veritatem editi in forensibus controversiis canonicis & civilibus, in quibus in urbe advocatus, pro una partium scripsit, vel consultus respondit*, Venetiis, apud Paulum Balleonium, 1698.

DE SANCTIS F., *Storia della letteratura italiana*, Bari, Laterza, 1912.

— *Antologia critica sugli scrittori d'Italia*, edited by L. Russo, Firenze, Vallecchi, 1924.

DE VIO T. [Card. Gaetano], *Opuscula oeconomico-socialia*, edited by P. Zammit, Roma, Angelicum, 1934.

— *De cambiis*, in *Opuscula oeconomico-socialia*.

— *De eleemosynae praecepto*, in *Opuscula oeconomica-socialia*.

— *De monte pietatis*, in *Opuscula oeconomico-socialia*.

— *De societate negotiatoria ad eundem*, in *Opuscula oeconomico-socialia*.

— *De usura quaestiones sex*, in *Opuscula oeconomico-socialia*.

— *Responsio ad tria dubia ad Magistrum Conradum Koellin*, in *Opuscula oeconomico-socialia*.

— *Commentaria in Summam theologicam angelici doctoris sancti Thomae Aquinatis*, n.t.n.

DE VITI DE MARCO A., *Le teorie economiche di Antonio Serra: memoria del prof. A. de Viti de Marco, letta nell'adunanza 27 marzo*, Memorie del R. Istituto Lombardo di Scienze e Lettere, XVII, Milano, 1890.

DECIANI T., *Tractatus criminalis D. Tiberii Deciani Utinensis*, Venetiis, apud haeredes Hieronymi Scoti, 1614.

DEL GIUDICE P., *Studi di storia e diritto*, Milano, Hoepli, 1889.

DELIPERI A.C., *Sulle coalizioni o rasse nell'economia e legislazione medioevale sarda*, Sassari, Gallizzi, 1934.

DENUCÉ J., *Inventaire des Affaitadi: banquiers italiens à Anvers, de l'année 1568*, Paris, Leroux, 1934.

16

DENZINGER H.J.D., *Enchiridion symbolorum definitionum quae de rebus fidei et morum a conciliis oecumenicis et summis pontificibus emanarunt*, Friburgi Brisgoviae, Herder, 1900.

DI TOCCO V., *Ideali d'indipendenza in Italia durante la preponderanza spagnuola*, Messina, Principato, 1926.

Dizionario biografico universale: contenente le notizie più importanti sulla vita e sulle opere degli uomini celebri: i nomi di regie e di illustri famiglie; di scismi religiosi; di parti civili; di sette filosofiche, dall'origine del mondo fino a di nostri, edited by F. Scifoni, Firenze, Passigli, 1844.

DONADONI E., *Breve storia della letteratura italiana: dalle origini ai nostri giorni*, n.t.n.

DONI A.F., *Mondi celesti, terrestri, et infernali, degli academici Pellegrini*, Venetia, Appresso N. Moretti, 1583.

DU BELLAY J., *Recueil des plus belles pièces des poètes françois: depuis Villon jusqu'à Benserade*, Paris, Par la Compagnie des Libraires, 1752.

DUNLOP J.C., *History of prose fiction*, London, Bell, 1896.

EHRENBERG R., *Das Zeitalter der Fugger*, Jena Fisher, 1922.

ERRERA A., *Storia dell'economia politica nel secoli XVII e XVIII negli Stati della Repubblica Veneta*, Venezia, Antonelli, 1877.

FABIANO P. [Chiavari, Fabiano], *Trattato del Cambio di Lione, o di Bisenzone, diligentemente composto, e considerato dal Reverendo padre Frate Fabiano Genovese, Eccellentissimo Teologo, e procuratore nella corte di Roma di tutto l'ordine de Frati Eremitani di Santo Agostino*, in VENUSTI, *Compendio utilissimo di quelle cose, le quali a nobili e christiani mercanti appartengono*.

FANFANI A., *Riforma e capitalismo moderno nella recente letteratura*, «Rivista Internazionale di Scienze Sociali», XXXVIII, no. 4, 1930.

— *Caratteri delle regole in materia economica dettate dagli scolastici medievali*, «Rivista di Filosofia Neo-Scolastica», XXIV, fasc. III, 1932.

— *Le origini dello spirito capitalistico in Italia*, Milano, Vita e Pensiero, 1933.

— *Cattolicesimo e protestantesimo nella formazione storica del capitalismo*, Milano, Vita e Pensiero, 1934.

— *I mutamenti economici nell'Europa moderna e l'evoluzione costituzionalistica delle classi dirigenti*, Milano, Vita e Pensiero, 1936.

— *Storia delle dottrine economiche: il volontarismo*, Como, Cavalleri, 1938.

— *Indagini sulla "Rivoluzione dei prezzi"*, Milano, Vita e Pensiero, 1940.

FARINACCI P., *D. Prosperi Farinacii I.C. Romani Sacrae Romanae Rotae Decisionum ab ipso selectarum nec unquam alias impressarum tomi quatuor*, Aurelianae, Sumptibus Viduae & Haeredum Petri de la Rouiere, 1623.

FELICI S.G., *Le dottrine filosofico-religiose di Tommaso Campanella. Con particolare riguardo alla filosofia della rinascenza italiana*, Lanciano, Rocco Carabba, 1895.

FERRARI G., *Corso sugli scrittori politici italiani*, Milano, Manini, 1862.

FILIPPI G., *Statuti dell'arte degli speziali in Savona del 1592*, Savona, Tip. Bertolotto, 1890.

FIORAVANTI L., *Dello specchio di scientia universale, dell'eccellente medico & cirurgico M. Leonardo Fioravanti Bolognese*, Venezia, Andrea Ravenoldo, 1567.

FOLENGO T. [Merlin Cocai], *Theophili Folengi vulgo Merlini Cocaii Opus macaronicum notis illustratum, cui accessit vocabularium vernaculum, etruscum, et latinum*, Amstelodami, Sumptibus Josephi Braglia, 1768.

— *Le maccheronee*, a cura di Alessandro Luzio, Bari, Laterza, n.d.

FOLLERIO P., *Practica criminalis d. Petri Follerii i.v.d. celeb. dialogice contexta, secundum dispositionem capitulorum, constitutionum, pragmaticarum & rituum regni Neapolitani*, Venetiis, Apud Bartholomaeum Rubinum, 1568.

FORCELLINI M., *La vita di Sperone Speroni degli Alvarotti, filosofo e cavalier padovano*, in SPERONI, *Opere di M. Sperone Speroni degli Alvarotti*.

FORNARI T., *Delle teorie economiche nelle provincie napolitane dal sec. XIII al MDCCXXXIV. Studi storici*, Milano, Hoepli, 1882.

FOSSATI F., *Gli ebrei a Vigevano nel secolo XV*, «Archivio Storico Lombardo», XX, 1903.

FRATI L., *La vita privata in Bologna dal secolo XIII al XVII*, Bologna, Zanichelli, 1928.

FULIN R., *Breve sommario di storia veneta*, Venezia, Visentini, 1873.

GABRIELLI A., *Alcuni capitoli del 1547 per un banco di prestito a pegno tenuto dagli ebrei in Velletri*, Velletri, Stracca, 1917.

GAITO G.D., *Tractatus absolutissimus de credito ex libris, epistolis, cambiis, apocis, instrumentis publicis, obligationibus penes acta, omnique alia publica inter vivos scriptura, pignore, & hipothecis*, Venetiis, apud Iuntas, 1626.

GAMS P.B., *Series episcoporum Ecclesiae catholicae*, Ratisbonae, G.J. Manz, 1873.

GARIMBERTO G., *De' regimenti publici de la città*, Vinegia, appresso G. Scotto, 1544.

GARINO-CANINA A., *Il concetto di valore della moneta in Alberto Bruno*, «Giornale degli Economisti», May 1935.

GAROSCI A., *Jean Bodin, politica e diritto nel rinascimento francese*, Milano, Corticelli, 1934.

GARZONI T., *La piazza universale di tutte le professioni del mondo*, Venetia, appresso Gio. Battista Somasco, 1587.

GATTIOLI P., *Cronaca tra il 1638 e 1671*, in DE CESARE, *Un massimario d'economia sociale del seicento nel Trentino*.

GIARDINA C., *La vita e l'opera politica di Scipione di Castro*, Palermo, Tip. Boccone del Povero, 1931.

GIBERTI G.M., *Opera*, Hostilia, Apud A. Carattonium, 1740.

GOBBI U., *La concorrenza estera e gli antichi economisti italiani*, Milano, Hoepli, 1884.

— *L'economia politica negli scrittori italiani del secolo XVI-XVII*, Milano, Hoepli, 1889.

GONNARD R., *Histoire des doctrines économiques*, Paris, Valois, 1930.

GOTHEIN E., *L'età della controriforma: lo stato cristiano-sociale dei gesuiti nel Paraguay*, transl. by G. Thiel, Venezia, La Nuova Italia, 1928.

GRAF A., *Petrarchismo ed antipetrarchismo*, in *Attraverso il Cinquecento*, Torino, Chiantore, 1926.

GUERRINI P., *Gli ebrei a Verolanuova*, «Archivio Storico Lombardo», s. V, 1918.

GUICCIARDINI F., *Dialogo e discorsi del Reggimento di Firenze*, edited by R. Palmarocchi, Bari, Laterza, 1932.

— *Scritti politici e ricordi*, edited by R. Palmarocchi, Bari, Laterza, 1933.

GUIDICCIONI G., *Opere di Monsignor Giovanni Guidiccioni Vescovo di Fossombrone*, Genova, Tarigo, 1767.

HAUSER H., *La modernité du XVIᵉ siècle*, Paris, Librairie Félix Alcan, 1930.

HECKSCHER E.F., *Il mercantilismo*, Torino, UTET, 1936.

HUBER K., *Die Anfänge des Liberalismus im Mittelalter*, Leipzig, Voglrieder, 1936.

Il XL anniversario della Enciclica "Rerum Novarum", Milano, Vita e Pensiero, 1931.

KAWAN L., *Gli esodi e le carestie in Europa attraverso il tempo*, Roma, Bardi, 1932.

LANCELLOTTI S., *L'hoggidi overo il mondo non peggiore, ne più calamitoso del passato del padre d. Secondo Lancelloti da Perugia abbate olivetano. Accademico insensato, affidato, & umorista*, Venetia, Guerigli, 1658.

La vita italiana nel Cinquecento, Conferenze tenute a Firenze nel 1893, Milano, Treves, 1919.

Le encicliche sociali di Leone XIII e Pio XI: testo latino e traduzione italiana della "Rerum Novarum" e della "Quadragesimo anno" con riferimenti ad altri documenti pontifici, Milano, Vita e Pensiero, 1933.

Li statuti di Valtellina riformati nella citta di Coire nell'anno del Signore 1548, nel mese di genaro per li mag. signori commissarij a cio specialmente eletti nella publica Dieta fatta nella medesima citta nell'anno precedente nel mese d'agosto, Poschiavo, per il Podestà B. Massella, 1668.

LOTTINI G.F., *Avvedimenti civili*, Firenze, Bartolomeo Sermartelli, 1573.

LUZZATTO G., *Storia del commercio. Dall'antichità al rinascimento*, vol. I, Firenze, Barbèra, 1914.

— *Storia economica. L'età moderna*, Padova, Cedam, 1934.

MACHIAVELLI N., *Opere complete di Niccolò Machiavelli*, Milano, Oliva, 1850.

— *Il Principe*, in *Opere complete di Niccolò Machiavelli*, vol. I.

MAGGI R., *Note all'opera di Antonio Serra*, «Annali di Scienze Politiche», IX, 1936.

Magnum Bullarium Romanum, Augustae Taurinorum editum, Sumptibus Seb. Franco et Henrici Dalmazzo, 1857-1872.

MAGONI G.B., *De recta iudicialiter patrocinandi ratione tractatus*, Ticini, apud Petrum Bartolum, 1609.

MANDICH G., *Delle fiere genovesi di cambi particolarmente studiate come mercati periodici del credito*, «Rivista di Storia Economica», IV, 1939.

MANSI G.D., *Sacrorum conciliorum nova, et amplissima collectio: in qua praeter ea quae Phil. Labbeus, et Gabr. Cossartius S.J. et novissime Nicolaus Coleti in lucem edidere ea omnia insuper suis in locis optime disposita exhibentur, quae Joannes Dominicus Mansi lucensis, congregationis matris dei evulgavit*, Florentiae, expensis Antonii Zatta, 1759.

MANZONI A., *I promessi sposi*, edited by P. Bellezza, Milano, Cogliati, 1930.

MANZONI DI ODERZO D., *Quaderno doppio col suo giornale secondo il costume di Venezia, 1540*, in *Opere antiche di ragioneria*, Milano, Monitore dei Ragionieri, 1911.

MARCUCCI E., *Prefazione*, in SASSETTI, *Lettere edite e inedite di Filippo Sassetti*.

MARGOLIS M.L. – MARX A., *Histoire du peuple juif*, Paris, Payot, 1930.

MARIANI M., *Lo statuto senigalliese dell'anno 1537*, «Le Marche», IV, 1910.

MARONGIU A., *Tiberio Deciani (1509-1582): lettore di diritto, consulente, criminalista*, «Rivista di Storia del Diritto Italiano», VII, 1934.

MARSILI I., *Hippolyti de Marsiliis Bononiensis i.v. splendidissimi doctoris ac criminalium studiorum professoris illustrissimi, Elegans et accuratus in titulum. ff. de quaestionibus compilatus commentarius*, Venetiis, al segno della Fontana, 1564.

MASI B., *Ricordanze di Bartolomeo Masi: calderaio fiorentino dal 1478 al 1526*, Firenze, Sansoni, 1906.

MAZZEI J., *Politica economica internazionale inglese prima di Adamo Smith*, Milano, Vita e Pensiero, 1924.

— *Principi etici ed economia*, in *Il XL Anniversario Della Enciclica "Rerum Novarum"*.

— *Schema di una storia della politica economica internazionale nel pensiero dei secoli 17, 18 e 19*, Torino, UTET, 1936.

MENOCHI J., *De arbitrariis iudicum quaestionibus et caussis, libri duo*, Florentiae, Pectinarius, 1571.

MENOCHIO G.S., *Institutionis oeconomicae ex Sacris litteris depromptae libri duo*, Lugduni, ex officina Rovilliana, 1627.

MOLMENTI P., *La storia di Venezia nella vita privata, dalle origini alla caduta della repubblica*, Bergamo, Istituto Italiano di Arti Grafiche, 1926.

MONTALBANI O., *L'honore dei collegi dell'arti della Città di Bologna, brieve trattato fisicopolitico e legale storico*, Bologna, Benacci, 1670.

MONTANARI A., *Contributo alla storia della teoria del valore negli scrittori italiani*, Milano, Hoepli, 1889.

MORONI G., *Dizionario di erudizione storico-ecclesiastica da S. Pietro sino ai nostri giorni*, vol. LXXIX, Venezia, Typ. Emiliana, 1856.

MORONI I., *P. Illuminati Moroni Bergomensis, e Strict. Obser. S. Francisci ... Centum responsa centum quaesitis: ex ijs, quae illi in dies deferebantur solvenda*, Venetiis, Combi, 1645.

MOZZI P.N., *Tractatus de contractibus Petri Nicolai Mozzii maceratensis*, Venetiis, ex officina Damiani Zenarii, 1585.

NATOLI L., *Paolo Caggio prosatore siciliano del secolo XVI*, «Archivio Storico Siciliano», XXI, 1896.

— *Paolo Caggio*, in *Prosa e prosatori siciliani del secolo XVI*, Palermo, Sandron, 1904.

NICOLINI F., *Aspetti della vita italo-spagnuola nel Cinque e Seicento*, Napoli, Guida, 1934.

OPERANS C., *Come nacque e morì la corporazione cittadina*, «Rivista di Storia del Pensiero Economico», II, 1935.

Opere antiche di ragioneria, Milano, Monitore dei Ragionieri, 1911.

PACIOLO L., *Trattato de' computi e delle scritture*, 1494, in *Opere antiche di ragioneria*.

PALEOTTI G., *Instruttione di monsig. illustrissimo e reuer.mo card. Paleotti arciuescouo di Bologna per tutti quelli, che hauranno licenza di predicare nelle ville, & altri luoghi della diocese*, Roma, Moneta, 1678.

PALMIERI M., *Trattato della vita civile*, in *Della educazione dell'uomo e del cittadino*, Venezia, Gondoliere, 1841.

PARUTA P., *Opere politiche di Paolo Paruta*, edited by C. Monzani, Firenze, Le Monnier, 1852.

— *Della perfezione della vita civile*, in *Opere politiche di Paolo Paruta*, vol. I.

— *Soliloquio*, in *Opere politiche di Paolo Paruta*, vol. I.

PASTOR L., *Storia dei papi*, Roma, Desclée, 1942.

PERAGALLO P., *Cenni intorno alla colonia italiana in Portogallo nei secoli XIV, XV e XVI*, Genova, Papini, 1907.

17

REFERENCES

PERTILE A., *Storia del diritto italiano*, Torino, UTET, 1896-1902.

PICOTTI G.B., *D'una questione tra Pio II e Francesco Sforza per la ventesima sui beni degli Ebrei*, «Giornale della Società Storica Lombarda – Archivio Storico Lombardo», XX, s. IV, fasc. 39, 1913.

PIETRA A., *Indirizzo degli economi, o sia ordinatissima instruttione da regolatamente formare qualunque scrittura in un libro doppio*, 1558, in *Opere antiche di ragioneria*, Milano, Monitore dei Ragionieri, 1911.

Politici e moralisti del Seicento: Strada, Zuccolo, Settala, Accetto, Brignole Sale, Malvezzi, edited by Benedetto Croce e Santino Caramella, Bari, Laterza, 1930.

POMPEATI A., *Per la biografia di Paolo Paruta*, «Giornale Storico della Letteratura Italiana», XLV, 1905.

— *Le dottrine politiche di Paolo Paruta*, «Giornale Storico della Letteratura Italiana», XLVI, 1905.

— *Saggi critici*, Milano, Dante Alighieri, 1916.

Primo Concilio Provinciale Milanese, in *Acta Ecclesiae mediolanensis*.

RAGIONERIA GENERALE DELLO STATO, *Elenco cronologico delle opere di computisteria e ragioneria venute alla luce in Italia dal 1202 sino al presente*, Roma, Tip. Nazionale Reggiani, 1886.

RANALLI F., *Vita di Paolo Segneri*, in SEGNERI, *Quaresimale del Padre Paolo Segneri*, edited by F. Ranalli, Prato, Dalla Tipografia Guasti, 1841.

RATZINGER G., *Geschichte der kirchlichen Armenpflege*, Freiburg, Herder, 1868.

RODOLICO N., *Il ritorno alla terra nella storia degli italiani*, «Atti della Reale Accademia dei Georgofili di Firenze», 1933.

Regesti di bandi, editti, notificazioni e provvedimenti diversi relativi alla città di Roma ed allo stato pontificio, Roma, Cuggiani, 1920.

ROSA S., *Satire, odi e lettere di Salvator Rosa*, with notes by G. Carducci, Firenze, G. Barbèra, 1860.

ROTA E., *Gli ebrei e la politica spagnola in Lombardia*, «Bollettino della Società Pavese di Storia Patria», VI, fasc. III, 1906.

SALVIOLI G., *Storia del diritto italiano*, 8th ed., Torino, UTET, 1921.

SANTINI E., *L'eloquenza italiana dal Concilio Tridentino ai nostri giorni*, Palermo, Sandron, 1923-1928.

SANUDO M., *I diarii*, Venezia, Visentini, 1879.

SAPORI A., *Il taccamento dei panni franceschi a Firenze nel '300*, in *In onore e ricordo di Giuseppe Prato*, Torino, R. Istituto Sup. di Scienze Econ. e Comm., 1931.

SARPI P., *Ricordi del P. Paolo Sarpi, dell'Ordine de' Servi, al Prencipe e Senato veneto intorno il modo di regolare il governo della Republica*, Friburgo, Stamperia Italiana, 1767.

SARRI F., *Il venerabile Bartolomeo Cambi da Salutio (1557-1617), oratore, mistico, poeta*, Firenze, Bemporad, 1925.

SASSETTI F., *Lettere edite e inedite di Filippo Sassetti*, raccolte e annotate da Ettore Marcucci, Firenze, Le Monnier, 1855.

SAVONAROLA G., *Confessionale reveren. fratris Hieronymi Savonarolae ordinis praedicatorum... per Reverendum D. Alexandrum Saulium Theologum, collectis et revisis*, Pavia, apud Hieronymum Bartholum, 1571.

SCHAFFSTEIN F., *Die allgemeinen Lehren vom Verbrechen in ihrer Entwicklung durch die Wissenschaft des gemeinen Strafrechts*, Berlin, Springer, 1930.

— *Tiberius Decianus und seine Bedeutung fur die Entstehung des Allgemeinen Teils im Gemeinen deutschen Strafrecht*, «Deutsche Rechtwissenschaft», 1938, pp. 121-148.

SCHIAVI L.A., *Gli Ebrei in Venezia e nelle sue colonie: appunti storici su documenti editi ed inediti*, «Nuova Antologia», s. 3, 1893.

SCHULLERN-SCHRATTENHOFEN H. v., *Die theoretische Nationalökonomie Italiens in neuester Zeit*, Leipzig, Duncker & Humblot, 1891.

SCHUPFER F., *Il diritto delle obbligazioni in Italia nell'età del risorgimento*, Torino, Bocca, 1921.

SEGARIZZI A., *Relazioni degli ambasciatori veneti al Senato*, Bari, Laterza, 1912.

SEGNERI P., *Opere del Padre Paolo Segneri*, Venezia, Stamperia Baglioni, 1773.

— *Il Cristiano istruito nella sua legge*, in *Opere del Padre Palo Segneri*, tome III.

— *La manna dell'anima*, in *Opere del Padre Paolo Segneri*, tome I.

— *Quaresimale del Padre Paolo Segneri*, in *Opere del Padre Paolo Segneri*, tome II.

— *Prediche dette nel Palazzo apostolico, e dedicate alla santità di nostro signore papa Innocenzo duodecimo*, in *Opere del Padre Paolo Segneri*, tome II.

SEGRE A., *Storia del commercio*, Torino, Lattes, 1923.

SERRA A., *Breve trattato delle cause, che possono far abbondare li regni d'oro et d'argento dove non sono miniere*, in *Scrittori classici italiani di economia politica: Parte antica*, Milano, Destefanis, 1803.

SERRANO L., *Correspondencia diplomática entre España y la Santa Sede durante el pontificado de S. Pio V*, Madrid, 1914.

SERTILLANGES A.D., *La doctrine catholique et les clauses du travail dans le Traité de paix*, Paris, Revue des Jeunes, 1919.

SFORZA G., *Cronachetta massese del sec. XVI ora per la prima volta stampata*, «Giornale Storico e Letterario della Liguria», III, 1902.

SFORZA PALLAVICINO P., *Istoria del Concilio di Trento*, Roma, per Biagio Diversin, e Felice Cesaretti librari all'insegna della Regina, 1663.

SMITH A., *An Inquiry into The Nature and Causes of The Wealth of Nations*, Milano, Cofide, 1998.

SOLMI A., *Storia del diritto italiano*, Milano, Società editrice libraria, 1908.

SOMBART W., *Die Juden und das Wirtschaftsleben*, Leipzig, Duncker & Humblot, 1911.

— *Der Bourgeois: Zur Geistgeschichte des modernen Wirtschaftsmenschen*, München, Verl. Duncker & Humblot, 1920.

— *Les juifs et la vie économique*, Paris, Payot, 1923.

SOMMERVOGEL C., *Bibliothèque de la Compagnie de Jésus*, Bruxelles-Paris, Schepens-Picard, 1894.

SPERONI DEGLI ALVAROTTI S., *Opere di M. Sperone Speroni degli Alvarotti tratte da mss. originali*, Venezia, Appresso D. Occhi, 1740.

SPIZZICHINO J., *Magistrature dello Stato pontificio (476-1870)*, Lanciano, Carabba, 1930.

Statuti dell'Arte di Por S. Maria del Tempo della Repubblica, edited by U. Dorini, Firenze, Olschki, 1934.

Supino C., *La scienza economica in Italia dalla seconda metà del secolo XVI alla prima del XVII*, Torino, Loescher, 1888.

— *Le idee economiche nei "Promessi sposi"*, «Rendiconti dell'Istituto Lombardo», s. II, fasc. XII, 1923.

Tacchi Venturi P., *Storia della Compagnia di Gesù in Italia*, Roma-Milano, Albrighi-Segati-Civiltà cattolica, 1910-1922.

Tamassia N., *La famiglia italiana nei secoli decimoquinto e decimosesto*, Palermo, Sandron, 1912.

Tangorra V., *Il pensiero economico di Niccolò Machiavelli*, in *Saggi critici di economia politica*, Torino, Fratelli Bocca, 1900.

Tasso T., *Il forno, overo della nobiltà, dialogo del s. Torquato Tasso*, Vinetia, presso Aldo Manuzio, 1583.

— *Il padre di famiglia*, in *Opere di Torquato Tasso*, Pisa, Capurro, 1832.

Tilgher A., *Le travail dans les moeurs et dans les doctrines: histoire de l'idéee de travail dans la civilisation occidentale*, Paris, Alcan, 1931.

Toniolo G., *Scritti scelti di Giuseppe Toniolo*, edited by F. Meda, Milano, Vita e Pensiero, 1921.

— *L'elemento etico nelle leggi economiche*, in *Scritti scelti*.

— *Scolastica ed umanesimo nelle dottrine economiche al tempo del Rinascimento in Toscana*, in *Scritti scelti*.

Tononi A.G., *Il Padre Segneri nei ducati di Parma e Piacenza*, «Rassegna Nazionale», IV, 1895.

Tornari G., *Del pensiero politico e delle dottrine economiche di Giovanni Botero*, Torino, Politecnica, 1907.

Trecca G., *Legnago fino al secolo XX*, Verona, Gurisatti, 1900.

Treves P., *La filosofia politica di Tommaso Campanella*, Bari, Laterza, 1930.

Turmann M., *Léon XIII, les catholiques sociaux et les origines de la legislation internationale du travail*, Milano, Vita e Pensiero, 1931.

Valensin A., *L'encyclique Rerum Novarum et les clauses ouvrières du pacte de la societé des nations*, Milano, Vita e Pensiero, 1931.

Vento S., *Le condizioni della oratoria sacra del Seicento: ricerche e critica*, Milano, Dante Alighieri di Albrighi Segati, 1916.

Ventura C., *La prima (-seconda) parte del Thesoro Politico in cui si contengono relationi, istruttioni, trattati, e varii discorsi pertinenti alla perfetta intelligenza della ragion di stato ... Raccolto per Comin Ventura da essemplari dell'Acad. Ital. di Colonia*, Milano, presso Girolamo Bordone, 1600.

Venusti A.M., *Compendio utilissimo di quelle cose, le quali a nobili e christiani mercanti appartengono*, Milano, G. Antio degli Antonii, 1561.

— *Discorso d'intorno alla mercantia*, in *Compendio utilissimo di quelle cose*.

— *Institutione de' Mercanti*, in *Compendio utilissimo di quelle cose*.

Verga E., *Storia della vita milanese*, Milano, Moneta, 1931.

Vida M.G., *M. Hier. Vidae Cremonen. Albae episc. Dialogi de rei publicae dignitate*, Cremonae, in civitatis palatio apud Vincentium Contem, 1556.

VON SCHEEL H.F.W.J., *I concetti economici fondamentali del corpus juris civilis*, in *Biblioteca di storia economica*, diretta da V. Pareto.

WADDING L., *Scriptores ordinis minorum*, Roma, apud Linum Contedini, 1806.

WEBER M., *Die protestantische Ethik und der Geist des Kapitalismus*, Tubingen, Mohr, 1920.

ZANONI E., *La mente di Francesco Guicciardini nelle opere politiche e storiche*, Firenze, Barbèra, 1897.

— *Paolo Paruta nella vita e nelle opere*, Livorno, Giusti, 1904.

ZDEKAUER L., *I Capitula hebraeorum di Siena (1477-1526)*, «Archivio Giuridico "Filippo Serafini"», V, 1900.

ZONGHI A., *Statuta artis lanae terrae Fabrianae (1369-1674)*, in *Documenti storici Fabrianesi*, Roma, Rossi, 1880.

ZUCCOLO L., *Dialoghi di Ludovico Zuccolo*, Venetia, Ginammi, 1625.

ZUMBINI B., *Vita paesana e cittadina nel poema del Folengo*, in *Raccolta di studi critici dedicati ad Alessandro d'Ancona*, Firenze, Barbèra, 1901.

INDEX OF NAMES*

---

* The following index is based only on Barbieri's text.
[1] Also known as Saint Austin.

---

[2] Called Merlin Cocai too.

[3] Probaby Antonionotto, Milan' Fregoso family founder, Fregoso's family comes from Genoa.

---

[4] Called Missaglia too.

TABLE OF CONTENTS

CITTÀ DI CASTELLO • PG
FINITO DI STAMPARE NEL MESE DI NOVEMBRE 2013